Economic Strategy
and National Security

Excerpts from the book:

"As heartening as these statistics are for us technological "haves," we should not forget that half the world's population has yet to make a telephone call. Accordingly, certain dangers will emerge from the path we are on. Most critically, any skills gap with respect to information will have huge consequences for social stability."—*Dave McCurdy*

"Even as capital and finance are becoming more international, politics is becoming more local. As individual citizens despair of participating in public policy decisions affecting international finance, they revert to demanding greater control of their neighborhood lives."—*Gary Hart*

"Success for the United States in the first half of the twenty-first century will be a function of the evolution of the Sino-American relationship. China's trajectory to world power transcends any analogy to the rise of Germany, Russia, and Japan in the first half of the twentieth century. China's geopolitical challenges for the United States may be closer to the sum of these three former challengers."—*Nicholas Rockefeller*

"As of the end of 1998, some 40 percent of our exports go to the Americas including Canada, while 35 percent of our imports come from there. The region is more important to us tradewise than Japan and Germany combined, and by the year 2010 will be more important than Japan and the entire European Union combined."—*Eric Farnsworth*

"Moreover, U.S. venture capital-backed companies generate about three times more export sales per dollar of equity than more established corporations and are a key source of research and development spending and applied technological innovation."—*Jeffrey Nuechterlein*

"The United States's technological advantages may actually endanger the country. Ironically, because the U.S. military and society are most dependent upon information systems, they may be more vulnerable to attack. Attacks against communications, power, transportation, or financial systems could greatly disrupt U.S. society; countries with systems that do not work well enough to be taken for granted might barely notice attacks against them."—*Lawrence Greenberg*

Economic Strategy and National Security

A Next Generation Approach

edited by

Patrick J. DeSouza

A Council on Foreign Relations Book

Westview Press
A Member of the Perseus Books Group

Copyright © 2000 by Council on Foreign Relations

Published in 2000 in the United States of America by Westview Press, 5500 Central Avenue, Boulder, Colorado 80301-2877, and in the United Kingdom by Westview Press, 12 Hid's Copse Road, Cumnor Hill, Oxford OX2 9JJ

Find us on the World Wide Web at www.westviewpress.com

Library of Congress Cataloging-in-Publication Data
Economic strategy and national security : a next generation approach /
edited by Patrick J. DeSouza.
    p.   cm.
  Includes bibliographical references and index.
  ISBN 0-8133-6834-0 (alk. paper)
  1. United States—Economic policy—1993– .   2. National security—
United States.   3. Capital market—United States.   4. United States—
Foreign relations.   I. DeSouza, Patrick J.
HC106.82.E274 1999
338.973—dc21   99-38483
                                                                              CIP

The paper used in this publication meets the requirements of the American National Standard for Permanence of Paper for Printed Library Materials Z39.48-1984.

10   9   8   7   6   5   4   3   2   1

Contents

Acronyms

APEC	Asia-Pacific Economic Cooperation forum
ASEAN	Association of Southeast Asian Nations
C3I	command, control, communications, and intelligence
CEO	chief executive officer
CFIUS	Committee on Foreign Investment in the United States
CFR	Council on Foreign Relations
CIAO	Critical Infrastructure Assurance Office
CIS	Commonwealth of Independent States
CoCom	Coordinating Committee for Multilateral Export Controls
COTS	commercial off the shelf
CPU	central processing unit
CSRC	China Securities Regulatory Commission
DARPA	Defense Advanced Research Project Agency
DoD	Department of Defense
EMU	European Monetary Union
EU	European Union
EXIM	U.S. Export-Import Bank
FAS	Foreign Agricultural Service
FASB	Financial Accounting Standards Board
FCPA	Foreign Corrupt Practices Act
FDI	foreign direct investment
FDIC	Federal Deposit Insurance Corporation
FEC	Federal Election Commission
FLAG	Fiber Link Around the Globe
FTAA	Free Trade Area of the Americas
FTC	Federal Trade Commission
FX	Foreign Exchange
GAAP	Generally Accepted Accounting Principles
GATT	General Agreement on Tariffs and Trade
GDB	Global Business Dialogue
GDP	Gross Domestic Product
GNP	Gross National Product
GPS	Global Positioning Satellite

IAEA	International Atomic Energy Agency
ICBM	Inter-Continental Ballistic Missiles
ICC	Interstate Commerce Commission
ILSA	Iran Libya Sanctions Act
IT	information technology
ITA	Information Technology Agreement
IW	information warfare
MAI	Multilateral Agreement on Investment
MFN	most favored nation
MIA	missing in action
NAFTA	North American Free Trade Agreement
NAS	National Airspace System
NASDAQ	National Association of Securities Dealers Automated Quotation
NATO	North Atlantic Treaty Organization
NEC	National Economic Council
NGO	nongovernmental organization
NIPC	National Infrastructure Protection Center
NIS	New Independent States
NPT	Nuclear Non-Proliferation Treaty
NSC	National Security Council
NTM	New Transatlantic Marketplace
OAS	Organization of American States
OECD	Organization for Economic Cooperation and Development
OPEC	Organization of Petroleum Exporting Countries
OPIC	Overseas Private Investment Corporation
PC	personal computer
PCCIP	President's Commission on Critical Infrastructure Protection
PLA	People's Liberation Army
R&D	research and development
SCADA	Supervisory Control and Data Acquisition
SEC	Securities and Exchange Commission
SOE	state-owned enterprise
U.N.	United Nations
Unicom	China United Telecommunications
USTR	U.S. Trade Representative
WIPO	World Intellectual Property Organization
WTO	World Trade Organization

Foreword

In 1992, President Clinton and Vice President Gore were elected as our first leaders born after World War II. It was nothing less than a generational shift in our nation's political leadership, reaffirmed four years later in 1996.

With this change came a new approach to international affairs. The world has changed dramatically since the onset of the computer age, and we must take note of and respond to the new realities we face in the twenty-first century. For example, the United States is now an information-based economy, where political and economic relationships are changing at every level. On the one hand, citizens have greater access to the world than ever before. Capital markets are fully integrated. Transportation and telecommunication links are opening new horizons to untold numbers across the globe, as I saw for myself with President Clinton during an Internet demonstration at a *favela* school in Brazil. On the other hand, changing technology and a changing polity mean that individuals are becoming, in some ways, more isolated, the so-called "bowling alone" phenomenon. In addition, the line between foreign and domestic policy has increasingly blurred—from trade and investment to narcotics, to the environment, to immigration, to labor rights and other non-traditional issues—and, as a result, the very conceptualization of U.S. national security continues to evolve. The world is changing from the one we once knew. That's why in 1992 we immediately positioned ourselves to take full advantage of the world we now face, while minimizing its downside, by strengthening our economy and putting people first.

We took a hard look at the budget deficit, passing the historic deficit reduction plan in 1993, and now, for the first time since man first walked on the moon, our budget is in surplus. We addressed the loss of U.S. competitive leadership and saw our nation once again reclaim the honor of being the most competitive nation in the world. And we saw the strategic importance of trade and investment, on which fully a quarter of our overall economy depends. Accordingly, we passed NAFTA on a bipartisan basis to shore up our strategic North American base and give us a platform from which to conclude the Free Trade Area of the Americas by 2005. We passed the Uruguay Round of the GATT, the largest tax cut in history, which created the WTO at the same time. And we invigorated APEC with agreement to form a regional trade area by 2010–2020.

In short, change is inevitable as we cross over to the twenty-first century, and as a result we face a fundamental choice: Either we can sit idly by and allow change to overwhelm us, or we can actively engage the world to shape and mold inevitable change to our best, lasting advantage.

Still, there is much to do, and so it is critical that even as the baby-boomers begin to reach middle age, we actively reach out to work hand in hand with those who follow behind. I wholeheartedly endorse, for example, the idea expressed in the 1996 annual report of the Council on Foreign Relations: Leadership must be perpetually renewed to be sustained. We must begin to include the voice of a new generation in the national debate—men and women with new ideas and approaches. Many authors in this volume have already contributed to the national debate by helping to form and implement a vision shared by internationalists of both parties, in addition to contributing thoughtful chapters here.

Encouraging and promoting a new generation of leadership is a central purpose for the book you have in your hands. It represents the first effort of the Council's Next Generation Program. Importantly, this volume opens discussion on a cricital area for the next generation: integrating economic strategy and national security. It touches on the influence of technology and telecommunications in changing the dimensions of politics, economic interest, and national security. It discusses challenges inherent in globalization, including aging populations, the rule of law, information terrorism, and others. And it points to opportunities in emerging markets—China and Latin America—that will shape our individual and collective well-being years into the future.

With this collection, the Council begins a bipartisan multi-generational debate to help orient our national discussion as we build that famous bridge to the twenty-first century. It is therefore a distinct pleasure and privilege that I commend to you this volume, *Economic Strategy and National Security: A Next Generation Approach.* It is, perhaps, the opening salvo of this nation's emerging leaders in international affairs.

Mack McLarty
Washington, D.C.

Acknowledgments

Approximately three short years ago, the Council on Foreign Relations (CFR) celebrated its seventy-fifth anniversary. Over the course of a remarkable century that, as Gary Hart notes in his essay, "has produced more history than it ever possibly could have consumed," the CFR has been a leading voice in trying to make sense of and to explain an interesting, sometimes tragic, but ever beautiful world. It has done so through a variety of communications vehicles such as *Foreign Affairs*, books, radio, television and, now, the Internet. In doing so, it has tried to help shape U.S. engagement in the world by blending an appreciation for the currents of history with "new realities" evident in economics, politics, military affairs, and technology.

The CFR's Annual Report for that anniversary year boldly kicked-off an effort to develop a somewhat untapped vein of insight regarding foreign policy: the ideas of the next generation. Various statements in the report communicated the CFR's deep commitment to the effort. Such leadership animated our efforts in the following pages.

Peter G. Peterson, in his chairman's letter, announced the establishment of a $2 million Next Generation Fund, which supported this project and many others.

Bob Hormats noted that, as one of the early participants in the CFR's Term Member Program—an effort to reach out to young men and women to participate in the grand foreign policy debate (and a program in which many in this volume have participated)—he was struck seeing the then stewards of U.S. foreign policy such as John McCloy, Averell Harriman, and George Kennan exchanging ideas with young members. We have had similar experiences with distinguished senior members such as Cyrus Vance and Henry Kissinger.

In his statement for the report, Hormats conveyed the "sense that [the] legacy [of these stewards] was the next generation's responsibility to continue ... [and that] we in this generation ... have the responsibility now to transmit that message to the next generation of foreign policy practitioners." It is this fundamental consideration of continuity and change and need for leadership in conveying a message of responsibility that is the basis for this project. Through his efforts in chairing our inaugural meeting on U.S. international economic strategy and through his essay on the Internet, our next frontier, Hormats set a standard for our work.

Leslie Gelb played a vital role by giving us our conceptual push. In his president's letter, Gelb elaborated on his, Peter Peterson's, and Maurice Greenberg's vision of the Council being the "Home to the Next Generation, and the Next." He argued that there was a need to build on the work of the "successors to the World War II generation ... [by focusing on] overall U.S. foreign policy and strategy." It is useful now to consider the agenda he set forth in those pages approximately three years ago.

> Little progress has been made on understanding the policy effects of the computer and telecommunications age beyond saying "it has changed everything." While we see the rising power of money, we are uncomfortable with the trade-offs between, say, trade and security interests in China. We grasp national, cultural, and religious grievances but have not begun to cope with their worst manifestations—ethnic conflict and terrorism.

In the subsequent pages, we have begun to examine these concerns and others from a "next generation" perspective. Moreover, we have discussed some of the new twists on this agenda such as the influence of information technology on items like tribalism and terrorism. There is, however, still much to be done; and the time available to think through such issues seems to be shrinking as technology accelerates the variety of decisions that public and private actors can take and structures the playing field for U.S. and international interests.

As we stand back, though, and survey our collective efforts over the past three years, we are all proud of this volume and its attempt to energize the public debate about American leadership in a new world that is on Internet time; largely, we have our respective families to thank for the support that they have given us during this period and throughout our lives.

Moreover, we all wish to thank the Council on Foreign Relations—the premier foreign policy think tank in the world—for creating an amazing environment that encouraged, in fact provoked, debate, over the future of American foreign policy. This institution, steeped in tradition and filled with leading individuals—captains of industry, former government leaders, and brilliant academicians—nourished us through an innovative and bold program initiated by its Next Generation Fund. In fact, this CFR project balanced participants who have been stewards of American foreign policy with younger upstarts who also aspire to make a contribution to the grand national debate.

There are certain individuals to whom we would like to express our gratitude but who deserve a whole lot more. These individuals participate in such efforts at the Council out of a true sense of public service. Bob Hormats led our group and kicked off our efforts by introducing our first discussion section. Gene Sekulow and Carter Beese, as chairpersons of the project, provided excellent guidance on its development. Former members of Congress Dave McCurdy and Gary Hart provided the lead articles as well as an invaluable perspective that gave the project a lift. Dan Tarullo, Jeff Shafer, Jeff Lang, and Jules Katz offered interesting executive branch perspectives. Jacob Heilbrunn of the *New Republic,* one of those Next Generation leaders, along with most of the contributors to this volume, chaired one of our most dynamic sessions.

Al Fishlow, our economics advisor, provided the same firm but kind guidance in pushing us to better analysis as he has done for his graduate students in economics at Berkeley and Yale.

David Kellogg, Lawrence Korb, Gary Hufbauer, Elise Lewis, April Wahlestedt, Teresa Aguayo, Dooley Adcroft, and Sean Costigan assisted in numerous ways in organizing the project and offering generously the benefit of their experience in creating successful ventures at the CFR. Last, but certainly not least, we would like to thank Westview Press, especially Leo Wiegman and Barbara Greer, for shepherding us through this demanding volume. Westview's professionalism and attentiveness made this project a reality.

Patrick J. DeSouza
New York, New York

Chapter 1

Introduction and Overview

Patrick J. DeSouza

On October 31, 1997, the Council on Foreign Relations (CFR) held a panel discussion among former National Security Council (NSC) advisors to commemorate the fiftieth anniversary of the NSC. During the event, Ambassador Winston Lord, former CFR President and Assistant Secretary of State for the Far East during President Clinton's first term, raised two central and related policymaking problems with the panel: How would the NSC, in coordinating the work of various governmental agencies for the president, deal with the continued rise of economic issues as integral to United States security? Also, what would be the agenda for U.S. foreign policy as the concept of security continued to evolve over the next generation?

The NSC was founded under the National Security Act of July 26, 1947, to coordinate foreign and defense policies and to reconcile diplomatic and military commitments. During the height of the Cold War, economic strategy was linked to national security primarily in *negative* terms—to deny the Soviet Union opportunities for indirectly subsidizing its military effort, including through the use of sanctions. The Reagan Administration's National Security Decision Directive 75 is one example of this approach; it built on the premise that adversaries needed to be contained.

With the end of the Cold War and the emergence of new economic challenges for the twenty-first century, this approach is now clearly obsolete. One approach currently being considered is that of *engagement* with adversaries to influence behavior. From this perspective, economic strategy is linked to national security in *positive* terms—to offer incentives for democratic reforms through market reforms. In contrast to the Cold War approach, engagement builds on a premise that adversaries can be transformed.

The exchange of visits between President Clinton and Prime Minister Zhu Rongji of China during June 1998 and April 1999 leading to a U.S.-China trade deal on November 15, 1999, and U.S. support for China's entry into the World Trade Organization (WTO) is one example of this alternative approach; a commercial agenda with Vietnam is another. The Chinese relationship is particularly challenging because it occurs against the backdrop of allegations of illegal satellite and nuclear weapons technology theft by the Chinese.

To be sure, these are crude characterizations of Cold War and post–Cold War approaches. President Nixon offered positive economic inducements to the Soviet Union to promote cooperative behavior. Meanwhile, President Clinton has implemented economic sanctions relatively frequently and against a variety of countries: India, Pakistan, Cuba, Iran, and Libya.

There is, however, a growing realization that in the twenty-first century, economic relations and economic policy tools will play a more central role in defining and preserving the peace than traditional military or diplomatic efforts. Ever increasing degrees of financial and technological integration are influencing the political and economic dynamics between and within nations. In this context, the United States has an important role to play. One may argue that it is through the "new economic and social realities" produced by networking technologies, advances in telecommunications, electronic commerce, and the global spread of venture capital efforts that the American vision of individual empowerment and democracy will spread throughout the world in the new millennium.

Recent financial and technology-related crises underscore the changing agenda for a twenty-first century security policy. On the financial side, because of increasingly integrated capital markets, volatile circumstances such as the 1995 Mexican peso crisis, 1997–1998 Asian financial crisis, 1997–1998 weakening of the Russian and Brazilian economies and on-going formation of the European Monetary Union have produced regional tensions. Moreover, during such crises, economic resources were abruptly reallocated among interest groups within the affected countries producing internal conflict. Also, contagion effects have produced negative economic consequences that have been transferred to the United States through lower demand for U.S. exports, devaluation of U.S. investments abroad, and possible increases in illegal immigration, organized crime, and drug shipments as a result of foreign attempts to find ways to counter the domestic impact of their respective economic downturns. It is illustrative to consider that the widespread ramifications of economic dislocation at our border motivated the Clinton Administration to define the Mexican peso crisis as a national security threat.

On the technology side, security issues also lie just below the surface of economic transactions. For example, the commercial licensing of satellite technology to countries such as China helps U.S. commercial interests but also may trigger regional arms races. Or, the sale of U.S. encryption technology, while good for Silicon Valley and the development of an electronic commerce industry, may assist global criminal organizations with money laundering or information terrorism in the United States.

The Clinton Administration has appreciated these "new realities" driven by economics from the beginning of its term. On January 21, 1993, President Clinton made a major innovation in the policy coverage of the NSC. In Presidential Decision Directive 2 (PDD–2), President Clinton increased the membership of the NSC to include, among others, the secretary of the treasury and the newly created office of Assistant to the President for Economic Policy. With this innovation, President Clinton not only acknowledged a broader agenda for the post–Cold War period, but also ensured a greater emphasis on economic issues in the formulation of national security policy.

In addition, on January 25, 1993, President Clinton issued Executive Order 12835 that established a National Economic Council (NEC). Foremost among the functions listed for this new organization was to "coordinate the economic policy-making process with respect to domestic and international economic issues." Moreover, to bring greater security policy coherence to such issues, some staffing would be shared between the NSC and the NEC. In these ways, President Clinton went beyond previous efforts to integrate economic policy and national security.

Yet, gearing up organizationally for a "next generation" agenda is still quite different from actually successfully addressing such issues or even understanding what U.S. interests are in these issues. Given the current turmoil produced by globalization, it may be necessary to go further and reconsider the concept of security as we enter the new century. Should we, for example, expand understandings of security that focus on military matters to include traditionally domestic economic concerns such as Americans' retirement savings? After all, volatility of integrated capital markets in which U.S. pension plans are invested creates new transnational threats to the well-being of U.S. citizens. Alternatively, from a foreign policy perspective, could currency speculation by global financial players constitute a security threat to the United States? After all, such attacks on currencies are destabilizing to U.S. capital markets because of the volatility they produce abroad.

While U.S. policy elites have begun to recognize the priority of these new and expanded security concerns, the public dialogue among the executive, Congress, and the electorate to explain and prepare for these new realities has been woefully inadequate. Moreover, partisan domestic politics threatens to disrupt President Clinton's policy innovations to attend to a new range of twenty-first century issues. It is an open question among some Republicans whether more bureaucracy, such as the NEC, is needed to address the new agenda. They argue that institutional growth results only in more access for special interest groups to influence policy away from deliberations of the national economic interest. On the other hand, some Democrats would argue that enhanced policy tools are needed to respond effectively to a twenty-first century foreign economic agenda that blurs the lines between what is domestic and what is international. As alluded to above, global integration has led to a new set of security problems regarding trade leadership, financial volatility, corruption, and information terrorism. These problems will affect the U.S. electorate of the twenty-first century in ways not felt by citizens living in the second half of the twentieth century.

Lord's concerns at the CFR event represented the tip of the proverbial iceberg. The panel of former NSC advisors identified certain related topics to be studied: the need for a strategic approach to foreign economic policy; the new instabilities produced by financial volatility, trade friction, and grinding poverty; the changing concept of security; the need to integrate domestic and international approaches to common concerns; and the problem of communicating such integration to the American people. Yet, even though different panel members acknowledged that the effective integration of economic concerns in national security policymaking was critical for U.S. interests in the twenty-first century, none really provided solutions for identifying or addressing these new concerns.

This volume takes as its point of departure, the fiftieth anniversary of the NSC and makes an effort to better understand the new agenda in which finance and technology play a central role in a twenty-first century conception of security. It arises out of a two-year series of roundtables held by the CFR with senior policymakers, businesspersons, and a "next generation" of participants in the grand debate regarding national security. This book is intended to enhance the public dialogue about new issues for a twenty-first century policy agenda.

Current Conception of National Security

In setting the baseline for the following discussion, it is important to lay out the Clinton Administration's current perspective on integrating economic issues with security policy. Section 603 of the Goldwater-Nichols Defense Department Reorganization Act of 1986 requires the president to publish a report setting forth our national security strategy. In May 1997, such a report was published and set the tone for President Clinton's second term. This report, *A National Security Strategy for a New Century*, is considered especially important in light of its timing at the beginning of the second term as the president reaches for his legacy in foreign policy. The preface indicated three core objectives of the Clinton Administration: 1) "to enhance our security with effective diplomacy and with military forces that are ready to fight and win"; 2) "to bolster America's economic prosperity"; and 3) "to promote democracy abroad."

The second and third items juxtaposed against each other are illuminating in understanding the administration's vision for integrating economic strategy with security policy. The focus of democracy-building efforts is promotion abroad. The assumption is that a system of states with common political values would contribute to peace and stability. By contrast, the report makes it clear that the priority for economic strategy is inwardly focused: "The strength of our diplomacy, our ability to maintain an unrivaled military, the attractiveness of our values abroad—all depend in part on the strength of our economy . . . our primary economic goal remains to strengthen the American economy" (at p.15).

By way of contrast, note that the driving focus of the report is *not* coordinated prosperity among states as a way of reinforcing U.S.-led capitalism and building markets. To be fair, however, this inward focus for economic strategy did respond to outside analysis of the kind described below. Moreover, as discussed below, as a result of international financial crises, the administration's views have evolved somewhat over time.

The primary focus on prosperity at home, as key to defining U.S. twenty-first century security strategy, is likely to be relatively less important as we head into the new century. Sustained growth at home for the decade has restored U.S. economic strength. Meanwhile, the United States has become more dependent on foreign economic relations abroad for its continued strength as trade and investment become drivers of U.S. prosperity. Strong and stable economic partners are needed for American exports and investment. Rather, an internationalist strategy is now needed to manage a twenty-first century agenda, especially in light of recent "contagious" financial crises.

Such a shift toward an internationalist strategy would require us to ask certain types of questions in crafting policy. For example, what is the U.S. vision of a post–Cold War world of capitalist states with which we must interact? After all, the European Union (EU) and Asian visions of capitalism are different from the United States and are more likely to emphasize state-led growth and sectoral policies. For example, the *Economist* has recently pointed out that "A world in which the American government collects taxes equal to 34% of the GDP and the Swedish 63% [of GDP] clearly retains considerable variety in capitalist arrangements."[1] On the other hand, Latin America's vision regarding the relative weighting of the government's participation in the economy, meanwhile, is evolving and becoming the focus for EU and Asian competitive influences. Regulatory differences among regions may be seen particularly with respect to the development of new industries such as electronic commerce and venture capital. Thus, how to shape international relations in ways favorable for the "American" version of capitalism becomes a relevant "next generation" question now that the threshold question of capitalism or communism has largely been settled over the course of the twentieth century.

Another example of the different types of questions raised by an "internationalist" perspective would be the question of how to make trade-offs between diplomatic and democratic core objectives and economic policy. During the Cold War it was necessary to sacrifice a degree of prosperity in the United States, such as through the use of economic sanctions, to achieve increased security. As the concept of security further broadens to take into account economic concerns, it is not clear to what degree a zero-sum perspective will be applicable for the post–Cold War. In an interdependent world, achieving mutual economic gain may enhance security for all.

What is clear is that the twenty-first century will bring policy problems involving a messy set of international economic, technological, financial, and legal issues that will intersect and be much more difficult to sort through conceptually. Two current examples illustrate the complexities.

First, most prominently, the Clinton Administration has been facing criticism and congressional oversight as a result of its prior granting (though subsequently revoked) of government licenses to the Hughes and Loral corporations to have commercial satellites launched on Chinese rockets. What makes the circumstance even more controversial is that Loral is one of the largest contributors of campaign funds to the Democratic Party. Because of allegations during the first quarter of 1999 that over the last fifteen years Chinese spies have stolen U.S. nuclear weapons secrets and have had inappropriate access to U.S. weapons laboratories, the U.S.-Chinese relationship has become twisted at a critical juncture for assessing the proper balance of U.S. economic and security interests. On one hand, China must be brought into the World Trade Organization—

an international institution through which the United States will be doing business in a fluid world of coalitions in the twenty-first century. On the other hand, membership and economic integration require public confidence that China will play by international rules—whether intellectual property or dispute resolution.

Different authors of this volume take on issues that inform the Chinese satellite and nuclear controversies from different angles. On one hand, Sekulow and Hormats note that the United States does have an economic interest in promoting advanced telecommunications and information technology (IT) products. These are leading-edge sectors of the economy that create jobs and contribute positively to the trade balance. Moreover, as Rockefeller and Helweg argue, the United States has a strategic interest in bringing China within a web of trading relations. In a fluid, integrated, and global marketplace, it is unlikely that IT that is useful for weapons development, such as powerful desktop computers, can be kept out of Chinese hands anyway. Greenberg's discussion of countering information terrorism has applicability here as well. On the other hand, there are high negatives surrounding the Chinese commercial relationship. Against the backdrop of the unsuccessful Chinese sales of missile technology to Pakistan (unsuccessful because of proactive tactics by the United States), detonations of nuclear weapons in May 1998 by India and Pakistan, and continued conflictual relations with Taiwan, the United States may be viewed by some as indirectly contributing to instability in Asia by working with the Chinese. As Murdock explores, campaign contributions in the U.S. electoral system, such as that made by Loral, may be distorting rational calculations of the national interest. Bass' call for U.S. policymakers to step back and gain perspective is critical for this key twenty-first century relationship.

Similar intersections between economic strategy and national security are also on display in Latin American policy development. Banana-producing islands in the Caribbean have traditionally received market access preferences in Europe as part of post-colonial compensation. Yet in 1997, in trying to get free-market trading rules right and secure economic interests of U.S. banana marketers, such as Chiquita, the United States (joined by Central Americans and Andeans) won a suit in the WTO to dismantle the European system of preferences. While U.S. economic interests in free trade have been advanced, the result may have created a security problem for the United States. One may argue that unless rapid creation and diversification of exports to balance global competition in bananas is achieved in the Caribbean, the unintended consequence of creating relatively greater U.S. prosperity for a few select companies such as Chiquita is that the Caribbean islands may turn to narcotics trafficking to make up for the lost banana revenues for which they are critically dependent. Such behavior would only serve ultimately to threaten U.S. national security. In addition, current U.S. responses of raising tariffs on European luxury goods to prod the EU to hasten implementation of the WTO ruling have exacerbated transatlantic trade tensions. Critics of the current policy outcome have also pointed out that Chiquita is yet another big contributor to the Democratic Party and that prioritizing Chiquita's WTO economic interest has undermined U.S. diplomatic efforts on other fronts noted above.

These examples, and others described in the various chapters, raise the need for better understanding the parameters of our economic "engagement"—a concept that is supposed to capture the essence of the Clinton Administration's security policy in the same way that "containment" summarized the Cold War effort. In some ways, the Clinton Administration, or for that matter, any future administration, is faced with a "no-win" position as international economic interests increasingly blend with security considerations. On one hand, the president will face criticism by some if he does not push the interests of U.S. companies and, ultimately, of American workers in the global economy. On the other hand, he will face criticism if U.S. companies create a foreign backlash by displacing local companies in unstable areas or if the transfer of U.S. technology strengthens a potential adversary. It would seem then, that one theme that will be tested continually during the twenty-first century, when economic and security concerns collide, is whether a rising tide of engagement will lift all boats.

To be sure, a strong U.S. economic base is fundamental to giving the United States the wherewithal to proceed internationally. However, it is quite clear, as the 1997 Clinton Administration report cautions, that "economic and security interests are inextricably linked" and that "prosperity at home depends on our leadership in the global economy"(p. 14–15). These caveats, while noted, need to be further developed, especially with respect to a range of "next generation" issues that will be raised in this book. In light of the global financial crises of 1997–1999, and new "networked" communities being brought together around the world with ever increasing speed through technology, this volume supports the idea that emphasizing successful management of economic interdependence around the world will be the new key to achieving the goals of prosperity and stability—the focal points for security—in the twenty-first century.

A "new reality" is that prosperity in the post–Cold War world, much like peace in the Cold War era, must be indivisible. More strategic thinking is needed in terms of economic and technological engagement abroad to produce a coherent and effective security policy. Ultimately, in articulating a twenty-first century approach, we must revisit the fundamental economic concept of "mutual gain"—that prosperity abroad is as important to us for our national security as prosperity at home.

Economic Areas of Engagement

As noted above, the primary economic goal articulated by the administration at the beginning of its second term in discussing national security—strengthening the U.S. economy—was inward looking. In many ways, this focus (as President Clinton once said, "like a laser") has been successful; the U.S. economy has enjoyed a period of extraordinary, uninterrupted growth. The budget deficit has gone from close to $200 billion per year to a surplus. In the last four years, exports have generated more than one-third of U.S. economic growth. To reiterate, the inward-looking priority responded to past recommendations regarding what the United States should do during the 1990s. The question going forward is whether it is time to relax those assumptions.

Partial Response for the 1990s.   Ten years ago, at the beginning of what seemed would be an "Asian Century," Fred Bergsten, among others, offered a strategy for the restoration of U.S. "power" and "leadership" in the 1990s and beyond.[2] His two-part strategy was titled "Competitive Interdependence." First, as a priority, Bergsten recommended certain "domestic" legislative measures: 1) reduction of the budget deficit and 2) support for export expansion. These domestic measures were to be the "Competitive" part of the strategy and were geared toward the restoration of U.S. economic power.

Supplementing these measures was an "international" portion. Among the recommendations included: 1) coordinating national economic policies in ways that would eliminate international imbalances while sustaining global growth and stability; 2) achieving equilibrium levels for the dollar and other key currencies; 3) improving the international monetary system; 4) alleviating Third World debt; and 5) expanding the role of international financial institutions. These international measures represented the "Interdependence" part of the strategy and were geared toward the application of U.S. leadership.

As noted above, the Clinton Administration has done a remarkable job with respect to the "Competitive" dimension of the strategy, especially in terms of eliminating the budget deficit and promoting exports. Strategic investments through government spending on education and technology and through infrastructure projects were made to reinforce and sustain growth. As a result, one might conclude that, to a large extent, U.S. economic "power" has been restored.

As various authors in this volume argue, there is mixed opinion with respect to the administration's success in the "Interdependence" part of the strategy. This concern is especially true with respect to the goal of coordination in macroeconomic policies and achieving an equilibrium value for the dollar and other key currencies. As a result, while U.S. economic "power" may have been restored, there still remain questions regarding U.S. international economic leadership.

A Complementary Response for 2000 and Beyond. At the beginning of his second term, President Clinton chose to make the case for U.S. economic engagement in shaping security policy by focusing on the personal pocketbook interests of Americans. We will discuss in this volume whether the "democratization" of the world has forced security policy to become "kitchen-table" matters. For example, the first foreign economic policy discussed in the president's 1997 national security report is that of increasing access to foreign markets. That seemingly international policy objective was defined in terms of domestic interests, *not* mutual gain:

> In a world where over 95 percent of the world's consumers live outside the United States, we must export to sustain economic growth at home. . . . [o]ver the next four years, the Administration will continue to press our trading partners—multilaterally, regionally and bilaterally—to expand export opportunities to U.S. workers, farmers and companies. (p. 15)

The report notes that it is the U.S. objective to "expand U.S. exports to over $1.2 trillion by the year 2000, which will mean over five million new American jobs and a total of 16 million jobs supported by exports" (at p. 17).

To be fair, the 1997 report does acknowledge that "as national economies become more integrated internationally, the United States *cannot thrive in isolation from developments abroad*" (p. 17). Moreover, as international financial crises during 1998 threatened the U.S. economy, the October 1998 update to the report ("Update") shifted its focus somewhat to the problems created by economic interdependence. The Update acknowledged directly that U.S. "future prosperity depends upon a stable international financial system and robust global growth" (Update p. 5). Importantly, the Update also made the link to tying the fate of foreigners to U.S. security interests: "If [foreign] citizens tire of waiting for democracy and free markets to deliver a better life for them, there is a *real risk that they will lose confidence in democracy and free markets. This would pose great risks not only for our economic interests but for our national security*" (Id. emphasis added).

These acknowledgments, however, are not the same as orienting policy toward a concept of mutuality that will be the hallmark of the twenty-first century. Even in the Update, the priority policy prescriptions are focused on the impact of global economics on the U.S. domestic economy. The Update acknowledges "over the next decade the global economy is expected to grow at three times the rate of the United States economy." The punchline, though, is domestic and is zero-sum: "If we do not seize these opportunities [emerging markets], our competitors surely will" (Update p. 33).

There are areas in which the Clinton Administration has taken action in stimulating international cooperation and in shaping a forward-looking, international economic agenda. The administration has supported the development and activity of international institutions such as the WTO and the IMF. The administration has also worked with multilateral banks to target resources for social programs that address some of the "by-products" of globalization such as growing inequality and poverty, environmental degradation, and corruption. These by-products are threats to democracy and stability.

Still the Clinton Administration's efforts in articulating the integration of economic and national security strategies have emphasized its domestic vision. To some extent, as we will see through the essays presented in this volume, the domestic flavor of the administration's foreign policy may be a political requirement for future policy development as demanded by the American voter. After all, analysts noticed that during the 1996 presidential debates the only foreign countries triggering questions were Mexico, Haiti, and Cuba—among our nearest neighbors—and the only salient security issues were "kitchen-table" issues—drugs, immigration, and transnational crime. It is fair to conclude that the Cold War agenda that had been driven by the Soviet Union and NATO—usually a staple of presidential debates—had been replaced, or at the very least dominated, by "inward-looking issues."

A Next Generation Agenda

The volume is divided into five parts that discuss some of the principal issues involving the growing intersection between economic strategy and national security. The articles in each part are meant to spark discussion of future challenges and opportunities facing a "next generation" of policymakers.

The volume first offers some perspectives on the changing concept of security and the requirements for U.S. leadership in the twenty-first century. Part II sets forth certain constraints that will shape our approach to the "new realities" of globalism. These constraints force American policymakers to acknowledge the pressures for "populist" reform, driven by those not included in the new global economy.

The volume proceeds, in Parts III and IV, to consider key dimensions—finance and technology—along which economic strategy and national security concerns will intersect in the twenty-first century. To some degree, the global financial crises of 1997–1999 and the recent technology controversies with respect to China are illustrative of the challenges that American policymakers will face along these dimensions. By contrast, in terms of opportunities, U.S. leadership in finance and technology may permit an American vision of the twenty-first century to take root. From the finance side, such vision would entail fluid, high-quality markets capable of sustainable growth for all, including those vulnerable populations at both ends (young and old) of the savings spectrum. On the technology side, an American vision would empower individuals through development of electronic commerce and the promotion of entrepreneurship.

Part V attempts to capture the dynamics of key emerging markets. First, by focusing on China and the NIS (New Independent States), especially Russia, we consider some of the greatest challenges facing us as we tend to the unfinished business of the Cold War. Strategic stability in the twenty-first century will depend on our ability to manage the transition of these two regional hegemons into the community of capitalist, liberal democracies. Because of their respective nuclear capabilities and abilities to create regional chaos, minimizing their respective political, economic, and social instabilities must be, for better or worse, part of our own calculus. Finally, in considering Latin America, we are looking at our greatest source of opportunities for the twenty-first century. Economically, politically and demographically, the Americas may offer a buffer against some of the volatility present in the international system.

Discussion along these five dimensions will hopefully open up the public debate on the terms of America's engagement with the world in the twenty-first century. It is a debate that illustrates the risk of insularity but also the great reward of material gain around the world. We are at a moment in history in which American leadership can make a difference in shaping the path along which human affairs are conducted. We have the opportunity to shape security policy in positive terms based on individual empowerment around the world rather than in negative terms of protecting ourselves from foreign influences, both welcome and unwelcome.

U.S. Leadership and
Twenty-First Century Concepts

The rapid rise of IT and the power of networking are fundamentally changing the U.S. approach to security and what constitutes the national interest. Moreover, the new economic, political, and social realities brought on by technology are forcing policymakers around the world to reconsider the applicability of present forms of institutions and politics to such new circumstances.

Dave McCurdy sets forth the basic themes of this volume with a discussion of the requirements of U.S. leadership for the next century. He calls for a new compact between the American people and the government that reflects new technological realities. Without the necessary adjustments, the changing dimensions of social organization and power brought by networking technologies and the Internet may create instabilities both at home and abroad. Some of these shake-ups, though, may be healthy for democracy and the marketplace of ideas. With greater decentralization through networked communities, the comparative roles of the public and private sectors in driving a security agenda may change with nongovernmental actors taking more of a prominent role.

Security threats will take on forms reflecting these new realities brought on by technology. First, conflict will not disappear. Instead, it will likely take on local rather than national forms. As individuals and local communities become empowered through decentralized access to information, "tribalism" may be reinforced. Second, traditional poverty concerns will have broader ramifications in the information age. Cleavages produced by the differences between the "information rich" and the "information poor"—concepts developed by James Wolfensohn in his tenure as president of the World Bank—may lock entire sections of humanity out of the future with no hope of catching-up. Already, in the United States, the "digital divide" is remarkable and is drawn along both income and racial lines.[3] In such a world, "skills" gaps, because of the instabilities they introduce, may have implications for security as profound as those resulting from missile gaps in the twentieth century.

McCurdy's focus on the driving influence of networked societies reinforces the work of other public commentators, such as Thomas Friedman, who argue that partisanship in the twenty-first century will be based on concepts such as "integrationist" and "separatist" that relate to the decisions about the processes of globalization rather than "democrat" or "republican" that pertain to decisions about the role of the state in national life.

Gary Hart enriches McCurdy's presentation by offering a philosophical approach for understanding the politics and the challenges of security in a new age. He points to a need for a new ideology that frees us from "tired" ideas in this "Age of Transition." Pragmatism in massaging "liberal" and "conservative" or "democrat" and "republican" labels will not be enough. Like McCurdy, Hart seeks a sharp break from "reform politics as usual" so that policy may be responsive to the new realities of the twenty-first century. He also reinforces McCurdy's point that as economics becomes more global, politics is becoming more local as networking technologies bring added empowerment to individuals to act outside the control of government within self-chosen communities.

Hart argues for four foundational principles around which to organize policymaking in the twenty-first century. The first two are the result of politics becoming more local with the emergence of IT. In the tradition of Jeffersonian democracy, Hart blends the principles of "classical republicanism" and "radical democracy" respectively. Drawing on the former, he argues that "civic virtue"—that is, participating in the life of the republic—is necessary. In this regard, innovative ideas are currently circulating among social scientists for using Internet technology to allow citizens to express their preferences regarding policy choices.

Hart also looks to democratic principles based on the concept of "ward republics" to underpin the American polity of the twenty-first century. Greater participation by the American public at local levels in defining economic and security policies is possible and can be encouraged without undermining the national interest. In this respect, one already sees localities such as New York or Silicon Valley or, for that matter, Redmond, Washington, carrying on trade relations that the national government is trying to accommodate. Moreover, localities relevant for citizens of the twenty-first century may not be tied to geography. Private Internet companies are currently setting-up "virtual communities" that may operate much like ward republics of the eighteenth century. Already, one sees communities and nongovernmental organizations coalescing on the Internet to develop effective relationships across borders to solve security problems such as land mines—an achievement that was honored with the 1997 Nobel Peace Prize.

Hart invokes, as the third and fourth principles, the concepts of "generational accountability" and "intergenerational compact." Such communitarian obligations focus attention on the "by-products of globalization." In this light, issues such as improved education standards for the information-based society of the future, environmental sustainability through climate change initiatives, and the economic security of aging populations around the world move to the forefront of the next generation agenda. Hart uses these types of issues to update the Burkean compact of citizenship: "It is the duty of each generation to leave for the next generation a better society in every respect than it found." With this goal in mind, we will focus on such an expanded twenty-first century agenda throughout the book.

Tony Blinken translates these challenges of politics for a new age into the requirements for a public dialogue to gain consensus for the path ahead. Such dialogue is absolutely necessary for future policy development with respect to security. Most agree that liberal democracy—one of the great achievements of the twentieth century—will likely continue to be the dominant form of government in the twenty-first century. However, as noted above, there is still significant variation among capitalist states. To give twenty-first century democracy content, leaders must translate the "new realities" in ways that provide meaning for the electorate's concerns regarding security.

Blinken presents a central paradox for foreign policy development: As the forces of integration proceed at an increasingly rapid pace, American citizens are becoming more disinterested in international matters—or "at least the media believes this to be so." In fact, there is a real danger that American disinterest about international concerns may turn into hostility as citizens fear rather than deal with transnational problems such as terrorism, drugs, and corruption. Such fears extend to what outcomes globalization will bring and were evident in Seattle in December 1999 with the violent protests outside the WTO meetings.

Blinken sharpens Gary Hart's challenge of shaping a twenty-first century America that fosters civic virtue. Blinken argues that one way to reinforce public engagement is to bring home the understanding that there is no longer a dividing line between foreign and domestic policy. To do this, security policy must be explained in a way that encourages analysis and the construction of a worldview that better captures the new realities that will shape the twenty-first century—the essence of this project.

Response to Globalization

After considering these conceptual underpinnings for policymaking, this volume then discusses certain constraints and policy areas that will shape our approach to dealing with the "new realities" brought on by globalization. One may argue that the foremost constraint limiting policy choices is fear of the future. As noted above, if democracy and free markets are to be sustained during the next century, policymakers must be sensitive to the discontent that is brewing among voters who live under the "new realities." Democracy must "deliver," as pointed out in the Clinton Administration's 1998 Update on national security strategy.

Trade and corruption are two key areas where there is a growing resentment by the American public about outcomes produced by globalization and the central role of economic interests in making foreign policy. Leadership and a public dialogue are needed to understand international integration. Without such leadership, some political aspirants will try to manipulate fears of the future. Already, some such as Pat Buchanan are campaigning for the 2000 presidential election with rallying cries against the free movement of goods, capital, and people. Such movement, Buchanan claims, would create a "global hiring hall" in the United States for Latins and Asians.[4]

The section begins with a consideration of the current policy baseline. The Clinton Administration's priorities thus far seem to have been: 1) the integration of the NIS and China into the international economic order; 2) nondiscrimination in trade practices; and 3) cooperative efforts to deal with the by-products of global change such as labor dislocation, environmental degradation, and aging populations. The administration's priorities for the twenty-first century thus reflect a progressive shift rather than a sharper break from the Cold War agenda that McCurdy and Hart suggest.

It also has been a priority of the Clinton Administration to stave off the American public's fear of the global economy. Most contributors to this volume believe that policymakers should learn from the populist counter-reaction to the growth of the U.S. national economy at the beginning of the twentieth century to prevent a similar counter-reaction today with respect to the growth of the international economy. Citizens need reassurance that their government can provide an effective regulatory framework that provides a sense of economic security during this period of transition—that democracy delivers.

Albert Fishlow and Patrick DeSouza open this section by discussing trade. In many ways, trade has become the lightning rod at home and abroad for U.S. foreign economic relations. Contrary to conventional wisdom that believes that the U.S. economy is too big to be influenced by globalization, trade has, in fact, altered the character of the American economy. Since 1970, the United States has realized a greater increase in the ratio of trade to national product than any other country. Trade is increasingly responsible for driving growth and creating high-wage jobs. Moreover, U.S. trade leadership has been responsible over time for a global system of wealth creation based on the premise of limited government (lower regulatory interference through tariffs and so forth) and the creation of efficiencies through open exchanges of goods and services.

Recent domestic discontent with increased U.S. "exposure" to the world has been driven by fears of low-wage competition stealing jobs and environmental degradation by foreigners eager to compete. Such popular discontent has taken root with "economic nationalists" who have relied on emotional arguments based on prejudice to undermine U.S. global trade leadership. The failure of fast track trade authorization for President Clinton in 1997 and

1998 is the clearest manifestation of the power of this "populist counter-reaction" to the global economy. Moreover, the financial crises of 1997–1999 and efforts by the United States to smooth out such volatility with official financial assistance have led "economic nationalists" to frame the counter-reaction in terms of "Wall Street" versus "Main Street." These tensions, as well as the underlying distributional concerns they represent, must be addressed to build the underlying consensus needed to project U.S. economic leadership. Such leadership is irreplaceable in that the United States is the only country whose trading relationships are so extensive in every region of the world as to provide enough leverage to promote a global system of wealth creation.

Brian VanDeMark provides some insight into United States history as we consider precedents on how to deal politically with such populist counter-reaction. VanDeMark looks back at other political reactions to changes in the structure of the U.S. economy. He points out that reform movements such as Populism and Progressivism were based on a set of convictions "embedded in American history and culture—above all, the vision of a chosen people uniquely entitled to enjoy the fruits of labor." He traces the roots of both movements to the fierce conviction of displaced farmers, laborers, and shopkeepers that they could reverse the course of history by returning power to the people. The worldview of each movement saw history as "an unending struggle between the virtue of ordinary people and the forces of corruption." These themes are manifest today in the rhetoric of economic nationalists who claim to be waging a crusade for restoring U.S. prosperity to the middle class whose interests are being given away by Wall Street and American politicians who are in the service of foreign interests such as the Chinese.

Deroy Murdock adds to our understanding of the current populist counter-reaction to globalization by focusing attention on the important issue of governmental corruption. As indicated above, questions about public integrity have animated much of populist reactions against economic change throughout United States history. To some degree, this could be expected: the American people expect a fair, level playing field, especially during transition periods, and rely on their elected representatives to ensure that. Murdock argues that the perverse incentives of the U.S. campaign financing laws and lobbying system actually create the possibility for "legal bribery" in the United States, as former President Jimmy Carter once termed such political behavior in a CNN interview. Whether or not substantiated, Main Street believes that special interest groups, foreign and domestic, are using American public officials to gain benefits from the global economy at the expense of working men and women. Such images exacerbate tensions already produced by globalization.

This reality that globalization produces unfortunate by-products and divides societies into "new" winners and losers, has been best understood to date by Western leaders such as Tony Blair (UK), Fernando Cardoso (Brazil), and Bill Clinton. It is also likely to be understood by those who espouse "compassionate conservatism." To illustrate, the principal theme of the April 1998 Santiago Summit of the Americas was that of promoting "Second Generation Reforms" such as the rule of law and educational reform. This theme emerged in response to hemispheric concerns that the first Summit of the Americas in Miami in 1994 produced a policy direction of free markets and democracy for the Americas that was not coupled with supporting institutions. These supports were needed to withstand the adverse by-products of globalization such as international crime, lack of skill-sets for an information age, and environmental degradation.

This section ends with a closer look at sanctions policy—one of the tools available to address security issues. As noted above, "engagement" through trade, as opposed to containment, seems to be a general approach favored by most of our group to attend to twenty-first century adversarial situations. To be sure, this is a sweeping generalization that demands case-specific evaluation in constructing policies. However, "engagement" recognizes that in a world in which technology is rapidly integrating financial and goods markets, a policy approach that relies on isolating adversaries must be selective and achieve broad adherence so as not to become a "paper tiger."

Diana Helweg argues that sanctions policy, especially during the last quarter of this century, has become a catchall substitute for "policy creativity." Moreover, in many cases, sanctions have become a proxy for the demands of special interest groups instead of being a reflection of strategic policy development. For example, it may be argued that economic sanctions with respect to Cuba are a reflection of the interests of Cubans living in the state of Florida as opposed to a strategy for achieving free markets and a democratic civil society in Cuba.

One should come away from this section about the constraints on policymaking created by the by-products of globalization with an appreciation that the gains of the last decade in confirming the triumph of free markets and democracies around the world is under some challenge. Questions are being raised about the *Washington Consensus*—an ideological framework for economic decisions pointing to balanced budgets, prudent monetary policy, stable exchange rates, and open economies in terms of trade and investment. For example, the International Monetary Fund (IMF) has undergone severe criticism for some of its *Washington Consensus*–styled recommendations in addressing the Asian financial crisis. Some argue that knee-jerk recommendations, such as sharply raising interest rates to support currency, have actually harmed Asian economies more than helped.

In Latin America, left-wing intellectuals have begun to develop an alternative ideological framework—the *Buenos Aires Consensus*—to push populist economic policies such as more progressive taxation, higher social spending, and greater regulation of international capital. In Asia and Latin America, as well as in the United States, a populist counter-reaction against globalization is gathering steam. This steam must be diffused because, despite such by-products, open markets and limited government have produced, and will continue to produce, mutual gains throughout the world in terms of per capita growth.

Challenges and Opportunities: Finance and Technology

The volume then focuses on the two issue areas—finance and technology—that hold the greatest challenges and opportunities for the United States and for the world. In both areas, the United States is the acknowledged leader in terms of policy development and having a private sector that can provide cutting-edge services. Moreover, each area has influenced the other, as we shall discuss in this volume. For example, electronic trading has redefined stock markets and dramatically lowered the transaction costs involved with capital mobility. Alternatively, venture capital financing and the ability to tap into foreign savings has made possible the revolution in IT.

On the other hand, recent foreign financial crises and illegal technology transfers have raised warning flags with the American electorate over what role the United States should play in these developing areas. Moreover, recent crises have actually provided Main Street with more ammunition to support the notion that special interest groups have captured the system under the guise of adjustments to globalism.

On the financial side, Main Street and Wall Street have already squared-off. Many observers have raised concerns about perverse incentives created by the United States acting as a lender of last resort to cover the financial mismanagement of other countries. For example, many have cited IMF and U.S. financial support of Russia during the 1990s as policy decisions that have had little effect on reinforcing capitalism. Rather, public sector loans are believed to have wound up in the offshore bank accounts of corrupt Russian officials and to have repaid unwise loans by Western banks.

On the technology front, Main Street and Silicon Valley have also tangled. While it is clearly in the U.S. economic interest to sell sophisticated, high-margin products, such as encryption technology, to foreigners, concerns have been raised that we are "selling the wire that will be used to hang ourselves" as Greenberg notes using Lenin's rope analogy. In this circumstance, Main Street argues that an updated security policy should put export controls on encryption technology because such technology is likely to be used by potential adversaries such as China or by foreign criminal organizations trying to operate in the United States.

The contributors to this volume provide a forward-looking approach to these domestic cleavages and argue for continued engagement to address the effects of globalization.

Financial Relations.   International financial integration is a primary force in shaping U.S. relations with the world for the twenty-first century. Jeffrey Shafer focuses on policymaking considerations in shaping the U.S. approach to international financial relations. Shafer presents the wide range of possible policy nodes: bilateral financial flows, multilateral lending, regional economic cooperation and private investment flows. However, he also underscores a dangerous and growing divergence that is affecting policy options: As private financial linkages with the world have grown, U.S. public linkages have atrophied decreasing opportunities to shape international financial outcomes.

In addition, certain U.S. institutional constraints further inhibit the ability of the United States to address international financial problems. First, there is no coherent U.S. governmental approach to dealing with international financial problems. Fragmented bureaucracies try to cope with issues implicating different regulatory jurisdictions. Second, congressional support for engaging in international financial issues has dramatically decreased as pent-up domestic demands on the federal budget have displaced support for an international financial policy agenda.

As evidenced by the "Asian contagion," integrated capital markets make it impossible to compartmentalize foreign and domestic financial markets. Although countries still try to shield themselves from external volatility, the United States must not fall into a trap of acquiescing to such attempts. Shafer makes the important point that the current fascination with the "quick fix" of capital controls is misplaced. Such controls only reinforce a fallacy that it is possible for a country to "go it alone." Rather, financial balkanization will likely be the only result of multiple, incompatible, and futile approaches by countries to shield themselves from foreign financial volatility. It will be critical for the United States to show leadership and develop coalitions to support reformist policies that maintain the free flow of capital.

Fishlow and DeSouza focus next on ensuring financial security for aging populations around the world—an emerging policy problem that illustrates how seemingly domestic financial issues are now linked to international behavior. "Saving social security" has been a rallying cry in the United States. However, opportunities for policy development extending to the international side have been missed even though they are increasingly integral to the problem.

The importance of certain international dimensions to retirement savings should be noticed. First, recent international financial crises have threatened the savings of American seniors as pension funds with exposure to emerging markets have seen their assets dramatically reduced as a result of external volatility. Second, around the world, countries are facing a similar social security shortfall. The issue of savings for aging populations was placed on the agenda of G-7 nations at the 1997 Denver Summit; in fact, the problem is actually more serious abroad, as a relative matter, than it is in the United States. A crisis in social security funding abroad may have a collateral effect on "traditional" military concerns because of the budgetary compromises that would be needed to satisfy domestic constituents. Especially in Europe and Japan, greater budgetary commitments for powerful retirees' lobbies might come at the expense of necessary defense expenditures such as support for NATO. To avoid negative security consequences triggered by social choices made abroad, U.S. leadership will be needed on this seemingly "domestic" issue.

On a broader front, U.S. leadership is absolutely necessary to find solutions to international financial volatility. Uneven macroeconomic policies have been exacerbated by misplaced regulatory policies that have sought to achieve a competitive edge for foreign capital through a "race to the regulatory bottom." In a world of integrated capital markets, such flawed regulatory strategies eventually feed back into the U.S. economy, creating economic security concerns. Carter Beese discusses the careful balance that must be crafted between prudent regulation and competitiveness. He advocates that the United States must provide leadership in helping create high-quality markets around the world. Leadership would be based on U.S. core principles of full, fair, and open disclosure and strong corporate governance. Such reform efforts would encourage transparency of corporate behavior by creating international standards, especially in terms of accounting.

Beese also offers an interesting link between the finance and technology issue-areas. He points out that advances in telecommunications, IT, and the Internet have reshaped the concept of stock markets. Screen-based transactions on "virtual exchanges" can increase exposure instantaneously on any market around the world. Investors are able to rapidly reallocate savings in seeking opportunities. In addition, technology has added pressures for consolidation in the financial industry as institutions have tried to eliminate transaction costs to remain competitive. These changes require dramatic regulatory changes at home and abroad as we head into the new century.

As evidenced during the financial crises of 1997–1999, technology has left countries with questionable macroeconomic fundamentals open to blitzkrieg speculative attacks on their respective currencies. Countries around the world are treating such attacks as matters of national security. In reaction to such threats, some emerging markets have begun to look for ways, principally through capital controls, to insulate themselves. Julie Katzman takes on this economic security issue by focusing on the use of a common currency—in this case the dollar—as a tool to smooth the volatility in financial markets. Through this approach, Katzman tries to preserve the free movement of capital while minimizing the scope for speculators.

Dollarization, by definition, eliminates the possibility of playing-off currencies against each other. However, it has clear foreign policy implications that must be considered when weighing policy options. First, sovereignty issues will arise, as countries adopting the dollar will be, to varying degrees, foregoing monetary tools to adjust macroeconomic performance. Second, other regions, such as the EU and East Asia, will watch closely any attempt by the United States to expand its influence through its currency.

Recent financial crises have threatened to feed back into the U.S. economy producing instability and threatening the sustainability of U.S. prosperity. It is clear that in this area, U.S. leadership is critical as countries sort through the trade-offs to be made. While emerging markets care a great deal about autonomy in monetary policy, in a world of integrated capital markets and ever-powerful trading technologies such autonomy can only be preserved at the unsavory choice of bearing the cost of limiting the movement of foreign capital through controls or remaining open to speculative attack.

Strong leadership by President Clinton and Secretary Rubin averted global financial meltdown during the fall of 1998. However, the dangers stemming from integrated capital markets called attention to the need for a new financial architecture. On February 26, 1999, in a major foreign policy speech in San Francisco, President Clinton put the task of creating such a financial architecture for the twenty-first century on the agenda of the G-7 nations. President Clinton underscored the populist pressures for reform by discussing the harsh impact of financial volatility on working men and women. Creating a new architecture, however, will require solutions for the daunting task of balancing sovereignty concerns with the need to smooth volatility of capital markets.

The threats discussed here are key topics for a new financial architecture. First, given the reality of aging populations worldwide and the macroeconomic stress arising out of efforts to honor every generation's commitment to their seniors, serious attention must be paid to the international dimensions of the retirement savings problem. Second, given the importance of public markets in terms of capital formation and attaining higher rates of return for invested funds, including perhaps retirement savings, it will be critical to develop high-quality markets based on the U.S. experience. Finally, because ever improving trading technologies and the integration of capital markets will increase volatility and open countries to speculative attacks, alternatives for smoothing such volatility must be considered carefully. Fear of such speculation is leading some to an isolationist call for a return to controls and away from open markets. Alternatives such as common currency must be considered to balance the objectives of smoothing volatility with the continued free movement of capital. At stake is a difficult public dialogue on the nature of sovereignty given the "new realities" of globalization.

Technology. The dissemination of IT will also create "new realities" influencing security policy development in the twenty-first century. The rise of new technologies and advances in telecommunications will influence every issue-area and produce changes in the way decisions are made at all levels of the public and private sectors. Such advances will raise distributional concerns. The most severe of these concerns is whether information "have-nots" can catch up or whether they will be locked out of future economic growth contributing to instability.

New technologies and new industries arising therefrom present great opportunities for shaping economies around the world. Such industries will affect the composition of U.S. investment, the direction and level of exports, and efforts to reach cooperative agreements. We will focus in this volume primarily on aspects of the IT business (telecommunications, electronic commerce, and venture capital); note that advances in life sciences are proving to be as transformative, though commercialization is proceeding at a slower pace relative to information technologies. In all these areas, U.S. leadership is unquestioned.

The current dynamism of the telecommunications industry, in terms of the variety of products and services being offered and developed, is in effect reinventing the sector. Recent mergers between telecommunications companies and networking companies are radically transforming the concept of audio, video, and data transmission. To some degree, the Clinton Administration has recognized this opportunity and made the distribution of telecommunications services for the twenty-first century a domestic and an international priority.

Domestically, the Telecommunications Reform Act of 1996 created subsidies for the wiring of schools to the Internet. The Clinton Administration's belief was that such subsidies would encourage the development of necessary skills for the future economy. This approach has been copied abroad, especially in Latin America through the 1998 Santiago Summit agenda. Moreover, on the international side, the Information Technology Agreement and the WTO Telecommunications Services Agreement have been important achievements of the administration, unlocking hundreds of billions of dollars of trade and investment as countries around the world privatize and deregulate based on U.S. principles.

The importance of technology affects not only our policy choices, but also those of our allies and adversaries. For example, it is said that one reason for Gorbachev's acquiescence to capitalist reforms, which were ultimately uncontrollable, was his acknowledgment that the revolution in the electronics industry could not be duplicated in the Soviet Union under the command economic system. Today, current resistance in APEC and Latin America to U.S. initiatives on electronic commerce stems from fear that U.S. companies will dominate forcing certain policy choices. Such fear often overrides a realization that advances in IT and telecommunications make a difference in economic growth paths for development. From the U.S. perspective, fear of the ramifications of technology dissemination also exists—in this case fear of empowering potential adversaries.

Gene Sekulow focuses on telecommunications and argues that there are several difficulties to be resolved before U.S. interests in international telecommunications reform may be achieved. The chief difficulty is one that foreign nations must address: How to balance the economic need to privatize and to import capital so as to build and upgrade telecommunications infrastructure against the political need to reassure domestic audiences that their "fundamental" rights to basic phone service would not be impaired by private or foreign control.

Emerging markets have the additional problem of determining what should be the optimal mix, given their resource base, of high-end and low-end telecommunications equipment and services. To shape the environment surrounding such decisions, U.S. foreign policy must work with other governments to raise their comfort level regarding the utility of an open market approach to telecommunications services and equipment.

The stakes are high for those resisting such an open market approach. The Internet is currently changing the nature of the telecommunications industry and, more broadly, the nature of economic transactions. In July 1997, the Clinton Administration outlined its approach to the emerging area of global electronic commerce (GEC). The administration's approach is one that seeks private sector leadership. The president's framework recognizes that electronic commerce has the power to transform societies, not only in terms of increased sales of goods and services, but also in terms of using the Internet to enhance societal values such as better education and healthcare delivery. Moreover, because it empowers all individuals, the Internet has the ability to convey an American vision for democracy and liberty.

Throughout the world, countries believe that GEC is important and inevitable. However, as Bob Hormats discusses, countries have been reluctant to embrace the principles that the Clinton Administration has articulated. As noted above, many countries fear that U.S. firms will dominate the provision of Internet infrastructure and services to the exclusion, rather than empowerment, of local entrepreneurs. Certain regional organizations, such as the EU and APEC, have considered their own versions of electronic commerce. These versions are more "state-centered" involving the creation of new bureaucracies. Hormats analyzes the competitive responses of the United States, EU, Asia, and Latin America and the possibilities for promoting the U.S. approach in the years ahead. Because of the enormous possibilities for the Internet to shape life in the twenty-first century, it will be important for the United States to fight for its private sector-led approach.

U.S. leadership in driving the creation of new technologies will also influence international financial relations through the promotion of venture capital—a financing approach that, as currently practiced, is uniquely American. Venture capital will be critical in the next century as countries seek to encourage entrepreneurship in small- and medium-sized businesses to sustain economic growth. Moreover, the venture business will offer important synergies with other issue-areas outlined above as countries try to boost savings rates through the private equity markets or try to develop new industries such as electronic commerce. Like telecommunications and the Internet, venture capital also has the ability to reinforce democratic principles through its entrepreneurial ethic promoting individual rights. More than any other "next generation" issue-area, venture capital has the possibility of conveying an American vision for the twenty-first century.

Like Sekulow and Hormats, Jeff Nuechterlein explores the competing approaches of EU and Asian countries in building venture capital industries. He offers a rich analysis of the contrasting approaches and offers some recommendations on how to develop U.S. interests. Importantly, he points out that government, through financial institutions such as the Overseas Private Investment Corporation (OPIC) and legal regimes such as that protecting intellectual property, does have an important role to play in the development of the industry. As a result, as with the shaping of electronic commerce, U.S. leadership is critical for ensuring an effective, private sector-led approach to venture capital worldwide.

Finally, Lawrence Greenberg presents the double-edged sword of promoting our leading-edge sector of IT as a matter of economic strategy. The dissemination of "off-the-shelf" IT creates vulnerabilities for U.S. security. With simple technology, hackers abroad may be able to create chaos by disrupting institutions such as financial exchanges and air-traffic control systems. Greenberg's essay is a useful reminder that the sense of boundless economic opportunities in a technological world sometimes masks a set of unintended consequences that must be addressed.

Technology is an area that will require some careful policy development so that the best path through the twenty-first century may be chosen by governments. The jockeying in Europe and Latin America to put more of a "statist" spin on electronic commerce is a prime example of the importance of the United States fighting for its private sector led-vision from the start. It is an area that stresses individual empowerment, entrepreneurship, and democracy in its ability to create previously unheard of access points for all. In light of such stakes, distributional concerns must not be overlooked.

Changing Markets

There are a variety of opportunities for developing U.S. interests in markets that are in economic transition. Three such markets will be explored here—the NIS, China, and Latin America. Russia and China represent the unfinished business of the twentieth century. Latin America, by contrast, represents the opportunity for a bold beginning to the new century as we integrate with our "own backyard."

The NIS presents the highest risk of near-term instability. As John Tedstrom points out, the United States has a fundamental, long-term security interest in having the NIS (especially Russia) develop from transition states to modern, market democracies rather than slide into rogue or failed states. Despite current public criticism, it must be acknowledged that Russia has made significant efforts toward reform. Russia has continually worked to stabilize its currency and has privatized approximately 70 percent of its economy. It is Tedstrom's assessment that Russia will not return to a Soviet-style regime.

Tedstrom, though, raises an important question regarding the kind of capitalism that will develop in the NIS. Tedstrom points out that, in Russia and the Ukraine, there is currently a fluid relationship among actors in business, government, and organized crime. In this respect, the above discussion of attending to the "by-products of capitalism," especially public integrity, is relevant for our approach to economic strategy with respect to the NIS. It is apparent, though, that Russia and Ukraine have much more to do given the current structure of their respective economies.

As troubling as the circumstances of Russia are, one could conclude that the United States has a handle on the issues involved because of its decade-long experience in working with the Russians
to make the transition from Soviet rule. By contrast, China presents
a problem of a different order of magnitude. First, given U.S. political history, we cannot truly appreciate the problems of economic
and political organization for over 1 billion people. Second, even if
we did begin to appreciate the issue of scale, our limited level of
regularized contacts with the Chinese make it difficult to have any
real insight into Chinese thinking on policy issues and to form expectations regarding economic interaction.

Jim Bass draws on his experience in China to call for a more mature, nuanced understanding of China rather than wild swings
based on over-reactions to the prospects for economic gain or dangers of instability. Calm analysis will be important as the
U.S.–China relationship has gotten bogged down in charges of
spying and illegal political influence. Bass emphasizes the element
of *caveat emptor* when looking at Chinese markets. In his estima-
tion, the Chinese will invite foreign investment but not readily liberalize because of their need for control. Their most pressing task,
he believes, is to ensure social stability through providing employment for 700 million laborers.

Any calculations by the United States of putting in place over the
next couple of years a complete framework of relations that sets
long-run expectations and a "web" of interests through "engagement" is misplaced. Because of China's priority of preventing social unrest among hundreds of millions of people, China is likely to
take only measured steps for the immediate future. We should expect no more. As Bass puts it, "The U.S. government will not be
able to change China—China will tend to that." In this light,
China's entry to the WTO should be considered as a policy driven
by mutual gain in terms of trade and investments rather than as a
carrot that will produce collateral concessions in future years.

Nicholas Rockefeller, however, offers the sobering thought that
because of its size and ambitions, the rise of China in the twenty-
first century may transcend any analogy to the rise of Germany,
Russia, and Japan at the beginning of the twentieth. Given this
possibility, Rockefeller challenges us to continue to search for and
to build alternative "economic levers" for dealing with China. In

this way, he too is a proponent of "engagement" as a twenty-first century security strategy.

Rockefeller argues for a U.S. focus on the cultivation of civil society and middle-market enterprises as key dimensions in which the United States has relevant experience, having shaped the democratic transitions in Germany and Japan after World War II. He points out that currently the United States has no policy initiatives targeted in this direction. Rockefeller finds this lack of a civil society approach startling given the variety of voluntary associations in the European context that permit contacts and points of cooperation. He also offers the comparative context of current policy reform in Latin America where formerly statist approaches have given way to the development of civil society. In offering policy recommendations, Rockefeller outlines a variety of U.S. governmental levers for working with U.S. business to cultivate small and medium-sized business relationships in China.

While Russia and China represent unfinished business, more than any other region, Latin America may represent the future for U.S. strategic interests. It may be surprising to realize how important Latin America is to U.S. economic strategy and security. In 1997, trade with Mexico surpassed Japan as our second largest market and Venezuela passed Saudi Arabia as our number one supplier of oil. Based on 1997 data, the United States exported more to Brazil than it did to China and more to Chile than it did to India. Before the 1998 financial crisis, it was projected that by 2010, Latin America would be more important to the United States with respect to trade than Europe and Japan combined.

Eric Farnsworth discusses the new opportunities for a sustainable and meaningful partnership in the hemisphere. Such a partnership has been deepening during the 1990s. The 1994 Miami Summit reaffirmed the region's commitment to vibrant democracies and open markets. Importantly, the 1998 Santiago Summit reinforced this commitment through a variety of "second generation reforms" in education, rule of law, and modernization of institutions that are necessary to support democracy and robust markets. These second generation reforms are also important for addressing concerns about the "by-products" of globalization. The leaders of the hemisphere committed in Santiago to an agenda that included combating corruption, enforcing labor standards, creating antipoverty programs, and strengthening climate change efforts. The Santiago Summit also produced the launch of negotiations for the completion of a Free Trade Area of the Americas by 2005. Juxta-posed against the 1997–1998 Asian financial crises, Latin America has been a model for making tough macroeconomic choices to re-inforce sustainable economic growth. To be sure, Latin America is susceptible to the Asian contagion as the case of Brazil makes clear. However, it must be remembered that, unlike Asia, Latin economic policy fundamentals are still quite strong.

Conclusion

Against the backdrop of the fast track trade debate, Asian financial instability, and, now, the chaos of the Seattle WTO meetings, the critics of globalization have multiplied. One such critic, Robert Kut-tner, offered this stark assessment:

> Naive globalism creates a bias against the mixed economy. . . . Un-regulated capitalism yields monopolies, gouges consumers, fails to invest adequately in public goods, and produces socially intolerable distributions of income and wealth. . . . The global money market, not the democratic electorate, becomes the arbiter of what policies are "sound.". . . What are the proper terms of engagement between a national, democratic polity and a global economy?. . . [I]f you want to see real economic nationalism—the ugly kind that leads to Cae-sarism and war—watch what happens in the IMF's wake.[5]

With this kind of assessment of the state of the world, Winston Lord's concern about policymakers' ability to understand and deal with the continued rise of economic issues as integral to U.S. secu-rity is quite prescient.

Each of the articles in this book begins to address different issues raised by Kuttner. Together, the articles seek to respond to those critics who want to reduce U.S. exposure to the world. Still, there was much left undone during the decade to create opportunity for all people based on an American vision of a community of twenty-first century liberal democracies. During the 1990s, the emphasis of policy development has been on restoring United States power through domestic-oriented economic policies that improved U.S. *competitiveness.* For the next generation, we would argue that the emphasis should be on projecting U.S. leadership through policies that manage *interdependence.*

With respect to the variety of concerns outlined by Kuttner, chapters by McCurdy, Hart, and Blinken are especially useful for getting at "the proper terms of engagement between a national, democratic polity and a global economy." McCurdy sets the stage with his discussion of the changing conceptions of security and the requirements for U.S. leadership in a networked world. He argues that persuasion will be the key element of leadership in the information age and that moral authority will be critical for credibility. Hart deepens the discussion by providing a philosophical underpinning for twenty-first century democracy through his principles of civic republicanism. Blinken focuses on the communications aspect of policy development in a democracy and the importance of U.S. leaders' ability to discuss the "new realities" of globalism with the American people. He challenges the conventional wisdom that Americans are disinterested (at best) in international affairs. All three, especially Hart, acknowledge the concern expressed by Kuttner that the "global money market" not the "democratic electorate" is becoming the arbiter of policies.

Various authors follow, taking seriously the importance of attending to the by-products of globalization. Each is mindful of the effect of democratic processes in the making of U.S. foreign policy and is quite aware of Kuttner's concerns about the rise of an "ugly" economic nationalism. Pat Buchanan's self-styled economic nationalism brings such ugliness to the fore with his characterization of the "great hiring hall" filled with Asians and Latins. Fishlow and DeSouza discuss U.S. trade policy and the failure of fast track in this light, noting that the data indicate that wage stagnation for labor is caused not by imports, but rather by the introduction of new technologies that increase productivity, changes in education, and immigration patterns. From the security standpoint, Helweg offers ways in which economic engagement through trade can actually be used as an effective foreign policy framework by creating incentives among parties, including adversaries, for cooperation.

VanDeMark calls attention to and analyzes precedents in American history where populist counter-reaction emerged during periods of economic transition. VanDeMark characterizes such movements in terms of the struggle of ordinary people seeking to share in the fruits of growth against the forces of corruption. In this light, Murdock's focus on the deterioration of public integrity and the need for campaign finance reform to prevent special interest groups from siphoning economic benefits away from average Americans is to the point.

In turning to international relations, various authors try to respond to Kuttner's concerns that the global money market, not the democratic electorate, becomes the arbiter of what policies are "sound." Shafer offers recommendations of how to make U.S. policymaking institutions more responsive to global financial problems that are emerging. Fishlow, DeSouza, Beese, and Katzman then try to address specific policy issues that come in line with Kuttner's concerns about a "naïve globalism" undermining the success of the mixed economy over the last century.

Increased volatility arising out of the development of sophisticated trading technologies and the integration of capital markets pose a range of problems requiring development of a financial architecture. In designing such architecture, the United States may lead by example in some neglected problem areas. The need to generate adequate savings for aging populations around the world and to protect such savings from the volatility of integrated capital markets is an emerging international problem that currently is being thought of in domestic terms by policymakers. In addition, as markets around the world deregulate in an effort to remain competitive in attracting foreign capital, policymakers must be concerned with a "race to the bottom" phenomenon. Beese reaffirms the need for U.S. leadership in ensuring high-quality securities markets that at the same time are competitive. Finally, as President Clinton has noted, working people in emerging markets (but increasingly also in the United States) live in fear of economic volatility triggered by attacks on currencies by speculators. U.S. leadership in the hemisphere through dollarization may be an important alternative to currency controls. Such controls, bred by fears of international integration, would likely only provide an ineffective method of retreat against the global marketplace.

Articles by Tedstrom, Bass, Rockefeller, and Farnsworth put the discussion of economic strategy and national security in a regional context. Each of the emerging markets described offer special challenges for the United States. In the near term, there is great risk that Russia will slide into economic chaos as the institutions of capitalism have not yet taken root. It is in this context, especially, that Kuttner's fears of an economic nationalism that would lead to Caesarism and war are most likely to be realized. Over the long run, though, it is likely that the rise of China will be the focal point of U.S. security concerns. Because of its immense size, nationalist tradition, and limited points of contact with the United States, the evolution of the U.S.-China relationship may prove to be the most difficult task facing the next generation.

Finally, while the integration of Russia and China into the community of liberal democracies represents the unfinished business of the Cold War, the strengthening of the Americas partnership may represent the great opportunity of the twenty-first century. Already the hemisphere contains our fastest growing trading relationships, our largest sources of energy, and some of our strongest supporters in multilateral diplomacy. It also should not be missed that Latin America offers an important case study in terms of a common reform agenda that combines the deepening of capitalism with the reform of institutions that support the rule of law, education, and humane markets.

We emphasize that security is not only about preventing certain threatening actions, it is about creating opportunities and a preferred set of circumstances for American interests and mutual gain. In this respect, the Internet and venture capital—as described by Hormats and Nuechterlein—are two emerging sectors that have the power to transform the world and to project an American vision of the twenty-first century. Electronic commerce, as conceived in President Clinton's framework, contributes to individual empowerment across a variety of areas from education to sales of goods and services. Venture capital, in its promotion of entrepreneurship and self-determination, has uniquely American characteristics.

Yet, even in this area of informatics, Sekulow and Greenberg remind us of sobering realities. There are distributional concerns involved in building a technological world. It is quite possible, as Kuttner would probably agree, that "information have-nots" will produce serious instability as frustration mounts over being locked out of twenty-first century wealth creation. On the other hand, from the security standpoint, the opportunities for individual empowerment through the widespread distribution of IT may actually be used against us someday.

The articles in this volume thus are meant to be provocative and to encourage discussion about the rise of economic issues as integral to the development of U.S. security policy. As we explore more closely in the following essays the changing concepts of security, the by-products of globalism, and the challenges and opportunities ahead, we may be able to better formulate our "Next Generation" agenda.

Notes

1. *The Economist,* "The 20th Century," September 11, 1999, p. 42.

2. See C. Fred Bergsten, *America in the World Economy* (1988), pp. 189–90.

3. The Commerce Department notes that 60 percent of households earning $75,000 or more had Internet access compared with less than 10 percent of households earning less than $20,000. Whites were more likely to have Internet access than African-Americans and Hispanics across all income levels. See U.S. Department of Commerce, *Falling Through the Net: Defining the Digital Divide* (July 1999).

4. Patrick Buchanan, *The Great Betrayal.* (Boston: Little Brown 1998) at p. 61.

5. Robert Kuttner, "Globalism Bites Back," *American Prospect,* March-April 1998, pp. 6–8.

Part I

Conceptual Underpinnings

Chapter 2

American Leadership in the Information Age

Dave McCurdy

Introduction

New international realities, based on the explosive rise and dissemination of information technology (IT), are propelling us into the twenty-first century. Pundits like Paul Kennedy, Peter Drucker, and Alvin Toffler tell Americans that to maintain our living standards and to preserve our security, we had better prepare for this new age. Yet under the current system, it is not clear that the United States will be prepared to take on these challenges. U.S. policies and institutions, especially with respect to our foreign relations, must be reformed to reflect the new realities that we face if we are to successfully shape our future.

The silicon chip, and the information-based economy it drives, is becoming a more accurate measure of national wealth, power, and

---

I participated in two excellent study groups which produced several reports that I will refer to throughout my discussion: Stimson Center, "The Partnership Imperative: Maintaining American Leadership in a New Era," "Alternating Currents: Technology and the New Context for U.S. Foreign Policy," and CSIS, "Information Revolution and National Security."

economic vitality, than traditional indicators such as capital and labor. For this new economy, the comparative roles of government and private sector are changing at a lightning pace. For example, there are currently several hundred satellites in orbit. Traditionally, these have been mostly government launched and operated. In 1997, however, we witnessed the passage of an important threshold. For the first time, more commercial money was spent on space than government money.

Over the next ten years, the number of satellites in orbit is projected to increase to over 2,000. Moreover, within the same time, the commercial use of space is projected to increase 300 percent. Most of this increase will be funded and operated by commercial multinational consortia. The space telecommunications business alone is valued at $1 trillion after deregulation by the end of 2000. The estimated "untapped" telecom market could be as much as a few billion people. It is just one component of the dynamic future of electronic commerce that knows no national boundaries and represents the new reality of globalization.

This new dynamic forces us to look at policy formation in a different way. Historically, government provided the impetus for economic dynamism through research and development (R&D) funding and demand for systems that supported remarkable technological innovation. Whether it was space assets, supercomputers, or the Internet, the government pushed progress in technology. The reality today, however, is that commercial innovation outstrips government innovation, resulting in approximately eight technology cycles in the private sector for every one policy cycle. Moreover, because of the competitive pressure in the private sector to maintain market share or stay ahead of the competition, twenty-first century business must have ever shorter development-to-product cycles creating additional stress on policymakers to remain relevant.

The truly successful ventures of the next generation will be nimbly reacting to changing markets as well as generating time-sensitive customer research to assist in the development of products and services. Government, on the other hand, will seem ever slower by comparison. This dynamic should not be surprising. Madison in the *Federalist Papers* even wrote, "promptitude in the legislature is more often an evil than a benefit." Government agencies, even with the efforts to streamline and shorten their regulatory red tape and cumbersome procedures, will be unable to keep up with the explosion of the technology revolution. Furthermore, innovation in the IT sector will result in "discontinuous development" that will virtually spawn entire business sectors. By the time government tries to regulate a new technology or industry, it will often be too late or misplaced. One conclusion has become apparent to most observers: Government's role should focus on areas in which it can be effective—funding basic research, protecting intellectual property, and promoting open marketplace rules.

The information revolution and globalization will require the United States to "nimbly react" by making a sharp, rather than gradual, break from the past. We will need new conceptual categories to properly understand the world, including new indicators of power and the creation of new, more accurate measures of economic activity. We will also need new policy approaches to be able to make informed choices and reach new understandings of the compact between the American people and government and, importantly, to confidently project our influence into the world. On the grand stage, the new realities are forcing the United States to rethink its approach to foreign policy and, ultimately to leadership in U.S. politics.

The Clinton Administration has had the difficult chore of helping the American people make the transition to a new age. In many ways, it has done well. The president has personally raised the visibility and awareness of the information age with his campaign to build a metaphorical "bridge to the twenty-first century." The administration has emphasized making public investments oriented toward the future. In many cases, the administration's forward-looking policies have been directed inward toward improving America's skills through education, financial security through balancing the budget and reforming social security, and infrastructure through telecommunications reform. Developing and articulating a strategy to help shape the world, though, has been episodic. As a result, we have not been fully able to make the sharp break necessary to better position the United States for the twenty-first century.

In moving from "grand design" (such as it exists) to practical policies, the Clinton Administration's international agenda has been erratic. In certain fora, the shift toward a twenty-first century agenda has been clear. The 1997 Denver G-7 Summit highlighted new global issues such as aging populations and the spread of communicable diseases. At the 1998 Santiago Summit of the Americas, the administration focused hemispheric attention on education, technology, and international financial stability.

On the other hand, the U.S. Congress, increasingly fragmented in its attention and approach to the twenty-first century globalization, has slowed these efforts. Specifically, the extreme wings of both major parties have slowed our embrace of the international economy so as to proactively shape outcomes.

The most salient example of this inward focus was seen during the congressional defeat of fast track trade authority sought by President Clinton in 1997 and 1998. Some parts of the Democratic Party, in fact, have become well known for their opposition to free trade, leading the way in defeating fast track. The Republicans have fared no better. USA ENGAGE, a group dedicated to promoting international trade, reported that based on a number of recent votes such as fast track, International Monetary Fund (IMF) funding, and use of unilateral sanctions, support for global economic engagement can no longer be considered an article of faith in the Republican Party, especially among social conservatives.

In long-standing security areas, such as China and Russia, the unfinished business of the Cold War—integrating former communist states into the world community, reducing stockpiles of nuclear weapons, and more—has delayed the shift to attending to the concerns of a new age. The administration has been slow to develop a policy that both recognizes the emerging power and role of China in Asia and the world, and is capable of dealing effectively and consistently with the ambiguities of China itself. The United States can and should play a role in helping steer China toward the right fork in the proverbial crossroads, one in which China is a cooperative and responsible international actor. Only recently, though, has the administration focused attention on today's rapid changes driving China. These administration efforts continue to be hamstrung by congressional accusations of special treatment for campaign donors, security breaches at U.S. nuclear weapons labs, and Chinese hostility over issues such as the inadvertent bombing of the Chinese embassy in Belgrade.

With respect to Russia, the administration spent the bulk of its energy bogged down in trying to integrate Russia and Central Europe with the North Atlantic Treaty Organization (NATO). Meanwhile, criminal organizations have allied with former communist bureaucrats to mute economic liberty and political democracy. Such corruption, when bundled with the economic crisis fueled by the Asian contagion, led to a collapse of credible leadership and the return of the old *nomenklatura*-style leadership. The Russian financial crisis sent economic tremors our way during 1998. Furthermore, the opportunity to secure greater reductions in and control of nuclear weapons, materials, technology, and expertise may have been squandered by lack of bold leadership and little support from the U.S. Congress.

Moreover, while the United States and Russia have been spending significant time and resources making limited progress on reducing nuclear weapons, "technically talented" India conducted five nuclear tests without detection by the U.S. intelligence community. The administration responded in 1998 with tepid economic sanctions aimed at Indian effrontery to the nuclear club's admonitions against proliferation. The United States and the international community were equally weak in persuading Pakistan, which has the technical skills required but is resource poor, not to respond in kind. The irony is that U.S. economic sanctions against Pakistan, which feels directly threatened by the Indian nuclear program, could have a much more debilitating effect on its weak economy creating greater strategic instability.

In addition to the distractions produced by the unfinished business of the Cold War, the economic crisis in Asia has spread to other continents threatening the economic and political liberalization of the post–Cold War era. The global financial turmoil has reinforced the fears of globalization and political retrenchment. In Indonesia, we witnessed the fall of dictator Suharto, but other autocrats, such as Malaysia's Prime Minister Mahatir have used capital flight as an excuse to crack down on political rivals and opposition. The linkage between economic and political freedom has never been so strong. The immediate effect of the almost instantaneous and unfettered flow of significant amounts of money gives credence to the call for a new Bretton Woods model. The world is looking to the United States for strong leadership and to demonstrate that it recognizes that this crisis requires more than mere expressions of concern and empathy.

This article focuses on the international dimensions of preparing our citizens for America's leadership role in the twenty-first century. After first considering the conceptual changes required to better appreciate "new realities," this article will identify some new indicators of power and policy approaches. I will then articulate an approach to U.S. leadership for the next generation. While everyone understands that the world is changing, policymakers underappreciate the pace of change and the firmness of the grip of the past in defining the required agenda.

New Realities and Concepts

New Realities

The new realities of the twenty-first century are changing the way we look at the world and our understanding of the meaning of power. We are headed toward a world in which social reality is defined by "networks" based on an individual's ability to exchange a new currency—information—with chosen communities. The ascendancy of networks undermines traditional hierarchical organizations by instant access to information and activities anytime, anywhere, and without regard to physical or political boundaries. Moreover, this trend is accelerating because of technological innovation.

To gain some perspective on the pace of change produced by IT, consider that over 30 million Americans now use the Internet at work every day, and almost 40 million use it at home. Internet bandwidth demand is growing 1,000 percent per year—in part because of the explosive growth in websites whose number may hit 100 million by 2002–2003. Business-to-business e-commerce is expected to approach $1.5 trillion by 2003.[1]

As a result of such rapid changes, technology is shrinking the world through globalization and integration. We are seeing greater collaboration through shared networks. Paradoxically, we are also simultaneously becoming more individualistic as such empowerment is rending the ties to traditional institutions and relationships, especially government. According to Regis McKenna, a pioneer in modern business marketing, "for business and branches of government serving the public, the important media of the past were channels for broadcast. The vital new media, by contrast, are channels of access."[2] Access to media and information is democratizing but, as Joe Nye has pointed out, it can potentially be very destabilizing to traditional institutions and organizations.

United States Transition to the Information Age

By now, it is well recognized that the United States is moving rapidly from a post-industrial, service-based economy to an information-based economy. To gain some perspective on the rapidity of change that IT is creating, consider that the number of phones in the world (currently about 800 million) will double in the next decade. In addition, the cost of computing has been falling at thirty percent per year in real terms for about two decades. Computing power is thus only one-hundredth of one percent as costly today as in the early 1970s. As a result, there has been a proliferation of personal computers (PC). The number of Internet-connected computers expanded globally to about 16.5 million in January 1997. There may be, by some estimates, 200 million Internet-connected users in the United States within a few years. With such change, what is emerging is the development of the "meganet": an array of telecommunication technologies linking most individuals in the world and making the movement of goods, capital, people, and ideas easier and cheaper.

Information itself now has "intrinsic value" and is considered a commodity. Moreover, technology that efficiently transfers the "commodity" will create new sources of wealth for the United States. First, the entire economy has benefited greatly from the proliferation of IT . Manipulation of information in real time has led to greater efficiencies in sourcing, R&D, production, marketing, and transportation. The U.S. Department of Commerce estimates that IT industries are growing at double the rate of the overall economy and, during the 1990s, were responsible for a quarter to a third of all real U.S. economic growth. Productivity has begun to accelerate, too, growing more than 2 percent annually in the late 1990s after years of stagnation. Many analysts credit IT with the productivity surge.[3]

Second, the development of IT has unleashed an entrepreneurial ethic that has, in turn, driven further innovation and wealth creation. There has been an explosion of growth in the telecommunications, electronics, computer, software, and service industries. To put this in perspective, only one-third of the companies on the Fortune 500 list fifty years ago still exist today and more than half of the top twenty computer companies in the United States were not in business twenty years ago.

The United States has become an information-driven economy and in some respect, has already paid the price of transformation from an industrial workforce to an information-based workforce. Peter Drucker stated in his article, "The Age of Social Transformation," that "America's industrial workers must have been prepared to accept as right and proper the shift to jobs that require formal education and that pay for knowledge rather than manual work, whether skilled or unskilled. In the United States the shift had by 1990 or so largely been accomplished."[4]

Such a shift, however, comes at a price. Drucker argues, "a society in which knowledge workers dominate is under threat from a new class conflict: between the large minority of knowledge workers and majority of people, who will make their living traditionally, either by manual work, whether skilled or unskilled, or by work in services, whether skilled or unskilled." A person who uses a computer at work makes nearly 20 percent more than his or her counterpart who does not. A more striking example of the gap is the *Economist* report stating that the average house in the San Francisco area costs over $300,000 and is a prime area for Silicon Valley elites, but that the city now has over 15,000 homeless living on the streets. Optimists, however, believe that the investment in technology and readily available training and education programs will eventually lead to a reduction in the gap.

International Challenges of
Technological Change

Technological change is not only transforming the American polity but influencing every corner of the globe. With a mouse click, anyone may obtain information as deep and broad as one wants. This flexibility gives enormous access to relatively isolated individuals. According to Peter Drucker,

> the knowledge society will inevitably become far more competitive than any society we have yet known—for the simple reason that with

knowledge being universally accessible, there will be no excuses for nonperformance. There will be no "poor" countries. There will only be ignorant countries. And the same will be true for companies, industries, and organizations of all kinds. It will be true for individuals, too. In fact, developed societies have already become infinitely more competitive for individuals than were the societies of the beginning of this century, let alone earlier ones.[5]

The spread of modernity through technology, however, will offer difficult challenges. Rapid communication of ideas will create, and sometimes force, reactions across national borders. The political and social values born in the West will reshape international relations and norms of governance across the globe, but it is not clear to what end. According to the U.S. Department of Commerce, international sales of U.S. software and entertainment products became the largest industry sector with over $60 billion in sales in 1996. Especially in terms of economic ideas and values, the varying background conditions in different corners of the world will raise difficulties for ensuring that technological change is used for good purposes.

Importantly, the spread of economic values through IT will intensify the effect of social and demographic trends. Even without the compounding effect of technology, rapid population growth in developing countries and aging populations in the industrial world are challenging economic and social stability. For example, it is estimated that by 2021, over half of the world's population will be urban, concentrated in 300 cities of a million-plus inhabitants, of which 45 will be megacities of over 5 million. There is a likelihood that there will be an explosion of "slumburbs," as cities will be unable to provide basic services, much less information-related services. In such slumburbs, there will be a youth bulge—an abnormally high number of people between the ages of 15 and 25—that will create stress on the ability of governments to provide adequate education, jobs, housing, and political participation.[6]

IT may serve to magnify the potential disruption of such social patterns in developed and developing nations by heightening public awareness of the inability of governments to cope with the widening gulf in interests between young and old. Moreover, given that the young are more likely than the old to adopt IT, an ever-widening divide will be created between those who can manipulate their environment (i.e., information) and those who cannot. The worst case scenario for those currently holding power would be that young, disaffected members of the slumburbs will hold the key to manipulating the new levers of power.

In addition to producing a divide based on information haves and have-nots, technological change will also produce unstable "centrifugal" and "centripetal" forces. In a particularly provocative article, "Jihad vs. McWorld,"[7] Benjamin Barber argues that the two axial principles of our age—tribalism and globalism—introduce contradictions at every point except one: they both threaten democracy because of the instabilities they introduce. Such instabilities are further accelerated by IT.

On one hand, information serves to raise expectations and awareness. Such empowerment can disrupt identities. As we are witnessing, modern communications is fueling an increase in tribal, religious, ecological, and ethnic passions.

On the other hand, the "new" McWorld is "demand[ing] integration and uniformity . . . with fast music, fast computers, and fast food—with MTV, Macintosh, and McDonald's, pressing nations into one commercially homogeneous global network: one McWorld tied together by technology, ecology, communications and commerce." These stresses on polities must be taken into account in policy development to meet the challenges of the next generation.

It should be noted, though, that even though the dangers of economic and demographic change will be heightened with the spread of technology, there will be created potentially new sources for institutional support. Newly rich nations, nongovernmental organizations (NGO), and multilateral organizations—will help manage change and address the large international and transnational challenges. These supports should be encouraged even though they create more actors that the United States needs to bargain with to achieve preferred outcomes for the United States.

New Concepts

The cornerstone of the information age is currently the Internet. The Internet accelerates the diffusion of political and economic power outward, away from central elites. New concepts are needed to understand this diffusion. The dissemination of information and power "outward and down from central elites"—is leading to the creation and maintenance of autonomous communities that share the new currency—information. In thinking about this dynamic, I would identify the concept of "network societies" as a driving force in shaping policy directions for the twenty-first century.

In defining "network societies" one must focus on organizational networks, mainly the "all-channel" design where all members are connected to and can communicate with each other. Social scientists commonly use the term *chain and star designs*. A better term may be *cybernets*.

David Rondfelt, an analyst at RAND, wrote a thought-provoking essay "Tribes, Institutions, Markets and Networks: Evolution of Social Organizations." In this essay, he describes the evolution of different forms of organization. The basic organizing unit for society was once the clan or tribe. Rondfelt argues that this unit is still dominant in many societies. Tribes, though, were limited in scope by their nature. As a result, historically, hierarchical institutions emerged to provide organizational structure. Examples included the Catholic Church, monarchies, and military organizations. These hierarchical organizations with centralized management actually enabled nation states to emerge. Hierarchical units, however, were also limited by the amount of information they could simultaneously process. Rondfelt asserts that, in response to this limitation, more efficient markets with diffused decisionmaking evolved, expanding the ability of societies to progress. His basic point is that modern societies are built based on a combination of tribes, institutions, and markets. Extending this evolutionary path, I would argue that the explosion of technology and media has fostered the development of the next great organizing structure—the network.

In network communities, the key relationships are between information creators and disseminators. The driving process is one of disintermediation—eliminating the need for middle-men—because individuals are empowered to use technology to achieve their own ends. In this kind of world, relationships are characterized by delayering and flattening of organizations, business, and hopefully—government.

Network societies allow groups to connect to each other to the exclusion of outside entities that might exert control. In this respect, network societies create great challenges for the constitutive structure of any nation. An emphasis on the network reduces national authority in favor of tribalism. On the positive side, if the philosophical underpinning of the nation is local self-governance, then network societies may actually be beneficial for returning autonomy to the local level. This is an angle that Gary Hart explores in the next essay.

New Indicators of Power

The new realities and concepts shaped by IT require us to reconsider what might be the indicators of power in the twenty-first century. Changes in indicators of power will have varying implications for U.S. security. Only by understanding these changing dimensions might the United States engage in effective policy development.

In the twenty-first century, the importance of the old benchmarks of national power, such as labor, natural resources, military forces, and industrial output, will change. Some economists have already begun using information-age measures such as "tele-density"—the number of telephones per person in a country—to evaluate national strength. Other measures readily come to mind such as a country's use of computers and electronic data.

Changing Economic Power

Global economic issues are playing an increasingly central role in U.S. foreign policy. Moreover, the composition of global economic issues is shifting, requiring different priorities for policy development. Ultimately, increasing economic interdependence and deepening the integration of markets are about ideas rather than land, resources, labor, and tradable goods.

As indicated earlier, the United States has become an information-driven economy with a clear edge in IT. By contrast, the EU and Japan have not yet fully made the transformation and are still regarded as stratified industrial economies. For example, the EU has 47 percent of global manufacturing exports, but only 7 percent of the world computer market. The net effect is that the United States continues to gain advantage in computer-related services as the industrial nations buy U.S. knowledge products and services. In fact, that dominance is likely to grow.

The *Economist* has projected that the global information business will grow to $3 trillion by this end of the decade, equivalent to 1 of 6 dollars of worldwide product. U.S. information services companies have a 46 percent share of global trade and an annual growth rate of 13 percent. Because of this economic reality, it has been important for the U.S. to focus on services (banking, tourism, insurance, data services, and telecommunications traffic) in the General Agreement on Tariffs and Trade (GATT) and World Trade Organization (WTO).

As heartening as these statistics are for us technological "haves," we should not forget that perhaps half of the world's population has yet to make a telephone call. Accordingly, certain dangers will emerge from the path we are on. Most critically, any skills gap with respect to information will have huge consequences for social stability. In our information society, those at the top of the income distribution are reaping huge returns while those at the middle and bottom of society are realizing comparatively few. Already one-fourth to one-third of the college–high school wage differential is caused by the loss of high-wage blue-collar jobs in the goods-producing sectors. These differentials and resulting social discontent will only be magnified internationally creating a great divide between the information rich and information poor.

In addition, there may be other negative by-products of the information age. While IT has made possible complicated global production and distribution networks, it has also produced a new breed of criminal. Intellectual property is now better understood as a store of value that is at risk. Theft and leakage of corporate and industrial secrets trebled during the mid-1990s resulting in losses of $24 billion per year. In areas such as the NIS and China, where economic institutions are underdeveloped, the young information industry offers a focal point for organized crime.

Finally, the increased dependence on and vulnerability of communications systems is now a major concern for national security. The U.S. leaders have become increasingly aware and concerned about the vulnerability of critical economic infrastructure, public and private, to attack either by information warfare (IW) or weapons of mass destruction. The bombings of the World Trade Center, the Federal Building in Oklahoma City, and the recent failure of the PanAm Sat's Galaxy IV satellite only heighten such concerns.

Changing Military Power

The United States currently remains the only true superpower. It is inevitable, though, that major competitors will emerge. Early adopters of IT may create the dynamics for a significant shift in the balance among militaries.

Conceptual Shift.   IT is changing our perspectives on military power. Traditionally, the U.S. military conceived of itself in the following ways: First, its mission was to use forces to repel attacks against U.S. territory and against U.S. interests abroad. Second, the military served to help to stabilize relations between U.S. friends as well as reduce regional concerns about the rise of hostile, militarily dominant powers. Third, the military's forward-deployed forces played a key role in stabilizing regions. Finally, U.S. forces could be used cooperatively with other states to teach military professionalism and to inculcate values, civilian control of military, and respect for human rights.

After the collapse of the Soviet Union and the end of the Cold War, the United States reduced its defense budget and presence overseas. Yet despite the dramatic reduction in resources, the United States has maintained a high operational tempo, increasing peacekeeping activities while clinging to the concept of being successful on two fronts simultaneously. Given the budget constraint, something has had to give: R&D and acquisition of future technology and systems have declined.

The central question is whether future adversaries will challenge U.S. and allied strength, as in the Gulf War, or look to probe U.S. weaknesses and vulnerabilities. Because information has no boundaries, U.S. technological dominance is not assured. The challenge for U.S. military leaders is to ensure that the defense organization (and culture) can keep up with the revolutionary pace of change in IT. Moreover, much of the change is generated by innovations in the commercial, not defense, market. This is a market that the military has no control over in that consumer demand, not warfighting demand, drives it. Hardware and software is available "off the shelf." Regardless of how adept we are in the manufacture and integration of technology, there will be those who can acquire it through commercial sources and are not so dumb as to "fight the last war." As a result, the next war could involve far different technologies and increase the vulnerability of high-tech societies.

In the *Army After Next* wargames, conducted by the U.S. Army to study alternative futures, different military scenarios were considered for the 2010–2020 time frame. The opposition always opted for asymmetrical attacks choosing not to play to U.S. strength-information superiority. Instead, the opposition tried to find ways to undercut or limit the U.S. edge. The "Information Operations" experience in these forward-thinking exercises has raised numerous policy issues, ranging from "no first use" to the involvement of international treaties on telecommunications. The Department of Defense (DoD) has slowly recognized these and other operational issues and has created a new post, Deputy Assistant Secretary for Information Operations, to review offensive and defensive operations. It is a step in the right direction, but there are far more questions than answers at this point.

The information revolution calls for a paradigm shift for the twenty-first century military. It is not clear at this point what the parameters will be. Over the ages there have always been shifts in military objectives corresponding to the shifts in the dominant mode of economic activity. For example, objectives in pre-industrial war were predicated on seizure or control of territory. In industrial age war, destroying the opponent's means of production and manufacturing more than one's opponent were central. Now, policymakers and analysts are trying to figure out how objectives will change in the information age war. The Joint Chiefs of Staff and Joint Vision 2010 are currently discussing the importance of incorporating information-age technologies and plans. The question remains, however, whether institutional change to meet the new realities can be achieved given the entrenched nature of the defense culture.

Most analysts acknowledge that the key to military strategy in the twenty-first century will be control of information and knowledge assets. Former Secretary of Defense, Bill Perry and Admiral Bill Owens are leading advocates of moving toward a "System of Systems." This approach would involve a union of components that would collectively provide "information superiority."

Currently, there is a whole new vocabulary of clichés: cyberdeterrence, digital battlefields, netwars, and information warfare or IW. A cottage industry of IW has sprung-up based on improved battle space awareness, information dissemination capabilities, and ubiquitous smart weapons. We have seen vast improvements since the Gulf War in interoperability, integration of the many diverse Command, Control, Communications, and Intelligence (C3I) systems and the dismantling of institutional barriers that separated intelligence from operations. In this context, there has even been a shift in the philosophical underpinnings for approaching the use of military power. There has been a resurgence in the theories of Karl von Clausewitz who believed that the role of knowledge in warfare is a "factor more vital than any other" and Sun Tzu who focused on principles of superior intelligence, deception, and knowledge of the enemy mind.

One illustration of how IT is changing the way the military thinks about the application of military power may be helpful. The Army Digitization of the Battlefield effort (Appliqué) argues for constant real-time intelligence linked through a laptop. Global Positioning Satellite (GPS) data transmitted to soldiers could synchronize their actions with the flow of the battle without a hierarchical and bureaucratic command and control system. No commander can expect perfect knowledge or awareness on the battlefield. However, with new technologies, he will be able to manage the knowledge gained.

The result of such distributed information is that "decision cycles" for commanders and soldiers on the field will be compressed and enriched, accelerating the operations tempo of warfighting. Forces will be able to focus and concentrate fire from distributed locations and platforms. Such an environment will demand more initiative-based, decentralized decisionmaking and decrease the need for manpower in the field and on staff.

The introduction of technology and networked decisionmaking will require the effective development of leaders. It is going to be a serious challenge to recruit, train, retain, and motivate a new generation of leaders who have the essential technical competence and judgment to make real-time decisions. As a result, the federal government is going to be in for the human resources fight of its life.

Military Design Changes.   There is an ongoing debate within the Defense Department about how much risk DoD is willing to take to develop new systems and to leverage technology. Because the United States is in the unusual position of having no real competitors on the military front, it has the luxury of looking farther out into the future and investing in the most advanced systems and practices. The question is, how much risk is the United States willing to take? Because of our current relative strength, we can rely on a reduced number of legacy systems and direct more investment into future capabilities. However, unless the DoD breaks out of its current "Cold War Lite" organization and invests in R&D and future modernization, all the talk of information dominance may be just that.

The area where we can see an immediate return is in reforming the structure of the logistics operations. The reality is that operations and maintenance spending is crowding out new development. If there is a business and IT analogue that can be applied to DoD, it is in the total asset visibility arena and logistics. It is in this arena that the commercial companies, not the Defense Department, are world class. The debate about DoD outsourcing must be given serious consideration within the administration and Congress.

Can the DoD, or government as a whole, adopt business or corporate practices? According to most business consultants, the best companies avoid "big bang" projects taking three to five years that are characteristic of the defense sector. Instead, commercial companies add infrastructure, develop custom applications, or implement standard systems through a series of regular deliverables, often every 90 days, and ensure that major projects take no more than two years to complete. Of course in business, people drive the projects and are on the hook for the results. In the fast moving world of business, "perfect" is often the enemy of the "good."

It is critical that the DoD fully incorporates these practices to shorten the development cycle of large systems. DoD even has incredibly long development and procurement cycles for non-weapon systems. The DoD should focus on those acquisitions that provide real leverage from the technology revolution. It doesn't make sense to continue to spend billions on upgrading conventional platforms that are not seriously threatened today. The real payoff is in accelerating revolutionary technologies, such as nonlethal weapons and advanced sensors, to deal with urban conflict.

IT can also provide new ways of handling and avoiding conflict. Tactics will have to change as well as force structures and military organizations. Given the return of forms of tribalism in the twenty-first century, what the United States really may need is a shift in policy and doctrine that recognizes constabulary and military operations other than war as well as warfighting. In effect, warfighters will also have to be peacekeepers. It will therefore be important to better understand the reality of conflict termination and conflict resolution.

The modalities of institutional cooperation will be key to future success under such scenarios. Hierarchical command structures and ponderous military-industrial bureaucracies, created to fit industrial-age needs, must give way to flattened networks that reflect the character of the information age and the locus of action residing in decentralized communities. Such a reorientation, based on the realities of the information age, will involve a major political and bureaucratic fight with the current "stove-piped" structure of the Defense Department. The real debate will be less over the viability of legacy systems but whether, in fact, the government is frozen in a legacy culture. There is hope that the increase in joint exercises and military operations will drive the necessary change.

Peter Drucker stated the challenge, "uncertainty in the economy, society, politics—has become so great as to render futile, if not counterproductive, the kind of planning most companies still practice: forecasting based on probabilities." I would submit, as did the National Defense Panel reviewing the Quadrennial Defense Report, that such uncertainty also applies to defense planning. I agree with the panel's recommendation for the DoD to develop a special command that will introduce, develop, and field future weapon systems with relevant doctrine.

Critical New Modality of Power: Persuasion

The United States has a variety of foreign policy assets. The information age, however, will require the United States to project its power in ways different than it did during the twentieth century. I have long believed that the elements of power in the White House were a good reflection of the broader paradigm of national power. Unlike the conventional assumption that power is located principally in the office of the president, I believe the essential elements of power are broader than the office. In addition to the office, ideology and character make a difference. These are bully pulpit factors.

First, the power of the office has been reduced in recent years by the emergence of a bolder Congress and the more confrontational media. Not since FDR, who enjoyed extraordinary power because of the double national emergencies of the Great Depression and World War II, have we seen a White House that possessed truly formidable power and influence.

Second, the ideology or philosophy of the president or administration creates "rules-of-the road" for decisionmaking. The most recent example is the Reagan Presidency, in which Ronald Reagan may not have been a policy wonk, but people knew where he stood and that he had core beliefs, even if they disagreed with him. His consistent views and action against communism accelerated the demise of the Soviet Union.

Third, and as important, is character. In this case I use character to mean more than honor, integrity, and honesty, but characteristics that lend to moral authority and credibility. We often think of Jimmy Carter has being a moral person, but Truman's character gave him greater strength and eventually, more success.

These three elements shape the broader application of national power, that is, the ability to persuade. The United States may be enjoying military and economic dominance, but its political ability to brandish them as weapons or tools is limited by an inability to marshal the elements of power. In this context, it is especially important to keep in mind that the real legacy and ultimate influence of the United States is derived from our ideology: liberal democracy and free trade. How we use such ideology will be important to the success or failure of the twenty-first century model of a freer, more prosperous world where humans cooperate to address the challenges facing us all—demographics, environment, and ethnic unrest.

Effective persuasion, using IT, may require the United States to make greater use of moral authority. In the information age, there will be benefits that derive from being a country that stands for more than material ends. Because of the ability to project images instantaneously, there will be a special power that is derived from being a powerful country that plays by the rules. The United States largely projects such authority. However, because of current beliefs about the relativity of moral values, the commitment to use such authority may be in jeopardy.

It is important to remember that just having more data or information does not translate into improved knowledge, much less wisdom. In many areas, the political emphasis on slogans and political hot or wedge issues has undermined and confused U.S. foreign policy positions. Leadership by consistent example is still more persuasive than bluster.

Another way in which the United States can expand its global influence is by nurturing and renewing its domestic values. The important message of protecting human rights internationally has more resonance when American domestic society does not appear to be plagued by violence. The United States surely wants to project an image of more than guns and television violence (real or Hollywood) and must continue to strengthen the family and social fabric at home. The challenge and hope for U.S. leadership to influence world events is to harness our nation's moral capital and communicate its values through the new information age vehicles.

United States Policy Objectives

Technology-driven change is rapidly reshaping the world's economic, social, and political relations. It is doing so at a pace that threatens to outpace the ability of twentieth century institutional structures to adjust. In this light, one must ask how the next generation of U.S. leadership will address the rise of IT and networked societies.

As noted above, the dissemination of IT reinforces independence, autonomous communities, and to some extent, tribalism. It certainly allows individuals to find fellow believers, regardless of knowledge, intentions, or geography. We have already witnessed the dramatic increase in the number of activists and special interest organizations effectively using these networks to their advantage. Recent violent protests by environmental and labor advocates at the WTO meetings in December 1999 was a prime example of such effective organizing. In such a world, using national authority to pursue clear objectives is made more difficult.

Given these new realities, it would be useful to consider some priorities for the twenty-first century. First, managing violence will continue to be our number one priority. Since the end of the Cold War, most large-scale conflict and violence has, in fact, been internal. By our count there have been about 140 wars between 1945 and 1989, which may have killed as many as 23 million people. However, it is estimated that there were more people killed by internal repression than all the wars combined. Trends toward tribalism, which will be accommodated and somewhat encouraged by IT, could possibly magnify the problem. The centrifugal forces outlined above may play a larger role in generating and spreading conflict.

The twenty-first century concept of autonomous communities and cultural fragmentation gives new meaning to current assessments of threat. Chemical, nuclear, and biological weapons proliferation, especially for the benefit of criminal syndicates and terrorist groups, will be more difficult to manage. Moreover, such groups will have additional targets such as communications networks and the information that these networks hold and transmit.

It is important to harness IT as a positive force and, therefore, the next generation Internet capabilities should be ubiquitous and not burdened by regulation and taxes. Recent efforts by state and local governments to subject the Internet to new taxes have the potential to burden the one vehicle, if used wisely, that has the potential to link the world. The focus should be on using this tool to improve education and training, thus increasing economic opportunities and growth. Productivity, competitiveness, and innovation of a country and its people will be important. By enlarging the economic pie and communicating common approaches, people will have some incentive to band together for productive ends. By contrast, with greater income disparities, there will be more incentive for disruptive, autonomous communities.

To maintain leadership, the United States must work to forge partnerships and coalitions. There is a strange paradox in the United States. On one hand, we take great pride in the prestige associated with superpower status. On the other hand, we, as a nation, don't want to pay the price of leadership. We ask our allies to shoulder a larger part of the burden, but are unwilling to sacrifice some sovereignty to promote coleadership or viable coalitions. It is axiomatic that U.S. leadership is required to build the necessary coalitions and bring all the resources and power to bear on the disparate challenges of the twenty-first century. It is equally important, however, that the United States more effectively use strategic partners and multilateral organizations to focus leadership on those threats that may not involve classic national security or vital interests. Coercive tools, such as military force and economic sanctions, may not be the weapons of choice to confront the non–Cold War challenges. We must dedicate the resources and leadership to develop new economic tools, unilateral and multilateral, to create the right incentives for positive behavior and norms.

The federal government is still frozen in its hierarchical Cold War structure. It is difficult to imagine it adopting the flexible decisionmaking process of the flattened network model. The government's current vehicle of choice to deal with difficult policy issues affecting multiple jurisdictions is the interagency process. At best it is cumbersome and is often unable to deal with complicated real-time policy challenges. Such limitations, though, have been recognized. For example, Congress, concerned with the lack of effective and coordinated action to combat weapons of mass destruction, created the Commission to Assess the Organization of the Government to Combat the Proliferation of Weapons of Mass Destruction. The commission examined the structure and process of government agencies, potential technological solutions, and resource allocation. The commission found pockets of expertise, talent, and technology residing within the government. Such pockets, though, lacked the critical coordination of agency leadership and action.

President Clinton, shortly after failure of the Galaxy IV satellite and after reading Richard Preston's *The Cobra Event* about biological terrorism, reportedly became concerned about U.S. vulnerability. He ordered a beefed up national response naming Richard Clarke, a National Security Council (NSC) staff member, as the new national coordinator for security. The problem of inadequate coordination, however, calls for more than the appointment of a NSC deputy who lacks supervisory or budgetary control.

The Defense Science Board Task Force on Transnational Threats called for the DoD to address this emerging class of threats through a response strategy that included defining an end-to-end operational concept and system-of-systems structure. The task force believed that twenty-first century technology and architectures could be effectively organized to confront growing threats, including international terrorism, narcotics trafficking, the proliferation of weapons of mass destruction and organized crime. The task force's call for an interactive global information system, built with existing state-of-the-art technology, is unlikely to be developed, however, because of the classic competition among stovepiped agencies. The fact that this potentially effective tool has not been supported is a clear example of the need for revolutionary, not incremental, reform in strategy and organizations.

Resorting, however, to special commissions or a task force is often inadequate for addressing our national interests. These entities often make recommendations that are politically unpopular. However, such recommendations have been considered "reasoned." The hope is that such a body can provide political cover for those "constitutionally responsible" for the decisions, that is, elected officials. In an era of real-time demands, the quiet and scholarly approach offered by special extra-governmental entities falls short of the requirements for flexible and decisive leadership.

As a member of the Armed Services Subcommittee that wrote the Goldwater-Nichols DoD reorganization plan legislating greater joint military operations, I believe it is time to consider a Goldwater-Nichols II. We have come a long way in fostering greater service cooperation, but Congress should go further and look at ways to break down interservice "stovepipes" and to "disintermediate" layers of delay. In government, it is a maxim that there are few people who are in a position to make affirmative decisions, but any number who can veto them. An effort concentrating on removing those layers is badly needed. Alternatively, building partnerships between government and NGOs, linked by IT, may be the most effective way to cut through the classic "stovepipe" structure.

American Leadership and the Democratic Process

Marked by the expanding influence of IT, the twenty-first century will produce a variety of contradictions that U.S. leadership must work to resolve. First, fundamental to our polity and leadership around the world, there will be new tensions based on our people's insecurity over the degree and locus of loyalty. New mechanisms will be needed through which government can better communicate with the people. This will be especially true as technology blurs the lines of communication between what is going on outside U.S. borders and what is going on within.

Thomas Friedman has an interesting heuristic that illustrates the new dimensions of political life. He defines the politics of the twenty-first century as making the labels of democrat and republican obsolete. Rather, new conceptual categories should be used to capture the changed dynamics of how people politically relate to the world around them. Friedman's heuristic sets forth a matrix of four quadrants.[8] The defining polar features of "Integrationists" and "Separatists" lie along one axis and the polar features of "Social Safety Netters" and "Let-Them-Eat-Cakers" lie along the other axis. In this framework, people place themselves within the matrix based on how they feel about globalization and technology.

I would fall—as I believe, most participants in this volume—on the "Integrationist" line, midway between the "Social Safety Netters" and "Let-Them-Eat-Cakers." Technology allows us to transcend borders in productive ways that support innovation, further democracy, and link open markets. However, the instabilities produced by tribalism and growing disparities between haves and have-nots require some level of government intervention to create a level playing field or a social safety net. Such a safety net, though, cannot be a substitute for competition and individual liberty.

From this perspective, I would argue that the United States must reform its democratic institutions to meet the challenges of the information age and to protect the interests of a free and open society at home. This will require the United States to acknowledge the development of network societies and to design policy organizations to be adaptive, flexible, and agile. As noted above, we should be concerned about the legacy culture imbedded in government. We must also communicate the value and responsibility of leadership. As the line between technology and globalization blurs, purely domestic and international issues are increasingly difficult to distinguish. A public dialogue, led by the president, must be sustained regarding this blurring of domestic and international.

Such a public dialogue will not be easy because the very role, if not the structure, of government has changed. The Clinton Administration and Republicans in Congress have agreed that the federal government should be smaller and have a different focus. This agenda involves a serious attempt to make government less bureaucratic, more relevant, and more citizen or consumer friendly. Domestically, to better prepare young people for the future, local governments and community-based organizations have experimented with new approaches to educational challenges, such as charter schools, "school to work," and injecting competition into a model that has been static for generations.

On the international front, the president will need to begin a new dialogue with the American people to explain what our national interests are in the world. In addition to economic well being, mutual interests, and U.S. leadership, certain unifying values such as moral purpose in our policymaking need to be reaffirmed to reinforce our views of the meaning of "national." Unlike the historical "broadcast" view of government, the twenty-first century variety is more about education, dialogue, and consensus building.

Yet, as with any effort to navigate a transition, there are dangers that must be avoided through careful public deliberation. The classic conflict between self-interest and national interest will need to be reconciled. Technology may be harnessed to give citizens more input. Increased communications, cyberdebate, and instantaneous referendums might be workable on some social issues, such as the death penalty; but what about fiscal policy? Do citizens want a referendum on setting prime interest rates or dealing with the long-term viability of Medicare? History has shown that making foreign policy by opinion polls is not an effective way to govern.

The debate must begin, however. IT is transforming the variety of integrationist issues, such as fast track authority for international trade, into kitchen-table issues. How we deal with these and other global or interconnected issues in the post–Cold War transition should be of great concern to American citizens. The traditional model of democratic institutions that our parents knew has changed. For instance, the very nature of the U.S. Senate has changed from one where individual senators were specialists (knowledge agents) and wielded enormous power. Today, senators are even more individualistic than their predecessors but subject to the pressures of interest groups (who are organized and wired) and the media. They are more partisan and polarized, resulting in less reflection and debate on long-term security issues. Accordingly, there is serious organizational gridlock.

As with any revolution, there may also be a counter-revolution that arises from fear of a twenty-first century agenda. Fear may produce nostalgic calls for a day long-lost and a wish for policies inappropriate for our nation's future. In this light, there are many who cling to the "Separatist" side of Friedman's framework, hoping that IT and changing demographics will go away. Unfortunately, there exist emerging background conditions that may create a receptivity to "Separatist" ideas among policymakers. For example, 60 percent of the new members of Congress did not hold passports in taking office and most do not care about "foreign" issues even as technology brings such issues closer to home. It is likely that such members will not be receptive to labels such as "Integrationist." In fact, as many Republicans as Democrats voted an isolationist line in the last session of Congress.

In this light, the decline of civility in Congress is devastating: the new bumper sticker is "Don't debate, investigate." In addition, the "politics of scandal" has become an increasing focus of the media and a very effective partisan weapon. Foreign policy and defense issues have taken a back seat to domestic and sensationalistic front-page stories.

In 1994, I campaigned for the U.S. Senate in Oklahoma on three issues: the decline of institutions, the skills gap, and the melting pot—the need to include all in the benefit of a high-tech, high-wage society. My opponent campaigned on God, Gays, Guns, and Clinton. My opponent won. I believe, in a way, that it was a fear of the future brought by technology and globalization that made the difference. Such fear must be overcome if we are to successfully embrace a future that could have limitless positive possibilities.

The United States Congress remains the greatest deliberative body in the world and individual members have a responsibility to put national above personal or partisan interest. Citizens should not forget what the conservative Edmund Burke wrote: "Your representative owes you not his industry only, but his judgment and he betrays, instead of serving you, if he sacrifices it to your opinion."

The amount of available data and information is growing exponentially. As Chairman of the Intelligence Committee in Congress, I challenged witnesses from the National Security Agency (NSA) with the statement that the United States was data rich but information poor. In the twenty-first century, the United States will not be information poor, but challenged with sorting out knowledge from noise. Technology is making it easier to extract knowledge from information, but only humans can insert wisdom. As Bran Ferren, the head of Walt Disney Imagineering, likes to say, "the human is a wide-band, sensing, fusing machine." Our challenge is to improve the human-computer interface, not in the traditional "techie" sense, but in the way we use technology to expand the opportunities and vision of humankind.

Big ideas have driven the explosive growth of technology. It is time we apply bold new thinking and wisdom gained from our experience to the global issues facing humankind. The time is ripe for leadership. As President Clinton stated in a speech to WTO Ministers in Seattle in December 1999, ". . . information has already been globalized and citizens all over the world have been empowered. And they are knocking on the door, saying 'let us in and listen to us.' This is not an elite process anymore."

Notes

1. Figures from *Computer World Online*, April 15, 1999; *Red Herring*, May 1999, p. 88; and *Business 2.0*, March 1999, pp. 83, 110.

2. Regís McKenna, *Real Time: Preparing for the Age of the Never Satisfied Customer*. Boston: Harvard Business School Press, 1997, p 56.

3. U.S. Department of Commerce, *The Emerging Digital Economy*. Washington, D.C.: Commerce Department, April 1998, pp. 1, 6; Michael Mandel, "The Spoils of the New Economy Belong to the High Tech," *Business Week*, August 16, 1999, pp. 37.

4. Peter Drucker, "The Age of Social Transformation," *Atlantic Monthly*, November 1994, available at http://www.theatlantic.com.

5. Drucker, *ibid.*

6. See Wilson P. Dizard, *Meganet.* Boulder, CO: Westview Press, 1997.

7. Benjamin Barber, "Jihad vs. McWorld," *Atlantic Monthly*, March 1992, available at http://www.theatlantic.com.

8. See Thomas L. Friedman, *The Lexus and the Olive Tree.* New York: Farrar Straus Giroux, 1999, pp. 353–355.

Chapter 3

The Spirit of the Age

Gary Hart

Introduction

Having produced more history than it could ever possibly have consumed, our century was tired. It now gives way to a new century and an, as yet, undefined age. And the search is on for ways to make traditional politics work in an "Age of Transition."

Various attempts have been made over the last decade to gain a better philosophical understanding of where we are headed in the world. Today, policymakers are debating the viability of the *Washington Consensus*—limited government and free markets—to organize a polity and an economy. Concepts such as the *Buenos Aires Consensus* with its populist prescriptions are being tested in Latin America. There are also vague references to *New Democrats* in the United States and a *Third Way* in Europe.

These various efforts to think about the underpinning elements of policy development, remarkably, mostly discuss alternatives within a box. By seeking only to preserve New Deal and Great Society social programs, liberalism has become reactionary. By seeking only to end those programs and return to the laissez faire of a simpler time, conservatism has become simply nostalgic. "Moderates" seek to mediate between liberalism and conservatism searching for a pragmatic center.

But "moderate centrism" is bound to fail. It is destined to fail in its mediating role for the same reason traditional liberals and traditional conservatives are going to fail. They are all seeking solutions in programs and policies rooted in a past that is fast disappearing. Programs derive from policies and policies derive from political belief systems called ideologies. Therefore, programs and policies debated at the end of the twentieth century are the products, directly or indirectly, of traditional conservatism, liberalism, or some faint reflection of very moderate democratic socialism—all belief systems derived from the Age of Enlightenment or from political reactions to it. Unfortunately, this Age of Transition does not recognize any of these ideologies as relevant to emerging realities.

Politics in democracies works only to the extent that there is congruence between the ideas it produces and the realities experienced by individual citizens. Most of the liberal programs of the rapidly disappearing twentieth century, and the laissez faire alternatives to them, are not conceptually designed to address the new realities of the emerging twenty-first century. Thus, as the United States considers a "Next Generation" foreign policy, it must first start afresh with some thoughts regarding political philosophy and the message that it wishes to communicate to the world.

New Realities

What are the realities that require radical new political thinking? Why is our age different from those of the recent past? Five themes, touched on throughout this volume, must be considered.

First, we now acknowledge information technologies, not traditional manufacturing, as the engine driving economic growth. The last such transformation was the mid-nineteenth century industrial revolution. But these technologies are disintegrating old networks, such as the entire chain from raw materials to finished products, old educational processes, even traditional communications networks. They are integrating new networks, such as new systems of communication, international financial networks, and cross-border transactions. And they are creating a new class of transnational elites.

Second, international markets are driven by systems of capital supply and demand that know no national laws or interests. Capital recognizes no political (or even moral) imperative. It recognizes no citizenship or special national obligation. It seeks only to maximize its own return. Despite the threatened collapse of major national and regional economies, sovereignty (perhaps itself an increasingly obsolete notion) has so far prevented the evolution of international financial regulatory institutions.

Third, even as capital and finance are becoming international, politics is becoming more local. As individual citizens despair of participating in public policy decisions affecting international finance, they revert to demanding greater control of their neighborhood lives. Thus, the authority of nation-states and confidence in traditional political institutions declines.

Fourth, human conflict in the form of traditional wars between nation-states declines even as low-intensity, largely urban conflict between and among tribes, clans, and gangs mushrooms in the post–Cold War nonpolar world. We all know the litany of Kosovo, Bosnia, Somalia, Haiti, Rwanda, and even East Los Angeles. Most students of the history of tribalism, nationalism, fundamentalism, and the clash of civilizations expect this type of conflict to grow.

Fifth, among thoughtful social and cultural critics there is a rising sense of the spiritual limits of the scientific method and the beginning of the end of the Age of Enlightenment. The twentieth-century age of mass slaughter—featuring the dedication of sophisticated instruments of science to purposes of wholesale destruction—did more than anything else to erode the notion of the evolution of human reason.

The list could go on at considerable length, but the point is obvious to anyone who has any sense of these revolutionary times. Yet if these are not ordinary times, then why do we think we can govern with ordinary—albeit "moderate," "centrist,"—policies? Those seeking the center of a horizontal—that is to say, static left-right—axis are condemning themselves never to participate on the cutting edge of change. To govern in the twenty-first century is to begin with the knowledge that life is not lived on a horizontal, left-right plane. It is lived on a vertical, future-past axis. To govern well in a revolutionary age is, by definition, to be revolutionary—not to seek the moderate center between the extremes of outdated ideologies of left and right, but to create revolutionary new political systems on the outpost of change.

Ideas for Governing in the Future Age

Reforming political systems to meet new challenges cannot be done by producing policies and programs based on ancient ideologies that no longer possess sufficient intellectual energy to make themselves relevant or compelling. Therefore, as a means of establishing the framework for truly innovative governance in this Age of Transition, let's consider some elements of a twenty-first century ideology, a political belief system that relates deepest traditional values to revolutionary new realities.

Consider four foundational principles that can form the framework of a new political ideology: first, from classical republican theory, the ideal of civic virtue—the citizen whose duties and responsibilities require participation in the public issues of the day; second, from radical democratic principles, the ideal of the ward republic, the immediate government in which all citizens can participate to achieve social progress and inclusiveness; third, also from radical democratic principles, the Jeffersonian concept of "generational accountability"; and fourth, from traditional conservatism, reinterpreted in light of the need for generational accountability, the notion of "intergenerational compact"—the moral imperative of leaving to the next generation a better society than the one inherited. This latter principle is especially important for it is the glue for a social compact that should form the standard for judging all proposed public policies.

Civic Virtue

The first pillar in a new ideological structure is restoration of the ideal of civic virtue—civic duty and citizen participation—from classical theory established 2500 years ago as the centerpiece of republican government. We are a republic—a democratic republic to be precise. This means our government is based on the principle of the many electing the few to represent them. It is not—or at least it should not be—a government controlled by an unrepresentative, unelected monarchy, oligarchy, church, or Washington elite. But classical republican theory—from the Greek city-state where it originated, through the Renaissance, to the English and Scottish Enlightenment, through the early U.S. republic until today—

assumes certain citizen obligations. It assumes citizen responsibility, civic duties, and civic virtue.

These are not platitudes to be memorized for a middle-school "civics" exam and then forgotten. They are central to the proper functioning of our form of government. Citizen responsibility and civic duty require participation in the life of the republic. That means something more than mere grudging payment of taxes or expectations that your neighbor's son or daughter put on a uniform if the nation is attacked.

It means, at the very least, voting—participation in the selection of leadership. Advocates of "centrism" believe that voters are driven away by political extremism, and this is undoubtedly true. But if so, then why, in 1996, when voters were given the most "moderate," "centrist" candidates imaginable, did 51 percent of those eligible to vote stay home? This was one of the lowest voter-participation percentages in modern democracy and a great shame on the U.S. republic. It is also a referendum rejecting mere "centrism."

It was fashionable in the late twentieth-century United States to pour scorn on politics and government. Many take the position that if one has nothing to do with it, then our government will simply go away. This fashionable libertarianism may suit the trendy businessperson. But it is no way to run a republic. Indeed, it is exactly the way to run a republic into the ground. Civic virtue means caring for, and therefore participating in the life of, the republic, the society, and the nation. It means fulfilling the citizen's responsibility to strengthen, nurture, and improve the political structures and public institutions by which the American people govern themselves. Absent this sense of civic virtue, the republic perishes.

Opinion-shapers on the right are fond of lecturing the public on the topic of virtue. It has turned into a lucrative business for some. But where, among all the sermons on personal virtue, is the sermon on *public virtue*—the debt and the duty of the citizens to the society of the republic. If one claims to believe that government is the enemy, then it becomes complicated to advocate participation in public affairs. Traditional conservatives have overcome this contradiction, and remained true to the republican ideal, by opposing large government, not all government. The "new right," however, is against all government and therefore finds itself outside the perimeters of classic republican theory.

Ward Republics and Generational Accountability

But we are also a democracy. Therefore, let's look to democratic principles for the second and third pillars of a new political structure. Taken literally, democracy is a radical notion in the grand scheme of human affairs. Nothing is more radical than the notion "that all men [and women] are created equal, that they are endowed by their Creator with certain unalienable Rights, that among these are Life, Liberty and the pursuit of Happiness." Again, the temptation is to say we studied all that in school.

Taken literally, though, nothing upsets established hierarchies and "courts"—whether political, religious, or cultural—than the notion of true equality, genuine individual liberty, natural rights, and human dignity. In the abstract, virtually everyone confirms these principles. It is in practice that these ideals become revolutionary—even today. One of their most radical promoters, Thomas Jefferson, understood this difficulty better than most. Inconsistent and too ready to compromise on slavery for the sake of union and independence, and largely absent from the constitutional deliberations that enshrined political paradox in American polity to this day, Jefferson nevertheless—as the Bill of Rights testifies—remained consistent in his belief in the radical nature of democracy.

From radical Jeffersonian democratic ideals, then, let us take two more pillars for our new twenty-first century ideology. The first is the ideal of the ward republic. Jefferson believed in the theory of the republic, a government of the many electing the few. He also believed in civic virtue, duty, and citizen participation. He opposed Hamilton's concept of a centralized federalist government because it concentrated power in the hands of the unelected few of position, property, and influence, and because it was too impervious to the participation of the ordinary farmer, laborer, and mechanic. Therefore, the best republic was the local republic, the "ward (or township) republic," the arena in which all could and should participate and in which civic virtue should be exercised. As many decisions as possible were to be made by as many citizens as possible participating in these local "grassroots" units of government.

Such democratic ideals are given new meaning as we enter the new century. Today, economics are migrating upward, as capital, labor, materials, fabrication, marketing, advertising, and consumption are all becoming internationalized. However, politics in democracies is migrating downward. Either people will reclaim the responsibility for self-governance, or democracy, and the republics in which it is presumed to be practiced, will continue to stagnate and decline. The first two primary elements of a new ideology for the twenty-first century, then, respond to the ongoing constitutive process of politics. They foresee a new political reality fashioned from the oldest of ideals: classical republican civic virtue and citizen responsibility on one hand, and "ward republics" or newly empowered local governments based on radical Jeffersonian democratic theory on the other hand.

Yet, Jefferson had another radical democratic idea that leads to the third pillar of this new ideology. He believed that every generation should have the responsibility to decide for itself the fundamental laws, indeed even the structure of government, it would adopt. Jefferson believed that one generation could not bind another, and that the past should not dictate to the present. "The earth belongs always to the living generation," he wrote to Madison in 1789. "Every constitution and every law naturally expires at the end of 19 years." As radical as the notion of ward republics is today, so also is the notion of generational liberation from the past.

To force each generation to reconsider its laws and underlying constitutions is to force the ultimate in civic responsibility. The underlying political principle is deeper than the notion that we can do anything we choose. It is supplemented by an equally valid moral corollary: We are *responsible* for our own lives. As a practical matter, except in extreme circumstances such as economic upheaval or world war, most Americans, being basically conservative by nature, will opt for the status quo. They may even choose, as they seem to be doing today, to abandon previous experiments in social equity and inclusiveness. Whatever the outcome, according to this principle of accountability, collective citizen involvement in self-governance would be encouraged if not, in an ideal sense, actively required.

If the idea of generational accountability is joined with the notion of the ward republic and active local government, then there is little justification for the failure of civic duty in the form of citizen participation. Are we not a nation, one people united in a common society with common interests, goals, and a common destiny? What of the notion that we are all in this together?

This new ideology retains a crucial role for central government. That role is to establish and enforce acceptable national standards for education, health, environment, public safety, and other social undertakings by local governments. No community should be able to subject its citizens to conditions inferior to those deemed by the national government to define a modern civilized society. How the ward or township will achieve these goals is for its citizens to decide.

It is unrealistic to assume, in any case, that the citizens of one community would willfully permit its conditions to decline materially compared to its neighbors or the nation at large. Enlightened self-interest would be the stabilizer. For those communities with inadequate tax bases, it should be the further responsibility of the central government to distribute national revenues according to an equitable formula designed to ensure that every local government has sufficient resources to meet its social obligations.

Intergenerational Compact

Jefferson's idea of generational accountability leads to the final pillar in a new ideology, an element traceable to an icon of traditional conservative thought, Edmund Burke. According to Burke, there is at all times a partnership among generations according to which the duty of the present generation is to preserve the values, structures, and institutions inherited from the past and to convey them unchanged to the next generation. For Burke, this was the ultimate means of conserving the past in an age of revolutionary upheaval. It was the social and moral compact linking generations.

Differently interpreted, in the light of Jefferson's own generational imperative, this notion of a partnership *across time* can become the central organizing principle, the moral imperative of a new twenty-first century ideology. We are accustomed to thinking in terms of partnerships at any given moment in time with other nations or political entities. Simply stated, a new ethical dimension for judging public policy would be this: It is the duty of each generation to leave for the next generation a better society in every respect than it found. This principle applies to every aspect of public policy and social life, from education standards to public health, from lower poverty rates to lower crime rates, from environmental quality to the strength of national defense, from lower public debts to the security of retirees. All public policies should be judged by the degree to which they achieve a greater common good for the next generation.

In this present age of self-aggrandizement, we judge every issue by its effect on us, right now or at least in our lifetime. But we also claim to care about our children. Most of us define our care by the private legacy we leave our children. We spend increasing amounts of time and energy on such matters as avoidance of inheritance taxes, life insurance, property conservation, and so forth. But why do we not also consider the *public* legacy we leave? Why are so many blind to the irony of bequeathing greater private resources in a world of increased poverty, pollution, and political corruption?

Whether we care to acknowledge it or not, we all leave two legacies, a private one and a public one. A genuinely concerned parent and citizen would be at least as concerned for the public legacy as for the private one. That necessarily means participation in the public business of the day, in the decisions that affect the public legacy left for the next generation. Whether we care to recognize it or not, we have a moral imperative to future generations not merely to preserve the values and institutions of the past but also to pass on a society, a nation, that we have made every effort to *improve* for our children and their children.

Conclusion

These four ideals or principles are interrelated. Civic virtue and citizen participation are best exercised in a local republic that has as its common good the commonwealth of the next generation. Some will say this ideological framework is radically conservative. Others may say it is radically liberal. Both will be right, and both will be wrong. This ideology clearly draws from classical principles that some have interpreted, to serve their own biases, to be conservative or liberal. They will certainly be right that this ideology is radical in the purest sense of the word. This ideology returns to root ideals and values. That is what radical means. Isn't it strange that we live in an age that considers returning to root principles to be extreme? For that is what radical has come to mean these days.

For the earliest Greeks, creators of a universe of gods and goddesses and great myths, the ideal of a republic where the many could themselves elect the few to govern them was radical in every sense of the word. For European monarchists and loyalists, Jeffersonian ideals of universal equality, individual liberty, and the natural rights of man were radical. Even for his more conventional revolutionaries, his ideas of ward republics and generational accountability were about as radical as the American Revolution would become. They would not be incorporated into the United States Constitution, although a radical Bill of Rights would be.

And now for a nation of consumption and instant gratification, nothing could be more threatening to its values than the thought that our collective public duty to our children takes precedence over our interest in consuming and acquiring material wealth for our gratification in our own time. This proposed moral imperative and social contract is indeed radical.

And so I propose the framework of an ideology for the twenty-first century that is radically rooted in principle and theory. It is meant to take serious account of the true meaning of both republic and democratic governance. It is neither conservative nor liberal in either traditional or modern meanings of these terms. It is most certainly not meant to find a "moderate," "centrist" position among what have finally become irrelevant, outdated, and state ideologies. Moderation in an irrelevant political arena is nothing more than irrelevant moderation.

Ideologies are organized systems of political belief and therefore must have a solid basis in political theory. But to survive and provide the basis for practice—for public policies and the programs they produce—they must be practical. Individuals do not produce ideologies. They are produced by the complex interaction of ideas, prejudices, beliefs, and experiences. They are difficult to evolve. But the spirit of our age is one of transformation and, therefore, our imperative is to think anew, to disenchant ourselves from corrupt and irrelevant politics, and to enchant ourselves once again with the hope of human progress.

Chapter 4

Is Anybody Out There Listening?

Communicating Foreign Policy in the Post–Cold War Era

Antony J. Blinken

Nearly a decade into the post–Cold War period, those who formulate foreign policy and those who communicate it must contend with a central paradox. On the one hand, powerful forces of integration are changing the world more rapidly and more profoundly than ever before. As a result, what goes on beyond America's borders affects what happens within them more than ever before. Yet the American people are more disinterested in matters international than ever before—or at least the media believes this to be so. This gap presents foreign policymakers with a special responsibility: not only to make the right choices, but to make those choices resonate with the American people.

The New Interdependence

Economic integration is the easiest to demonstrate, because it is the easiest to measure. On any given day, traders, buyers and investors move more than a trillion dollars around the world. Over the last six years, trade has driven one-third of America's strong growth. Yet, by the measures of merchandise exports and foreign direct investment, the world arguably was, in relative terms, just as interdependent at the turn of the last century as it is today[1]. From this, one might conclude that the much-trumpeted phenomenon of globalization has been overblown.

In fact, these quantitative measures do not adequately reflect the qualitative change in the nature of interdependence. Not just economically but also politically, culturally, and socially, we are more interconnected than we ever have been. Consider: whereas economic output has increased dramatically over the past several decades, the physical weight of the goods produced has barely changed. The world's new wealth largely comes from the power of ideas, which flow more freely than ever. Three decades ago, phone lines could accommodate only 80 calls at one time between Europe and the United States; today they can handle one million. Today, every day, 500,000 airline passengers, 1.4 billion e-mail messages, and 1.5 trillion dollars cross national borders.[2] And the combination of CNN and satellites has created a common culture of images in real time, accessible from Israel to Iceland, from Brazil to Botswana. Once prosperity primarily was a function of cheap labor or abundant natural resources. Increasingly, it is a function of free societies and educated people, linked by technology and invigorated by open markets.

The result is extraordinary opportunities for political progress and economic prosperity, both deep and wide. This dynamic, idea-based global economy offers the possibility of lifting billions of people into a worldwide middle class. As technology shrinks the distance between us, it extends the reach of democracy, human rights, and the rule of law. But this promise has a flip side of peril. In a world with falling barriers and increasingly fluid borders, technology and openness can be put to the service of evil as well as good; a tremor in a market halfway around the world can make all of us tremble; the choices one nation makes about the air it breathes, the food it eats or the hours it works can affect citizens, consumers, and workers on other continents; fast-flowing surges of capital can recede just as quickly, leaving economic dislocation in their wake. In such a world, more than ever, trouble on the far end of town can become a plague on everyone's house.

The New Indifference

It should follow from these facts that Americans are more concerned about the world around them than at any time in their history. Yet, there is strong evidence that Americans—or at least the media that informs them—are more disconnected from the world than ever. For the first time in 60 years, foreign policy no longer dominates American public opinion as the nation's top concern. Social issues do—such as crime, health care, education, drugs, welfare, immigration.[3] Either as a reflection of this phenomenon or, perhaps, a cause of it, broadcast media devote dramatically less time to the coverage of foreign policy and international affairs:

- Between 1990 and 1997, coverage of international news on the three major networks has dropped from 32 percent of coverage—with a 50 percent spike during the Gulf War—to 20 percent.
- In 1990, the networks gave their foreign bureaus 4,000 minutes of broadcast time—in 1996, 1,600 minutes. In 1990, they devoted 3,500 minutes to stories on U.S. foreign policy, versus 1,100 minutes in 1996. And in 1990, there were 4,300 minutes of network news time on stories about international subjects, against 2,200 minutes in 1997. [4]

To be fair, there are moments when matters international break through. For example, when China's President Jiang, leader of the world's most populous nation, came to Washington in the fall of 1997 for the first summit meeting with an American president in nearly a decade, a major international news story dominated the evening news: the British Nanny trial, which captured 34 minutes, versus 29 for Jiang.

The most compelling and obvious explanation for this phenomenon is the end of the Cold War. In the absence of an overwhelming and unifying threat from abroad, most Americans prefer to focus on problems at home. A critical question for foreign policymakers and those who communicate it is whether the media simply reflect this preference or fuel it by shifting coverage to the home front.

The Foreign Policy Gap

Recent polling from the University of Maryland and the Pew Research Center concludes the existence of a "foreign policy gap" between the media and foreign policymakers on the one hand (who believe the American public is disengaged) and the American people themselves, who consistently and strongly support broad global engagement. For example, contrary to the belief of policy practitioners, the majority of Americans support a foreign policy of broad global engagement; approve of the United Nations, want it to be stronger, and believe the United States should pay its dues; and back international peacekeeping operations and favor contributing a proportionate share of American troops.[5]

These polls don't tell the whole story. As noted above, for the first time in sixty years, a host of social issues precede foreign policy as the top concern of the American people. So while the American people may very well still support active engagement, in *relative* terms their interest has declined—and the media is simply giving expression to this phenomenon.

But the gap between what policymakers and the media think the American people are thinking and what they actually think is real. It may be that the challenge of making sense of a world of diverse, disconnected dangers—instead of a world with one overriding, existential threat—is too hard a story to tell. Or it may be that policymakers and the media are not trying hard enough.

Whatever the cause, the problem requires a solution. As President Clinton has said, "Most of the benefits we seek for our people in the global economy require us to cooperate with others. And most of the challenges we face will result from threats that cross national boundaries and so require international solutions."[6]

Consider the administration's effort during the course of 1997 to renew Fast Track trading authority—an effort that failed to engage the American people. Granted, free trade is not always a simple sell as the tear gas and broken glass at the recent WTO Summit in Seattle remind us. In the short term, some distinct, identifiable group—

say, the widget industry—may well lose out, as it is forced into more open competition with foreign manufacturers who may pay their workers less or abuse the environment more. The widget industry floods the airwaves with advertisements, warning of the dire consequences of liberalization. Meanwhile, the winners in this process—that is to say, everyone else, as the beneficiaries of lower prices, new jobs and the freer flow of goods and services—do not engage in the debate, as they are not a distinct, identifiable, or organized group.

Nonetheless, in the Fast Track debate, the administration had a strong set of facts on its side. During the first four years of the Clinton administration, an aggressive free trade policy resulted in more than 200 trade agreements.[7] Because America has maintained, in the aggregate, the most open markets in the world over the past fifty years, these new agreements had the net effect of righting a historic imbalance—opening the markets of other countries more to America than America opened its markets to them. American exporters—and so their suppliers, their employees and ultimately, the American economy—were the beneficiaries. For example, by 1996, in the sectors where the administration reached new trade agreements with Japan—such as medical supplies, automobile parts, and computers—U.S. exports increased some 85 percent, or twice as much as our overall exports to Japan.[8] In toto, one-third of America's growth since 1993 can be attributed to trade. It should have followed that giving the president the authority he needed to strike new trade agreements would be an easy sell.

Looking to the future, the case for Fast Track was even more compelling. Americans make up just over 4 percent of the world's population, yet account for 20 percent of its wealth. To maintain this standard of living requires reaching out to the other 96 percent of the world's population who live beyond our borders—especially because, before the international financial crisis struck, foreign markets were projected to grow three times as fast as America's. [9]

Yet the Fast Track debate utterly failed to engage the American public. Instead, it remained an inside-the-beltway game, in which narrower—which is not to say unimportant—interests carried the day.

More broadly, public support for international engagement may be as soft as it is wide—and it could turn in a heartbeat. Until half way through this century, the current of isolationism ran deep in American history. Then, it was because the world didn't matter enough. Next time, it could be because the world matters too much. Those left behind in the global economy combined with those who fear America is being left behind by an abdication of sovereignty are a growing political force, muted for now by the longest and broadest peacetime expansion in American history. If we fail to adequately explain the benefits of the new interdependence to the American people and deal forthrightly with its downsides, their relative indifference to international engagement could turn into hostility.

Strategies of Engagement

From a communications perspective, there are three ways to bridge the foreign policy paradox.

The first is to erase the dividing line in people's minds between foreign and domestic policy. Put another way, we should work harder at showing how our engagement abroad can make a real difference in the lives of our people at home. The primary preoccupation of most Americans may well have shifted away from foreign policy, but what has it shifted to: crime, drugs, immigration, the environment. Are these issues domestic policy or foreign policy? When an American president meets with his or her Mexican counterpart and they discuss the drugs coming into America from Mexico, or maintaining legal migration while cracking down on illegal migration, or cross-border pollution problems, is that foreign or domestic policy? Pointing out the connections and putting them in real terms is one key to getting people and media to tune back in.

This is especially vital in the area of foreign economic policy. When times are good, as they are now, protectionism loses its appeal. But its resurgence is no more than a recession away—and perhaps even closer; witness the success of Patrick Buchanan's presidential campaign in 1996. The plain fact is that economic integration is neither inherently good nor inherently bad, but it is inevitable. We can go faster or slower by seeking more or fewer trade agreements. We can do more or less to cushion the negative effects of globalization by strengthening or shrinking our social safety nets, protecting or undermining the environment, setting or ignoring labor standards, and investing more or less in education and training. But we cannot turn back. Integration will take place with or without us. If we try to will it away, it will wash over us, and others in Europe and Asia will ride its tide. The fundamental question America must answer is whether we will use our unique position of prominence in the world to channel the currents of globalization in our favor. That is a debate that should engage the American people.

A second solution is to present America's foreign policies as a singular foreign policy. With the happy demise of the Cold War, the search is on for a unified theory of foreign policy to replace containment—a sound bite or bumper sticker explanation for America's role in the world. The lack of one exacerbates people's tendency to tune out: what they don't understand, they'd just as soon not think about, and the media would prefer not to waste time on.

Unfortunately, today's more complex international environment may defy a simple slogan. That may not be so bad. Containment got the big picture right, producing victory in the Cold War. But arguably, in allowing policymakers to define anything and everything in terms of containment, it produced some bad results: a "one size fits all" foreign policy by doctrine, not analysis.

The absence of a bumper sticker does not relieve policymakers of the obligation to explain what they're doing and where they're going. When the American people do tune in to our engagement abroad, the effect is a little like channel surfing: an eye blurring onslaught of disparate and seemingly disconnected images. Security alliances like NATO. Arms control regimes like the Chemical Weapons Convention and the Comprehensive Test Ban Treaty. Open trade pacts like the World Trade Organization and the Information Technology Agreement. International coalitions to fight terror, crime, and drugs. Binding commitments on the environment and human rights. Policymakers need to connect the dots. For example, each one of these initiatives is good in and of itself— it advances a specific American interest. It might be argued that, taken together, they do even more: they constitute new international rules of the road for the twenty-first century, protecting those who adhere to them while isolating those who do not. In this manner, a big picture begins to take shape, making it easier for people and the media to focus on foreign policy and understand what they are looking at.

Finally, a third option: find a new enemy and use "rally round the flag" rhetoric to get the attention of the media and the American people. Take China, a tempting target for demonization because its system of values deviates from our own, especially with regard to human rights. This is a path fraught with danger—treat someone as an enemy and you may well create one.

A better candidate for enemy status is a nexus of new threats—rogue states, terrorism, international crime and drug trafficking, the spread of weapons of mass destruction. This presents its own problems: how to make the case without terrifying people; how to sound resolute without over-promising; how to put a face on a diverse and complex problem. Consider Saddam Hussein's weapons of mass destruction program. It isn't hard to paint Saddam as the mother of all villains, or his chemical and biological weapons as a grave threat to our security. But if at the end of the day Saddam is still standing and his arsenal still intact, the result is a gap between words and deeds that will leave people disquieted and disconnected—even if in fact, a policy of containment does just fine in preserving our vital national interests.

This is an especially challenging time to be in the business of communicating foreign policy. Simply put, the challenge is to help make sense of a radically new world to the American people. To explain why it is so important that America continue to play a leading role in that world—why it will make a tangible difference in peoples' lives. To convince wary taxpayers that money spent on international affairs is not money wasted. In short, to shed some light on just what America's mission is in the world at a time when that mission is changing, our country is changing and the world is changing faster and more profoundly than ever before. It's an interesting story—and if we tell it right, we just may find that it has a very large audience.

Notes

1. See, e.g., Beinart, "An Illusion for Our Time," *The New Republic*, October 20, 1997. For example, merchandise exports by industrialized countries were 13 percent of GDP in 1913 versus 14 percent in 1992.

2. President William Jefferson Clinton, Commencement Address, University of Chicago, June 12, 1999.

3. See The Charlton Report, "Does America Have a National Vision?" January 1997, www.charltonresearch.com. A survey based on multiple focus groups and telephone sampling of 1,000 people.

4. See Tyndall Report, October 29, 1997; *Center for Media and Public Affairs Media Monitor,* Volume XI, Number 3, July/August 1997.

5. "The Foreign Policy Gap: How Policymakers Misread the Public," a study by the Program on International Policy Attitudes at the University of Maryland, as published in *The Polling Report,* Volume 13, Number 24, December 22, 1997; PEW Research Center Report, September, 1997.

6. President William Jefferson Clinton, Answers to Questions in Joint Press Conference with President Henrique Cardoso, Brasilia, Brazil, October 14, 1997.

7. President William Jefferson Clinton, Remarks on Fast Track Authority, The White House, September 10, 1997.

8. "Security Ties and Reciprocal Trade with Japan," in Clinton Administration Foreign and Security Policy Fact Sheets, August, 1996.

9. Clinton, op. cit., remarks on Fast Track.

Part II

Response to Globalization

Chapter 5

Updating Our Conception of Trade Leadership

Albert Fishlow and Patrick J. DeSouza

Introduction

Global trade has grown sixteenfold since 1950, far outstripping the growth in Gross Domestic Product (GDP). The period since the end of World War II has seen the largest expansion of international exchange of goods and services ever, even outstripping the period before World War I. Indeed, since 1970, the United States has more than doubled the ratio of trade to national product, realizing a greater increase than any of the other industrial countries. By contrast, over the same time, Germany increased its trade by 24 percent and France by 43 percent; for Japan, the comparable value is negative 17 percent.

More than even the growth of global financial flows, the growth of global trade has come to symbolize the triumph of capitalism at the end of the twentieth century as the defining economic and political ideology. This freer exchange of goods and services across borders is not only based on the premise of limited government but also reliance on private response to market signals.

Contrary to the propaganda of economic nationalists, who have pejoratively labeled the General Agreement on Tariffs and Trade (GATT)—the post-war mechanism for regulating international trade and predecessor of the current World Trade Organization (WTO)—the "Magna Carta of multinationals,"[1] globalization has produced positive results for American workers. Job creation in the export sector has increased during the 1990s at a rate four times faster than the overall rate of job creation in the private sector.[2] Moreover, workers have received approximately 15 percent higher pay in firms that export than firms that did not export.[3] Further, a number of studies have pointed out that wage stagnation in this country has been a function of technological progress, educational change, and immigration rather than imports.[4]

Trade has been productive, and not only for the United States. The European Union (EU) gives compelling evidence. Free trade among the European Community has even led countries to the recent acceptance of a common monetary base. Developing countries have also dramatically reduced their protective barriers in recent years in an effort—highly successful in East Asia—to compete effectively.

Given this record, one might think that international trade would be the least of our worries as we consider a "next generation" agenda that moves beyond the post–Cold War triumph of capitalism. Yet, as we head into the next century, there are renewed pressures, not only here but around the world, to retreat from the free trade formula. In this country, environmentalists, labor activists, populists, and nationalists are part of a newly forming coalition that sees trade as the problem rather than the solution. Greater governmental intervention in the production and sale of goods and services is sought by such groups to slow down the pace of change.

This coalition's influence far exceeds its limited numbers as evidenced by the circus-like atmosphere created during the recent WTO meetings in Seattle. An increasing number of studies show that average Americans are ambivalent about trade's effect and in the end pay little attention, preferring to focus on drugs, crime, and immigration.[5] Thus it is not surprising that critics of trade often try to gain greater influence by playing on the fears of the public. Critics paint a causal path from trade with foreigners to the "importation" of social problems such as illegal labor and corruption. For example, Pat Buchanan has sounded warning bells that global trade agreements would create a "global hiring hall" in industrial countries for hundreds of millions of Asians and Latin Americans.[6] In addition, he makes the obnoxious assertion that Americans and Asians differ in their attitudes toward bribery. As a consequence, most Asian nations "engage in bribery, shakedowns, and extortions as the conventional tactics of trade wars."[7] Given the large Japanese and Chinese trade surpluses with the United States, these statements play on emotions and are heard. Such efforts at generating fear of international integration are being replicated in countries around the world, and by similarly composed groups.

We disagree with such free-trade backsliding. The straightforward reality is that the current trade regime has produced mutual gains for nations, and especially for the United States, and has been a major global engine of growth. Yet it is important to realize that if we are to stave off wholesale attempts to undermine international trade relations, we must be sensitive to these undercurrents and update our conception of international trade leadership. As has been discussed throughout this book, the concept of national security must be broadened to deal with the adjustments needed to cope with globalization.

In this brief essay, we focus on two principal dimensions along which trade policy should be shaped for the next generation.

First, from the domestic angle, policymakers, businesspersons, and analysts will need to focus more on sensitive issues like labor and the environment, as well as technology and capital. Managing these new variables raises the importance of public sector help to make the necessary adjustments to globalization and to stave off self-serving propaganda by domestic interest groups.

Second, from the international side, we explicitly consider foreign policy as we think about how to translate an evolving U.S. ideal of free trade into a stronger, wealth-maximizing global system. The fundamental issue, in this respect, is how regional efforts at expanding trade—which may discriminate in certain priorities—can be productively linked to a global free-trade agenda.

Before we discuss these two dimensions, it will be useful to look back and take a broad view at the importance of free trade to the development of international relations in this century. Without renewed U.S. leadership on trade in the twenty-first century, many of the hard-fought gains achieved during the past 50 years may quickly be eroded.

Evolving Conception of International Trade and Its Political Implications

It has been a bumpy ride toward freer trade for much of the twentieth century. The century opened positively, continuing a major expansion in international exchange that began around 1870, with many analysts optimistically opining that economic integration through trade would bring peace. More trade and economic links, less reason to go to war. That formula was soon seen to be naïve as the world plunged into World War I.

The new post-war respite was short lived. A little more than a decade later, came a worldwide depression that created the conditions for fascism, the U.S. retreat from free trade through its increased Smoot-Hawley Tariff and expanding barriers around the globe. And shortly thereafter came an even more destructive and broader Second World War. At its conclusion, in conjunction with establishment of the United Nations, came a failed attempt to set up a new International Trade Organization. The United States was not yet ready to commit fully until the Cold War and Marshall Plan had become realities. Then the General Agreement on Tariffs and Trade (GATT) was organized to enforce freer trade. Under its aegis, and led by the United States, restrictions to trade continuously fell. That was one of the reasons for the rapid recovery of European capitalist democracies and Japan.

Subsequently came a period of rapid extension of trade and investment greater than any that had preceded. Foreign competition introduced new ways of organizing work. U.S. mass production techniques eventually gave way to Japanese "just-in-time" inventory techniques. A European Common Market took form and flourished. Economic integration soon shaped the way prosperous individuals around the world lived their lives and felt about their economic security.

The link between international economic relations and social organization was particularly pronounced in the developing world. In the 1970s, after the first rise in international oil prices under the

Organization of Petrolium Exporting Countries (OPEC), an important North-South debate came to a head. Industrial countries had recovered and grown rapidly; developing countries had not. The developing countries argued that they were being exploited by advanced countries; because of the imbalance in political bargaining power, comparative advantage relegated developing countries to produce low-value commodities that did not allow for rapid and continuous improvements in the standard of living for their citizens.

This debate diminished in the 1980s. That decade saw two divergent characteristics among the developing countries. Those in Asia, including China and India, did relatively well, exporting in larger amounts and benefiting from the expansion of intraregional trade. Those in Latin America were subjected to a debt crisis that lasted for almost a decade until the Brady Plan provided for modest relief. With capitalism's definitive triumph over communism, punctuated by the fall of the Berlin Wall, all countries were launched into a competitive world market. The philosophical assumptions of this new world order were that the market, combined with limited government, would provide solid macroeconomic fundamentals and the right incentives for private economic agents to increase per-capita income. On the other hand, the problems of income distribution remained.

Symbolic of this definitive resolution has been the political journey of President Fernando Henrique Cardoso of Brazil. During the 1960s, as an academic, Cardoso wrote a seminal book on "dependency." Its central point was that free trade and investment had the unacceptable cost of locking developing countries into an inferior status as producers of low-value commodities. Government was needed to intervene and to shape market outcomes so that higher-value activities could be performed. Today, as a re-elected president, Cardoso has committed Brazil to the free movement of trade and investment and broad privatization as a primary strategy to achieve economic growth. In the new Brazil, the government's primary role is to pursue the investment of capital to achieve better health and education.

As we head into the new century, the industrial world as well as the developing have serious questions about whether such commitment to free trade and investment will endure. In both worlds, interest groups are now arguing that they have not seen the benefits of relying on the market; all they see are trade deficits and the need to conform to external financial pressures at whose hands incentives are skewed.

The Domestic Side:
Backpeddling on the Triumph of Capitalism

The demands of the anti-free trade coalition have already registered with politicians and have altered the U.S. political landscape. Most dramatically, this change was manifest in October 1998 as Congress denied President Clinton fast track authority to conclude trade agreements. Such authority would have permitted trade legislation to be expeditiously considered, without amendments, thus maximizing chances for passage. Although the outcome was basically a foregone conclusion as a result of the political debate during the fall of 1997 and the decision to avoid a vote, the Republicans wanted the issue before the American people before the 1998 mid-term elections. For the first time during the 43 years of post–World War II free trade, the U.S. Congress backed away from the prevailing consensus on free trade. This outcome has reverberated around the world because the United States had consistently led the way in shaping a global free-trade agenda.

While the Clinton Administration's tactical response to the 1998 financial crisis has been stellar, its strategic planning for reinforcing U.S. resolve toward free trade going forward has not been ideal. A brief look at the politics of the 1997–1998 fast track effort offers a useful perspective.

Two fatal errors were made. One was the decision to approach the subject quietly during the summer of 1997. It was believed that the North American Free Trade Agreement (NAFTA) had been oversold—despite its success in generating large increases in trade—and that private interests might be garnered in support of fast track without fully engaging the American public. The other was taking excessive time to decide what kind of bill would be submitted. The choices centered on a fast track bill that simply authorized the president to pursue a free-trade agreement and a bill that introduced "social" concerns into the application of presidential authority to pursue trade agreements. The former bill was one that most Republicans favored. The latter bill was a version that required labor and environmental safeguards in any agreement that the president would negotiate. The delays in deciding which bill was more likely to succeed only doomed the effort to failure by ceding the public relations initiative to the opposition.

This early debate and the later vote raised new and difficult domestic issues. For the first time, fast track authority was denied. Moreover, the issue arose in the midst of the international financial crisis that evolved in Asia, Russia, and Brazil. When the trade debate re-emerges, as it will in the presidential campaign of 2000, one will soon see whether public support for free trade is only a heritage of the past rather than a driving influence on twenty-first century international relations.

Some have already concluded that the United States may have reached its breaking point in terms of its willingness to lead on free trade. In 1997, the U.S. trade deficit in goods and services reached $114 billion. In 1998, it was larger. And in 1999, in the aftermath of the global financial crisis, it is projected to be still higher. In politically sensitive industries involving merchandise trade such as steel, autos, and textiles, the sectoral deficit was actually greater than the total trade deficit. This merchandise deficit was compensated by a surplus in services—banking, accounting, consulting—that has now reached close to $100 billion annually. This evolution of the U.S. economy toward services has increased the tensions between Main Street and Wall Street and further weakened the domestic consensus on free trade.

The Clinton Administration has sought to address such tensions, especially during the financial crisis of the fall of 1998 when some argued that U.S. foreign economic policy was geared to bailing out bad financial decisions by Wall Street. The administration has argued that tolerance for an expected surge in relatively cheaper Asian imports is needed in the short run to help those economies recover. Such recovery, former Secretary of Treasury Robert Rubin has reminded critics, is in the economic interest of the United States so that "[Asian countries] can once again become good markets" for the United States.[8] It is unlikely that any other nation would have been able and willing to bear such balance of payments costs. Thus, free trade goes together, inseparably, with U.S. financial leadership.

As domestic politics has already revealed, there are two fundamental pressures on support for expanded trade. One is the increasing opposition of labor, as domestic manufacturing production is reduced in favor of imports; the other is increasing environmental concerns and insistence on equivalent intervention to counteract potential negative effects abroad.

As already mentioned above, much research has been done on the role of trade in preventing rises in workers' wages over the past decade. The economic results actually strongly negate opposing arguments to continued openness. They show that technological change has been overwhelmingly the most important source of changed relative prices associated with changing patterns of trade. The results also indicate that trade with the industrial countries continues to account for something on the order of two-thirds of U.S. imports. Workers are affected. The next generation will specialize in other activities. But in the interim, technical progress in automobiles, steel, and so forth retains for our country a continuing production role. These activities have not, and will not, simply disappear. But inevitably their weight in imports will rise, as workers switch to activities where comparative advantage favors U.S. skills and capacities.

What workers have seemed increasingly to want—a "level playing field" defined in terms of equal wages and work conditions abroad as a prerequisite for free trade—is patently impossible. Labor abroad offers competition, but even in the Mexican case, where with NAFTA, Ross Perot predicted "a great sucking sound" of departing jobs, a careful tabulation shows a very limited effect. And this is despite an unanticipated Mexican trade surplus in 1995 and 1996 in the wake of exchange rate devaluation.

On the environment, one has seen adaptation occurring abroad, and more rapidly in recent years. One cannot anticipate that poorer countries will have the capacity to invest the large sums that one has already seen devoted in the United States, for example, to elimination of harmful gas emissions in energy production. Standards of living are different. But, and again to cite the NAFTA experience, in the original agreement—before additional measures were imposed—there is some justification to Ambassador Carla Hills' assertion that NAFTA "is the 'greenest' trade agreement ever negotiated."[11] Certainly NAFTA went beyond GATT or the Uruguay

Round, and compared with the efforts of the European Community it deals more effectively with environmental issues.

Progress has occurred. Technology has been transferred. And that is one of the reasons that the same unanimity of labor opposition is less characteristic of environmental groups. That precisely shows the difference between the two issues. In one, modification is possible; but in the other, relatively less can be done, except for the provision for job retraining and sharpening public scrutiny on child labor.

In the next century, one must continue to rely on technological change and productivity advance for free trade to continue to flourish. The United States has already shown an extraordinary capability in reacting to these new forces as it has expanded the role of international trade in the economy. That capacity will be more essential in the future.

Moreover, as services evolve, there exists the possibility for great trade expansion in the electronic age. The electronic commerce revolution is here. The market for the sale of goods and services over the Internet has been estimated at $250 billion by 2002; and daily that amount is being revised—upward. For instance, Christmas Internet sales in 1998 far exceeded expectations. Such results are the reason for the extraordinary multiples based on future earnings that the stock prices of companies operating in cyberspace have enjoyed.

Electronic commerce may make trade friction obsolete by making it far easier to exchange goods and services. Currently, there are no duties on Internet commerce. In addition, taxing electronic transmissions will be difficult. Although the Hormats article in this volume goes into the area in great depth, it should be noted that the Clinton Administration has exercised great foreign policy leadership in attempting to keep electronic commerce duty-free. The test in the aftermath of the collapse of the WTO concensus in Seattle will be to achieve an extension of the moratorium on electronic commerce duties.

Foreign Policy Dimension: Regional Linkages

As outlined above, and noted throughout this volume, leadership in building a new domestic consensus on trade will be critical for policy development as we enter the new century. Equally important will be leading its international evolution as an interactive system of free exchange. The secret here is making the rising regionalism compatible with an eventual global market. In all parts of the world, Latin America, Asia, and Europe, there are powerful forces calling for trade restrictions to strengthen local industry. What is special about the United States is its strong trade with all of these areas. That is additionally what gives the United States undisputed leadership in this issue-area.

A brief survey of these different regional efforts will illustrate the reality that the political stakes are high in each. We spend more time below on the Americas, and especially NAFTA, because Canada and Mexico are our number one and two trading partners. In addition, the Americas represent the fastest growing market for exports in recent years.

The Americas

In many ways, NAFTA is the touchstone for U.S. trade leadership in the twenty-first century. NAFTA is bold in its vision of an integrated market based on dissimilar economies that can complement each other extraordinarily well if effective leadership is maintained. It is also a case in which two different administrations showed bipartisan leadership reinforcing the consensus that liberal economics and liberal democracies go hand in hand.

Contrary to the arguments of economic nationalists, the effect of NAFTA has generally been positive. NAFTA provided an opportunity to create a model agreement with new standards for international trading rules going beyond those for trade in goods, as contained in the GATT, to deal with trade in services, intellectual property, and investment.

NAFTA has been a victim of poor public relations. As noted above, the measure of the success of NAFTA has been the issue of jobs. And, because of the special political and economic events of 1995 and 1996, it remained neutral as to net job numbers instead of achieving the promised 200,000 increase in U.S. employment. These narrow criteria, though, will likely show improvement over time.

NAFTA, however, has had a broader meaning. The goals of NAFTA focused on influencing Mexican political and economic incentives for the twenty-first century. Integrating Mexico into the North American economy would support emerging democratization measures and would foster economic growth in an important neighbor. Politically, because of the long, common border shared with Mexico, NAFTA had to be bold to create the necessary social and demographic stability that could address concerns regarding U.S. security such as illegal immigration and trafficking of narcotics. Economically, it was believed that NAFTA would encourage and lock in reforms already underway in Mexico.

The bet placed on Mexico, in our judgment, has proved successful. Mexico has faced tremendous challenges over the past several years—economic crisis, civil unrest, and political turmoil. Despite seemingly overwhelming odds, the Zedillo government has continued to promote reform, especially in terms of pluralism and the rule of law. Since 1994, elections, including those held during 1997–98 for a variety of national, state, and local positions, were widely recognized to be free and fair. For the first time in many decades the ruling PRI party lost its majority in the Lower House in the Congress as well as the important position of mayor of Mexico City.

As noted above, because of NAFTA, during its 1995 peso crisis, Mexico did not close its borders to imports, nor did it default on its debt as it had done in previous crises. Despite an economic decline that was the worst since the 1930s, Mexico undertook tough domestic measures including fiscal reform. It was able to achieve a recovery in little more than a year in contrast to the five-year recession it suffered after the 1982 debt crisis. Importantly, in January 1997, Mexico repaid early the U.S. emergency loan for the 1995 peso crisis. The economy is still growing, enabling it to weather the market turbulence of the fall of 1998.

In the six years since NAFTA entered into force, trade among the parties has grown by double-digit percentages. By the end of 1997, Mexico moved from third to second as the most important export market for the United States. Total trade between Mexico and the United States reached $157 billion in 1997, an increase of 20 percent over 1996. Since 1993, the year before NAFTA went into effect, total U.S.-Mexican trade has grown by almost 93 percent, this despite a 9 percent decline in U.S. exports to Mexico in 1995 because of the peso crisis.

NAFTA also has had an important effect on industry integration in various sectors. Production sharing has increased efficiencies in the use of resources. The automotive, textiles and apparel, electronics, and chemicals sectors, in particular, have benefited. Industry in these sectors has been able to strengthen their competitive position not only in the regional market but globally.

The automotive industry, which is the largest single manufacturing employer in all three countries, has been one of the greatest beneficiaries of NAFTA. More important than the removal of tariffs has been the dismantling of the highly restrictive and cumbersome Mexican Auto Decree, as well as Canadian and U.S. regulations that distorted trade and investment decisions of the industry. Manufacturers are now free to locate production of auto parts and assembly operations in the most rational way. The benefits of this new situation flow not only to the major companies, but also to many independent parts producers in all three countries.

Although the Mexican leg of the NAFTA triangle poses the biggest challenge, Canada has also played an important role. Canada is the largest trading partner of the United States. By the time NAFTA entered into force at the beginning of 1994, the United States had already gone through half of the ten-year transition period for removal of trade barriers under its bilateral free trade agreement with Canada.

In the past ten years, U.S.-Canada trade has grown by 136 percent. In the six years of NAFTA, trade between Canada and the United States has grown by more than 50 percent, reaching $320 billion last year. The movement of goods and services across our northern border is now running at close to a billion dollars a day with the movement of people reaching 500,000 daily. Meanwhile, Canada's trade with Mexico was at very low levels before NAFTA—less than $2 billion. It has doubled in value since then, but remains at low levels relative to the other two partners. About 80 percent of Canada's trade is with the United States, and its exports account for almost 40 percent of Canada's GDP.

The most visible measure of the success of NAFTA in providing leadership is the explosion of trade that has taken place within the region as compared to trade with other partners. Trade *within* the region has grown substantially faster than trade by the parties with the rest of the world (43 percent versus 33 percent for the years 1996 over 1993).

Mexico and Canada, though, have not been content to limit themselves to NAFTA and have sought a number of bilateral free-trade agreements with other countries in the hemisphere. Mexico and Canada have concluded their own free-trade agreements with Chile. Such linkages must be seen in the context of similar efforts occuring throughout the hemisphere. Mercosur—a grouping of Southern Cone economies—has pushed for free-trade agreements with the Andean Pact countries, Central American countries, and Canada. Mercosur has already integrated Bolivia and Chile as associated states. And even in the aftermath of the Brazil devaluation, negotiations are still occurring between Argentina and Brazil to ensure continuity of their substantial increase in bilateral trade.

Such leadership outside the United States has been necessary while President Clinton and Congress have been sparring over fast track authorization and the urgency of free trade agreements. These intraregional trade efforts have provided some momentum for efforts to negotiate and conclude a Free Trade Area of the Americas agreement (FTAA) by 2005. The FTAA process was initiated at the Miami Summit in 1994 and has continued as a major undertaking. The Santiago Summit in April 1998 officially launched negotiations to complete the FTAA. The next milestone will be for the countries to achieve "concrete" negotiating progress by 2000. It will be important for President Clinton, despite Seattle, to reengage the American people on trade before this marker is reached.

In the absence of strong U.S. leadership in the hemisphere with respect to free trade, Mercosur, led by the Brazilians, has tried to fill the vacuum. While it is important for regional institutional-building that leading Latin economies "buy-in" to the free-trade regime, there is no substitute for the United States. Without the United States to lead the way, the politico-economic character of the FTAA may shift. By far, the United States has been the most market-oriented participant in its conception of free trade. By contrast, Mercosur, like other trade groupings in the world such as the EU, has more of a sectoral approach to trade. In this context, government has a larger role in managing trade relations and promoting key sectors. This difference between market-led and government-led trade liberalization will have to be resolved through negotiation before the next Summit of the Americas in 2000/2001. And without fast track, the United States is substantially hindered in using its leadership.

Along these lines, the United States must closely monitor two dynamics. President Clinton fully appreciates both. First, there is an emerging triangular game between the United States, Latin America, and the EU on economic matters that will require skillful diplomacy. The final resolution of the current trade dispute over EU preferential treatment of banana exports from the Caribbean vis-à-vis the United States and Central America, especially in light of the WTO ruling that such treatment is in violation of WTO rules, is a primary example of upcoming diplomatic challenges. Improved economic relations with Cuba will be another. As noted below, the EU is quite interested in securing Latin economic markets for itself, as evidenced in the discussions emerging from the EU–Latin America Summit in June 1999. Such challenges in "triangular diplomacy" for the next generation economic agenda may be contrasted to the U.S.-Russia-China dynamic with respect to security matters during the 1970s and 1980s.

Second, Latin leadership on critical wedge issues such as labor and the environment will be important, not only for the region, but also for "swing" constituencies in the United States that must be brought in to any future debate on trade. On one side, Argentina has shown leadership on environmental matters as they affect developing economies, hosting a global conference on climate change in November 1998. On the other, Brazil and Mexico will need to demonstrate further leadership on labor standards as the next round of negotiations on FTAA proceeds.

Asia

The Asian-Pacific area has been following a somewhat different path to free trade. Three important differences may be noted. First, because the region is much more a mix of developed and developing countries, and of different internal structures, there has been less policy constancy. Note that China has worked to join the WTO. Second, the region is subdivided into different areas. ASEAN, for example, has maintained a degree of internal trade organization within the broader APEC framework. Third, the Asian crisis since 1997 has made movement toward free trade less continuous. A number of the countries—Thailand, Korea, and Indonesia—have been badly affected. And this has slowed the movement initially thought to be achievable by the year 2010 for developed members and 2020 for developing countries.

Moreover, APEC seems to be evolving less as a regional trading bloc and more as a catalyst for trade liberalization in the WTO and elsewhere. The focus has been on achieving sectoral free-trade agreements, which would be global and subject to most-favored-nation (MFN) treatment. One product of this latter approach has been the agreement to establish through the WTO free trade in information technology goods, a critical and extremely valuable sector for the twenty-first century. In November 1997, the APEC trade ministers agreed to seek reduction of trade barriers in some 15 additional sectors, including such areas as environmental goods and services, medical equipment, chemicals, and forest products.

APEC, additionally, has important political and military content. This explains why there has been a regular annual meeting of heads of state, in contrast to the less regular FTAA case. The nature of the problems vary from obvious concern with the China/Taiwan relationship to the broader issue of implicit United States/Japan competition for leadership of the APEC countries. The United States wishes to assure multilateral continuity of the group rather than its restructuring under Japanese aid and trade credits.

For these reasons, APEC is assured of continuing interest, regardless of the availability of a fast-track provision for the United States. But the degree to which it can be used to push forward a policy of free trade will depend on economic recovery within the region, including Japan, as well as a strong commitment of members to the trade agenda.

Europe

Developments in the foregoing emerging markets have produced an interesting reaction in Europe. Not wishing to be excluded from the increasingly integrated and growing Western hemisphere market, and developments in Asia, the EU has made several tactical moves designed to avert its isolation. It inaugurated biannual Europe-Asia summit meetings, which seem to have a general objective of strengthening relations rather than a specific negotiating agenda.

The EU also initiated negotiations with both Mercosur and Mexico, which paved the way, as noted above, for the EU-Latin America

Summit. The prospects for free-trade outcomes post-Summit are uncertain, primarily because of Europe's notorious common agricultural policy, complicated by prospective enlargement negotiations with countries of Central and Eastern Europe.

More recently, Sir Leon Brittan took the lead in the European Commission to propose a broad-scale agreement with the United States for a so-called New Transatlantic Marketplace (NTM). This is a complex proposal with elements both of bilateral agreements and commitments for multilateral negotiations. It calls for 1) widespread removal of technical barriers to trade in goods through an extensive process of mutual recognition and harmonization, 2) a political commitment to eliminate by 2010 all industrial tariffs on an MFN basis through multilateral negotiations, provided that a critical mass of other countries join in, 3) bilateral free-trade area in services, and 4) liberalization beyond multilateral agreements in the areas of government procurement, intellectual property, and investment. Significantly, agriculture, and audiovisual services, sometimes referred to as cultural industries, were explicitly excluded from the proposal.

Europe, newly fortified by the successful beginning of the Euro and by broader trade discussions with other areas of the world, is rapidly emerging as a major source of potential cooperation as well as a source of contention in the trade area. Clearly, as in the recent past, any further movement in the direction of free trade will require European and United States association. How to attain this, consistent with the important push toward regional identity—with the forthcoming expansion of the EU to Eastern Europe—is a major task at the beginning of this century.

Conclusion

We are at a critical juncture in the evolution of U.S. trade policy. While it is true that trade is expanding more rapidly now than at any previous time in history, clouds are gathering on the horizon threatening to undermine such progress. Such clouds are different because they implicate the U.S. conception of security and the preferred world order that it has been trying to shape.

For the first time, Congress has denied the president fast-track authority to negotiate trade agreements. The rest of the world has noticed. As a result, an inherently domestic issue of internal income distribution now has much broader international consequences. Working Americans' fears center on the "new realities" of globalization—noted throughout this volume—and the possible emotional invocation by Buchanan and the like of the "great hiring hall" that may alter Americans' economic well-being in favor of "Asians and Latins."

A public dialogue is imperative so that the United States may build the domestic consensus needed to lead again. The positive economic story of free trade, along with abundant retraining assistance for needed adjustment, must be effectively retold.

What is more difficult to deal with is the foreign policy aspect of trade. For all the economic arguments in favor, free trade is based as well on the positive political and social interactions with foreigners that inevitably result. Nationalism and prejudice are emotional factors that numbers sometimes have trouble pushing aside. In fact, the very argument of economic nationalists is based on the principle that national identity, and not mutual gain, should be the touchstone for America's leadership in the world.

This contest is a fundamental "new reality" for the next century.

Notes

1. Patrick Buchanan, *The Great Betrayal* 61 (Boston: Little, Brown 1998) (hereinafter *Great Betrayal*).

2. Bruce Stokes, *Future Visions for U.S. Trade Policy,* (New York: Council on Foreign Relations Book), at 6.

3. *Future Visions*, at 6.

4. *Future Visions*, at 8.

5. *Future Visions*, at 9.

6. *Great Betrayal*, at 61.

7. *Great Betrayal*, at 50.

8. Reuters Business Briefing, *Rubin Tolerant on Export Surge From Asia,* November 20, 1998 (reprinted from Kyodo News, November 20, 1998).

Chapter 6

Economic Transformation and Political Reaction

Globalization in Historical Context

Brian VanDeMark

Introduction:
Deepening Anxieties Among Americans

A new industrial revolution is underway. Advances in information technology (IT) and telecommunications press on relentlessly, shrinking distances, eroding national boundaries, and enlarging the domain of the global economy. The world economy has become more integrated in the past few decades than it used to be. Trade is one striking example. In the United States, the share of exports in the output of manufactured goods has skyrocketed from 6 percent in the 1950s to nearly 20 percent in the 1990s. Fully 30 percent of U.S. economic growth since 1993 has been caused by expanding involvement in the global economy. The daily turnover on the currency markets now often exceeds the global stock of official foreign-exchange reserves. A global economy, in today's terms, is globalized production by international corporations.

No one seems to doubt the new power of international market forces. The debate about "globalization" is whether it is a good thing or a bad thing, whether to embrace it or to resist it. A growing backlash against globalization is evident almost everywhere today, from Indonesia to the New Independent States (NIS) to the United States.

The vast impersonal forces of the global economy generate deep anxieties in many Americans. Global integration depends on freer trade at a time when lower-skilled Americans fear competition from developing economies. Washington increasingly finds itself called on to help secure the stability of world financial markets at a time when its less affluent citizens resent the influence of Wall Street. No longer is there an unchallenged belief among Americans that they are better off when their economy is open and the world is better off when the United States takes the lead. At a time when American prosperity increasingly depends on managing economic change, stabilizing the world financial system, and spurring global economic growth, the American public has become less and less willing to maintain allegiance to the country's post–World War II internationalist tradition.

Analysts are reading American public opinion as being more pessimistic. Policymakers are responding to a degree, trying to better explain the anxiety in coping with globalization. Yet, increasing numbers of Americans blame globalization for a slowdown in their incomes and a decline in their standard of living. Studies of U.S. Census Bureau data show a shrinking middle class. At the same time, studies find a rapidly widening gap between the rich and the poor. In the past two decades, rich and poor families have been increasing as a percentage of the population, while the percentage of middle-class families has declined.

Trade, especially cheap imports, is widely blamed for downward pressure on the employment prospects of the unskilled. This focus of blame will only get worse as the global financial crisis of 1998 will lead to a wave of cheap imports hitting American shores as foreign countries try to right their economies by importing less and exporting more. Average Americans increasingly believe that a transition to a global economy without an adequate social safety net can sacrifice American productivity in the name of progress. These grievances underscore feelings of isolation and the insignificance of the beleaguered American in an increasingly global economy.

Such sentiments were given powerful voice in early 1998 in a much-publicized speech at Harvard University by House Minority Leader Richard A. Gephardt, Democrat of Missouri. Gephardt called for a "new internationalism" that adhered as much to "American values" as it did to the dictates of the marketplace. "In a new era of globalization, the forces of commerce and technology are weaving the world closer together but . . . pulling our own people further apart," Gephardt said. "Our challenge is once again to link capitalism with values and standards." The globalization that seemingly promised economic well being for the United States has set in motion powerful cultural and political counterforces that threaten fragmentation and isolation.

The stresses and resentments that build up during times of economic change—such as today—generate broad and deep political pressures that, if left to fester, will only grow more destructive over time, as evidenced by violent public protests during the WTO meetings in Seattle in December 1999. The internationalist consensus that has governed U.S. foreign economic policy since World War II could be jeopardized. Attention must be paid to the counterforces of globalization by a federal government that American citizens expect to respond to their concerns. Such a conviction is matched by the public's acute awareness of the relative success of the federal government in responding to similar economic and political concerns in the past. Without responsive policies by government, the current economic transition may generate so much resistance that the U.S. internationalist commitment will grind to a halt.

Economic Reform Antecedents in United States History

Economic change has triggered sharp responses before in U.S. history. During the half-century before the Civil War, the U.S. economy was essentially a "closed system," reliant to a modest extent on exports, more or less indifferent to the volume of imports. During the half-century after the Civil War, known as the Gilded Age, the nation rapidly transformed itself into a major agricultural exporter and a producer of a mammoth stockpile of industrial and consumer goods. Within a generation, the United States had joined Britain, France, and Germany as one of the world's leading industrial powers.

Statistics tell the story of unprecedented economic growth during this prior day. Between 1870 and 1900, total U.S. exports tripled from $450 million to $1.5 billion, and, even more significantly, the percentage of those exports that consisted of manufactured goods (rather than agricultural or raw materials) jumped from 15 percent to 32 percent. By 1919 Woodrow Wilson could say, "The financial leadership will be ours. The industrial primacy will be ours. The commercial advantage will be ours." He was right. By 1929 almost half the world's industrial production was located in the United States, while the international thrust of U.S. business continued apace. In just two generations, the United States had been propelled into extensive involvement with economies throughout the world.

This transformation of the U.S. economy was, at first, largely a matter of indifference to Washington. Post–Civil War Republican administrations of the 1870s and 1880s, sympathetic to corporate business, watched with admiration as captains of industry built first a mighty industrial, and then a mighty export, economy. Slowly, however, another view began to manifest itself. While improvements in the standard of living were real, so too were the economic and social stresses created by this transformation—particularly the decline in status among farmers, laborers, and shopkeepers. The obsolescence of their skills and the division of their work routines by efficiency-minded managers shattered an older artisanal culture of skilled craftsmen who considered themselves the backbone of America.

Real wages rose 25 percent in the 1880s, but in the same decade textile workers could not support their families unless their wives also worked. Despite growing national wealth, most American workers managed on the slimmest of margins. The rich were getting richer, while American workers were not enjoying much of the new wealth being created. Working and middle-class Americans began to demand regulatory supervision of industrial consolidation and financial concentration through the political movements first of Populism in the 1890s and then of Progressivism in the 1900s and 1910s.

Populism and Progressivism rested on a set of convictions and emotions deeply embedded in United States history and culture—above all the vision of a chosen people, uniquely entitled to enjoy the fruits of abundance. The social seedbed of both movements lay in the conviction of farmers, laborers, and shopkeepers that they were being displaced and in their fierce determination to reverse the course of history by returning power to the people. At the heart of it was a view of history as an unending struggle between the virtue of ordinary people and the dark forces of callousness and corruption lurking in the halls of business and industry.

Populists and Progressives explained their second-class status under the rule of the "Money Power" by resorting to a highly charged moral language as old as the American Revolution. In a just economic system, the natural and proper workings of the market ensured a balance between energy expended and wealth acquired. It was only when this equilibrium was upset by greed or privilege that the natural system broke down and ordinary people suffered. Then it fell to the ordinary people of the country to enter politics and set matters right. Populists and Progressives declared themselves to be redemptive grassroots movements of the American folk, leading their fellow citizens to a just society across the roadblocks put in their path by a selfish minority of plutocrats.

An acute sense of immediate practical needs and the role of the federal government in meeting them matched such beliefs. Populists and Progressives sought to win elections and send to Washington representatives who would repair the economic system, clean up political corruption, and return to the "plain people" the management of the social order. Theodore Roosevelt was elected president in 1904 to implement effective government regulation of big business. Woodrow Wilson won election to the White House in 1912 promising to restore competition, make business more efficient, and release the individualism that had built the United States. National regulatory agencies created during this time, such as the Federal Trade Commission (FTC), greatly strengthened the hand of government by empowering it to conduct corporate investigations. The Federal Reserve Act assured stability and orderliness in the nation's banking system, which was then subject only to the regulation of the states. Gradually, the Federal Reserve System became a mechanism for regulating the amount of spending power available to the country.

After World War I, the country experienced a sharp economic downturn after the wartime boom. Farm income plunged and unemployment spurted up. These difficulties fueled the antagonisms between those who clung to traditional ways and those willing to accept change. Disillusioned by post–World War I turmoil in Europe, fearful of Bolshevism, and antagonistic toward immigrants bringing "alien" habits to the nation's shores, the great majority of Americans longed to insulate themselves from further contact with the outside world. The country rejected participation in the League of Nations and raised barriers to trade in the Fordney-McCumber Act of 1922 and the Hawley-Smoot Tariff of 1930, which reduced imports to the United States and undercut U.S. efforts to sell goods abroad.

The twin crises of the 1930s and the 1940s—the Great Depression and World War II—taught U.S. leaders several hard lessons: that economic isolationism and protectionism were bankrupt and dangerous, that disengagement was not a simple process, and that international affairs required more than paper promises to ensure economic and political stability around the globe.

After World War II, an undercurrent of anxiety tempered the great euphoria of victory. The Great Depression had left an invisible scar on the U.S. psyche, and the end of the war signaled to many citizens the reappearance of a time of economic troubles, a shaky fear about weathering the reconversion ahead. Predictions of gloom and doom filled the air: it was darkly said that 12 million veterans, trained to fight, would not meekly submit to the mass unemployment that seemed an all too likely consequence of the decline in war spending. U.S. leaders charged with the responsibility of guiding the nation through this time of worries and averting future world wars set out to create a free-trade system that surmounted destructive economic and political nationalism.

U.S. political leaders moved decisively, using as their compass the Wilsonian principles of political self-determination, free economic exchange, and international cooperation. Efforts to promote and regulate international trade became a prominent feature of U.S. foreign policy. The multilateral economic accords signed at Bretton Woods, New Hampshire, in July 1944—through American initiative—sought to encourage economic prosperity and political stability around the world through free trade, global finance, monetary cooperation, and development. Institutions created at Bretton Woods included the World Bank (which issued loans to the poorest nations) and the International Monetary Fund (IMF) (which helped to regularize transactions among the industrial powers). In 1947, the United States and other nations attempted to ensure an open trading system by entering into a General Agreement on Tariffs and Trade (GATT). Each member of GATT was to treat all other members the same way: the lowest tariff, the fewest restrictions, and the easiest access. Every U.S. administration since World War II has pursued a rule-based, multilateral, international trading system as a preeminent national economic objective. Free trade has remained a central tenet of American foreign economic policy ever since.

Current Difficulties

Today, the United States reigns as the world's dominant economic, cultural, and military force. But its power still has limits. As the world's largest debtor nation, the United States owes the rest of the world more than $1 trillion—much of it to Japan—and remains vulnerable to the whims of its creditors. While the United States remains the world's paramount economic engine, its share of the global economy is much smaller than in the days after World War II, when the United States accounted for a quarter of world output. The resistance to U.S. leadership generated by U.S. policies—for example, U.S. efforts to impose unilateral sanctions on countries that do business with Washington's list of pariah states—shows that American power does not always translate into persuasive influence. Trading partners reject the idea of having the United States tell them where they can and cannot invest.

At the same time, a culture of technology and management increasingly governs the industrial world. National borders mean much less today than they used to with respect to the flow of technology. It is increasingly difficult to create new technologies that will stay contained within national boundaries in a world where technological sophistication is widespread. Modern international business operates on a scale, and at a level, that lifts it above the

nation-states in which it locates its operating units. Economic linkages and relationships have leaped over national boundaries.
Trade has broken down the compartmentalization of the world. As
noted above, a global economy, in today's terms, is globalized production by supranational corporations.

A globalized economy presents problems that transcend the regulatory reach of the nation-state. Today, technological innovations
are bringing about ever larger and more rapid flows of production
and communication. This forces supranational corporations to
seek ever wider and deeper forms of organization. Supranational
corporations are becoming more organized and more planned.
Governments and international institutions respond by developing wider and deeper forms of regulatory supervision.

Countries like the United States that depend increasingly on the
workings of a globalized business system cannot, however, easily
interfere with the dynamics of that system. The principles of the
market mechanism and free trade retain their powerful influence
in the world economic system. Moreover, efforts to interfere with
the natural flows of business threaten to dampen the expansive
forces of the emerging international economy.

Even a brief history of U.S. industrial growth—generated overwhelmingly by corporate enterprise—shows that such change
gradually stimulated the intervention of regulatory supervision, in
part to protect the market mechanism, and in part, to vitiate the
deleterious effects of technological change on the American work
force (i.e., serious problems of economic dislocation and social and
political unrest). This point is critical for thinking about what a
next-generation approach to economic strategy should look like.

Conclusion: Appreciating the
American Reform Tradition

To a greater extent than ever before, the United State's future is inextricably entangled in the changing structure of world economic
affairs. At the same time, the United States faces a greater need
than ever before to deal with the pressures and stresses that result
from globalization and to come up with realistic policies that address the significant inventory of resentments accumulated by the

losers in this process and those most vulnerable to economic change, such as children and the elderly. These resentments and vulnerabilities are as much political as economic. They are potentially dangerous: the perception that the United States is helpless in the face of a globalized economy erodes political faith in and support for the government in Washington. If ordinary Americans do not feel any benefits from globalization, then it will be difficult for U.S. leaders to sustain the economic direction they believe the country should follow. This reality was most evident during the failed effort by the Clinton Administration to obtain fast-track trading authority during 1997 and 1998. Moreover, in response to protestors in Seattle during the WTO meetings who complained that "history is moving under our feet," President Clinton acknowledged that "more people are going to demand to be heard."

The need to act soon is great because these pressures and stresses will only increase over time. The new globalization will certainly enrich many—but this class is likely to be dominated by the highly skilled rather than ordinary workers. Moreover, those who will fare worst among ordinary workers will be the unskilled, least able to fend for themselves. Globalization will widen inequality, exacerbate poverty, and lead to social exclusion. If the internationalist consensus that has governed U.S. economic policy for 50 years is to endure, globalization's losers must be mollified and its risks anticipated. For without adequate safety nets to cushion adjustment burdens, political support for globalization may be impossible to sustain. Then, the half-century of global economic liberalization and growth since World War II could stall or even be thrown into reverse.

President Clinton, in his widely publicized speech to the Council on Foreign Relations (CFR) on September 14, 1998, stressed this danger of retreat and the need to maintain U.S. leadership in the global economic system, a system that has benefited the United States more than any other nation for the last 50 years. "The United States has an absolutely inescapable obligation to lead," the president said, "and to lead in a way that is consistent with our values and our obligation to see that what we are doing helps lift the lives of ordinary people. . . . We can, if we do that, redeem the promise of the global economy and strengthen our own nation for a new century."

Chapter 7

Donations and Double Standards

Trade and Global Public Integrity

Deroy Murdock

Corrupting the U.S. Economic Model

As weighty Cold War matters of past decades have become more-or-less manageable, the U.S. economic model is now dominant. While local variations exist, once-socialist nations today sway to the economic gospel the United States preaches. Around the globe, nations are moving toward more limited government, increased private property rights, and more reliable legal systems to protect individual liberty and commercial activity. Brazil's recently improved patent rules illustrate this trend. So does privatization that has moved unproductive assets, such as Argentina's phone system, from political control to the guiding hands of for-profit managers and entrepreneurs.

Leaders worldwide are leveling playing fields so competition will lower prices, improve the quality of goods and services, and reward investors. In addition, slowly but surely, the rule of law increasingly compels governments to treat those who come before them with impartiality and without favor. One could say that today the sun never sets on the U.S. economic model. In fact, the April 1998 Santiago Summit, discussed by Farnsworth in this volume, set forth an entire agenda agreed to by the governments in this hemisphere to implement "second-generation" reforms—policies and supporting institutions that would reinforce capitalism and the rule of law.

That same sun, however, exposes a rift between the U.S. economic ideal and an unsavory reality. While free-market slogans ring loudly from Capitol Hill to the capital markets, the U.S. economic playing field quietly is being tipped in favor of the politically connected. Rather than simply compete in open markets, supporters of Democrats and Republicans alike have used campaign contributions to purchase tax benefits, export subsidies, and import restrictions that hinder competitors and keep foreign goods that American consumers might prefer outside U.S. borders.

This corruption of U.S. political institutions through what has been called "legal bribery" impedes United States diplomatic efforts to advance cleaner governance overseas. Moreover, the public favors bought with private campaign cash create economic distortions and sometimes even produce and exacerbate foreign-policy headaches for the United States.

While some might call it alarmist to describe this phenomenon as "legal bribery," it is interesting to consider one of its "early adopters." Former President Jimmy Carter indicated on CNN's "Late Edition" on October 19, 1997, that bipartisan influence peddling has created the "not always erroneous" sense that to get results in Washington, "you've got to contribute money in a so-called 'legal bribe.'" He added "extremely large contributors, as has been revealed in testimony before the Congress, expect some favor in return." In addition, Carter concluded: "I think this is the most embarrassing and debilitating thing that I have seen evolve in the political structure of our country."[1]

This problem of public integrity broadly conceived is not just an American one. Leaders around the world—faced with rent-seekers of their own—seem to recognize the quest for global public integrity as an important item on the twenty-first century diplomatic agenda. On February 23, 1999, Glenn R. Simpson of *The Wall Street Journal* reported that U.S. officials were aware of alleged bribe payments in 239 international contract competitions between May

1994 and April 1998. This problem is a costly one. These contracts alone totaled $108 billion.

World leaders have responded to such bribery. On December 17, 1997, 34 Organization for Economic Cooperation and Development (OECD) nations signed an agreement to curb the bribery of public officials.[2] This agreement went into effect in February 1999. Officially known as the Convention on Combating Bribery of Foreign Public Officials in International Business Transactions, the treaty is the result of three rounds of negotiations held in July, October, and November 1997. The U.S. Senate unanimously ratified the treaty on July 31, 1998. The 105th Congress also passed enabling legislation to implement the treaty shortly before adjourning in October 1998.

According to a summary of the agreement prepared by the U.S. Departments of State, Justice, and Commerce:

> The convention obligates the Parties to criminalize bribery of foreign officials. This is defined to include officials in all branches of government, whether appointed or elected. . .
>
> Although the text does not specifically cover political parties, the negotiators agreed that the convention will cover business-related bribes to foreign public officials made through political parties and party officials, as well as those bribes which corrupt foreign public officials direct to political parties.
>
> The negotiators agreed to apply "effective, proportionate and dissuasive criminal penalties" to those who bribe foreign public officials. Countries whose legal systems lack the concept of criminal corporate liability must provide for equivalent non-criminal sanctions, including monetary penalties.

This deal was good news for U.S. businesspeople who long have argued that they were competing with one hand tied behind their backs. Since 1977, through the Foreign Corrupt Practices Act (FCPA), the United States unilaterally has prohibited the bribery of foreign officials who approve government contracts and other public goods. Meanwhile, overseas rivals of U.S. companies traditionally have been free to make such payoffs. Until their governments signed the OECD agreement, German and Canadian companies, for instance, could deduct foreign bribes from their taxes as business expenses. German officials calculate that their economy lost some $29 billion annually because of these *nuetzliche Ausgaben*[3] or "useful expenditures," as well as the costs of inflated contracts, kickbacks, and related tax evasion.[4] Until France ratifies the agreement, bribes will remain tax-deductible for its companies.

On the other hand, complying with U.S. law has not come cheaply for U.S. firms. A 1995 U.S. government report estimated that the FCPA had cost U.S. companies some $45 billion in overseas contracts because of their inability to compete with rivals whose governments permitted bribery of foreign officials.[5] According to *Business America* magazine, between 1994 and September 1996, there were

> significant allegations of bribery by foreign firms in 139 international commercial contracts valued at $64 billion. We estimate U.S. firms lost 36 of these contracts, valued at approximately $11 billion. Since these figures represent only those cases which have come to our attention, we suspect the magnitude of the problem is much greater than those estimates.[6]

In this context, it is important to reiterate that the United States is no innocent victim when it comes to graft. While the FCPA has discouraged all but a few U.S. managers from bribing foreign officials, "legal" payoffs to American politicians corrupt public affairs and distort the economy in functionally equivalent ways. As this issue grows ever larger in this new millennium, the United States must clean up its own house if it wishes to maintain any credibility in leading the world toward greater transparency and public integrity.

Old-fashioned, "Third World" Corruption and American Variants

U.S. executives and politicians often point to "third world-style" bribery. The last two decades of Republican and Democratic scandals have turned the accusatory finger back on the United States. This step back toward "immoral equivalence" has undermined U.S. leadership in combating this problem. For example, during an October 1997 visit to Brazil, President Clinton had to apologize for language in a U.S. government guidebook that said corruption was "endemic" in Brazilian culture.[7] This reference must have seemed especially hypocritical to Brasilia in light of the legal troubles of former Agriculture Department Chief of Staff Ronald Blackley that were underway at that time. Blackley's problems culminated in a December 2, 1997, conviction on three counts of lying about $22,000 he received from lobbyists for industries the department regulated in exchange for over $400,000 in subsidies.[8] Blackley received a jail sentence of 21 to 27 months for his crimes.[9]

Variations on a Theme

A classic example of the third world-style bribery is that of Melida Aleksic Molina. Ms. Molina is a former Venezuelan judge who ran into trouble in April 1995 for exchanging bribes for favorable court decisions. At that time, one defendant was so outraged at Molina's prices that he approached the anticorruption police who arranged a sting operation. After he paid the bribe she demanded, police knocked down her front door. Judge Molina took the evidence (about $5,880 worth of Venezuelan bolivares) and tossed it out the window of her seventh-story apartment. She claimed that she thought robbers were breaking into her home and disposed of the cash to prevent them from stealing it. The authorities apparently recovered only about $10 as Judge Molina's neighbors enjoyed a windfall on the sidewalks below. To this day, Caracas newspapers call this episode "The Night It Rained Money."[10]

In contrast, U.S. politicians rarely accept bags or bundles of cash. More likely, those seeking favors from officials practice bribery, American style. They make donations to campaigns and political party war chests with large bank drafts, nearly all of which are reported to the Federal Election Commission (FEC) and available for public inspection. Public Disclosure Inc., a nonpartisan, Washington-based campaign research group, maintains FEC Info., an online database on political donations at http://www.tray.com/fecinfo/indiv.htm. In this sense, these donations are perfectly transparent and almost always perfectly legal.

And yet, one wonders what donors want in return. Surely, some generous contributors give money to candidates because of ideological kinship or faith in politicians' personalities and leadership skills.

Campaign reformers complain that it is difficult to make direct connections between donations and favors. Officials typically deny such links, saying that campaign cash and government goodies are linked by coincidence, if at all. They often add that policies that help political donors also create jobs, boost exports, or prevent "unfair" trade. In one example of this sort of decoupling, President Clinton declared at a March 7, 1997, press conference in the East Room of the White House: "I don't believe you can find any evidence of the fact that I had changed government policy solely because of a contribution."[11]

Too often these days, though, the campaign finance system resembles the very same bribes-for-favors machines around the world that the aforementioned convention on combating bribery is designed to eliminate. Contributions to the Democratic and Republican campaign committees buy donors exclusive "access" or quality time with politicians. Government business, subsidies, and protection from competitors—foreign and domestic—often follow. These cozy relationships among generous corporate favor-seekers and politicians with access to other people's wallets create atrocious economic distortions that harm average Americans. Consumers pay higher prices for products while foreign suppliers are barred from U.S. markets after "favorable" regulatory barriers are put in place.

Three Examples from Emerging Markets

In this volume, essays on emerging markets consider China, the New Independent States (NIS), and Latin America. When reading these analyses, it also will be useful to keep in mind examples of how the current campaign contribution rules invite unscrupulous individuals to try to influence policy in these regions. Moreover, neither Democrats nor Republicans are immune to such questionable dealings.

To date, there has been little evidence of policy being altered *directly* in exchange for campaign donations. However, average Americans find it increasingly plausible that threats to U.S. national economic interests are being made from within. It will be important for a next-generation foreign policy—one rooted in a domestic consensus as has been stressed in various essays here—to address the threat *before* policies are changed.

China. Congressional investigators and the U.S. media have focused on the prospect that Chinese officials influenced the U.S. political system through concealed campaign donations. Fundraiser Johnny Chung generated for the Democratic Party some $366,000 (that it subsequently returned as suspicious). Chung visited the White House 57 times by his own count.[12] Chung also escorted People's Liberation Army (PLA) Lieutenant Colonel Liu Chaoying to a July 1996 California fund-raiser where she met and was photographed with President Clinton.[13] Liu—a reputed arms dealer, official with state-owned China Aerospace Company, and daughter of the PLA's senior commander, General Liu Huaqing—allegedly gave Chung $300,000.[14] He, in turn, confessed to federal officials that he funneled $100,000 of these funds to the Democratic Party in 1996.[15]

This transfer to Chung "was done by Liu Chao-ying acting as an individual," China Aerospace spokeswoman Zhang Libul confirmed to the *Christian Science Monitor* in Beijing. "She used her own financing rather than China Aerospace funds."[16] Whether Liu used personal or corporate money is legally irrelevant. It is a violation of U.S. law for campaign donors to launder contributions given by foreign nationals residing outside the United States. These laws ensnared Johnny Chung who pleaded guilty on March 17, 1998, to making illegal payments to the 1996 Clinton-Gore campaign. He also pleaded guilty to bank fraud and tax evasion related to his political philanthropy.[17]

The NIS. Roger Tamraz, a Lebanese-born oil man, donated $300,000 to the Democratic Party. He then tried to influence U.S. policy in an effort to promote a Caspian Sea oil-pipeline project.[18] On direction from the White House, Department of Energy analyst Kyle Simpson evaluated Tamraz's proposal and eventually recommended *against* backing the plan. However, it is important to note that Tamraz visited President Clinton at the White House six times and did try to influence policy. Such attempts require Americans to consider carefully the dangers to public integrity posed by economic interests that increasingly predominate in foreign policy.

Latin America. Now, let us ponder bananas. On March 19, 1997, the World Trade Organization (WTO) sided with the United States and Latin banana producers such as Ecuador—the world's largest exporter—in their banana trade dispute with the European Union (EU) and Caribbean growers. On April 12, 1996, then-U.S. Trade Representative (USTR) Mickey Kantor asked the WTO to support Cincinnati-based Chiquita Brands International, Inc. (the famous banana distribution company) in a case involving the EU and banana growers from Jamaica and Belize. Chiquita said it was victimized by EU rules that favor bananas from these former European colonies. *The very next day* after Uncle Sam gave Chiquita this big boost, Chiquita began donating a total of $415,000 to two dozen state Democratic parties across the United States.

The cozy preference scheme that allowed Europe's former colonies to supply it with bananas cannot be defended on free-market grounds. To be fair, it is conceivable that the WTO's March 19, 1997, ruling in favor of Chiquita's interests might have transpired without U.S. action. Banana producers such as Ecuador could have led the WTO action. Still, by visibly intervening in an area where the United States has no direct national economic interest, the United States is now involved in a highly divisive trade conflict with its European allies. In April 1999, Washington imposed 100 percent tariffs on $191.4 million worth of European imports such as bed linens and bath salts.

This U.S. brand of lawful bribery has a direct bearing on world trade. Wasteful, abusive corporate welfare programs keep inexpensive imports out of the hands of American consumers while denying overseas manufacturers access to the lucrative U.S. market. Meanwhile, export subsidies help U.S. firms sell their products abroad with government assistance. This makes it even harder for international competitors to compete on a level playing field and undercuts American efforts to gain similar even-handed treatment for U.S. firms.

Recommendations

While America has spearheaded international efforts to adopt an antibribery treaty, such an accord is unlikely to succeed if it only focuses on old-fashioned, "paper sacks of cash"-style graft. The United States should lead by example in an effort to get other nations to sever the tie between political donations and governmental gift giving. There are several concrete steps America should take in this direction:

First, the United States must adopt campaign finance legislation that will prevent the legal bribery of U.S. politicians and parties. Campaign reforms have failed in recent sessions of Congress, even though cleansing this system is as crucial as ever. Critics of reform correctly argue that some anticorruption remedies would jeopardize citizens' First Amendment rights to support the candidates they prefer. While the specifics of campaign finance reform go beyond the scope of this essay, it is both possible and vital to design a system wherein legal bribery would be dramatically reduced and Americans could *increase* their political freedom of speech.[19]

Second, the federal government should terminate its corporate welfare programs including distorting tariffs and import restrictions. So long as the state has goodies to give away, donors will line up for pieces of the action. The less government has on the auction block, the fewer bidders there will be.

Third, international watchdog groups like Transparency International and the creators of several economic freedom indices should be encouraged to continue scrutinizing the government ethics of the United States and its trading partners. The United States could benefit from being reminded that in the latest Transparency International survey of global corruption, the United States was the 18th most honest nation out of 99 evaluated.[20] At the 82nd percentile, America earns a B-minus in public integrity.

In some cases, sorting out "legal bribery" will be easy, as it will be clear that the transaction sought will not benefit America's broad economic interests. In other instances, judging a policy's contribution to the general welfare will be difficult to determine and will require careful scrutiny. More and more frequently, the commercial and security interests of the United States collide. For example, on February 23, 1999, the Clinton Administration reversed itself and a practice that spanned the Reagan and Bush Administrations and decided *not* to permit the sale of a commercial satellite by the Hughes corporation to a business group tied to the Chinese government. Although the $450 million satellite was designed to establish a mobile telephone system over Asia, it also appeared capable of assisting the Chinese military's efforts to improve the accuracy of its Inter-Continental Ballistic Missiles

(ICBMs). It is clear that campaign contributions to both parties over time pressured regulators to find such gray-area sales compliant with U.S. national security policies. As this volume will explore in the section involving telecommunications and technology, and, as best explained by Greenberg, globalization will create the dynamics whereby we may be selling the "wire" by which we hang ourselves.

In evaluating where the United States' national destiny lies, we must take steps to ensure that policymakers always act in America's best interests. The United States should set the global standard for public integrity by insisting that overseas governments treat their citizens and companies equally before the law and lawmakers. Perhaps the best way to assure that the United States succeeds in this role is for its friends to insist that America take a long look in the mirror.

Notes

1. Love, Alice Ann, "Carter slams 'legal bribes.'" *The Oakland Tribune,* October 20, 1997, page A1.

2. Daley, William M., "The Battle Against Bribery." *The Wall Street Journal,* December 17, 1997, page A22.

3. "Commercial Corruption" (editorial). *Wall Street Journal,* January 2, 1997, page 6.

4. Mitchener, Brandon, "Germany Says Business Bribes on the Rise." *The Wall Street Journal,* April 14, 1997, page A12.

5. Lewis, Paul, "No Consensus on Global Anti-Bribery Treaty." *New York Times,* May 20, 1997.

6. "Transnational bribery." *Business America,* September 1, 1996, page 112.

7. Douglas, William, "Brazil Protesters Pelt Clinton Car." *Newsday,* October 15, 1997, page A17.

8. "... and stay on the cutting edge of corruption." (Editorial) *The Washington Times,* December 21, 1997, page 36.

9. Vorman, Julie, "Ex-USDA official faces jail for lying about gifts." Reuters, March 18, 1998.

10. "Venezuela bribery case highlights court corruption." Reuters, April 24, 1995.

11. "Press Conference of the President." Official on-line White House transcript, March 7, 1997.

(http://www.pub.whitehouse.gov/uri-res/I2R?urn:pdi://oma.eop.gov.us/1997/3/7/26.text.1)

12. O'Reilly, Bill, Interview with Johnny Chung. "The O'Reilly Factor," Fox News Channel, August 16, 1999.

13. Gregorian, Dareh, "Campaign bombshell: Chung claims Chinese army backed Bill with 100G: report." *New York Post*, May 15, 1998, page 5.

14. Myers, Lisa (correspondent), "China Trail." NBC Nightly News, May 26, 1998.

15. Gregorian, *supra*.

16. Orin, Deborah, "China admits its 'spy' gave money to Dems." *New York Post*, May 19, 1998, page 6.

17. "Democratic Fund-Raiser Guilty." Reuters News Summary, March 17, 1998.

18. Lacey, Marc and Jackson, Robert L., "Ex-Aide Tells of Pressure on Donor's Behalf." *Los Angeles Times*, September 18, 1997, page A1.

19. Murdock, Deroy, "Solving the Campaign Finance Dilemma." *Headway*, June, 1997, pages 19–20 .

20. *The 1999 Transparency International Corruption Perceptions Index* (Berlin, Transparency International) October 26, 1999. (http://www.transparency.de/documents/cpi/cpi-bpi_press-release.html)

Chapter 8

Taking Sanctions into the Twenty-First Century

M. Diana Helweg

Reforming U.S. Sanctions Policy

Today's global economy has rendered the U.S. current sanctions policy largely ineffective by making it more difficult to isolate targeted nations.[1] The near extinction of communism has also eliminated the Cold War paradigm—a primary justification for sanctions—that dominated U.S. foreign policy after World War II. These changing dynamics have uprooted the international architecture that enabled sanctions to be a frequently used U.S. foreign policy tool over the past quarter century. Unfortunately, sanctions are still continually imposed, creating significant problems for a next generation foreign policy. The continuing U.S. preference for sanctions despite changed circumstances has, in fact, undermined and further weakened sanctions by leading to their overuse and, consequently, misuse on nonsecurity issues.

Despite the inefficacy of sanctions in recent times, the United States should not do away with the tool. Instead, it should reform

131

its use, narrowing its application to those rare circumstances when sanctions can be useful and effective in altering a regime's behavior. Simultaneously, the United States should implement a policy of constructive engagement that blends political and economic engagement together with other types of restrictive policies, including, but not limited to, sanctions. By creating a "web" of additional incentives, "constructive engagement" will allow the United States to continue to influence and lead the rest of the world in the promotion of core U.S. values, such as democracy and freedom. By retaining its economic leadership in the emerging global era, the United States will also enhance its national security.

This chapter creates a framework for reforming sanctions and making them part of a comprehensive policy of constructive engagement. First, to provide some perspective on the U.S. application of sanctions, the chapter gives a brief history of the use of sanctions and places current sanctions use in the context of the relatively new world the United States faces. Second, this chapter lays out the reasons why sanctions so often fail to achieve their stated objectives, despite their frequent use. Third, the chapter prescribes some remedies that should be applied to U.S. sanctions policies to restore their effectiveness. The factors include multilateral support, the timing of imposition, targeting, and a realistic assessment of the goals to be achieved. Finally, the chapter proposes using sanctions and other economic penalties as part of a broader policy of constructive engagement on trade and security issues with other countries.

The Life and Times of U.S. Sanctions

Sanctions have always been a part of international relations: thousands of years ago, the ancient Greeks employed sanctions against their enemies, refusing the Megarians access to their land, their markets, and their seas.[2] The United States, meanwhile, has employed sanctions at different times and against different constituencies, virtually since it declared itself a nation in 1776.[3] The modern concept that economic sanctions could substitute for the use of military force, however, began after World War I, mainly under the authority of the League of Nations, which sought to use collective action to settle disputes among member states.[4]

In most of the post–World War II situations where economic force was brought to bear against misuse of military power, [5] the United States substituted for the defunct League of Nations as the international policeman. For example, the United States unilaterally coerced colonial powers to step aside in favor of independence movements in countries in Africa, the Middle East, and Asia in the late 1940s and 1950s; forced France and the United Kingdom out of the Suez Canal in 1956 by blocking their International Monetary Fund (IMF) assistance; and tried unsuccessfully to prevent Fidel Castro from expropriating foreign-owned industries in Cuba in 1960.[6]

Sanctions rapidly increased in use and public awareness in the latter half of this century during the Cold War when the Western powers sought to contain or isolate communism. In those cases, the United States primarily used sanctions to prevent border skirmishes, destabilize governments, and influence other military actions.[7] Sanctions often targeted Communist regimes or nationalist movements. Institutions were even created to support the enforcement of sanctions policy. For example, the NATO countries plus Japan, and later Australia, started the Coordinating Committee for Multilateral Export Controls (CoCom) in 1949 to prevent the Soviet Union and the Warsaw Pact nations from obtaining advanced military technology. The cooperative organization was intended to prevent the Communist countries from seizing the lead in critical defense sectors. By forcing the Soviet Union to spend massive amounts of money on efforts to achieve military parity with the West, CoCom's denial of military technology contributed to the economic collapse of the Soviet Union and the end of the Cold War.[8]

In the 1960s, U.S. sanctions policy reached a watershed. For the first time, the United States began to employ sanctions to achieve nonmilitary foreign policy goals such as improving human rights in Latin American countries, settling expropriation claims in Cuba, changing civil rights in South Africa, improving labor standards in Asia, and protecting endangered species all over the world.[9] In some countries' eyes, the United States had metamorphosed from international policeman to international enforcer of morality.

Following the fall of the Berlin Wall in 1989, American sanctions policy continued to evolve. U.S. use of all kinds of sanctions increased so rapidly that some now deem sanctions as a U.S. foreign policy of first resort.[10] This allegation is not unfounded. The United States frequently finds itself imposing sanctions carelessly and hastily against regimes that the United States does not like or as chits in election campaigns to garner certain domestic voting blocks. The recent spate of sanctions, however, have rarely worked.

The Prodigal Sanction

The current U.S. adoration of sanctions is analogous to the biblical father's feelings for his prodigal son: despite many obvious short-comings, they are still loved. As sanctions shifted from targeting security-related issues to individual rights and environmental issues, they correspondingly became less effective. Too often now, the United States casually invokes sanctions for counterproductive reasons: to satisfy a domestic constituency or to assuage American consciences regarding injustices abroad, such as with Cuba, Haiti, and others. Thus, policymakers have begun to "squander" U.S. military, political, and diplomatic power by misusing sanctions.[11] To bring the prodigal sanction back into the family of foreign-policy tools, the United States must reevaluate what sanctions can actually accomplish and then apply them in a discriminating manner.

Expanded Use and Overuse

Most of sanctions' favor derives from congressional predisposition towards them as a foreign-policy tool. All too often, members of Congress view sanctions as inexpensive and relatively painless statements against unacceptable foreign behavior. Although senators and representatives have become more involved in foreign policy since the Vietnam War,[12] they are often less informed about all sides of the issue, preferring to focus on the repercussions in the domestic election campaign cycle and on their particular constituents, instead of the nation as a whole. In addition, there is no longer an overarching paradigm that dictates a cohesive national interest. As a result, congressional use of U.S. foreign policy for domestic power brokering has led to increased introduction of sanctions legislation on behalf of vocal, small, or single-issue constituencies.[13]

A particularly striking example of a law passed to satisfy a domestic constituency is the Cuba Libertad Act (known most commonly as Helms-Burton). In 1996, domestic outrage over the Cuban downing of two Miami-based "Brothers to the Rescue" planes encouraged Congress to push through and force the president to sign into law the Cuba Libertad Act. The law punishes countries, including U.S. allies, that trade with Cuba. The act imposes sanctions on companies that invest in Cuba as well as on their executives by barring entry by such executives into the United States. The law was originally drafted in response to concern from the Cuban-American community that the increased foreign investment in Cuba in the early 1990s involved former U.S. properties that had been confiscated by Fidel Castro. Although President Clinton had considered redesigning his Cuba policy during his first term to promote more engagement, he felt obligated to sign this legislation because of the domestic push by Cuban-Americans in an election year and Congress's promise to override any veto.[14]

Recent sanctions laws, including Helms-Burton, have targeted not only the country in question with a primary boycott, but also American allies that do not comply with U.S. sanctions. These "secondary" boycotts apply U.S. law either to prohibit U.S. trade and investments with a country, including a U.S. ally, that does business with the targeted country or to sanction a foreign company for investments in the targeted country.

Another example of this type of sanctions law is the Iran Libya Sanctions Act (ILSA). Also signed into law in 1996, ILSA targets any investments in oil and gas development in Iran or Libya, including those of U.S. allies, over a threshold amount of $20 million. Initially formulated by the pro-Israel lobby to target investments that would enrich Iran, the law was expanded by Senator Edward Kennedy to include Libya as a gesture to the families of the Pan-Am 103 bombing. By doing so, Senator Kennedy turned ILSA into a bill about terrorism.[15] Congress and the president then felt compelled to pass the law to show their support in combating terrorism, especially in the wake of the midair explosion of TWA flight 800.[16] The cause of that crash has not been finally determined, but no evidence has surfaced that it was a terrorist attack, much less a "state-sponsored" terrorist attack.[17] Yet, the tragic accident served as the catalyst for passing a law that requires imposition of U.S. sanctions on non-U.S. companies that invest in Iran or Libya.

In addition, the recent proliferation of sanctions has tended toward nonsecurity issues. Specifically, sanctions abound to protect human rights, civil rights, labor rights, and the environment abroad. This trend has been borne out in several sanctions of questionable effect passed in this decade. Examples include sanctions invoked against human rights abuses of the Cedras regime in Haiti, the recently passed Freedom from Religious Persecution Law that targets the treatment of religious minorities in many nations including those of U.S. allies, sanctions against the current political oppression in Cambodia, and laws that protect sea turtles from the Caribbean shrimp industry.

Members of Congress recognize that sanctions appeal to the American public because they satisfy domestic desire to reprimand those who do not share traditional U.S. values. The pressure for sanctions has increased as the media has brought more and more of the actions of other governments, and any resulting horrors, into Americans' living rooms. Such attention leaves American citizens with a corresponding desire to act, and sanctions usually seem to be the appropriate level of response. As a result, sanctions garner much public support because they allow the United States to be on record as objecting to events without going so far as entering into military conflict with those with whom it disagrees. Americans generally oppose going to war, and they have even recently increased their opposition to U.S. involvement in multinational military interventions. Sanctions, therefore, seem like the perfect middle ground. They offer a lower risk and a lower cost option to military intervention, but they still go beyond either taking no action or merely engaging in verbal opposition.[18] The public thus perceives sanctions as quick, inexpensive, and painless solutions to what bothers them.

The Problems with Overuse

There are three main reasons why sanctions often do not succeed in this post–Cold War era. First, in today's era of globalization and integration, the United States does not have the leverage that it once did to enforce a comprehensive sanctions policy. The United States has lost its status as the "premier" trading partner. U.S. exports have declined from 15 percent to 12 percent of the world's exports in the 29 years from 1968 to 1997.[19] Other countries now actively seek to exploit any restriction on U.S. capital or goods overseas. Multinational joint ventures have increased the power of previously national or regional companies to do business around the world. Americans in business abroad have seen this diversification of trade happening all over Asia, and it is beginning now in the Middle East.

Nor has this global integration bypassed the United States, further reducing U.S. leverage. Today, the United States is more financially dependent than ever on the markets and regimes that it seeks to sanction. In 1995, exports lost by U.S. companies totaled an estimated $15 to $19 billion, and affected 200,000 to 250,000 jobs.[20] Another study, looking more broadly at the implications of sanctions, found that sanctions imposed from 1993 to 1996 cost the United States an estimated $800 billion in access to export markets.[21] These figures do not even contemplate U.S. profits and jobs lost in markets where new business ventures automatically go to international competitors because U.S. companies are barred from bidding on them.[22] In this time of uneven economic growth, U.S. sanctions often mean denying American companies access to certain fast-growing markets with significant potential for profits. Correspondingly, sanctions often limit the U.S. government's ability to have a constructive dialogue with certain regimes on various national security issues. As a result, U.S. sanctions often hurt U.S. interests as much as those of the targeted countries.

Second, with the end of the Cold War, the United States has greater difficulty trying to encourage its allies to join U.S. efforts to isolate or punish certain regimes. The international political dynamic has shifted from superpower confrontation to globalization and integration of markets and interests. Many nations no longer need U.S. protection, and the formerly bipolar world is now divided into various, frequently shifting coalitions. In any given situation, some nations are only interested in the financial bottom line; others do not share U.S. values; while still others believe that they can promote the same values through economic engagement alone. Moreover, many nations are reluctant to resort to sanctions or to following a U.S.-led policy. This is especially true of policies targeting social issues such as human rights reform, civil rights reform, improved labor standards, and environmental protection.

Third, without the Cold War battle lines of democracy and communism, the United States and the world have developed fractured foreign policies where there are no clean boundaries which delineate what to support and what to reject. The U.S. government has not yet developed a cohesive, bipartisan policy response. Traditional allegiances carry less weight than ever before, and finding common ground among American citizens as well as allies presents difficult challenges.

To succeed in this new era, the United States must focus on understanding the goals of the government whose behavior it wants to change and then, using psychology as much as sanctions, find options that appeal to that country's needs and desires.[23] Thus far, the Clinton Administration has done this on a case-by-case basis. Examples include using the Chinese desire to have the Tiananmen Square sanctions repealed as leverage for progress on proliferation issues; linking the Vietnamese-desired bilateral trade agreement to improved access to missing-in-action (MIA) remains and more effective processing of emigration petitions; using Taiwanese desire to accede to the World Trade Organization (WTO) as leverage for progress on regional security issues; and focusing on the interests of Hungary, Poland, and the Czech Republic in joining the North Atlantic Treaty Organization (NATO) as an incentive for obtaining necessary reforms in their respective economies. Now the U.S. government must turn this *ad hoc* engagement policy into an affirmative, comprehensive foreign policy. The first step is reforming U.S. sanctions policy.

Recipe for a New Sanctions Policy

Sanctions can serve as one of many useful tools in the U.S. foreign-policy arsenal. If the United States can remedy the sanctions overuse problem by limiting their imposition to those situations where sanctions actually have the possibility of working, sanctions will regain some of their strength. Such change will enhance U.S. credibility in foreign policy and enable the United States to develop other successful economic, political, and security strategies for the twenty-first century.

The framework set out below recommends three elements for an effective sanctions policy. First, the United States should strive, whenever possible, to impose multilateral sanctions. Second, the government should impose sanctions swiftly, and for a fixed period. A positive finding of effectiveness should determine whether or not they continue. Third, sanctions should always target a sector of the adversary's economy where the United States can expect to inflict the most harm. These elements must be balanced and examined in the context of each situation. Through such an approach, the United States can return sanctions to their core focus on altering behavior related to military and security issues such as weapons proliferation and regional instability. Using sanctions to promote change on issues like individual rights and the environment rarely work, and those issues should be addressed through other means such as positive incentives in constructive engagement.

Multilateral Sanctions

As seen in South Africa, Iraq, and Bosnia, multilateral support for sanctions can make an enormous difference in their ultimate effectiveness. The nature of today's global economy allows targeted countries to obtain the goods and capital they need from other countries when the United States bans its nationals from doing business there. As a result, unilateral sanctions usually serve as nothing more than a statement of protest against a regime. This may be the desired objective in the face of exceptionally egregious behavior by a particular country. The United States should understand that fact in evaluating policy options, rather than pretending that the paper tiger of unilateral sanctions has teeth.[24] Unilateral sanctions might have an effect if the United States is so heavily engaged in trade with a targeted country that it cannot adjust to the U.S. cessation of business. That, however, is rare in today's markets.

Unfortunately, making the effort to foster consensus on sanctions policy among nations can slow the actual imposition of the sanctions as well as significantly water down the provisions.[25] Policymakers must consider this possibility when deciding to impose sanctions. If the benefit of multilateral support would be gained at the cost of taking a long time to impose sanctions, then the costs might outweigh the benefits, making the entire effort futile. Nonetheless, the United States must recognize that the best results are usually won through multilateral efforts.

In addition, the United States should not legislate secondary boycotts, which cost far more than they are worth and eliminate any possibility of multilateral support. The most recent examples of such boycotts, Helms-Burton and ILSA, have arguably had some influence over the investment decisions of American allies, but at an extremely high political cost to U.S. relations abroad. In fact, those laws have done more to force the United States to defend itself against its allies in international court, than to change the behavior of Cuba, Iran, or Libya. Ironically, in previous international disputes, such as the case of the Arab League boycott of Israel, the United States has argued that these kinds of secondary boycotts are contrary to the procedures of the General Agreement on Tariffs and Trade (GATT). Now, it finds itself before the WTO, defending these laws that appear to take action against rogue regimes, but in reality have had very little positive effect on any country's behavior.

Timing and Review

The United States should impose sanctions as quickly as possible given other criteria such as multilateral support. The less time a regime has to prepare for the imposition of sanctions, the more likely sanctions will have an effect. Two comprehensive studies of sanctions have shown that the speed with which sanctions are imposed is directly related to their effectiveness.[26]

The need for surprise was demonstrated in the case of Iran, after its revolutionaries seized the U.S. Embassy in Tehran in 1979, and the case of Libya, after terrorists acting on behalf of the government bombed Pan Am flight 103 in 1988. Because public debate delayed the imposition of sanctions, Iran and Libya reduced the effect of the impending sanctions by using the delay to remove assets from reach, to hoard necessities, and to negotiate with their allies to circumvent some of the penalties.[27]

Once imposed, sanctions should also have a built-in review provision requiring policymakers to analyze their application and to make a positive finding of effectiveness for continuation. Congress, however, has almost always opposed any sunset provision that would automatically terminate a law's application.[28] As an alternative, an annual written report from the administration to Congress incorporating public comment could detail whether or not a particular sanctions policy had made progress towards achieving its objectives. If not, then Congress would have to repeal the sanctions; if so, the sanctions would continue.[29]

Policymakers must think carefully about which measures are most effective and most in the national interest because the longer sanctions go on, the less likely they are to work.[30] After a long period, the targeted regime becomes insulated from the pain of sanctions for a number of reasons. Sometimes, other countries begin to feel sympathy for the target and do whatever they can to alleviate the restrictions on goods; in other cases, the country itself uses the sanctions to promote nationalism and encourage sacrifice by its people; or even worse, a regime may not care if its people are harmed by the sanctions and will continue to resist even in the face of the illness and death of its people. Policymakers must evaluate an inevitable "sanctions fatigue" and factor it into any lengthy application of sanctions. [31]

Timing also affects the public perception of costs that the United States may pay for choosing this policy option. On the domestic front, the longer the sanctions go on and the more they cost U.S. businesses and consumers, the more likely the United States will have to consider compensation for U.S. businesses. The United States may even have to compensate other nations indirectly harmed. This was the case when the United States decided to pursue a multilateral effort, through the United Nations (U.N.), to impose sanctions against Iraq. Realizing that the coalition had to alleviate the extremely high costs inflicted on Egypt, Turkey, and Jordan by banning trade with Iraq, the United States proposed an Economic Action Plan that ultimately provided about $20 billion in multilateral assistance to those countries.[32] Paying such compensation for lost business may make the costs of sanctions unbearably high. Policymakers on Capitol Hill and in the administration should require a rigorous cost-benefit analysis that includes an impact statement analyzing the effect on U.S. businesses and other indirect costs illustrated above before imposing sanctions. This should *precede*, but not replace, the annual review to determine whether or not the sanctions are having a positive effect.

Targeted Sanctions

Once the United States decides to apply sanctions, it should target certain sectors of the other country's economy, rather than invoke a blanket ban on all trade. Targeting a sector of the economy or an aspect of a country's military preparedness allows the United States to focus its efforts, refine its tools, and achieve a greater effect. Also, targeted sanctions reduce the unintended consequences for ordinary people living under a regime by focusing the application. To the extent the United States is seeking multilateral support, targeted sanctions will also improve the chances of consensus by presenting less room for contentious wrangling. Furthermore, the United States can then easily evaluate a focused application of sanctions to determine whether or not they work and what adjustments it should make to the current policy.

Targeting efforts have the most effect when the United States applies sanctions within the broader context of economic engagement. When an ongoing bilateral relationship exists, targeted sanctions signal disapproval and serve as a warning of potential future pain. At the same time, however, the ongoing relationship increases the importance to the target of having the sanctions lifted and acts as an incentive for the target to change its behavior. A targeted nation is more likely to comply if it has something of value to lose.

Within the compendium of targeted sanctions, there are many possible options, but financial sanctions, such as freezing assets and denying official credits, appear to have the best results for two reasons.[33] First, they affect the elite of a country before the ordinary citizen because they tend to hit decisionmakers who have access to the nation's money. Second, financial sanctions are less likely to affect any one domestic U.S. constituency, which makes imposition an easier decision for Congress and the administration. The use of financial sanctions, however, demands quick imposition, given the speed of electronic transfers and the ability of a targeted nation to move money rapidly to protect itself from the grasp of a sanctioning country. In this global marketplace, use of financial sanctions also requires an especially careful analysis so as not to disrupt the international banking system or cause unintended consequences in unrelated regions.

Members of Congress should also restrict themselves to legislating sanctions that target national security issues rather than social issues that have become so popular recently. These social issues include human rights, civil rights, improved labor standards, family planning, environmental rights, and so forth. By comparison, the sanctions that focus on weapons proliferation, regional instability, and other security threats are much more likely to result in changed behavior, as well as receive multilateral support. Arguably, most countries perceive national security threats as "objective" and find them easier to support than the "subjective" concepts of individual rights and how a nation should use its own natural resources. For example, although the sanctions against Iraq have not worked perfectly, there has been multilateral understanding and acceptance of the need to prohibit Saddam Hussein from terrorizing the Middle East or spreading weapons of mass destruction. The continuation of sanctions against Iraq is under debate within the U.N. Security Council, but international consensus exists that Iraq's threatening behavior is unacceptable. That would not be the case if Iraq's human rights record were under discussion.

Economic sanctions can be a powerful tool in this era of globalization. As they displace military force, sanctions should undergo thorough analysis commensurate with their potential role in the U.S. policy arsenal. If policymakers apply the three elements discussed above to U.S. sanctions policy, they will likely use sanctions more carefully and with restraint as a discrete policy option.

Constructive Engagement: An Alternative to Sanctions

To fill the policy vacuum left by the reduced use of sanctions, the United States should adhere to a policy of political and economic engagement that balances "sticks" such as sanctions and other restrictive measures with additional "carrots" of trade and aid. Only broader economic engagement can open up the relationship with a country and create the mutual economic and strategic benefits that will enable subsequent restrictive policies to encourage the targeted regime to change its undesirable behavior.

Stated most simply, engagement is the opposite of isolation. It includes the flow of ideas, goods, and money under the umbrella of official diplomatic relations. Engagement can be effected through strategic and political dialogue, investment, trade, and even joining forces on appropriate issues in multilateral fora. Since the fall of the Berlin Wall in 1989, the United States has pursued a policy of political and economic engagement with some previously isolated regimes through dialogue, investment, and support of free trade. In doing so, the United States has indirectly helped promote democracy, freedom of association, freedom of speech, and civil and human rights. To be sure, progress has occurred slowly and with differing degrees of success. Although difficult to measure, engagement with democracies provides the citizens of closed countries the opportunity to learn what types of political freedoms and economic successes are possible. The past decade is replete with instances of ordinary people using that education to try to change their political worlds from Eastern Europe to Latin America and from Africa to Asia.

Countries that have initiated trade and diplomatic relations with the United States have definitely benefited more than those that remain isolated from the United States. For example, compare the civil reforms that have accompanied economic reforms in the former Soviet Union that have been triggered by Western investment and trade, against those that have yet to occur in an isolated Cuba. The same dichotomy can be seen when comparing the improvements in quality of life in a virtually capitalist China thriving on foreign investment with an unstable, famine-stricken North Korea. This argument does not suggest that further significant reforms are still not needed in Russia and China, but there have been improvements over the last decade. One of the keys to the gradual improvements in the Chinese and Russian regimes has been the coupling of economic and political engagement with economic restrictions for behavior incompatible with international norms.

Secretary of State Madeleine K. Albright has argued that a U.S. policy of economic engagement with a country does not mean endorsement of its regime.[34] In fact, the U.S. version of engagement is different from countries, such as France and Japan, which often practice a policy of *unlimited* economic engagement based on the rationale that unfettered trade and investment best promotes democratic values for the targeted nation, and financial success for themselves. By contrast, U.S.-"style" engagement must be coupled with a range of policy tools that includes the targeted use of economic restrictions. In other words, it is a variation on the traditional carrot and stick approach rather than one or the other.

Engagement, coupled with the availability of discrete penalties, establishes a functional dialogue and practical relationship between the United States and the targeted government. It constructs a bilateral relationship that the targeted country values and wants to preserve. In the context of that relationship, the United States has more opportunity and more credibility to potentially influence a country's behavior. The targeted country has more at stake, in the form of economic profits, enhanced security, and even international status. It, therefore, has more reason to adapt its policies to maintain a good relationship with the United States. Studies over the years have shown that sanctions combined with a healthy trade relationship often succeed in getting a targeted country to change its offending behavior before it loses more business.[35]

A policy of constructive engagement can also serve as a useful nexus between a forward looking economic strategy and improved U.S. national security. As evidenced by the failure of the United States to change the behavior of Libya, North Korea, Cuba, and others, the United States has only a limited ability to isolate countries in today's global markets. On the other hand, economic and diplomatic engagement coupled with discrete tools offers the possibility of affirmatively promoting national security in three ways.

First, the act of merely being engaged with a nation lessens the chances of military conflict with that country. Nations that have a relationship, especially democracies, are less likely to go to war with one another than countries that are neither democratic nor engaged.

Second, by being engaged with a country, the United States increases its credibility and can thereby play more of a role in regional security discussions. If the ongoing relationship is worth preserving, the United States has the leverage to persuade a country to modify its behavior. This was evidenced in the successful U.S. discussions with China over its sale of ring magnets to Pakistan for use in a nuclear reactor not under International Atomic Energy Agency (IAEA) supervision.[36] The United States suspended availability of U.S. Export-Import Bank loans for infrastructure projects in China and threatened to impose sanctions on exports of technology to Chinese enterprises suspected of supplying Pakistan with military technology. In the wake of the 1996 Taiwan Straits showdown, China wanted to improve relations with the United States. As a result, the threat of sanctions coupled with the prospects of further deterioration in the U.S.-China relationship worked to change China's behavior.[37]

Third, in a context of constructive engagement, nations have more incentive to return to accepted norms of nation-state behavior even if they believe that they have to partially deviate from them to ensure their own security or survival. This is especially true if they have ongoing constructive relationships with countries that do live by those norms. For example, although economic engagement plus the threat of sanctions did not prevent either India or Pakistan from each testing nuclear weapons in May 1998, the multilateral policy of sanctions plus ongoing engagement did help bring them back to the negotiating table once they had ensured their own security.[38] In September 1998, both countries agreed to resume a dialogue and each made commitments to sign the Nuclear Non-Proliferation Treaty (NPT).[39] Each country wanted the sanctions lifted; each wanted to be treated again as a respected nation; and each wanted to continue to play a role in the U.N. and other multilateral entities.

Making the Transition

Without reforming its sanctions policy and engaging with the nations it wants to change, the United States will miss its opportunity to define the future. Too much has changed. In a world of integrated markets, if we abdicate shaping economic incentives, others will fill the vacuum.

It will not be easy to change the trend of the current U.S. approach to sanctions. Congress will incur significant pressure from special interest groups and small domestic constituencies to impose U.S. sanctions against regimes that do not necessarily share U.S. values. To alleviate some of this pressure, Congress should focus public attention on the weaknesses of sanctions. Legislators should authorize government-business hearings and bipartisan studies to determine the effectiveness of sanctions currently in place. Once Congress undertakes the challenging task of educating the American public that the legislation of sanctions almost never succeeds in attaining human rights, civil rights, and environmental reform, then the U.S. government can be more creative in its policy formulation. Congress and the administration will have more flexibility to find ways to influence a regime's behavior through gaining an understanding of what motivates the targeted regime and ascertaining its long- and short-term objectives. If the United States understands the motives of a targeted country, it can then work with that country to attain its goals as well as those of the United States.

This approach has worked well in the negotiations for a bilateral trade agreement between Vietnam and the United States. The United States has conditioned the conclusion of any agreement on improved access to remains of U.S. servicemen missing in action during the Vietnam War, and the Vietnamese have responded positively.[40] In addition, the United States linked Vietnam's performance on the repatriation of Vietnamese refugees from Hong Kong to the availability of EX-IM Bank financing for U.S. businesses that would invest in Vietnam. That linkage resulted in Vietnam's offer to process the emigration petitions of these refugees before exit visas were granted.[41] This significantly loosened up the process for emigration and has enabled many more people to have their cases heard. The bilateral trade agreement is still under negotiation, but the United States government has successfully leveraged Vietnamese aspirations for concluding an agreement and acceding to the WTO to obtain U.S. policy objectives through the negotiations. Using this type of constructive engagement with a regime requires more work and takes longer than legislating a boycott to force action. As evidenced in Vietnam, it has the potential to work.

Cuba would be a good place to try this constructive engagement policy again. The United States can promise a gradual removal of sanctions in return for economic and political reforms in Cuba. The increased dialogue with Castro's regime would bring more progress on trade, investment, tourism, and discussions on security issues than the current embargo has in forty years.

The United States should pursue its foreign policy and national security by examining the goals, the political situations, and the economic needs not only of the targeted countries, but also of the United States itself. Once the United States updates its national interests to meet twenty-first century realities and moves beyond relying on sanctions as a general substitute for foreign policy, it can then effectively shape the world for the next century. In this new era, the United States must get engaged if it wants to lead.

Notes

1. This chapter focuses on sanctions that are economic, political and military, and designed to deter or compel action by a targeted country. This chapter does not address sanctions that are used solely to gain market access or trade agreement compliance.

2. Gary Clyde Hufbauer, Jeffrey J. Schott, and Kimberly Ann Elliott, *Economic Sanctions Reconsidered: History and Current Policy Reconsidered*, 2nd ed. (Washington, DC: Institute for International Economics, 1990), pp. 4–5 (hereinafter "Hufbauer").

3. Richard N. Haass (ed.), *Economic Sanctions and American Diplomacy* (New York, NY: Council on Foreign Relations, 1998), p. 3 (hereinafter "Haass").

4. Hufbauer at p. 5, and Table 1.1 (for example, Greece was successfully persuaded to cease occupying Bulgaria in 1925, while Italy refused to agree to leave Abyssinia in the mid–30s).

5. As John C. Sharfen points out in his book, *The Dismal Battlefield: Mobilizing for Economic Conflict*, (Annapolis, MD: Naval Institute Press, 1995), p. 22: "In some instances, economic force is the principal instrument being used to influence an adversary. In others it may play a supporting role where military or political forces dominate."

6. Makio Miyagawa, *Do Economic Sanctions Work?* (New York, NY: St. Martin's Press, Inc., 1992), pp. 10–15 (hereinafter "Miyagawa"). In addition, see Hufbauer at p. 5.

7. Hufbauer at pp. 4–5.

8. While often credited with maintaining the Western alliance's military technology lead, CoCom was terminated in 1992 and replaced with the Wassenaar Agreement in 1994. This successor export-control organization counts Russia and other former Communist states as members with a revised mission of controlling exports to rogue nations such as Libya, Iran, Iraq, and North Korea.

9. Under the umbrella of the United Nations, the United States also participated in sanctions against racial discrimination policies in Rhodesia in 1966 and 1968 and against South Africa in 1977. Miyagawa, at pp. 10–15. See also Hufbauer at pp. 4–9.

10. Jim Hoagland, "Squandered Power," *Washington Post*, October 16, 1997, p. A19 ("The Clinton Administration and Congress have made sanctions the foreign policy tool of first resort. . . .")(hereinafter "Hoagland"). Citing a study that National Association of Manufacturers commissioned from the Georgetown University Law Center, Howard Lewis, vice president for trade policy at the National Association of Manufacturers, said, "Since 1993 roughly, there have been 50 different laws or executive branch actions imposing unilateral sanctions against 31 different countries." Cited in "Chicken Soup Diplomacy," *National Journal*, January 4, 1997, pp. 13–17, at p. 15 (hereinafter "Chicken Soup Diplomacy"); see also, Haass at p. 1 (citing the same study).

11. Hoagland at p. A19.

12. Haass at p. 209.

13. See "Chicken Soup Diplomacy" at p. 13; Haass at p. 3; and Report of the President's Export Council prepared with the assistance of Don Zarin and Meha Shah, *Unilateral Economic Sanctions: A Review of Existing Sanctions and Their Impacts on U.S. Economic Interests with Recommendations for Policy and Process Improvement* (Washington, DC: President's Export Council, June 1997) at p. 2 of Executive Summary (hereinafter "PEC Report").

14. See Haass at pp. 47–55 (Chapter by Susan Kaufman Purcell). The president announced in January 1999 that he would like to expand U.S. contacts with Cuba, a first step in the administration's efforts to change U.S. policy with Cuba from isolation to engagement. This expansion of contacts does not include the lifting of any sanctions.

15. Haass at pp. 87–92 (Chapter by Patrick Clawson) and pp. 142–148 (Chapter by Gideon Rose).

16. "Chicken Soup Diplomacy" at p. 13.

17. Don Phillips, "Flight 800 Hearing Looks at Navy Jet Fuel for Safety," *Washington Post*, December 13, 1997, p. A6 ("A 17-month investigation involving thousands of people and millions of dollars has failed to find any solid evidence of why the [plane's fuel] tank exploded."); Don Phillips, "Probers to Search Miles of Wire from Flight 800; NTSB Looks for 'Needle in the Haystack'," *Washington Post*, December 11, 1997, p. A3 (The NTSB tries to piece together the factors that caused TWA flight 800 to crash, but none of those factors include terrorism).

18. As the American Catholic bishops said, "Sanctions can offer a nonmilitary alternative to the terrible options of war or indifference when confronted with aggression or injustice." National Conference of Catholic

Bishops, "The Harvest of Justice is Sown in Peace: A Reflection of the National Conference of Bishops on the Tenth Anniversary of *The Challenge to Peace*" (Washington, DC: United States Catholic Conference, 1994).

19. International Financial Statistics Yearbook, pp. 126–27 (Washington, DC: International Monetary Fund, 1998).

20. PEC Report, at p. 2 of Executive Summary.

21. A National Association of Manufacturers Study, commissioned from the Georgetown University Law Center, cited in "Chicken Soup Diplomacy," at p. 15.

22. Presenting a contrasting viewpoint, Senator Jesse Helms (R-NC) takes issue with these statistics and the general argument that the United States has overused sanctions in his article "What Sanctions Epidemic?" in *Foreign Affairs*, Vol. 78, No. 1, at p. 2 (Jan/Feb 1999)(hereinafter "Helms").

23. The importance of psychology in foreign affairs and especially economic policy has been written about recently by George Soros in his new book, *The Crisis of Global Capitalism* (New York, NY: Public Affairs, 1998), and by Charles William Maynes in his article, "Squandering Triumph" in *Foreign Affairs*, Vol. 78, No. 1 at p. 15 (Jan/Feb 1999).

24. More often than not, U.S. policy reflects this description of a failed sanctions policy: "[C]onflicting pressures within the sender government often lead to an indecisive response, which neither emits the desired political signal nor imposes arduous costs on the target country." Hufbauer at p. 39.

25. Hufbauer at p. 95–96.

26. Hufbauer at pp. 100–101; Haass at p. 208–209.

27. Haass at p. 209.

28. Helms at p. 6.

29. The Enhancement through Trade, Security, and Human Rights through Sanctions Reform Act, S. 1413, still before the Senate, requires in Section 8, that the president submit an annual report to Congress that details (1) the extent to which the sanctions have achieved their objectives; (2) the extent to which the sanctions have harmed humanitarian interests in the targeted country; and (3) the impact of the sanctions on other U.S. foreign policy and national security interests.

30. Hufbauer at pp. 100–01; Haass at p. 203.

31. Haass at p. 205.

32. Haass at p. 115 (from chapter by Eric D. K. Melby, pp. 107–28); PEC also argues in its report that the USG should either provide for businesses to fulfill already-signed contracts or compensate businesses that are forced to break their contractual obligations for their committed costs. PEC Report at p. 4 of Executive Summary. Hufbauer, Schott, and Elliott concur with this as well. Hufbauer at p. 103.

33. Hufbauer at p. 70.

34. Secretary Albright coined the phrase "engagement does not mean endorsement" when discussing U.S.-China policy: George Lardner, Jr., "Clinton To Be 'Forceful' in China, Aide Says," *Washington Post*, June 15, 1998, p. A19 (quoting Secretary of State Madeleine K. Albright in an interview on CNN's "Late Edition").

35. Hufbauer at p. 64.

36. Haass at p. 27–28 (chapter by Robert S. Ross).

37. The policy of constructive engagement that the Clinton Administration has actively pursued with China is a good example of engagement plus sanctions. See Barton Gellman, "Reappraisal Led to New China Policy; Skeptics Abound, but U.S. 'Strategic Partnership' Yielding Results," *Washington Post*, p. A1; John Pomfret and John F. Harris, "Jiang Arrives Here to Begin Summit," *Washington Post*, October 29, 1997, p. A4.

38. The United States has little hope of influencing a country's behavior if the country believes that its national security or very survival is threatened, regardless of the policy used. Haass at p. 198.

39. Editorial Page, "Two for the Test Ban Treaty," *Washington Post*, September 27, 1998, p. C6; Pamela Constable, "To Sign or Not to Sign? India, Pakistan Must Answer at Home on Joining Nuclear Pact," *Washington Post*, October 14, 1998, p. A17.

40. Testimony of Douglas Peterson, U.S. Ambassador to Vietnam, before the House Ways and Means Committee, Subcommittee on Trade, on June 18, 1998, at p. 2 (testimony on Jackson-Vanik waiver for Vietnam) (hereinafter "Peterson Testimony").

41. Peterson Testimony at pp. 1–2.

Part III

Capital Markets

Chapter 9

U.S. International Financial Policy

Jeffrey R. Shafer

Introduction

U.S. financial linkages with the rest of the world have proliferated and grown stronger over recent decades. These ties raise issues of economic security to a level of foreign policy concern formerly reserved for defense issues. Policy thinking and the process for formulating and implementing policy, however, have lagged behind the reality of markets. This gap threatens U.S. interests and deserves to be given prominence in formulating next generation foreign policies.

The extent to which the United States has become financially interlinked with the rest of the world is indeed remarkable. The market value of foreign direct investment in the United States has gone from 4 percent of Gross Domestic Product (GDP) in 1982 to 20 percent in 1997. United States direct investment abroad has gone from 7 percent of GDP to 22 percent over the same period. Turnover in the New York foreign exchange market tripled between 1989 and 1998 according to Federal Reserve Bank of New York surveys. And ever improving transmission mechanisms make shocks in foreign economies felt in the United States as never before: Mexico's financial crisis knocked a percentage point off U.S. growth in early 1995 despite an unprecedented commitment of support for Mexico's stabilization effort. When a slide in the Hong Kong market in October 1997 triggered the second largest one-day drop in the Dow Jones Average in history, any thought that the United States was too big or too insulated to be affected by financial developments abroad went out the window. The paralysis of U.S. capital markets in the fall of 1998, following financial collapse in Russia, was yet another lesson.

While *private* financial linkages with the world have grown, U.S. *public* financial linkages have atrophied. U.S. official development assistance dropped from nearly 0.6 percent of GDP in 1965 to 0.04 percent in 1996—less than one-tenth as much. While bilateral assistance is arguably a failed tool of international financial policy in most circumstances, the astonishing decline of aid is a quantifiable indicator of a general trend of diminishing U.S. official financial engagement. This weakening of an official link is occurring despite the globalization of markets, which is making economic development and financial stability abroad, supported by liberal institutions, all the more vital to our prosperity. Without strong growth abroad, markets for U.S. goods and services will stagnate, the competition for remaining markets will become more intense and migration pressures will intensify. Thus one does not need to think very many steps ahead to see the security implications of benign neglect in public financial matters.

In such a world, protecting U.S. prosperity must be given a prominent place alongside protecting U.S. military security as an objective of U.S. foreign policy. Indeed, as noted above, economic security has become intertwined with traditional foreign policy concerns about military and political issues like never before. But when it comes to the question of how to pursue our interests given these changing financial dynamics, a hundred schools of thought contend: whether Washington should take an active role or leave the initiative to the private sector; whether to work through bilateral, regional, or global institutions; whether to regulate markets or liberalize them further; whether to give external conditions such as the dollar exchange rate weight in setting domestic monetary and fiscal policy or to focus on getting our own house in order; whether or not foreign aid can make a contribution to development and, if so, under what terms and conditions?

In this essay, I want to clarify the context in which financial policy interests of the United States need to be addressed and to identify some of the institutional deficiencies that have stood in the way of more effective pursuit of international financial policies. First, I will describe the broad scope of these policies, illustrating the various channels through which U.S. financial relations are managed. Second, I will identify the kinds of problems that arise today in deploying these policies to further our fundamental national interests in security, prosperity, and respect for values Americans cherish. Third, I will suggest five policy tests to guide the debate on specific measures in specific circumstances. Finally, I will offer some thoughts on the directions in which the process for policy formation should evolve in order to pursue U.S. interests more effectively.

The Domain of
International Financial Policies

There are at least two ways that one might define the domain of international financial policies. A *functional* approach would identify those policies that have an important influence on the size and composition of cross-border financial flows. An alternative *institutional* view would identify those policies over which the Treasury and Federal Reserve, as the lead financial agencies, exercise responsibility. Despite the different focus of these respective approaches, they produce similar results and thus suggest some institutional logic in the present allocation of responsibilities in our government. However, there are differences that illustrate the need for greater coherence in the policy process in Washington.

The following list, which is organized functionally and describes the allocation of executive branch responsibilities, shows the variety of activities through which international financial matters are considered in Washington. A Congress and general public that remain skeptical of either the stakes involved or the effectiveness of the policy tools or both are challenging some of these activities. In reviewing this list, it becomes apparent that it will be difficult for the United States to continue to do business in the same way, through the same institutional structures, given a global landscape that has changed beyond recognition over recent decades.

Consider:

- Exchange rate and macroeconomic policy coordination has historically been conducted in the G-7, G-10 and the Organization of Economic Cooperation and Development (OECD), with Treasury and the Federal Reserve playing the lead roles in these fora. The Council of Economic Advisors is also a player through its chairmanship of the OECD Economic Policy Committee and membership in its Working Party No. 3. In practical terms, however, the Fed's action with respect to interest rates is by far the most important official influence on exchange rates and short-term growth prospects; exchange market intervention and public statements are a sideshow. As regional finance ministry and central bank networks have developed—for example, within the Asia-Pacific Economic Cooperation Forum (APEC) and the Western hemisphere—macroeconomic policy has come onto regional agendas, where the issues tend to be common problems facing countries in a region. But to date these fora have remained talk shops, with concrete policy actions addressed in the context of the International Monetary Fund's (IMF) provision of conditional financing.
- Official multilateral financing through the IMF, World Bank, and regional development banks has become a front-burner issue in the wake of the emerging market financial crises of 1997 and 1998. These crises have brought the IMF and its fundamental mission to assist countries in dealing with balance of payment crises to public attention as never before. In addition, these crises have also put pressure on the World Bank and the regional development banks to provide support that essentially fills budgetary and balance of payment gaps, supplanting these institutions' traditional focus on projects with development impact. The logic for shifting the efforts of these institutions is straightforward: Failure to deal with financial crises threatens to set back development in affected countries by a decade or more. The challenge for international institutions is to adopt new missions and to coordinate their activities. This will be difficult. As international institutions take on this challenge, they will be in-

creasingly subject to closer public scrutiny. The terms and conditions of their lending—political as well as economic and developmental—and their governance will now be a matter of intense interest not only among specialists but also from elected officials, who have their own constituencies.

In the United States, the Secretary of the Treasury serves as the governor for these organizations and instructs the U.S. executive directors. Both formal interagency consultations and informal discussions inform policy decisions. Ongoing congressional consultations against the background of the appropriations process are a major force shaping policy, as are an increasing number of specific requirements written into authorization legislation and appropriations.

- Official bilateral financing is provided by a range of agencies to serve a number of specific programmatic purposes— U.S. Export-Import Bank (EX-IM) to support U.S. exports; Overseas Private Investment Corporation (OPIC) to remove political risk impediments to investment abroad; Foreign Agricultural Service (FAS) to support exports of U.S. farm products; and the U.S. Agency for International Development (AID) to support a range of U.S. foreign-policy objectives. The common denominator of these programs is the intense budgetary pressure that they have been under for a long time. Within tight budgetary limits, there is increasing tension between the pursuit of specific program purposes (often closely linked to sectoral business interests) and the pursuit of broad national objectives (by directing funds for financial stabilization or other foreign policy objectives).

The extent to which interagency consultation processes allow for general international financial considerations to influence policy under these programs varies from the formalized and close, in the case of EX-IM, to the informal and distant in the case of FAS or AID programs. Even more than with multilateral programs, congressional input is extensive and detailed. For example, individual project allocations for AID often are determined by congressional earmarks.

The Treasury's Exchange Stabilization Fund (ESF) and the Federal Reserve, through swap arrangements have also provided bilateral financing in exceptional circumstances. The most notable use of the ESF has been to provide a $25 billion line of credit to Mexico in early 1995, after the onset of the Mexican peso crisis. The authority to use the resources of the ESF rests with the president and the secretary of the treasury alone. Congress, however, has questioned the use of the ESF for financial stabilization and temporarily limited the president's authority to use the resources of the ESF following the Mexican support package. Its use continues to be controversial. Given this sensitivity, use of the ESF to provide financing is a matter of extensive consultation with the Hill.

- Multilateral, debt-rescheduling negotiations (the Paris Club) have become an important tool to forestall a reverse flow of official funds from developing countries as budgetary authority for new commitments has shrunk. For the poorest countries, debt reduction, as well as rescheduling, is now an option. Multilateral conditions are routinely imposed on debtor governments in the Paris Club framework through coordination with the IMF. Bilateral conditions are also imposed, reflecting particular U.S. interests. The State Department has the first chair in the Paris Club, with Treasury at its elbow and taking the lead with respect to financial issues.

- Negotiations on financial market opening have been pursued bilaterally with Japan and others and multilaterally in the World Trade Organization (WTO). A WTO financial services agreement was reached in December 1997. These negotiations have been the responsibility of Treasury and the U.S. Trade Representative (USTR), reflecting the former's lead role on financial issues and the latter's designation as negotiator of all U.S. trade agreements. As a matter of practice, Treasury has generally exercised the policy leadership on financial services, except for the insurance sector, where USTR has taken the lead.

- International financial regulatory matters are pursued by a hodgepodge of agencies—the Federal Reserve, the Comptroller of the Currency, the Federal Deposit Insurance Corporation (FDIC), the Securities and Exchange Commission (SEC), the Commodity Futures Trading Commission (CFTC), and the Treasury—reflecting dispersed *domestic* regulatory responsibilities within the United States. In the wake of the financial crises of 1997 and 1998, the technical international fora in which U.S. agencies work with counterparts in other countries have become a matter of broad interest and concern for the first time.

- U.S. investment abroad is handled by USTR or the Department of State depending on the forum. For example, USTR negotiates bilateral investment treaties. Also, State led the ill-fated Multilateral Agreement on Investment (MAI) negotiations in the OECD. In practice, foreign investment over the past decade or so has been unprecedented, reflecting growing recognition of the net benefits of foreign investment. Formal agreements entailing future commitments have lagged behind, however, reflecting specific sectoral concerns and a general reluctance of governments, even OECD countries, to make irreversible commitments. Thus we have seen the MAI negotiations stall, even as countries continue to liberalize.

- Foreign investment in the United States is subject to review as an exception to the principle of national treatment (a foreign company enjoying the same rights and being subject to the same restrictions as a domestic company) only on national security grounds under the Exon-Florio legislation. The limited scope of this review reflects a broad U.S. consensus in favor of open competition. The Treasury chairs the Committee on Foreign Investment in the United States (CFIUS), which implements Exon-Florio, with strong input from the Defense Department. Of course, foreign investment is also subject to the same reviews and regulations that U.S. investment is subject—for example, antitrust review and possible challenge by the Justice Department. There have been occasional efforts to legislate an "economic security" investment review as a part of a national industrial policy. But as the failure of such policies abroad have become evident, the pressure for the United States to go down this road has abated, at least for the present.

These are the main channels through which Washington enters the domain of international finance. The specific issues that arise range from the absolute first rank of U.S. foreign policy concerns—responding to the global financial crisis that began in Asia in the summer of 1997—to the arcane: negotiation and enforcement of the OECD consensus on interest rates that can be charged on official export credits. All involve, however, important U.S. interests and make demands on U.S. leadership.

Problems in Formulating and Implementing International Financial Policies

The international community has showed time and again that, without U.S. leadership, there will be no coherent response to regional or global problems. Moreover, especially because of increasingly integrated capital markets, these problems ultimately come home to the United States.

Constraints at home and abroad are making it more difficult to take effective action. For one thing, financial resources that can be mobilized at home have shrunk dramatically as pressures on the federal budget have intensified. In this respect, the situation in the financial arena is no different from that facing the defense arena. Yet it has proven much more difficult in the financial area to mobilize public and congressional support for the commitment of U.S. financial resources. This is unmistakable evidence of the failure of those who see the vital U.S. economic security interests at stake in the financial area to make their case. Too often, financial issues are treated as reserved for market specialists, an attitude that fuels public and congressional indifference or distrust. Defense issues are also treated largely as reserved for specialists; however, by contrast, the public and Congress accord deference to policymakers over these issues because of their traditional importance to U.S. sovereign interests.

In addition to this general bias against action, there are also conceptual and institutional problems that stand in the way of effective international financial policymaking. These can be grouped under four headings: 1) outdated thinking, 2) new players, 3) games being played, and 4) institutional obstacles to making efficient policy trade-offs.

1) Outdated Thinking

U.S. international financial policymaking is plagued by three kinds of out-of-date thinking. First, there exists the belief that the United States can do it alone. U.S. leadership is indispensable and on rare occasions, such as the threat of a Mexican collapse in early 1995, the United States may find it in its interest to shoulder a disproportionate burden when the alternative would be inadequate or tardy action. However, pursuing the fundamental U.S. interest in stable and efficient flows of capital generally requires the cooperation of others. For example, domestic financial supervision and regulation cannot fully protect the United States against failure of supervision elsewhere and runs the risk of simply driving activity to less regulated environments. As Beese points out in this volume, for any national market to be secure, global cooperation among financial supervisors is essential in a world of integrated capital markets.

To take another example of the need for others' cooperation, financial assistance to a country facing a liquidity crisis can speed recovery and limit global contagion *if and only if* the country involved takes strong action to deal with its problems as Mexico did in 1995 and Korea did in 1998. Russia's collapse in the summer of 1998 showed how international resources can be wasted when there is no political will or capacity to undertake the necessary steps to achieve financial stabilization. The costs of the failure of Russia were felt strongly in the United States and around the world. There was certainly no lack of U.S. interest in supporting Russia, even putting important security concerns to the side. But without real Russian cooperation, the probability was slim of achieving the objective of avoiding a meltdown. U.S.-sponsored IMF support simply postponed disaster, making the ultimate collapse all the more costly to the Russian people and disruptive to global markets.

Another important example of failure when the United States has sought to go it alone has been in the use of unilateral financial sanctions. As Helweg discusses in this volume, clear analysis of what financial sanctions can and cannot achieve, and at what cost, is essential if the pursuit of clear U.S. interests is to drive policy at this interface of economic, political, and military affairs. While there is a significant record of positive results when a critical mass of the world community has used sanctions, in concert, to induce a country to conform to international norms of behavior, the record when the United States has acted unilaterally is poor. Yet the United States has imposed a range of unilateral financial sanctions on a number of countries under increasingly inflexible legislation. The withholding of access to EX-IM Bank when other countries are actively pursuing business is a particularly egregious example of harming our business interests and our political relationships without furthering our intended objectives.

The second kind of outdated thinking is to believe that foreign and domestic financial markets can be compartmentalized. There is a U.S. version of this kind of thinking that would ignore economic problems in other parts of the world in the belief that U.S. markets are invulnerable to external shocks. To anyone close to the markets, the paralysis of the U.S. capital markets in September and October 1998 was an unmistakable lesson that events abroad, in this case the financial collapse of Russia and the precarious situation in Brazil, can seriously damage U.S. markets. The Federal Reserve lowered interest rates and the U.S. Congress passed IMF funding legislation just in time for the organization of a financial support package for Brazil. As a result, the market distress was alleviated before there was deep damage to U.S. investment, U.S. production, and U.S. jobs. But with the restoration of more normal market conditions, voices of skepticism have been heard almost immediately as to whether the threat had been real. It was.

In other countries, one hears another version of the compartmentalization fallacy: capital controls can insulate a country from the global markets and provide a tranquil environment for economic growth. Experience, though, shows that financial isolation can never be completely achieved. Moreover, as the effectiveness of barriers erodes over time, the costs of maintaining capital controls rise in terms of administrative costs, the efficiency of the financial sector, and erosion of respect for rules as financial players use new technologies. So, while controls may sometimes be the best available emergency response, they should have no place in the permanent architecture of the international financial system. What would much better meet the needs of all countries would be a collective effort to strengthen and reduce the instability of global markets combined with a determined effort by each country to create more resilient domestic financial systems. In this context, the multilateralization of financial market oversight is the most critical financial issue before the world today. Unfortunately, as noted earlier, the fragmentation of financial supervisory responsibilities within the United States makes it difficult for us to exercise effective leadership.

The third kind of outdated thinking is the continued failure to come to terms with the forward-looking nature of markets. The effect of a policy announcement is frequently much greater through its influence on the views of market participants regarding how a government will behave in the future than through its direct effect. This is the main reason that developments sometimes have much greater effect than would be expected given their immediate importance. Reputations are difficult to build but easy to destroy by failure to live up to them and the destruction of a reputation can have major implications for financial policies.

Hence, every policy action and its announcement must be carefully considered from the standpoint of how it will affect a reputation. For example, an unavoidable depreciation of the Mexican peso and collapse in the price of even dollar-linked Mexican debt were triggered in December 1994 when a new government announced a modest widening of its exchange rate band after repeated statements by the outgoing government that the peso would not be devalued. In retrospect, it appears that the government had succeeded in convincing many market participants that it could and would adhere to a policy that proved unsustainable. Against this background, what would normally be seen as a moderate policy change by the new government triggered a complete loss of credibility. It took a change of finance minister, an unprecedented U.S.-led financial support package, and a sustained period of rebuilding a record of policy actions consistent with statements to restore the credibility of the Mexican financial authorities. The costs to the Mexican economy were high.

One requirement for building and maintaining reputation, highlighted by Mexico's 1994 experience, is that policies should be, in technical terms, "time consistent." This means that what authorities say they will do under given circumstances is what they would rationally choose to do when those circumstances arise. If policies are not time consistent, they are unlikely to be credible. Only by following a foolish course can authorities build a bizarre kind of credibility. Even when credibility is established for a time, as in the Mexican case, the costs when policies inevitably change will be high.

Sometimes out-dated thinking can be updated in mistaken ways. Concern expressed today about moral hazard in financial markets is an example. It is argued that providing official support will lead to excessive risk-taking by borrowing governments, lenders, or both—reflecting the forward-looking nature of markets. Even if there were strong evidence that past liquidity support had this effect on investors (and there is not), those who would stop all liquidity assistance out of concern for moral hazard fail to address the time consistency issue. It is simply not in the U.S. interest, indeed I would argue that it is not moral, for the United States to refrain itself and to restrain the IMF from providing support that would mitigate an economic calamity under the circumstances that prevailed in Mexico in 1994–95 or in Korea in 1997–98. It is not credible that the United States would sit by and do nothing. In both of the cases mentioned, U.S. leadership in arranging international support backed by the strong policy actions of authorities in the countries concerned led to financial stabilization and to a much more rapid recovery than could be imagined otherwise. In these cases, assistance has been or is being repaid. Financial assistance did not in the end go to "bail out" investors but rather to bridge the loss of liquidity of the countries.

Moreover, there is little in the record of market commentary to suggest that investor behavior in Asia was significantly affected by the Mexico rescue and hence created the conditions for the Asian crisis of 1997–98. But concern about future moral hazard cannot be dismissed if large-scale support becomes more common and, especially, if it is not conditioned on a hard-nosed assessment of whether liquidity support is only bridging a gap, or whether it is plugging a solvency hole created by an unsustainable debt trajectory or unsound policies. In this respect, the withdrawal of support for Russia sent a clear, if belated, signal that international support is indeed conditional.

What is needed to contain moral hazard is not a cessation of liquidity support but more active policy review and oversight of financial markets to restrain government and market behavior that might be engendered by moral hazard. Ways have been developed to deal with this problem in other contexts: for example, the provision of lender-of-last-resort and deposit insurance support for banks in countries with developed national financial markets is accompanied by capital requirements and other prudential restraints. The development of analogous approaches in the global marketplace should now be a priority.

2) New Players

In the early 1960s, the G-10 countries (actually 11 countries—8 in Western Europe, the United States, Canada, and Japan) were all that mattered in the financial world. Since then the world has changed radically. Five of the European G-10 have formed a common currency with six others. Economies from Australia to Singapore to Hong Kong have emerged as financial centers. Developments in Thailand, Korea, Brazil, China, and Russia have moved global markets. Yet the structure of consultations among governments has not changed since the mid-1970s when the G-7 (a subset of the G-10) took shape.

Similarly, new markets have come to the fore in global finance. We no longer live in a world where global finance is dominated by a relatively small group of international banks that take deposits and lend funds. In that world, global systemic issues could be addressed by central bankers and bank examiners meeting at the Bank for International Settlements in Basel, Switzerland. When private sector involvement was called for, it was not difficult to put the players in a room. Today, the players in global bond, equity, and derivatives markets—securities underwriters, ratings agencies, institutional investors, individual investors, hedge funds, securities exchanges, and securities market regulators—are central participants in global finance. The number, as well as the diversity, of players is greatly expanded. Financial policymakers are struggling to update their ways of approaching systemic issues in the light of the expanded set of players. But they are far behind the curve.

The major issues of the day—effective supervision of globalized, securitized markets, and national policies that sustain growth—call for an expansion of the international financial network in terms of country and market representation. Reducing the proportion of Europeans in the existing fora would make room for new countries. This is but one change. Currently, it is the United States that actually poses a major barrier to a more coherent approach to financial market issues. The fragmentation of U.S. financial regulation among agencies, most of which are independent of the executive branch, limits policy development toward greater regulatory coherence.

3) Games Being Played

Coherent and effective policymaking requires a sound analysis of the nature of the strategic interactions among players and how each will pursue its defined interests. On a more theoretical level, game theory may be useful in clarifying the bargaining incentives of the actors. For these purposes, certain realities are illuminating.

First, there are multiple games being played simultaneously. The U.S. government is engaged on various fronts. The variety of actors include foreign governments, market participants, and various interests within the U.S. Congress. Moreover, congressional support is required whenever funding or legislative authorization is required to implement policy. All of these games have three attributes in common, which have a strong bearing on which strategies will best serve U.S. interests:

a. Each game has more than two players. As a result, success in forming coalitions is crucial. The United States cannot achieve its interests if it allows itself to be isolated, if it defies markets, or if the executive branch and Congress are unwilling to search for common ground on which a broad coalition can stand.

b. Each game is nonzero sum. This means that cooperative strategies can achieve greater gains than noncooperative ones. It may not always be easy to implement such a strategy, especially because it may be easy for small players to be free riders. Hence, achieving cooperative solutions may require policing by major players like the United States. There should be no mistake, though, that cooperation ought to be the objective.

c. The games are repeated from year to year with surprisingly little change. Funding international commitments and responding to financial distress are recurring activities in international finance. As a result, reputation matters. Lack of follow-through on threats and promises devalue future commitments to other governments and to markets. And follow-through is equally important for an effective political process at home.

The domestic political game has become especially problematic because of the structure within which it is played. Declining strength of the executive branch, combined with the growing strength of groups focused on a single aspect of U.S. global interests, have made it difficult to define, let alone pursue, a coherent vision of the national interest. This problem has been further complicated by the use of the international financial policy area as a battleground for domestic political issues. The intrusion of a separate abortion issue, on which Americans are sharply divided at home, into the IMF funding debate in 1997, is an outstanding example. In cases like this, international policy may become an incidental outcome of another game that carries higher stakes for motivated and mobilized participants.

On the other hand, those who see the world primarily in financial terms cannot blame all of their frustrations with policy on the process. There are other strong U.S. interests besides economic and financial interests, and the political process reflects them. Moreover, the reality is that policy embedded in enduring U.S. values is likely to prove more politically sustainable than policies that only reflect immediate economic and financial considerations.

4) Institutional Obstacles to Efficient Trade-offs

Achieving one objective almost always involves giving up something with respect to another objective. The proposition that each policy has one natural objective and that other considerations ought not to intrude is misleading and indefensible. For example, if the United States has an interest in reducing government corruption around the world, it may make sense to condition multilateral lending that furthers the U.S. interest in global growth on the implementation of policies that counter corruption. The issue ought not to be, as it is often posed, whether noneconomic objectives have any place in economic policy. This is an artificial distinction. The issue ought to be whether a policy strikes an *efficient* trade-off in the light of broad U.S. interests.

In light of the above example, U.S. interests are well served by putting anticorruption on the agenda of the IMF and World Bank. Any narrowing or slowing of lending programs as a sanction will be more than compensated by increased focus on a problem that threatens the development process in many countries. On the other hand, one could imagine setting a standard for disbursement of funds that was completely unrealistic and only served to paralyze multilateral programs. If this were the case, the objectives of lending programs would be lost and, ultimately, such a policy would not be very effective in curbing corruption. It is a matter of getting the trade-offs right, which is no easy task. The compartmentalization of policy formulation within the executive branch and the committee structure of the Congress make it difficult to make efficient trade-offs.

Another impediment to making efficient trade-offs is the reactive mode of most policymaking. When one issue jumps to the center— whether it is a financial crisis, a human rights showdown, or a political conflict—other objectives take a back seat. One then has outcomes like the Helms-Burton legislation, which has proven ineffective and costly as a way of achieving our objectives with respect to Cuba.

The costs and benefits of trade-offs are rarely considered, let alone given strong weight in the decisionmaking process. As noted above, this is most true when one objective is magnified by a sense of crisis. Often, if the trade-offs were analyzed carefully, the conclusion would be that the benefits are illusory and the costs substantial of using economic policies to pursue political objectives. But this will not always be the case. What is needed is a focus on the costs and benefits of the trade-offs involved in a particular cause.

Directions for Next Generation Policies

Moving from problems to solutions is a major undertaking. And the specifics of each policy area and context crucially matter. Thus it is difficult to offer general prescriptions. But drawing on the themes of the foregoing discussion, I would propose five general guidelines for international, financial policy formation by the United States.

1. *Policies should be coherent.* The same fundamental broad objectives must be kept in view when a decision is being made. We cannot, for example, press for cancellation of a loan from the World Bank because of a political issue with a country while continuing to provide bilateral financial assistance from FAS or EX-IM.

2. *Policies should be cost effective.* As discussed above, we must be careful to assess the costs and benefits of decisions and make efficient trade-offs. One area over time where there has been little careful evaluation of the trade-offs has been in the unilateral application of financial sanctions.

3. *Policies should be consistent over time and across institutions.* Reputation is built and leadership exercised through consistency of decisions. Such consistency reinforces credibility. Thus differences in the U.S. response to financial crises in Mexico, Thailand, Korea, Russia, and Brazil in 1997 and 1998 have confused governments and markets. To be sure, such crises must be handled on a case-by-case basis. This means there will be differences. But such differences should be grounded in fundamental interests and such interests need to be made clear to targets.

   In recent crises, responses have not been consistent because the legislative basis for the use of the ESF first became more restrictive and then subsequently eased, thus giving the executive branch different tools to work with at different times. Asian countries, for example, are largely unaware of how legislative interests have shaped U.S. policy responses. What they perceive as U.S. inconsistency leaves them confused and suspicious about our objectives.

4. *Policies should be connected to our domestic sensibilities.* If policy is going to enjoy political support at home, it must reflect fundamental shared values and be insulated from domestic issues on which Americans are fundamentally divided. I have previously cited the fight against corruption

as an example of the former and abortion policy as an example of the latter.

5. *Policy actions ought not to be taken in pursuit of objectives that are not achievable.* The imposition of automatic economic sanctions on countries exploding nuclear devices, which were recently triggered in the case of India and Pakistan, is a case in point. All Americans share the objective of nonproliferation. But economic sanctions were ineffective in dissuasion, leaving the United States with an embarrassing task of delaying their application. A generation ago, we learned the fundamental lesson that military forces should not be given an objective they cannot achieve. We need to learn that important lesson now with respect to international financial policymaking.

Updating the Policy Process for the Twenty-First Century

Policy direction is easier to propose than creating a process that steers consistently in the chosen direction. Our policy machinery reflects our democratic values and our distrust of unshackled power. These values put limits on what process is acceptable to Americans. But there are things that can be done that could put a clearer focus on international economic policymaking and generate more coherent policy outcomes.

Better interagency coordination is, of course, always desirable. But I would put the emphasis on three other areas simply because they have received less attention. First, little consideration has been given to the gains in policy coherence that can be achieved by embedding a broader policy focus in lead agencies. For example, the establishment of an environmental unit in the International Affairs bureau of the Treasury has enabled environmental issues to be incorporated into international financial policymaking. Such integration has occurred much more efficiently than would have been the case if policy development had occurred mainly through Treasury/Environmental Protection Agency (EPA) interagency confrontations at a late stage in the policymaking process. By the same token, it would be nice to see more financial sensitivity in agencies like the EPA. There is much scope for this broadening of agency cultures. This broadening promises to bring much more efficiency in policy tradeoffs.

The second area for process improvement is in executive branch interaction with Congress. Today, such interaction is far too piecemeal, with little effort to convey a consistent picture of how the president's international economic initiatives fit together. Interagency coordination of congressional consultation in the international economic area is arguably worse than coordination on other tasks.

The third area for reform is how Congress organizes itself. The fragmentation of committee and subcommittee responsibilities makes the executive branch look coherent by comparison. A consolidation of oversight responsibilities for international financial matters, if not through a committee reorganization then through a working group of relevant chairmen and ranking minority members, is crucial if Congress is to play its role effectively in a faster and faster moving world in which the previously unrelated are now intricately connected.

These are only a few thoughts on how to achieve more coherent and effective international financial policies for the next generation in the United States. Change will inevitably be incremental. The important thing is to have a clear national sense of the stakes in terms of U.S. prosperity and to look for every opportunity to push in the right direction.

Conclusion

This chapter began with some observations about how U.S. stakes in the functioning of a global financial system have grown over the past decade or so. This is not a process that will stop. Nor will it continue smoothly in a straight line. Just as the 1997–1998 crises in Asia forced a revision of views concerning the inevitability of continued rapid Asian growth, future developments will force views to change and U.S. policies to adapt in ways that we cannot anticipate.

We can foresee some forces acting on global finance. For example, aging populations in developed countries and birth rates in emerging markets are variables that will alter the global distribution of savings and investment opportunities in ways that underscore the interest shared by the United States and other nations in strong global financial markets. Funds will need to be moved from where savings are greatest to where they can be most efficiently invested in ways that do not threaten stability. This process can raise the return on savings in countries like Japan, which will very soon be facing challenges of paying for the needs of an aging population.

Pressures for international financial stability in light of aging populations is just one example of the stresses produced by rapidly integrating capital markets. Ultimately, the entire international financial architecture will need to be reexamined. Calls for such reexamination are already being made from all quarters. As I noted above, the multilateralization of financial market oversight is the most critical financial issue before the world today. Unfortunately, as I also noted earlier, the fragmentation of financial supervisory responsibilities within the United States makes it difficult for us to exercise effective leadership.

Another clear trend that needs further thought is that of European integration. With the creation of a common money (the Euro) for eleven countries, a more balanced bipolar financial leadership capability with the dollar is emerging. Such new capabilities call for new arrangements within which to pursue transatlantic and global cooperation. One variable in this mix will be the strength of the yen and the role of Asia in shaping the financial architecture of the twenty-first century.

Financial market oversight, stable savings for aging populations, and currency dynamics will be discussed further in this volume. Other developments will undoubtedly take us by surprise. As with national defense, one cannot overestimate the importance of an available and first-rate capability to react to the unexpected.

Chapter 10

The Internationalization of the Social Security Problem

Albert Fishlow and *Patrick J. DeSouza*

The rallying cries of the Clinton Administration and the Republican Congress of finally saving social security have now captured American public attention. For years, while there were budget deficits, the issue could not be touched. Now that the budget is balanced—largely by including the substantial current annual social security surplus—the issue has surfaced. President Clinton's major argument against a tax cut was the need to provide additional funds for social security. With a presidential election up for grabs, the issue is very much on the agenda.

The U.S. situation is similar to that of most other developed countries, but at the same time, as a *relative* matter, less pressing. That circumstance occurs for three reasons. First, the U.S. underlying change in a rising percentage of the dependent population in the future is much smaller than in Europe and Japan; the major reason, ironically, is the extensive immigration the U.S. has experienced. Second, the existing social security system in the United States is not as pressed as those of other countries providing greater assistance and at much earlier ages. Even on fairly conservative assumptions, the present system could continue to cover 75 percent of obligations throughout the twenty-first century. And third, there is much greater supplementary investment in private pension funds by a U.S. population persuaded that social security is no longer a generalized solution appropriate to all. Therefore, as income rises, the dependence on, as well as belief in, the system is less.

Nonetheless, there is a problem, even in our country. Something will have to be done; and that something will need to incorporate a solution to the internationalization of the social security problem as retirement savings become increasingly subject to the volatility of integrated global capital markets. Such volatility makes the problem far more vexing than a simple trade-off between raising taxes and cutting benefits to maintain the proper fund level. As outlined below, the social security problem impinges on the issue of national security as well as domestic prosperity. To date, internationalization is an aspect of the problem that has been missing from the public dialogue.

As the experience, post-Russian economic crisis, during the fall of 1998 indicates ever so clearly, global capital markets are increasingly integrated but also highly variable—a difficult mix for senior citizens whose continuing income security is as salient to them as international conflict is for 18–22 year olds. In this respect, the traditionally "domestic" issue of providing for older Americans has really been transformed into an international problem. It is inconceivable, no matter what domestic reform of social security is finally adopted, that it can provide continuing secure yields for American seniors if the rest of the world fails to grow and is unstable.

In this essay, we focus on the foreign policy imperative of addressing economic security for aging populations around the world—a key topic discussed at the Denver Summit of G-7 countries in June 1997. The Denver Summit Communique set forth the international problem clearly:

> Increased life expectancy and improved health among our elderly are two major achievements of this century. In the next century, these successes will present us with both opportunities and challenges, as longer life expectancies and lower birth rates significantly raise the proportion of seniors in our countries' populations . . . [with] differ-

ing implications ... for our nations' pension, health and long-term care systems.

Note, moreover, that this is a problem that transcends the industrialized countries. Leading developing countries in Asia, Latin America, and Africa will confront the same difficulty in the twenty-first century. Their circumstances are frequently ignored because the problem emerges much sooner in the already industrialized countries.

In outlining the question and possible approaches, we first consider the broad economic and national security implications of the issue. Next, we discuss the narrower economic dimensions of the "aging" problem and current attempts to address the subject. As we shall argue, these attempts have failed to account for the international side of the problem. Finally, we take up some potential approaches to this matter.

Economic and National Security Concerns

It is vital—as a matter of economic strategy—that the U.S. recognize the changed world that it presently inhabits. Vast quantities of resources—some $1.5 trillion at last estimate—now flow globally on a daily basis. We have seen how Japan's autonomous decisions on the level of sales taxes contributed to the Asian slowdown. We recognize the potential consequences of the creation of the Euro on the level and form of reserves held in Europe with attendant consequences on world interest rates. And we have clear evidence from the Federal Reserve's aggressive reductions in interest rates after the Russian economic crisis in Fall 1998: those decisions have seemed to stabilize not only the global economy, but also provide an increased position for the United States in foreign affairs. This stature has cast a positive shadow with respect to national security: international responses to American foreign policy decisions with respect to Iraq and Kosovo have been helped by the U.S. active role in righting world markets.

Peter Peterson, in an important article in the January 1999 issue of *Foreign Affairs* entitled "Gray Dawn: The Global Aging Crisis," suggested economic and military scenarios regarding our key allies that relate demographic change to international security. Peterson points out that "over the next decade, Japan's annual pension deficit is projected to grow to roughly 3 times the size of its recent and massive capital exports to the United States . . . caus[ing] wildly fluctuating interest and exchange ratios, which may . . . trigger a serious market crash" (p. 47). Another area of rising tensions would be Europe—a region considered a "safe-haven" during the 1998 financial crisis. Peterson indicates that the EU may be forced in the future to "penalize certain EMU [European Monetary Union] members that exceed the current 3 percent deficit cap" as a result of having to meet substantial and currently unfunded pension liabilities (p. 48).

Such fiscal imbalances of our allies can lead, not only to macroeconomic instability that affects U.S. financial markets, but also to dangerous compromises with respect to defense preparedness. Allied governments may cut back on military expenditures to a greater degree than currently planned in favor of shifting additional resources to senior citizens. Such choices are quite possible when Peterson reminds us that powerful retirees' interest groups in Europe and Russia have thrown their weight behind the social welfare promises of leftist parties (pp. 52–53). In a twenty-first century world where we will need our European allies to stand with us in the face of rogue states such as Iraq, the economic and political instabilities produced by the social security problem have wide-spread and ill-considered second-order ramifications as new coalitions of ruling parties emerge.

These "new realities" are part of the mingled challenge of economics and security that the world faces in the twenty-first century. They may not focus U.S. foreign policy minds in the same way as Iraqi terrorism does, but these new realities can lead to international dislocations every bit as serious not merely for the aging, but also for the world population as a whole.

The Economic Dimensions of the Problem of Aging

Aging has emerged as perhaps the number one "hidden" issue for this century. The problem is a large one, affecting the developed countries immediately as well as the developing countries subsequently.

"Pay as you go" has been the traditional way of financing old-age pensions. It has been part of the accepted "social contract between generations"—an important link that Hart develops in an earlier essay in this volume. This financing approach makes a great deal of sense in a world of constant rates of population increase. Under these conditions, the collection of funds from each current working generation goes to finance the pensions of a constant percentage of the aged. It is an on-going process that is intergenerationally equitable and fair.

There is much greater difficulty in meeting responsibilities, however, when population growth significantly subsides. Under those conditions, the ratio of retired workers to those actively employed dramatically changes, becoming much greater. To provide illustrative numbers, the ratio of workers to the retired in the industrial countries as a whole, now about 3:1, will fall by 2030 to 1.5:1, and in some of the European countries still lower. The change in Japan falls toward the bottom end.

Interestingly, the demographic problem in this country is much less severe than it is internationally. The projected percentage of the population over 60 in the United States will grow from 17 to 28 percent over the next 30 years or so, compared to 35 percent in those countries most affected. Frighteningly, the demographic trends are as difficult in developing countries that are presently even less likely than our G-7 allies to be able to manage the volatile mix. In Latin America, the rate rises from 7 to 24 percent by the middle of this century; China, the ratio rises from 6 to 26; India, it moves from 7 to an excess of 20. In Africa, where the effect is much delayed, the ratio changes from 4 to 28 percent over the course of the twenty-first century.

These estimates are based on current death rates. With medical advances, the age until death is much more likely to show continuing improvement over time. This will inevitably create still greater stress on resources. Older citizens will survive for longer periods, and place greater pressure not merely on health insurance, but on social security itself.

What makes matters worse is that another economic determinant of the viability of "pay as you go" schemes—the relationship between interest rates and the growth of wages plus population—is clearly moving *adversely*. Real interest rates are currently higher than they have been through much of the last fifty years, while wage-rate increases and population growth have faltered. In much of the developing world, one has moved not only toward positive real interest rates, but real rates that are much higher than those within the developed world. And the move to low inflation rates worldwide has brought with it a much-reduced capability for labor to achieve high rates of wage increase than at one time prevailed. And on top of that, productivity growth, the ultimate determinant of escalating real income, has fallen since the 1970s. The rise of information technology may change this latter variable.

The implications of such movements in these key variables is profound. Lower wage growth means lesser continuing contributions to finance pensions. Higher interest rates mean that the present value of a stream of future pension receipts is lower. Larger payments will be needed to compensate. Where will it come from? Not likely from deficits.

Here in the United States, a balanced budget is currently a reality. As noted above, among our allies, there has been pressure on the members of the European Union (EU) to cut fiscal deficits to qualify for the introduction of the Euro. Future deficits will not rise. In Japan, there is presently a larger deficit that reflects low growth and the need to stimulate the economy. But that will not persist, and, in fact, must shrink, particularly given the inevitable rise in future consumption as the population ages.

Out of this combination of factors emerges a pecking order of countries. The United States appears with virtually the most sustainable system among the developed countries. One option mentioned is an increase in the social security tax rate of little more than 2 percent to make the system viable for the next 75 years, and thereafter as well. And this is apart from the effects of lengthening the age of payment before eligibility or from reducing the price deflator used, or from making payments more fully subject to taxation. By contrast, Europe and Japan are in serious difficulty, with much larger increases in taxes being required.

During the spring of 1998, President Clinton urged the American people that a new dialogue on social security had to begin. He began to hold a series of town meetings to develop a strategy on how to address the current shortcomings of our system. Simply put: By 2033 there will probably no longer be the capability to meet the present legislated targets for payments to those who have retired. As discussed below, this process culminated in a two-day Washington meeting in December 1998 where some convergence began to emerge from those who started in far different positions.

This same dialogue has been held around the world over the last several years, most notably in Latin America where a number of countries led by Chile have moved to privatize much of the state obligation for social security support. Elsewhere, where privatization has not been chosen, as in Singapore, the system has been centralized to obtain the advantages of large public savings that have been used to social advantage. But in most of the developed countries, other than Australia and the United Kingdom, the reality has been "preferred avoidance." After all, as recognized by most political observers, leaders have short terms: the problem of an aging society occurs in the future. The problem is that such a future is coming closer and closer.

Social Security Reform in the United States

In the United States, the report of the 1994–96 Advisory Council on Social Security set in motion the present efforts to reach consensus on modifying the current system. That report definitively showed that there could be a serious problem with meeting current legislated benefits throughout the twenty-first century if projected trends of population and wage growth continue.

Three alternative schemes for dealing with this potential problem emerged from the Council's deliberations. Other plans have emerged previously and subsequently. But these three alternatives usefully define the range of potential modifications.

One way to change the system would be to make it financially viable while continuing to favor the poorer recipients of benefits. Social security currently keeps about 40 percent of older Americans out of poverty. Proposed alterations would make social security receipts subject to fuller taxation; gradually extend the period before retirement benefits were available; allow for slightly larger payments by workers; and, if necessary, permit centralized invest-ment of resources other than in government securities. Note that the rate of future productivity growth plays a very large role in defining the extent of the gap. Also, if wages were to rise more rapidly, a good bit of the potential future difficulty disappears.

A second alternative would be to move substantially toward privatization. Older citizens would retain their present benefits, but younger ones would commit to investment in securities whose average rate of return yielded a sum large enough to cover the current mandated obligations plus enable the next generation to do even better. This comes from the much higher average re-turn earned by investments in the stock market than in govern-ment obligations, something of the order of more than 7 percent annually since 1926, compared to a real rate closer to 2 percent earned by government securities. But, of course, there is the fun-damental liability of great variability in such earnings. Depending on the period chosen, results vary widely, and so would the pen-sions of those dependent on them. And in addition, there may be difficulties in financing the conversion: part of the contributions of the young would have to continue to be transferred to the elderly.

A third option, previously less widely supported, would be to add to the present payments into social security an additional per-centage of income. Such forced additional savings could be pri-vately invested, thereby potentially yielding a higher total benefit. But the largest bulk of social security resources would remain in-vested in government securities as in the present system. In addi-tion, it is argued that the country would be better off as a result of the increased national savings that potentially would emerge from the obligated increase in individual commitments.

At the December 1998 White House Conference, this last alterna-tive seemed to obtain increasing interest from each of the groups that had earlier been strongly committed to the other two posi-tions. One reason was the accumulating budget surplus that promised an unexpected addition to present social security funds. Another was the rise in productivity in recent years that promised smaller needed modifications to shore up the present system through increased taxation and reduced benefits. So it is now con-ceivable that a mutually satisfactory resolution might occur if all sides were prepared to commit themselves to finding a resolution.

Such a decision would have salutary consequences for the broader international situation. It is one thing for a dictator-led Chile in the 1980s to design a radically new program that sharply differs from "pay as you go"; it is another for the United States democratically to invent a way of merging the best of alternative approaches to the problem. There are no magic formulae that will be found in coming years to produce other, and better, ways out. Rather, decisions must be taken at an early point to benefit from the greater length of time the possible solution will be operable. Waiting until the last minute, much as it has current political benefit, has an accumulating cost.

The Missing International Dimension

Our current "national" focus on social security reform needs to be broadened. The December 1998 White House Conference was the *second* time in 1998, as we shall point out below, that the administration missed an opportunity to discuss social security in its international context. To be sure, the political judgment of building consensus among the American people first is important. However, social security is a classic example of a problem, seemingly so domestic, that in reality is much broader and international in scope, and must be understood as such to begin to devise an effective means for treating it. It is a reality that, as Blinken points out in an earlier chapter, must be communicated better to the American people.

Tunnel vision has been demonstrated abroad as well. Ironically, the European countries, even as they are coming together in monetary union, and are now beginning to explore the effects of different taxation rates in individual countries, have avoided confronting the broader issue. They presume that any decision is *national*.

As noted above, though, *in a global age, nothing is exclusively national*. Investments in large corporations are inherently multinational. Indeed, investments made by Americans, should the social security system evolve in that fashion, will inevitably have a large dependence on the performance of the rest of the world.

In other issue-areas, nations have already realized the interdependent nature of twenty-first century economic problems. For example, how do countries deal with balance of payments pressures? Not exclusively independently. How does one assure access to international flows of capital and to large levels of reserves required to avoid crises? By altering relative interest rates. Moreover, how do countries adopt more efficient policies? With modern communications and exchanges—"a networked world," to borrow from McCurdy's essay in this volume—nations learn from each other through "policy entrepreneurship." The rapid privatization of social security throughout Latin America over the last ten years is a prime example.

In addressing the "missing" international dimension, we would stress three lines of discussion for policy development: 1) greater macroeconomic coordination, 2) increased opportunities for learning in a comparative context, and 3) increased dialogue and media attention through a multilateral forum—an idea raised in Peter Peterson's recent article.

We deal with each.

Macroeconomic Coordination.   The placement of retirement savings in potentially volatile capital markets creates a need for greater policy acknowledgment of financial interdependence. Would not social security funds logically be placed abroad in Japan and Europe, and potentially in East Asia and Latin America, to diversify holdings? There has been much comment about the possible effect of a U.S. stock market decline for retirement earnings and, therefore, a pressure for at least an implicit public guarantee. What happens when the market in question is foreign, such as occurred with mutual fund holdings in the case of Mexico in 1994?

Economic reality puts an entirely new emphasis on pressures for internationally coordinated and consistent macroeconomic policy, not only within the developed countries but also the leading developing ones. It is possible to construct general equilibrium models, as the OECD has done, showing that there is a dramatic consequence of aging on savings. In these models, savings in Japan and other economies decline precipitately. They likewise do in the studies of other economists.

Inherently, such a national savings shortage will impose even greater dependence on international flows to compensate. But the countries engaged in capital inflows will possibly be the more attractive developed economies, using up their previously accumulated balances. In such a world, the relevance and importance of international consistency becomes much greater.

Learning in a Comparative Context.   Learning from the opportunities and limitations of other nations' efforts to solve problems enhances policy reform in any individual country. In this light, a brief consideration of the Chilean experience is instructive. For example, one of the reasons that the Chilean plan of independent accounts has proved so popular within the region, and beyond, is its presumed positive effect on the savings rate. Argentina has followed, as has Peru, Colombia, and more recently Mexico. But recent evidence has put this justification in doubt.

We noted above that the December White House Conference was the second missed opportunity in 1998 to discuss the international dimension of the problem. The first came during the previous April's State Visit to Chile and the Santiago Summit. A decision was made that it was premature for Presidents Frei and Clinton to host a public discussion on social security. At that time, town meetings were initiated by President Clinton in the United States to discuss social security reform. Such a discussion in Santiago, even at that early date in terms of U.S. policy development, would have helped illuminate the international dimension of the problem.

Again, to be fair, the decision to cultivate a domestic consensus first before attending to the international dimension was a policy trade-off. If our domestic consensus jells, as pointed out above, it will provide a significant leadership boost to other democratic countries illustrating that a solution may be negotiated and not imposed. We must be careful, however, that future opportunities to discuss the international dimension not be missed under the category of "trade-offs." The international dimension of the problem is too important.

In this context, three aspects of the Chilean plan are worthy of comment.

First is the need to note that the obligations, there and usually in other nations that have privatized social security, are much more modest because of demographics as well as the limited coverage of the total labor force. There is not a bulging older population; there is not universal membership. As a result, there really isn't much of a problem involved in conversion of the system. This would not be the case in the United States or other developed countries where the current public liability is huge.

The second observation is that a recent International Monetary Fund (IMF) study argues that privatization quite probably has had a negative, indirect effect on total savings: the consequence of each peso of increased public savings was a 0.5 peso reduction in private savings. One might also note that a subsequent assessment of the sources of savings in the Chilean scheme shows that the largest part of the increased savings realized occurred within the business sector of the economy, not by individuals personally. The message, then, is the need to assess the total effects of privatization, and not to exaggerate their significance.

The final point is that the positive Chilean results are the consequence of a historical period in which the average rate of return on invested capital was quite high. The scheme benefited from returns that averaged more than 12 percent per year. They were attainable in large measure because the principal investments were in government securities, purchased at prices much below their par values. Because policy worked to activate growth, these issues generated quite large capital gains. That strategy is a thing of the past.

We note that recent results of some funds in that country have now become negative. When stock market prosperity flourishes, results and expectations are positive; but it is not a continuous trend. That has certainly been true in 1998 and 1999 in Latin America, where some markets have been sharply down. It remains to be seen whether the earlier enthusiasm found within Chile, and the rest of Latin America, can survive negative results without creating a political reaction. It is for this reason that we come back to the importance of cultivating a domestic consensus for the remedy chosen so that the public may appreciate the risk/return trade-off. Such understanding will provide additional resolve during episodes of market volatility.

That is precisely the problem with *full* commitment to private investment—its higher average return is balanced by greater volatility. Assuring that those most dependent on the system are at least partially protected against the consequences of such variation is a direction that everyone can agree on. It is one that can be made compatible with privatization by assuring that there remains an important public component in any scheme.

A Summit on Global Aging. In addition to learning and consensus building in a comparative context, multilateral dialogue also can serve an important global consensus-building function. The interesting recent proposal by Peter Peterson for a Summit on Global Aging, replicating the recent attention granted to climate change, merits consideration. The objective does go further in building institutions: the establishment of a Summit process, with a broad mandate to examine the question and to publish a regular report that would update the full economic consequences and implications of a growing older population. This may be more than the current multilateralism traffic will bear. But very clearly, this is an issue whose time will clearly come, and in the not too distant future.

In thinking about the "sequencing" of various forward-looking policies, we believe, as we describe in our essay on trade in this volume, that first, the twenty-first century world must show its ability to sustain and expand the openness that has characterized the last 50 years. This is an important prerequisite for a broader and more communal response to the global aging question that will then not only seem appropriate, but indeed provide the basis for an innovative and effective economic solution.

Conclusion

In the last analysis, then, there is a major challenge that lies immediately ahead. It is to avert an old-age crisis that could set generation against generation in an increasing but futile struggle. As many have acknowledged, such a struggle would lead, in the worst case, to a revision of the social contract that has been the hallmark of twentieth-century liberal democracies. In this case, the triumph of markets, but not of democracy, may be the ultimate legacy of the post-Cold War.

As noted above, the social security issue is a unique one internationally. It appears to be totally domestic, but it is so large and involves such economic interdependence that inevitably the question extends into foreign policy. As the largest part of state expenditure, including health care, such outlays leave little for other purposes. Shafer has already indicated in a previous essay how development assistance has disappeared under lesser budgetary pressures. If social security is not shored up, we reiterate our earlier concern over the pressures placed on the guns and butter trade-off, especially as new threats arise such as the emergence of China as a major power in the twenty-first century.

In a world that has already become inherently global in terms of financial flows, and one that is about to be much more so in terms of the evolution of electronic commerce, social security will not remain an isolated domestic issue. Countries will inevitably follow carefully what others do, and what they do not choose to do. The EMU, barely established, is already leading new efforts to deal with different fiscal systems found in member countries. Pension systems will soon follow. And inevitably, issues of competition in trade and service flows will bring in other non-European countries. The new globalism of the twenty-first century is one that inherently reaches out to encompass what initially had been national concerns.

Chapter 11

U.S. Capital Markets Leadership in the Changing Global Economy

J. Carter Beese Jr.

Introduction

Once confined within boundaries and borders, capital is now capable of disregarding those restrictions as new developments in technology, consolidation of financial institutions, increasing liquidity of previously restricted capital, and harmonization of accounting standards accelerate the speed and size of cross-border capital flows. As capital markets continue to integrate, it is becoming harder for the United States—and the rest of the world—to distinguish between what is considered a "foreign" policy matter and what was once viewed as a traditional "domestic" concern. Moreover, U.S. and foreign investors have been increasing cross-border investments, further eroding those boundaries that used to segregate foreign and domestic issues.

Foreign holdings of U.S. securities have grown from just under $950 billion in 1990 to nearly $3,365 billion in 1998. Similarly, U.S.

holdings of foreign securities stood at $313 billion in 1990; by 1998, they had grown to over $1,604 billion.[1] In 1994, 204 non-U.S. domiciled companies were listed on the New York Stock Exchange; five years later, the total number of foreign listings jumped to 382.[2] Given this "new reality," the chairman of the New York Stock Exchange, Richard Grasso, has held preliminary discussions with several companies from the United Kingdom, Italy, and Germany about entering a pilot program that would list ordinary shares of select companies that now trade only American Depository Receipts.

Furthermore, in this evolving seamless global marketplace, financial institutions are being liberalized. For example, in late 1997, the World Trade Organization (WTO) announced a landmark initiative where banks, insurance companies, and other financial institutions would be opened up to foreign investment and ownership. Nearly $18 trillion in global securities assets and $2.2 trillion in insurance premiums will now be freer from excessive restrictions.

In this dramatically shifting global economic landscape, U.S. capital markets may no longer be the guaranteed destination of capital flow. Companies have more choices than ever as to the domicile of their issuance, and investors increasingly are searching worldwide for where and how to invest their funds. In a world where capital knows no boundaries, the cost and qualities of financial regulation have become keenly competitive factors. Moreover, because of U.S. domestic economic exposure to volatility created by foreign under-regulation to induce capital inflow, U.S. national security concerns are implicated.

To date, the United States has been able to develop—and to lead by example—some of the highest-quality capital markets in the world. The core principles of the U.S. capital markets—full, fair, and open disclosure and strong corporate governance—have sought to provide investor protection without imposing overly burdensome restrictions on issuers and investors.

If America is to maintain its leadership role of providing efficient and fair examples of capital markets, U.S. capital markets must continue to develop and establish the highest standards of corporate governance and disclosure, providing the most open and liquid capital markets in the world. This new financial order requires a forward-looking policy, one that will continue to promote capital formation, reduce regulatory constraints, and encourage transparency. On the other hand, as discussed in the next sections, the new financial architecture will need to address technological changes that make regulatory supervision problematic and add pressure for consolidation among financial services. Under such competitive pressures one must worry about a loss of quality in capital markets.

Changing Global Dynamics in Capital Markets

Perhaps one of the biggest challenges to U.S. capital markets foreign policy is the rapid deployment of information technology (IT). Dave McCurdy has developed herein some of the social and economic changes of our new "networked world." On the financial side, the acceleration of capital mobility, driven by advances in technology, have fundamentally altered the concepts of national boundaries and international competitiveness. Today, issuers and investors can avoid intermediaries by using a computer terminal on their desk to execute transactions, and access electronic equity, fixed income, and foreign exchange trading networks, electronic-based research and analytics, and initial public offerings (IPO) for smaller companies through the Internet.[3]

"Economics are going to drive us towards consolidation and towards electronics," predicts Wayne Wagner, President of Plexus Group, a consulting firm that advises institutional investors on creating cost-effective trading. Technology is becoming the driving force behind current merger possibilities for the securities exchange landscape. During the past few years, the energy-based New York Mercantile Exchange merged with the metals-based Commodities Exchange, New York's coffee and cotton exchanges announced a merger, and the Philadelphia Stock Exchange, the country's oldest exchange, agreed to join the proposed American Stock Exchange–NASDAQ combination.[4]

Simultaneously, stock exchanges are facing increased competition from technology-based competitors such as "electronic communications networks [ECN]." "You're seeing consolidation at the same time that a number of ECNs are coming into existence," stated Frank Baxter, head of the brokerage firm Jefferies & Co. "Instead of a static, administered marketplace, you have a boisterous, dynamic series of marketplaces."[5]

Technology is, in fact, fundamentally reshaping the traditional concept of stock markets. Screen-based transactions are replacing the "open outcry" system of futures markets, a revolution in the industry first set into motion by the London International Financial Futures and Options Exchange.[6] Off-the-shelf technology is helping create new "virtual" exchanges that can be established quickly and cheaply in any location, such as the Cayman Islands Stock Exchange. In addition, virtual exchanges are able to match bids and offers for more exotic forms of derivatives, such as mortgage-backed securities,[7] thus being able to increase exposure in almost any market. In fact, during an on-line investing conference in San Francisco, the world's first wireless Internet securities trading system was unveiled.[8]

On the investor's side, the traditional role of dependent market participants is giving way to independent individuals equipped with direct access to market activity around the world. Touted as the "new equalizer," the Internet allows unprecedented access to services and opportunities unheard of even a few years ago. With the push of a button, individuals can choose from the many on-line discount brokerage firms in the industry to place their trades. It is believed that at least 30 percent of all U.S. retail stock transactions take place on the Internet, with that amount growing to reach most of the transactions over the next few years.

Advances in telecommunications are also providing unprecedented access to distant markets. Wireless, data-delivery systems are allowing investors to access real-time market data without being immobilized by a standard phone line. Once considered a service reserved for the elite, the number of wireless subscribers is expected to reach 1.26 billion by 2005.[9] Likewise, software developers and information service providers are collaborating efforts to expand their financial product offerings and to meet the increasing demands of consumers and investors.

In addition, Web-based investment companies equip investors with research, news, and market information, as well as access to investment opportunities including venture capital, initial public offerings, and institutional-style electronic trading. The new players in the trading industry deliver "bundled" services, such as research and processing, allowing investors to more freely allocate transactions without considering the cost of additional services. For instance, Wit Capital, the first on-line investment bank of its kind, offers investors access to research, news, and an alternative stock market—the Digital Stock Market—which allows investors the opportunity to trade directly with other investors thus avoiding spreads imposed by traditional market intermediaries.[10]

Consolidation of Financial Institutions

Technology has also been a critical factor in the rapid consolidation of financial institutions. As the industry is reshaped by unprecedented mergers, one objective remains clear: to develop integrated, high-speed computer networks that can perform the daunting tasks faced by tying together so many products and services across a global marketplace. Such networks, as stated by Jim Dixon, president of technology at NationsBank, are "the fuel" of the bank consolidation drive. Customers, concluded Dixon, are demanding the ability to use banking products and services any time of the day or night and to use whatever vehicle they choose, be it a phone, home computer, automatic-teller machine, or other device, "and the race is to put that in place fully."[11]

In an environment where regulatory barriers to acquisitions are gradually being removed, financial institutions will continue to push forward, forming global, full-service conglomerates. "By our calculations, based on capital available and required returns," reported Peter Davis, consultant with the Banking and Capital Markets Group of Booz Allen & Hamilton, "twelve to fifteen banks now compete for a dominant global position that can sustain only six to seven."[12]

On the regulatory front, the Glass-Steagall Act, once a bastion of populism and the minimization of risk in capital markets, has fallen, in part due to the recognition of technological transformations in the banking industry. The April 1997 announcement that Bankers Trust would acquire Alex Brown was the first merger to apply expanded Section 20 privileges, and unleashed other transactions across the industry that ultimately led to legal reform in November 1999.

This process of overhaul began in 1998 as the merger trend reached a new level of regulatory consideration. The Travelers-

Citicorp merger represented consolidation on a global scale with assets topping $700 billion and revenues of $48 billion.[13] Indeed, the creation gave rise to a giant financial services conglomerate encapsulating insurance as well as retail and investment banking. The Citicorp-Travelers merger sparked a renewed consolidation in the financial industry. In April 1998, BankAmerica and Nations-Bank announced a $570 billion merger (total assets), and BancOne and First Chicago followed with a $230 billion proposal. Once these transactions turned into a tidal wave, the repeal of Glass-Steagall became inevitable.

Increased Availability of Capital

As Fishlow and DeSouza develop in a previous essay, all around the world, countries are reviewing their retirement planning systems and looking for greater returns on the capital invested. Even the American concept of social security is undergoing serious scrutiny. If reforms continue, there may be an increasing flow of available capital seeking open and liquid markets across the globe.

Chile was the first country in the Western hemisphere to privatize its system for retirement savings. In 1998, Chile had $33 billion under management, with reported annual returns averaging 11.8 percent since inception of the program.[14] Peru adopted an optional plan in 1993, Argentina permitted private accounts in 1994, and Bolivia reformed its system in 1996. Mexico adopted its plan in 1997, and in its first seven months, generated a retirement savings pool of $1.5 billion, with new fund management companies providing average real return of 8 percent.[15]

In the United States, the makeup of retirement funding is changing just as dramatically. The number of American citizens in 401K personal pensions programs jumped from 7.5 million in 1984 to 27 million in 1997.[16] Public and private pension funds have seen their assets swell from $130 billion to more than $1.6 trillion in just 25 years. Holdings in mutual funds, which could soon overtake corporate pension funds as the largest single group of investment institutions, have increased from 5.2 percent a decade ago to 12.2 percent of the total equity market.[17] A study by the Federal Reserve Board found that 70.3 percent who identified themselves as professionals have some form of retirement account, 26.1 percent own individual stocks, and 21.3 percent own mutual funds.

Pension-fund reform continues to build on its established momentum, and Americans now appear to be agreeing to a bipartisan effort on the issue of privatization of social security. The Center for Strategic and International Studies assembled the National Commission on Retirement Policy—a bipartisan group of politicians, businessmen, and policymakers—and presented a proposal that included raising the retirement age and diverting percentage points of the current payroll tax.[18] A poll taken in 1997 found that 75 percent of all Americans favored allowing workers to transfer 2 percent of their income from payroll taxes into private retirement funds. Moreover, 55 percent of Americans polled favored full privatization of social security.[19]

Furthermore, Europe has also been caught in the wave of pension-fund reform sweeping the globe. Countries including Great Britain, Sweden, Italy, and Switzerland have revamped their social security systems. And with the close of the consultation period on the European Commission's 1997 Green Paper on supplementary pensions, there seems to be an increasing prospect for privatizing pensions in the evolving European Union (EU).[20] With the growing weakening of government-run pension programs and lower interest rates, "you are looking at a set of circumstances that occur only a few times a century," noted Phil DeCristo, head of European operations for Fidelity Investments, who sees European pension reform as being a prime engine of growth over the next few years.[21]

New International Challenges: Need for Financial Transparency

Increasingly, events around the world are directly influencing American lives, business, and policies. The Asian economic crisis has shown that one of the world's regions can have a significant effect on American capital markets as well as other markets around the world.

The lack of rigid accounting standards and core corporate governance principles have drastically affected Asia, and as such, the rest of the global economy. Nearly all participants in the Asian capital markets suffered, from investors to issuers to banks. In many cases, Asian economies were focused more on building market share than on building net income. Many Asian currencies had a tendency to be overvalued because they were pegged to the U.S. dollar.

The IMF's prescription of bailouts, in excess of $100 billion to cover South Korea, Indonesia, and Thailand, did little more than suffocate Asian economies under the burden of high taxes and excessive interest rates. For true recovery to be sustained, those in a position to influence policy must prescribe reforms that will inject growth capital. For countries to obtain growth capital, they need to immediately institute transparency and accuracy in their financial practices. Foreign investors will not return to these markets to fuel the necessary growth until they can see a firm's entire financial picture. To help Asia rebuild and seek long-term success, Americans must realize that foreign policy should target the worldwide development and implementation of full and fair disclosure requirements and sound corporate governance principles as critical objectives.

The speed at which Asia transforms into a financial culture, more focused on the full disclosure of assets and liabilities and proper corporate governance practices, is the speed at which it—and the world—will build sustainable growth. As companies become more transparent, a renewed confidence in Asia's issuers and markets will be reborn. An environment will be created that is necessary to draw the much needed growth capital into Asian economies. Clear and comprehensive disclosure and accounting standards are vital and must be implemented.

As a former SEC commissioner, I suggest that the world's capital markets would be well served to focus on certain objectives. First, enhanced securities regulations must set forth clear guidelines and standards. Second, reliable and consistent enforcement of these enhanced rules should be mandatory. Third, the input of all the different market participants involved—investors, domestic financial institutions, and foreign firms—must be considered to provide the required flexibility and liquidity. Finally, to provide investors with the utmost confidence, securities regulators must be equipped with a broad range of investigative powers and enforcement remedies.

As Asia works to regain economic growth, competition for capital will continue to be intense. Waves of capital are still flowing around the globe looking for attractive open markets. Only those capital markets in the world that truly provide a level playing field will win the race to the top in attracting high-quality capital that becomes a long-term partner in a country's economic growth.

Adding to that dynamic is the reality that unlike Asia, which has experienced a serious financial collapse and is rebuilding, Europe is taking on new "gravitas." It was reported that London has replaced Tokyo as the largest equity investment center in the world, with funds under management in 1998 up 48 percent, to $1,808 billion.[22] Moreover, European capital markets are integrating financial landscapes, from currency to stock exchanges, and pushing forward in critical reforms ranging from pension-fund privatization to steps toward real-time settlement mechanisms. Corporate Europe is taking the lead by adopting U.S.-styled earnings reports, generally accepted U.S. accounting standards, and the concept of shareholder value.

"Japan and the rest of Asia are in a crisis now," said Frankfurt *Business Week* Bureau Chief Thane Peterson, "at least partly because they have avoided opening their companies to scrutiny and are taking painful restructuring steps that the best of corporate Europe has achieved."[23] The transition to the Euro is forcing a merger boom, and companies are already expanding across borders and converging their management cultures, styles of business, and corporate governance. In addition, caused by stringent economic requirements for becoming a participant of the European Monetary Union (EMU), governments across the continent have reduced budget deficits and reformed monetary policies. For the first time this century, interest rates and inflation have been converging across the European continent.[24]

The more progressive and innovative Euro market may pose a competitive challenge to U.S. capital markets. Given the current debate over one-day settlement, for instance, it is possible that Europe, rather than the United States, will become the driver of T+1 settlements. With the demands of Year 2000, the EMU, and decimalization pressuring operations and systems, the U.S. market consensus is that T+1 will not occur until, at the earliest, the year 2001. And while U.S. regulatory bodies debate settlement standards, Euroclear, an international clearinghouse in Brussels, and its Luxembourg-based rival Cedel, are already working together to develop real-time processing formats that would be used as the foundation for faster settlements.[25]

U.S. capital markets have moved to eliminate some restrictions in response to this new paradigm, but they must do more. The challenge for the United States will be to encourage growth of full and fair disclosure and strong corporate governance standards across the global economy, while remaining vigilant in our own innovation efforts.

U.S. Leadership in the Global Marketplace: Long-Term Structural Changes

How can the United States continue to maintain its leadership role in the face of the new global marketplace? By standing on the core principles that make U.S. markets some of the leading capital markets in the world: providing full, fair, and timely disclosure to investors, and open and accountable corporate governance standards. These principles, based on transparency and liquidity, should serve as an example to other countries seeking to assert and define their roles in the global economy.

In the area of accounting standards, fundamental differences still exist between U.S. standards and practices of other countries, particularly in terms of the purpose of financial statements. Some countries believe that financial reporting should serve social or political purposes, such as encouraging or discouraging investments in certain types of businesses, while others believe that financial reporting should serve as a basis for taxation. Agreement on a common objective is imperative if real progress toward harmonizing accounting standards is to be achieved.

U.S. capital markets have served as an example in the development of international standards and accounting principles. Under U.S. GAAP, the SEC is committed to maintaining high levels of investor protection; in addition, FASB is working to ensure that U.S. GAAP keeps pace with marketplace trends while promoting transparency through full disclosure. For example, under the U.S. GAAP, assets and liabilities are intended to represent real economic facts expected to result in future cash flows based on events that have already occurred. These parameters define financial reporting by precluding certain events or transactions from qualifying as assets or liabilities.

Upholding these high standards and maintaining a core set of corporate governance principles is the first issue that concerns U.S. regulators and businesses alike. The SEC is committed to ensuring that international accounting standards are nothing less than credible financial reporting. SEC Chairman Arthur Levitt has emphasized that the decision regarding IASC's international accounting standards would be based solely on the quality of the standards. As an entire set of generally accepted accounting principles, the IASC's set of standards must provide for financial disclosure as relevant and reliable as information prepared in accordance with U.S. standards.

On the liquidity front, the SEC has taken important regulatory steps in the past few years to attract foreign issuers to the U.S. markets. In April 1993, foreign issuers to the U.S. markets were placed on an equal basis with domestic issuers by reducing the threshold for short-form registration for foreign registrants from $300 million to $75 million. Even more important, the SEC allowed foreign issuers to use shelf registration to register debt and equity offerings. Thus, foreign issuers, similar to domestic issuers, were granted the flexibility to determine the size and type of an offering at a future date. This option enabled foreign issuers to "come to market" quickly when optimal conditions prevailed.

In addition, during the last several years, the SEC has taken steps to lower the regulatory cost to foreign issuers. In April 1993, the SEC recognized international accounting standard Number 7, the "Cash Flow Statement," as an acceptable alternative to U.S. GAAP. U.S.-listed foreign companies were permitted to prepare cash-flow statements in accordance with international accounting standard Number 7. Furthermore, the required reporting history was reduced from 36 months to 12 months provided that a company had filed at least one annual report.

In late 1994, the SEC adopted two more international accounting standards: Number 22, which addressed the issue of "business combinations" for cross-border stock filings; and Number 23, which dealt with the costs of borrowed funds and the effects of hyperinflation. Foreign issuers were thus allowed to use these rules instead of U.S. GAAP when filing to list in the United States.

However, perhaps the most important step in terms of regulatory streamlining has been the implementation of Rule 144A. Under Rule 144A, a foreign corporation can sell its securities to a large majority of U.S. investors without reconciling its financial statements. Rule 144A allows regulators to work within the parameters of integrated capital markets and streamline capital raising requirements without excessive regulatory oversight creating undue risk. Specifically, a foreign company can comply with Rule 144A securities by registering under the Exchange Act or by periodically submitting to the SEC information that the company is required to disclose by its home country regulator.

Enacted in 1990, the SEC adopted Rule 144A for two reasons. First, the SEC aimed to increase the liquidity and efficiency of the secondary market among large institutional U.S. investors for privately placed foreign and domestic securities that are not registered with the SEC. Second, the SEC intended to attract foreign issuers of privately placed Rule 144A securities.

Investors and companies from all over the world have benefited from the innovative, liquid, and transparent capital markets in the United States. Most have invested in these markets because they trust U.S. markets and place deep faith in their integrity. U.S. capital markets foreign policy should be centered on providing leadership to the changing global economy by encouraging worldwide use of strong corporate governance standards and full, fair, and open disclosure.

Conclusion

The United States has developed some of the world's highest quality capital markets by providing liquid and transparent marketplaces. The environment in which these markets operate, however, has fundamentally changed. As capital flows freely around the globe, national boundaries that used to define markets and companies are rapidly losing their significance. International competition, technological change, and more demanding consumers are collectively working to erode the significance of national boundaries and to create a truly global marketplace.

Given the growing importance of economic considerations in the U.S. foreign policy agenda, creating unbridled and transparent capital markets is an imperative. The United States should encourage other markets and countries to adopt full, fair, and open disclosure and strong corporate governance standards in their capital markets. At the same time, U.S. markets must also remain vigilant in maintaining their competitive advantage by pursuing innovative measures that will provide investors around the globe with the most liquid, transparent, and cost effective capital markets possible. Only by providing sophisticated, flexible, and open capital markets that can be used as examples around the globe, can the United States continue its foreign policy leadership in the financial arena.

Notes

1. *Securities Industry Factbook* (1999) at p. 80.

2. *New York Stock Exchange website* (1998).

3. Davis, Peter. "Dawn of a new era on Wall Street." *Booz Allen and Hamilton website* (1998).

4. Ip, Greg. "Philadelphia Exchange to Join Nasdaq, Amex." *Wall Street Journal*, June 1998.

5. Ip, Greg. "Proposed merger of Nasdaq, Amex may be followed by other markets." *Wall Street Journal* (1998).

6. Iskandard, Samer, and Edward Luce. "Liffe grasps the nettle of electronic trading." *Financial Times*, March 10, 1998.

7. "Caught in the 'Net.'" *Open Finance*, Summer 1998.

8. "IT is still changing the face of trading." *Financial Times*, March 24, 1998.

9. Yankee Group. *Cellular PCS Competitive Licensing Assessment and Global Forecast* (1999).

10. Wit Capital website (1998).

11. Murray, Matt. "Bank Mergers' hidden engine: technology." *Wall Street Journal*, April 23, 1998.

12. Davis, Peter. "Dawn of a new era on Wall Street." *Booz Allen & Hamilton website* (1998).

13. "System Overload." *Open Finance*, Summer 1998.

14. Pinera, José. "In Chile, they went private 16 years ago." *Cato Institute website* (1998).

15. *Amafore Pensions Research* (1998).

16. West, Maureen. "Taking pensions private; key Arizona lawmaker open to reshaping of social security." *The Arizona Republic*, May 31, 1998.

17. Waters, Richard. "Institutions becalmed amid Wall Street power shift." *Financial Post*, June 12, 1998.

18. "Social Security: And the work goes on." *Economist*, May 23, 1998.

19. *Democratic Leadership Council* (1997).

20. "Pensions: Insurance firms argue for equal treatment." *Financial Times*, June 3, 1998.

21. Andrews, Edmund. "Investing in Europe," *New York Times*, June 14, 1998.

22. *Technimetrics Research Report* (1998).

23. Peterson, Thane. "A giant leap for the new Europe." *Business Week*, May 18, 1998.

24. Andrews, Edmund. "Investing in Europe." *New York Times*, June 14, 1998.

25. Richardson, Portia Thorburn. "Is this time to be thinking about one-day settlement?" *Investment Dealer's Digest*, October 13, 1997.

Chapter 12

Dollarization

Julie T. Katzman

Introduction

In the last eighteen months, the world has seen the near collapse of numerous financial markets and economies as volatility and a crisis atmosphere spread from one corner of the globe to another. This article will address the repercussions of these crises and focus on the attendant volatility on Latin America—the fastest growing export region for the United States and intended partner by 2005 in a new regional trading area.

In evaluating recent economic circumstances, the severity of the 1998 Asian and Russian financial crises has had dramatic repercussions. Once the serious macroeconomic and business practice problems of Russia and Asia were exposed, investors who had lost substantial amounts of money in these markets drew down their balances elsewhere. Currency speculators began to take advantage of weaknesses in other emerging markets, particularly Latin America. Emerging market currencies, such as the Brazilian real, came under attack for being overvalued. Eventually, devaluation and a new exchange rate and monetary policy became necessary to stabilize the Brazilian market. These adjustments have had adverse consequences for real output in Brazil and in the region.

What we have seen over the last eighteen months may accelerate as the twenty-first century "new realities" of growing economic interdependence and the spread of information technologies (IT) make information increasingly available and global transactions instantaneous. As weaknesses in any given economy occur and become apparent, those weaknesses will be exploited, and quickly.

This situation has created a foreign-policy problem for the United States. Many of the currency speculators and market participants who have been the catalysts for these devaluations and the subsequent economic hardships that countries have experienced are based in the United States. At the same time, the United States has been one of the most vocal proponents of the free-market philosophy—the "Washington Consensus"—that many now blame for their economic and currency difficulties. From the vantage of the United States, such discontent is worrisome as U.S. economic security is highly dependent on healthy export markets. The U.S. share of exports to gross national product has more than doubled over the last twenty years. Any financial crisis abroad, therefore, will be significant for U.S. economic interests at home.

Despite its relative success in preventing a global financial meltdown, the current administration realizes that strong, forward-looking measures are needed to ameliorate the effects of globalization on the people living in emerging markets. In an important foreign-policy speech in San Francisco on February 26, 1999, President Clinton articulated five great challenges for the remainder of his term and for the new century. One was to "create a world trading and financial system that will lift the lives of ordinary people on every continent around the world." More precisely, the president set forth the following objective: "[W]e have got to find a way to facilitate the movement of money—without which trade and investment cannot occur—in a way that avoids these dramatic cycles of boom and then bust, which have led to the collapse of economic activity in so many countries around the world."

The United States has a distinct national interest in quickly finding a way to address the current economic and financial problems brought about by globalization. There is a real danger that some emerging markets may resort to the alternative of capital controls and other isolationist solutions as a way out of instability. This policy device only undermines the post–Cold War move to market mechanisms—something sought by policymakers over the last generation. Interestingly, a recent *Wall Street Journal* poll of a broad group of people from all over Latin America demonstrated the public's continuing strong commitment to free trade and open markets. However, one may wonder how long this popular support will last if daily life does not improve markedly.

We cannot turn the clock back from the integration of markets. It is only the rare country, like Malaysia, that can make a system of capital constraints work in even the short term. With almost 70 percent of its Gross Domestic Product (GDP) exported, Malaysia has unique access to foreign exchange flows outside this "isolationist" policy—a situation few others can replicate. For most of the world, advances in telecommunications and technology have allowed capital to become extremely mobile. Solutions to the problem of volatility must recognize and accommodate a twenty-first century world of economic interdependence where mutuality of gain should be the focal point.

In this context, a policy of "dollarization" should be considered as a tool to reduce capital market volatility in an interdependent world. Dollarization can remove the possibility of speculative attacks on currencies and the flight of capital seeking a safe haven, induce greater stability in key indices such as inflation and interest rates, and thereby add economic stability.

In the article that follows, the first section will discuss the volatility that has occurred over the last eighteen months. It will focus primarily on the Latin American experience. The second considers a framework for decisionmaking that allows us to develop a "next generation," win-win approach. It focuses on the policy option of dollarization as the alternative that best fits the need for such a cooperative framework. The costs and benefits of this policy to the participants are outlined. The third section then addresses some of the practical implications of implementation. Finally, the last section discusses the broader social context of dollarization.

Recent Volatility: The Effect of Currency Instability

In the wake of the Asian and Russian crises, Latin America's economies have spent the last year riding a roller coaster largely not of their own making. Capital available for investment in the local markets has decreased dramatically, interest rates have increased substantially, and GDP growth has moved into negative territory. These events demonstrate the widespread negative effect that unstable foreign exchange rates can have. From GDP growth of 5 percent in 1997, a high point since the early 1980s, growth for the region slowed to approximately 1–2 percent in 1998. A slower rate of expansion is foreseen for 1999. Interest rates increased as much as 200 percent between 1997 and year-end 1998 in efforts to support currencies. Corporate access to the debt and equity capital markets effectively ceased because of such volatility. Issuances declined from $23 billion in 1997 to approximately $8 billion in 1998 (99 percent of which was debt).

Countries themselves fared only slightly better. Brazil's devaluation at the beginning of 1999 marked the low point. From a value of 1.20 reals to the dollar, the value of the real shrunk vis-à-vis the dollar as the exchange rate soared to 2.20 before returning to a range of 1.75 to 2.0. Yet currency volatility throughout the region has occurred against a backdrop of economic progress that has resulted in more solid banking sectors, strong industrial capacity, and, for many of the countries, responsible federal budgets and manageable budget deficits.

Currency volatility in this period has had substantial ramifications. Sharply diminished access to foreign capital and sudden increases in interest rates have served to choke off economic growth that had become quite robust during the decade. Large and small enterprises have had a difficult time absorbing such shocks. Many large companies have a substantial portion of their liabilities denominated in U.S. dollars. Those liabilities have effectively grown as a result of devaluation. In addition, interest rates on debt denominated in local currencies have doubled in a period of weeks or months. As a result, companies experience an increase in their overall cost of capital, restricting the capital they have available for expansion and eroding their ability to create new jobs.

By way of illustration, consider the case of an entrepreneur trying to plan the future of his business even one fiscal year ahead. He budgets, plans, controls costs, and borrows what appears to be a prudent amount of money. Then, overnight, he sees his borrowing costs triple, quadruple, or quintuple. Small businesses cannot sustain such shocks during their formative years nor can individuals save securely for their futures when their currency may be devalued at any time. In combination, these events cause a decrease in income levels and job creation and a further divergence between the standard of living of developed countries and emerging markets; such a situation breeds discontent arising from failed expectations of partnership in the global economy.

This outcome is unacceptable for the United States' national interest. Latin America is critical to the U.S. economic future. As Farnsworth indicates in this volume, as of the end of 1998, approximately 40 percent of U.S. exports went to the Americas. Canada and Mexico are our number one and two trading partners. Moreover, it is estimated that by 2010, the region will be more significant to the United States in terms of trade than Japan and the EU combined. Ensuring that this region continues to grow and prosper is therefore an economic and foreign policy imperative. It will not be able to do so in an environment of financial volatility like that experienced over the last eighteen months.

Dollarization as an Alternative

In addressing the need for a responsive policy framework, from the perspective of the United States and that of the emerging countries of Latin America, dollarization is a tool that can achieve a number of strategic goals in one fell swoop—the ultimate "one plus one is greater than two." Dollarization is simply conversion of Latin American countries' current currency system to one that is U.S. dollar-based. It is akin to the current evolution of the European Monetary Union (EMU), but with the important distinction that the United States, not a regional institution, would lead the way. Why is it justified in the Western hemisphere? Under typical circumstances, a common currency would underpin large-scale flows: trade, investment, and labor—with common expectations of the movements in exchange rates and other monetary indicators such as interest rates. Of course, the participating countries would have the obligation of assuring that their policies did not deviate from those established in the United States; otherwise, their dollar balances would soon disappear.

It is important to note that in many Latin countries, particularly the Caribbean and Central America, forms of dollarization already exist; formal in the case of Panama and informal for the balance of the region. For example, relatives living in the United States sent roughly $1 billion to families living in the Dominican Republic in 1998. During the same time period the United States bought only $200 million in sugar and $270 million in cigars and tobacco from the Dominican Republic. Last year, immigrants sent more money to Latin American countries—Mexico, El Salvador, Columbia, and the Dominican Republic—than the U.S. government provided in aid to those countries from 1978 to 1994. Institutionalizing this practice would not involve a substantial change in the day-to-day activities of the local population and would result in substantial benefits.

More important, dollarization could transform the gradual process of regional integration. The existence of the North American Free Trade Agreement (NAFTA) with its positive effects on trade growth, would make Mexico an ideal candidate for a more formal approach to dollarization. In fact, many analysts believe that monetary union with the United States would solve Mexico's chronic historical problems of high inflation and devaluation at the start of almost every new president's term of office for the last 20 years—an event, incidentally, that will occur in 2000.

Although other countries in the region fail to satisfy the criteria as fully as Mexico, there is also scope for them to benefit from an institutional conversion to the dollar. Intensification of trade relations as is happening in the EU is a likely outcome of a common currency. Over time, with more rapid growth, the current illegal migration would also likely gradually decline preserving human capital and reducing political tensions.

From a financial markets perspective, dollarization of Latin America would decrease global financial volatility. Avoiding the advent of the next Brazilian crisis would benefit all players in the global marketplace because of the increasing integration of markets. Dollarization would eliminate the cycle of boom and bust, inflation and recession, and overvaluation and devaluation—goals outlined by President Clinton in his San Francisco speech. This would simultaneously create a more secure market for U.S. goods and for U.S. companies who have become substantial players in the domestic economies of Latin America.

From a U.S. foreign policy perspective, dollarization can be a tool that addresses and reduces the inequalities in Latin American society that ultimately threaten the long-term survival of free markets and democracy. The underlying stability fostered by dollarization, and greater and cheaper capital availability, allow for the growth and development of new businesses—and new jobs. In addition, it allows for the creation of "instruments" that are almost completely absent from most of our hemisphere today; long-term corporate debt and legitimate commercial mortgages, to name two significant instruments.

Costs of Dollarization

So, what is the cost to achieve these gains? From the perspective of Latin American countries, there are two primary issues: the psychological issues of sovereignty and the real lack of flexibility to address domestic crises using monetary policy. First, sovereignty. On one hand, the ability to print money has always been a defining characteristic of a modern nation-state. Therefore, giving up this right is a major hurdle for policymakers and the citizenry at large, as demonstrated by the comments of, say, Mexican Finance Minister Gurria. However, in focusing decisionmaking matrices of governmental elites, one must recognize that issues of national sovereignty preoccupy decisionmakers because much of their careers and authority derives from such concerns.

By contrast, many business leaders are more open-minded. Eugenio Clariond, chief of the influential Mexican Business Council (CMHN), has suggested to President Zedillo that dollarizing the economy would be a policy that would stabilize the economy. Clariond believes this policy will curb the flight of capital and stimulate the repatriations of an estimated $38 billion currently resting in U.S. bank accounts. He also believes that not only would inflation, over 18 percent in 1998, be curbed, but high interest rates, like the 22 percent rate on Treasury bills, would decline. The return of capital, lower inflation, and less prohibitive interest rates resulting from a dollarized economy would make capital more accessible to small- and medium-size companies.

Also of importance are the interests of non-elites, whether public or private—the working men and women who must live under the monetary regime chosen and who must cope with globalization. Value creation for the average citizen is based on stability of economic expectations so that they can save, invest, and achieve better lives. However, they too are affected by issues of national pride. In a broad poll conducted by the unaffiliated Mexican newspaper *La Reforma* in October 1998, 70 percent of the respondents were in favor of being paid their wages in U.S. dollars and having savings accounts denominated in U.S. dollars. The same percentage of respondents was also against eliminating the peso. This seemingly contradictory mindset is an illustration of the lingering psychological aspect inherent in dollarization. Nonetheless, government officials are not prepared to consider dollarization as a remedy to volatility. Chief executive officers (CEO) and working people would at least like to have a public discussion—the essence of democracy—on a policy that would move them to a form of dollarization. In crafting a next generation foreign policy, it is important to recognize that individuals and groups are important participants in discussions of the "new" financial architecture. As this volume has discussed, with the broad empowerment of technology, such as the Internet, foreign policy issues are now "kitchen-table" issues.

Second, as it relates to using monetary policy to address domestic crises, a number of things should be kept in mind. For one thing, the inability to use monetary policy as a tool becomes important only when such a crisis is not simultaneously affecting the United States. It may be assumed that the United States will have similar incentives to avoid crises. Also, counter-cyclical policy tools are available from the fiscal side. In addition, the frequency of such crises may decrease dramatically after dollarization, particularly with the on-going strengthening of major institutions in Latin America, including an independent judiciary, and the further strengthening of the banking system through the adoption of the Bank of International Settlements (BIS) capital and transparency guidelines. Ultimately, dollarization is a straightforward application of the strategic decisionmaking theory of "hands-tying." By removing the ability to make decisions on monetary policy from government bureaucrats in volatile economies, these countries will boost their credibility in the financial markets that, in turn, will translate into broadly available and cheaper capital.

Perhaps the best case study is Argentina. In the wake of the current Latin financial crisis, Argentina will certainly suffer some ill effects caused by the interrelationship between its economy and Brazil's. However, even with much lower exports to Brazil—its major trading partner, Argentina has defied all who were forecasting that they too would have to devalue. Rather, the Argentine government has reacted to this crisis by seeking ways to further its efforts toward dollarization. Why? Because Argentina alone among the Latin American countries has been able to access capital in late 1998 and early 1999 during the global financial crises. Argentina alone has a domestic mortgage market. It alone has had only 2.7 percent cumulative inflation since 1991. And, Argentina alone has managed through two regional crises without a single devaluation.

Of course, in accomplishing these impressive results, Argentina had the advantage of gold-standard experience, which is lacking in much of the rest of the region. That is what gives Argentina a leg up on possible dollarization and why Economy Minister Roque Fernandez has been so aggressive in encouraging discussions with the United States. But in the end, the political reality is that other Latin countries, with the possible exception of Brazil, have also shown an interest. How to move ahead is then the basic issue that we now take up.

Implementation

There are a number of ways, along a continuum, through which to bring about dollarization. First, in its broadest formulation—something the United States has not yet been willing to consider—dollarization could imply full monetary union with the United States. Through bilateral or multilateral treaties, individual currencies would be replaced with dollars. Then Latin American countries would have to enter into the calculations of the Federal Reserve Bank, exactly as many countries in Europe have just joined in a common currency with a single central bank.

Alternatively, a more modest formulation could mean a further deepening in monetary cooperation with the United States, allowing dollars and local currencies to circulate freely. In this circumstance, greater financial cooperation need not include the U.S. Federal Reserve acting as a lender of last resort. Such is the system in Argentina today where Argentina's currency is pegged at a 1:1 rate with the dollar and 100 percent backed by U.S. dollar reserves. The United States is not perceived and does not act as lender of last resort. In fact, from the U.S. perspective, the current Argentine example of effective dollarization demonstrates specifically that the United States need not take on undue risk to achieve this goal. Instead, Argentina has put in place a stand-by credit facility backed by governmental assets to provide liquidity in a crisis.

Finally, along the continuum, dollarization could be based on unilateral decisions by countries to withdraw their respective currency from circulation in exchange for dollars currently held as reserves. In this case, because of such unilateral action, it would be clear that the U.S. Federal Reserve would not act as a lender of last resort. This is illustrated by the case of Panama.

Practicalities of Implementation

To implement some variation of dollarization requires addressing a few practicalities. First, a country must have sufficient dollar reserves to back its currency or to exchange its currency for dollars. For those who lack sufficient reserves, one option is to simply borrow the money in global capital markets. A bond issue, the use of whose proceeds would be to establish a currency board or to dollarize the economy, could likely be sold at an interest rate well below that of the country's current borrowing rate—even in the case of Brazil in today's market. While the rate may be higher than ideal, the bond could be refinanced in a few years' time once global markets gained renewed faith in the country.

Second comes the choice between full dollarization (with or without U.S. cooperation) and a currency, board-type format. This choice may ultimately have more to do with the optics of sovereignty (not "giving up" your own currency) than with the realities of sovereignty (retaining the right to print money in major crisis). However, it also relates to the economic reality of seigniorage—the obvious gain associated with the issue of one's currency. A government would only choose to forego the seigniorage and dollarize fully if the premium it had to pay in the capital markets because it was not fully dollarized was greater than the income it would have to forego if it fully converted to dollars and lost the seigniorage.

The U. S. decision on how to address this issue will give a clear signal of the support it intends to give to dollarization. Inevitably, however, the issue will arise, and it will likely come through Mexico rather than from farther south.

Broader Implications

Despite Washington's internal electoral clock, the issue of dollarization may ripen early in Latin America. The public discussion on dollarization currently rages furiously on the streets of Latin America. One is just as likely to discuss exchange rates as soccer scores on the streets of São Paulo or eventual monetary union with the United States with a taxi driver in Mexico City; so important is increased economic stability to those who live in the emerging markets. Residents of many emerging markets up and down the socioeconomic pyramid are painfully aware of the local effects of the economic and foreign policy decisions of their own and the G-7 governments. Working men and women are dramatically engaged in these issues on the national agenda because the region's instability and resulting economic hardship have dominated their lives.

Latin-American leaders understand this political reality. Fernando Henrique Cardoso of Brazil achieved a constitutional change allowing him to run for reelection and was reelected because he had fought inflation successfully. His inability to pursue tighter financial policy, however, has turned out to be costly. Today, after the recent devaluation, he is fighting a renewed battle against inflation and recession. He seems to be winning, if one judges from recent Brazilian data. Recovery of Brazil may establish the ability to devalue modestly to adjust for currency misalignment. However, because markets initially overreacted substantially, and because Brazil and, in fact the entire region, has had to walk a tightrope, the dollarization position will continue to gain strength.

By comparison, Carlos Menem was not given the opportunity to run for president again. Nonetheless, the strength of support for his policies—by both major parties—is based on newfound growth and price stability in Argentina. It is no mystery that strong support for dollarization comes from Argentina. When the Peronist party suffered losses in the mid-term elections, Argentina was experiencing a new luxury: the ability after seven years of stability to vote based on concerns over corruption and security rather than economics.

The implications for the region of greater economic stability are thus far reaching. Deeper political dialogue over economic issues is one such benefit. Another is the development over an economic base that can advance a necessary social agenda. Latin America's educational, housing, and health infrastructures need improvement. The World Bank estimates that over $3 trillion will be needed over the next 10 years to build the necessary infrastructure for the region. The Inter-American Development Bank points out that the greatest way to increase earnings is to increase education—a long-term investment whose efficacy depends on economic stability.

As important as achieving a larger, more advanced, and effective educational structure, meeting the region's infrastructure needs and advancing the other areas of social investment requires capital, internally and externally generated capital. Dollarization and the stability it brings will contribute to increasing both of those sources. Internally generated funds will increase as businesses grow and new businesses are established and thrive, generating higher tax revenues. External investment will increase, and hurdle rates will decrease, as currency uncertainty is removed from the investment evaluation and allocation. Ultimately, as capital flows more quickly to those countries that dollarize, others will follow suit. Each of these actions reinforces the win-win situation around which successful policies—like successful deals—can and should be created.

Conclusion

If we are to consolidate the gains made by democracy and free markets, we must create a twenty-first century coalition in the United States and elsewhere that understands that globalization requires policies based on the concept of mutual gain. However, such understanding must be bolstered by results to avoid cynicism about politics. To this end, policymakers must ensure that globalization translates into tangible benefits and advancements for working men and women in the world.

Dollarization is a powerful tool that can do just that, fundamentally reshaping the hemisphere for the next generation. Dollarization will decrease regional economic volatility—something to which the United States is increasingly exposed in a world of integrated markets—as it stabilizes the economies of the United States' fastest growing trading partners. In addition, it will build broader economic foundations in each of these trading partners by beginning to address the substantial inequalities of wealth that exist by creating the domestic conditions necessary to spur the growth of businesses and jobs. Such per capita income growth in emerging markets is critical for creating consumers eager for U.S. goods and services.

Yet, today the United States is sitting on the sidelines, either out of a view that beating the dollarization drum would seem imperialistic or out of the belief that dollarization is a policy option that entails too much risk. This article argues that risks to the United States can be managed by choosing how and in what form dollarization should be supported. The substantial economic benefits to the United States and the Latin American countries merit further policy development in this area.

The alternative, espoused by such strange bedfellows as Hugo Chavez in Venezuala and Patrick Buchanan in the United States, is a return to capital constraints, currency protectionism, and a "seal-the-boarders" mentality. Such a mindset is out of step with the 24-hour-a-day, round-the-world global trading and capital markets that have developed and are here to stay.

Part IV

The Information Age

Chapter 13

Telecommunications

Eugene A. Sekulow

Introduction

Telecommunications has always been regarded as an intrinsic part of any national infrastructure and an essential growth engine. Countries understand that there is more than a casual relationship between the ability to communicate and economic development; a communications infrastructure enables more efficient economic transactions to be consummated. As Hormats will develop in the next chapter, the convergence of modern telecommunications and information technology (IT) will enable the revolutionary, trillion-dollar marketplace of electronic commerce to be a reality within the next few years.

Because telecommunications has traditionally been considered by most countries to be of strategic and fundamental importance, it has been typically categorized as a "sensitive" sector requiring government protection through relatively heavy legislation and regulation. Indeed, in Germany, for example, basic telephone service is a citizen's inherent right enshrined in the basic law. We reconsider here the applicability of heavy regulation, not the reality that it is a sensitive sector, in light of our changing world of information.

Telecommunications and the IT that supports it will be the lifeline of the twenty-first century. As McCurdy has set forth in an earlier essay, we are moving toward a new "networked" concept of society. Because of its priority of preparing citizens for the twenty-first century, the Clinton Administration has been attempting to ensure universal access to telecommunications in the United States. In fact, almost everywhere in the world, appreciation of our "networked" future has engendered solid political support for basic universal service.

This new "information" century will cause nations to value, more highly than ever before, both telecommunications capacity and virtually unlimited access for citizens. However, realization of the increasing significance of telecommunications is producing some difficult political and economic choices for developed and developing countries. First, in terms of *capacity*, countries are facing the dilemma of what is the optimal structure given the prevailing economy and resources available. Not all societies "need" the most advanced telecommunications services such as cellular data transmission. Rather, in certain circumstances, basic phone service that can be used by many would do more to increase growth rates and productivity than specialized features and functions that can only be used by a relative few. Concomitant with the question of optimal structure is the question of who—government or the private sector—should lead the way in creating the right kind of telecommunications environment and infrastructure.

Second, in terms of *access*, all countries will need to face the issues of how to allocate services and who should be doing the allocating. Will the public sector make such determinations or will the choices be left to the marketplace? The reality of the cost of service must be factored in. Yet, irrespective of allocation issues, all societies, for the sake of social stability, have a need to avoid a growing gap between the information rich and the information poor.

Despite the difficulty of these domestic choices, the telecommunications revolution will produce much opportunity for mutual gain in terms of economic growth, the dissemination of democratic ideas, and the spread of individual empowerment around the world. Because the United States is the leader of the information revolution, it will have a special ability to shape the world of the twenty-first century. However, such leadership will be looked at skeptically by most other nations out of fear that instead of mutual gain, the United States will use telecommunications and IT to dominate the world.

This article will focus on the opportunities available for the United States to shape the world of the twenty-first century. The United States must first develop a strategy that secures its fundamental economic and political interests. Such interests may actually collide under certain circumstances. On one hand, it is in the U.S. economic interest for its companies to sell as much sophisticated telecommunications products and services to the world as possible because such products carry the highest profit margin for American companies. On the other hand, it is in the U.S. political interest to promote democracy and individual empowerment through universal access and an appropriate mix of high and low technology. Advancing economic and political interests thus will be a challenge for U.S. diplomacy because "one size does not fit all." Under some circumstances, as a policy matter, margins may need to give way in priority to appropriateness.

One recommendation developed below to alleviate the constraints involved in the trade-offs between improving capabilities and broader access is that it should be a priority for the United States to work with other governments to bring down barriers to foreign investment. In this way, countries may tap into foreign savings to relieve their allocative constraints and finance a fuller range of telecommunications products and services.

Today's Telecommunications Reality

Increasingly, the telecommunications sector drives an economy through the pursuit of a straightforward goal of minimizing the importance of "time," "distance," and "place" for economic development. In this way, sophisticated forms of work, necessary for the global marketplace, may be accomplished without regard to restraints and inhibitors, controlling when, where, and how work is to be done. For example, schools may teach necessary skills to workers through distance learning using audiovisual transmission to the site where the job function is to be performed. Also, sophisticated design and manufacturing information may be conveyed irrespective of location. Complex tasks that can contribute to economic growth thus can take place when and where necessary.

There is, however, a premium to be paid in restructuring an economy to take advantage of such technological innovation in the ways of doing work. Investment in telecommunications technology is expensive and requires large financial outlays putting upward pressure on the cost of capital. Advanced telecommunications infrastructure must be laid so that data may be carried to the desired location. Such new equipment may be difficult and costly to install. Also, service providers must train people to use the new telecommunications equipment to carry out the tasks demanded. Such providers can charge higher rates for training because of the specialized nature of their business. Whether government or private individuals make the ultimate calculation, there is a cost-benefit analysis that must be made to decide what degree of restructuring is optimal.

One need only take a look at the expensive and complex undertaking known as Fiber Link Around the Globe (FLAG) to gain insight into the infrastructural effort that is required to respond to modern demands for state-of-the-art technology. FLAG is an international private consortium initiative that planned, designed, financed, and constructed an optical-fiber submarine-cable system between the United Kingdom and Japan having a total length of over 30,000 kilometers and a total cost of approximately $1.5 billion. FLAG lands in approximately fifteen countries, eleven of which can be regarded as developing economies.

At this stage in the revolution, governments are, by and large, still taking the lead in making telecommunications decisions because of their traditional role in protecting this sensitive sector. Increasingly, however, governments have concluded that they are not capable of effectively providing service and are granting to the private sector more responsibility for providing capacity. The FLAG example is a case in point.

Additionally, within the next few years, at least 30 countries will either fully privatize state-owned telecommunications companies or continue to privatize companies in which the transition from being a state enterprise has already begun. Some of the larger economies that will privatize 100 percent state-owned companies include Australia, Congo, Ecuador, France, India, Poland, Switzerland, Turkey, and Thailand. Countries continuing to privatize include Brazil, Germany, Greece, Israel, Italy, South Korea, and Portugal.

To be sure, governments will still play a regulatory role. However, the locus of decisions, especially regarding access, will necessarily change. While the private sector will be able to provide a higher degree of service, the cost of such service is likely to go up in the short-run reflecting market demand and influencing the distribution of service among the respective populations creating information haves and have-nots. Yet, if all goes according to schedule, privatization and competition should bring more service at affordable prices to most citizens over the long-run.

Questions of privatization and distribution of service will also be shaped by the reality that there are only a handful of leading-edge telecommunications equipment suppliers—Lucent, Motorola, Siemens, Ericsson, NEC, Alcatel, and Nortel; a significant portion thus being of U.S. origin. Because of this reality, another variable in the decisionmaking equation for governments will be lingering suspicions regarding foreign influence in their telecommunications sectors.

The shift to a global information age, then, has forced policymakers around the world onto the horns of a dilemma: They must rethink how best to maximize the role of telecommunications in the economy so as not to fall behind the information curve. In doing so, they will need to turn to foreign companies for solutions regarding increasing capacity. At the same time, policymakers will have a difficult time compromising what are viewed as "basic rights" that should be determined "inside" the nation by surrendering control over telecommunications development. For most countries, including the United States, foreign investment in telecommunications evokes concerns regarding national security.

The Market and U.S. Economic Interests

As noted above, U.S. companies are the leading suppliers of telecommunications equipment and services in the world. The potential market for such products is huge. It is estimated that the global market in 1998 for telecommunications equipment was $210 billion and for telecommunications services was $750 billion. With the number of Internet hosts increasing by a factor of ten over the last three years and with exponential increase likely over the next three, it is probable that there will be an explosive demand for telecommunications products.

During the Clinton Administration, the trade performance of U.S. companies within these markets has been outstanding. Since 1993 there has been a dramatic upswing in U.S. exports. Between 1994 and 1996, the trade surplus in telecommunications equipment increased from $901 million to $2.4 billion with U.S. exports reaching $15.7 billion in 1996. Finally, it is important to note that this sector represents a significant share of the U.S. workforce. For example, the Cellular Telecommunications Industry Association estimates that approximately 275,000 new jobs have been created in the wireless industry over the last decade.

Moreover, as of 1996, based on data from the International Telecommunications Union, the United States was an order of magnitude ahead of the next country—Japan—in terms of total telecommunications revenue. In fact, the telecommunications revenue in the United States was still a third higher than the next two countries—Japan and Germany—combined. These three countries were significantly ahead of everyone else.

The U.S. lead in telecommunications revenue should increase in the twenty-first century as satellite technology provides multichannel and superior audio and video quality to the market, especially areas underserved by cable operators. Although American companies have partnered with foreign companies, they still dominate the satellite systems projects that will compete for twenty-first century telephony: Iridium (Motorola, Raytheon, and Lockheed Martin); Globalstar (Loral and Qualcomm); Odyssey (TRW); and ICO Global (Hughes and COMSAT). Iridium and ICO Global are of questionable viability. In addition, work to be done by the Teledesic (McCaw, Gates, and Boeing) and Celestri (Motorola) projects could create a dominant position in terms of the delivery of Internet services in the twenty-first century. Note that while some may carp at U.S. dominance, such projects involve a substantial amount of risk capital (in the order of a hundred billion dollars). "Fairness" would argue that such projects should earn high rewards over the next two decades.

Transatlantic Marketplace

Currently, the satisfaction of demand for telecommunications services has focused more on "Western" developed countries. Based on data through 1996 provided by the International Telecommunications Union, European countries plus the United States and Australia have the highest penetration of main telephone lines per 100 inhabitants. In addition, as of 1997, the Scandinavian countries plus Australia and the United States have the highest percentage of subscribers of cellular service among economies with over 1 million inhabitants. With respect to other areas of the world, Hong Kong, Japan, and Singapore have significant percentages in both categories.

Not surprisingly, such capabilities have allowed for the United States and Europe to lead the way in terms of international interconnection. Such communication links have created economic and social opportunities. Data from the International Telecommunications Union indicates that, as of 1996, approximately three-quarters of the total minutes of international telephone traffic occurred in the United States (32 percent), Germany (11 percent), the United Kingdom (8 percent), Canada (6 percent), France (6 percent), Italy (4 percent), Switzerland (4 percent), and the Netherlands (3 percent). One may conclude that in terms of telecommunications, globalization seems to be driven from a transatlantic perspective. To be sure, the United States is the dominant actor. As of 1995, four of the top five international routes involved the United States (rank ordered: United States/Canada; United States/Mexico; Hong Kong/China; United States/United Kingdom; and United States/Germany).

Compared with the United States, telecommunications reform in Germany is more representative of the changes that "Western" developed countries are instituting to better prepare themselves for the twenty-first century. Germany represents about 25 percent of the European Union (EU) telecommunications market. It has a relatively high tele-density (lines per 100 inhabitants), reaching about 55 percent in 1996. The 1996 German Telecom Act accelerated the process of reform. That year, Deutsche Telekom completed the largest public offering in European history selling a quarter of its ownership. The capital provided by the sale was critical for capital projects necessary to modernize the system. Moreover, starting in 1998, there has been increased competition for the provision of services. Private network operators have been granted licenses to compete with Deutsche Telekom. American companies such as

AT&T, Airtouch, and BellSouth are competing in the German market. These changes promise to accelerate the provision of service so that the German economy may achieve higher productivity and growth.

Emerging Markets

Outside of the developed country context, there are a variety of emerging markets that offer the opportunity for high growth in the market for telecommunications services. As with developed countries, these markets are making commitments not only in terms of spending on telecommunications, but also in terms of the institutional and legal reforms necessary to support such efforts. Equally important, certain emerging markets also involve strategic considerations for the post–Cold War period that place a premium on successfully cultivating the processes of modernization. Although essays on key emerging markets—Russia, China, and Latin America—will be set forth later in this volume, it is useful here to focus on the telecommunications segment of these markets.

Russia has been trying to reform its telecommunications systems since the fall of the Soviet Union. Under the Soviet system, there was insufficient capacity, poor interconnection services, and obsolete equipment. In trying to modernize its economy, Russia has laid over 1,300 miles of radio-relay and cable lines, installed television relay stations, and activated 16 digital exchanges. Yet these changes mark only the beginning of a complete overhaul. Because of a low penetration rate in terms of lines per inhabitants (17 percent) and an emerging entrepreneurial class, there is pent-up demand for telephone equipment and services. Moreover, Russia is sensitive to the fact that it must reform its regulatory structure to permit sufficient transparency so as to encourage Western firms to enter the market and provide services.

China, also, has been trying to reform its telecommunications system within the context of state-led planning. Demand for telecommunications services is even more pent-up than in Russia. Penetration has only reached about 5 percent of the total market despite a current annual growth rate of approximately 40 percent. It is estimated that the Chinese Ministry of Posts and Telecommunications has spent over $90 billion for telecommunications during the last five years of the previous decade. Currently, China is attempting institutional reforms so as to maximize the chances for favorable outcomes that are hoped for with such spending. In 1994, the government set-up China United Telecommunications (Unicom) to promote "managed competition" in telecommunications. In addition, China began to relax its prohibition against foreign participation in the operations of communications networks. Currently, however, liberalization is being reconsidered. Over the next several years, nonetheless, one may expect Chinese laws and regulations to be revised in pragmatic fashion because of its realization that it needs foreign help to bring its telecommunications network to a stage that can support sustained economic growth.

Brazil is seen as the largest and most promising market in Latin America—the fastest growing region for U.S. exports. According to Price Waterhouse Coopers, more than 10 million people are waiting for phone service. Tele-density is currently only 8.5 percent. To satisfy such demand for services, Brazil expects to permit about $100 billion in direct investment over the next five years. In July 1997, a consortium led by BellSouth paid $2.5 billion for a 15-year license to offer cellular service in São Paulo. BellSouth felt that such a price was justified by the backlog of 1.8 million orders for basic and cellular phones. Foreign equipment providers such as Ericsson have reported record profits.

Like Russia and China, Brazil is willing to make the institutional and legal changes necessary to modernize its telecommunications system. While Brazil does not have the communist legacy of Russia and China, it does have the baggage brought on by a history of inefficient state bureaucracy. The year 1998 was marked by the privatization of Telebras, the largest government carrier in Latin America. Telebras was reorganized into four regional subsidiaries and sold off. In addition, the long-distance state-owned company Embratel will be sold off. Moreover, not only federal, but also companies owned by states such as Compania Rio Grandense de Telefonia (carrier for Rio Grande do Sul) are being sold (in this case to Spain's Telefonica for approximately $700 million).

In surveying the international telecommunications market, certain observations should be highlighted. First, the potential market for products is large with U.S. companies occupying a favorable position. Second, the regional focus to date has been transatlantic. Third, there are many opportunities in emerging markets for which the United States must develop a strategy. Such strategy will be necessary not only for maximizing economic return, but also for advancing foreign-policy considerations of promoting democracy and individual empowerment. Transforming emerging markets such as Russia, China, and Brazil, however, requires the United States to encourage continued institutional reform to permit direct foreign investment and to create certainty and transparency in laws so as to give the private sector the confidence necessary to make strategic investments.

U.S. Diplomatic Efforts: Multilateral and Regional

In light of these opportunities, the United States has made serious efforts to advance American interests in telecommunications trade. Two multilateral agreements should be noticed. First, the Agreement on Basic Telecommunications Services in the World Trade Organization (WTO), which was signed in February 1997, went into effect January 1, 1998. This agreement was the first multilateral agreement ever reached in this area and involves approximately 70 countries accounting for more than 90 percent of the world telecommunications services revenues. The agreement covers three general areas: 1) increasing market access and promoting the adoption of national treatment (foreign and domestic suppliers to be treated alike) for suppliers of services; 2) opening foreign ownership or control of services and facilities; and 3) enhancing competition in services markets.

Second, a corollary to this effort was the signature of the Information Technology Agreement in April 1997. This agreement eliminates most tariffs on IT and telecommunications products by the year 2000 and attempts to advance a plan for a Global Information Infrastructure. This agreement covers over 40 countries representing over 90 percent of the world trade in IT products. Together these two agreements will reduce the costs of restructuring telecommunications infrastructures around the world and, ultimately, the cost of information services.

The Clinton Administration has supplemented these multilateral efforts with regional action. The United States and the EU signed on June 20, 1997, the Mutual Recognition Agreement on Conformity Assessment. This agreement will help minimize a significant nontariff barrier to trade in telecommunications hardware by allowing manufacturers in the EU and United States to avoid cost and delay in having their equipment certified before it is marketed.

Meanwhile, with respect to Asia, the Asia-Pacific Economic Cooperation (APEC) Working Group on Telecommunications is developing initiatives to improve competition in the region by 2010. The efforts in APEC include creating Guidelines for International Value Added Network Services, harmonizing equipment certification procedures and a model mutual recognition agreement on conformity assessment of telecommunications equipment similar to that achieved in Europe. In light of the tendency toward protectionism in the aftermath of the Asian financial crisis, it will be important that progress continue to be made in APEC.

Finally, in North America, the implementation of the North American Free Trade Agreement (NAFTA) has dramatically opened the market for telecommunications. Significantly, NAFTA eliminated Mexican import tariffs on over 80 percent of telecommunications equipment and will phase out the remaining tariffs in 10 years. In addition, NAFTA lifted all Mexican restrictions on foreign investment in service providers and increased the level permitted in Canada to approximately 47 percent. NAFTA, more than any other regional effort, has produced strong results. The U.S. share of Mexican telecommunications imports increased from 64 percent in 1993 to 85 percent halfway through 1996. The U.S. share of Canadian imports has increased from under 67 percent in 1993 to about 75 percent in 1997. Such results indicate the value of regional agreements in keeping markets open and should be seen in the context of the discussion on trade outlined by Fishlow and DeSouza herein.

Policymaking Dynamics

Despite common international frameworks, different dynamics in regional markets require some thoughtfulness by U.S. policymakers in addressing the opportunities. Decisionmaking for most countries is largely based on the resource constraints present as each tries to position itself in the global economy. More specifically, the cultivation of democratic norms through universal access to communications technology has become a priority for U.S. domestic policy. By contrast, such cultivation is a luxury for most developing nations and subordinate to overall economic development.

Consider for a moment the national markets featured above. Each has made certain allocative choices based on its relative socioeconomic circumstances. Russia and China each realize that it would not be economically feasible to fully upgrade the communications infrastructure that is in place. Each has decided that it would be cheaper to build parallel networks based on radio or wireless networks rather than completely overhaul its current system with advanced technology.

By contrast, after the fall of the Berlin Wall, West Germany opted to bring East Germany up to or surpassing the overall infrastructure level of West Germany. The approach chosen was to leapfrog existing technology. The German government spent 60 billion marks on telecommunications alone; now eastern Germany has one of the most sophisticated telecommunications networks in the world.

In Brazil, President Cardoso has taken an approach similar to that of President Clinton. An emphasis is currently being placed on universal access while upgrading the system. One way around the allocative constraint for Brazil has been to privatize and open the telecommunications system to foreign investment. Moreover, upwards of $500 million from such privatization is being used for education so that all Brazilians may be more "informatics" literate and productive.

Along this continuum of telecommunications reform, it should be noted for comparison that the Philippines has taken a bold step toward implementing a twenty-first century vision that does *not* require high technology. To promote economic development and individual empowerment, the Philippine government has made it a national priority to put at least one payphone in every village. It is now even possible to equip such public payphones with Internet access.

In considering these markets, not only in terms of economic strategy, but also in terms of foreign policy, the United States must be sensitive to developmental concerns. As noted above, this remains tricky given the competitive pressures generated to promote high margin products from U.S. companies without consideration of what may be the appropriate mix of technology.

U.S. Political Interests

The telecommunications revolution also creates opportunities to advance U.S. political interests by reinforcing democratic tendencies around the world. As McCurdy discussed earlier, one may assume that telecommunications strengthens democracy by permitting the spread of ideas and the empowerment of individuals.

Domestically, the Clinton Administration has gone further than simply mouthing conventional wisdom that telecommunications also promotes democratic values. Through its shaping of the Telecommunications Reform Act of 1996, the administration has emphasized advanced universal access. The legislation subsidizes the wiring of schools to the Internet as a way of enabling all citizens to develop common perspectives through technology.

Internationally, as noted above, the United States has invested considerable political capital in advocating the same telecommunications philosophy that it fosters domestically. Free trade, deregulation, open markets, and revised settlement policy all underlie the same thrust for enhanced universal service on an international basis.

Vice President Gore most recently reaffirmed that a priority of the administration is for everyone to communicate inexpensively and easily. How this is to be accomplished, at what cost, and on whose tab is, however, yet to be disclosed. In itself quite noble, the universal access message lacks even a hint of addressing implementation issues. It fails to adequately take into account that principle and reality are somewhat at odds. Very few governments will deny the merits of universal access. Yet, very few governments are in a flush economic situation that would permit disregard for allocative choices. Current fiscal stresses in uniting the German Federal Republic are a painful example of budgetary constraints. The high costs involved are not always fundable through current revenue without surfacing distribution issues.

Developing countries, especially, do not have the luxury of focusing on the benefits for cultivating democracy while trying to strengthen their communications infrastructure with the latest technology. Developing countries and, importantly, their citizens, first need basics. As a result, considerations of universal access to high technology and promotion of democratic values have become secondary to ensuring that the telecommunications infrastructure is connected to the critical financial and manufacturing hubs in a country.

Attaining a proper mix of telecommunications technology is quite tricky and such efforts cannot be abandoned. James Wolfenson, president of the World Bank, has pointed out that telecommunications infrastructure must have a combination of high- and low-tech capabilities that match the range of local needs. Although this is not a very profound or arguable truth, it forces us to ask follow-up questions so that we can develop solid answers or significant guidance.

The main challenge then for economic development is how to move toward U.S. aspirations for the global spread of technology against the background reality that often 50 percent of the population of a developing country has never used technology. The allocation of national resources for economic and social development and the effective deployment of telecommunications infrastructure is a conundrum that plagues planners, promoters, and advisors alike. As with all such issues, there is no one correct answer and certainly, as noted above, no "one size fits all."

U.S. Strategy for the Twenty-First Century

It would be rather straightforward for the United States to focus on its pure economic interests and promote advanced telecommunications technology. However, as the leader of the post–Cold War world, the United States has multiple objectives. One is to support the conditions under which democracy and individual rights grow. Such conditions are created by the dissemination of telecommunications capacity and access for the general public.

Outside the United States, the issues facing policymakers are really quite formidable. As previously outlined, the fundamental choices are more often, too often, choices from among alternatives having nothing to do with technology but rather with economic realities in conflict with political imperatives and promises. Should a sophisticated state-of-the-art infrastructure that serves a high-end user market and that generates significant revenues from subsequent deployments take precedence over a bread and butter universal service? It is an option between POTS (plain old telephone service) and PANS (pretty awesome new stuff). It is also invariably a no-win situation.

It would seem, therefore, that the most useful U.S. policy would be one that addresses the alleviation of allocative constraints. In this way, a rising tide could produce mutual gain. For our purposes, following are some principles to guide policy development.

We should encourage the revision of inward investment policies and ownership. Such reform would create a hospitable climate for a shared commitment to produce mutual gains in the new "information century." Such commitment would be focused on basic network upgrades and the installation of leading-edge sophisticated network build-outs as a more or less simultaneous effort. This partnership arrangement—BOT (build, operate, and transfer)—could largely eliminate the compelling need to choose among some alternatives to the exclusion of others. Thus, it does lie within the reach of well-intentioned government to serve special interests (to be sure, economically enhancing and productive) and the general good (universal basic service for as many people as possible) at more or less the same time or at least with a minimum time lag between projects.

It is not banal to suggest that, in truth, U.S. policy does want the best for the world. It is also realistic to understand that what is deemed as "best" is frequently also self-serving. That, however, does not take away from the good intention. Our national ethos is in no way diminished if it serves us as well as the beneficiaries of our efforts. However, we must always and altogether be mindful that, in wishing for the best for others and ourselves, what we deem to be in others' best interest is truly that.

Optical fiber, open network architecture, Internet and expanded Internet, and on and on, offer entry into a new world. These technological features and functions should and will, over time, be available, of necessity, to all. But the pleasure-pain calculus suggests the need for an early strategy to alleviate suspicions that will limit countries' abilities to overcome resource constraints.

The telecommunications world may be, probably will be, a different world by 2010. The comfort and painlessness with which all players will ease into that new world will largely be determined by the experiences of the preceding ten years. The financial and social costs, the mistakes and lessons learned, the social adjustments and readjustments will be determinants. A balanced *economic and political needs* focus rather than the conventional wisdom of pushing only high margin business is what is required.

Chapter 14

The Foreign Policy of the Internet

Robert D. Hormats

Introduction

Rarely in history has a new technology posed greater challenges to conventional methods of communication, commerce, governance, and organization than the Internet. The explosive use of the Internet, together with revolutionary breakthroughs in biotechnology and the proliferation of intelligent microprocessors in all aspects of our lives, form a triad of dramatic changes that will define and drive progress in the coming era. These advances will vastly enlarge the human potential, greatly improve the quality of life, and dramatically broaden the scope of knowledge and experience for hundreds of millions of people.

The Internet will substantially diminish the influence of governments, traditional media, and entrenched bureaucracies in the public and private sectors. It will challenge the relevance of laws, regulations, and government policies tailored to modes of commerce, communication, and organization based on older technologies. What new laws, regulations, policies, and patterns of interaction take their place will be prominent issues for debate in national capitals and on global agendas well into this century. Such issues will become increasingly significant as the use of the Internet expands, commerce on it grows exponentially, and issues of content, privacy, taxation, intellectual property protection, and security provoke heated controversy. At home and abroad, the Internet and e-commerce are likely to become a highly contentious legislative and regulatory battlefield pitting the laissez-faire philosophy of business and technology advocates against governments' instincts to tax and regulate.

The questions to be addressed are many: What role should governments play in regulating this technology and the commerce and communications it facilitates? What role should individuals, businesses, or communities of users in the private sector play? How will government and private spheres interact? Can privacy and security be protected? How will piracy of intellectual property be prevented? Will children be guarded against pornography or worse? How can societies be defended against cybercrime and terrorism? How will the question of encryption be resolved? Will governments resist temptations to tax arbitrarily, discriminatorily, or excessively on-line Internet transmissions of services and data or Internet-generated sales of physical goods? Answers to these questions will determine the way societies, governments, and individuals relate to the Internet, the way it relates to them, and the way they relate to one another early in the twenty-first century.

If policymakers and users of this new technology proceed wisely to allow the Internet to achieve its full global potential, the results will have far-reaching political as well as economic implications. By hardening international political, ideological, and economic barriers, the Berlin Wall became the most prominent and powerful symbol of the Cold War era. By promoting global flows of information, ideas, and commerce, and by empowering the individual relative to his or her government, the Internet can become the most prominent and powerful symbol of this millennium era—signifying the collapse of barriers among nations and peoples and the emergence of the networking of individuals, businesses, educators, students, and scientists in ways that transcend geography and ideology.

The Internet also exemplifies the triumph of economist Joseph Schumpeter over Karl Marx. Marx advocated "command and control" economics. Schumpeter advocated "creative destruction" whereby new technologies emerge in a decentralized fashion, and old ones decline at a rapid pace. That is what is occurring now in an explosion of entrepreneurship in computer software and hardware, and in tens of thousands of e-businesses linked to and by the Internet and Web, as new technologies, new business models, and new companies displace older ones at a rapid clip. This also reinforces the need for what Nobel Prize-winning economist Douglas North terms "adaptive efficiency"—the capacity of individuals and institutions to constantly learn, innovate, and alter the ways they do business.

This chapter focuses on the international commercial aspects of the Internet and Web. Its basic premise is not just that the Internet has changed the nature of commerce, but also that it has profoundly changed the rules of the game and must sharply alter the way new rules are written. So far the Internet has developed in a virtually tax and regulation-free environment. But as it grows that is likely to change, with the attendant risk that governments will impose burdensome or mutually inconsistent national policies. That would be a tragic error. The Internet and e-commerce demand new attitudes toward regulation and government policy. Emphasis should be on self-regulation and market-based or technology-based solutions that allow users, entrepreneurs, and technical experts great latitude to advance the Internet and the way businesses and consumers use it. In many cases, constructive government–private sector collaboration will enable precisely those technologies that permit the Internet and e-commerce to grow so rapidly to solve the complex public policy challenges such rapid growth poses.

This chapter is titled "The Foreign Policy of the Internet." However, the author well recognizes that, in fact, the Internet can have no foreign policy because it has no boundaries and no geographic center. Rather, the Internet and e-commerce have a distinctly global character. How the international rules are shaped and by whom are what this discussion of the foreign policy of the Internet is about.

In particular, this chapter discusses the international initiatives that the U.S. government and private sector are pursuing to ensure that the Internet, the Web, and e-commerce can realize their full potential. It takes as a starting point the July 1997 e-commerce initiative of the Clinton Administration. It does so not because it is the only one of its kind. Indeed the European Union (EU) and Japan, as well as other countries such as Malaysia, Canada, Australia, and Indonesia, have put forward initiatives of their own. However, the administration's initiative embraces the widest range of considerations relating to the future of the Internet and global commerce. Moreover, the philosophical underpinnings of this initiative are the most conducive of any to establishing an environment of openness and regulatory restraint, giving users, service providers, and entrepreneurs the broadest range of possibilities for developing their own solutions to technological and regulatory challenges.

With his call for a minimally regulated, secure, duty-free environment for Internet information flows and electronic commerce, President Clinton put forward a doctrine of U.S. policy that is likely to have a profound effect on governance, the openness of societies, and the integration of economies around the world for decades to come. His *Framework for Global Electronic Commerce*, (hereinafter referred to as *Framework*, with page references added) could become one of his administration's most enduring legacies.[1] The *Framework*, prepared under the leadership of presidential assistant Ira Magaziner, has been the centerpiece of an energetic and systematic series of e-commerce initiatives by U.S. officials; these have substantially improved the environment for the globalization of the Internet and digital business.

The Clinton Administration's concept of "Global Electronic Commerce" was designed to respond to the growing use of the Internet in virtually every aspect of daily life: transmission of data, shopping, business-to-business links, banking, insurance services, stock trading, education, health care, and entertainment. To put the growth of the Internet in historical perspective, it took 38 years for the telephone to reach 10 million customers, 25 years for cable TV to do so, 9 years for cell phones, and only 5 years for the Web. In December 1995 fewer than 10 million people worldwide were connected to the Internet; the figure at the end of 1997 was about 100 million and by the end of 1998 it had risen to over 140 million. During the first decade of the new millennium as many as a billion people throughout the world could have access to the Internet. Traffic on the Internet has been doubling every 100 days. Commerce on the Internet was estimated to be about $200 million in 1995, $10 billion in 1997, and $200 billion in 1998—and is predicted to reach over $1 trillion in the U.S. alone early in the twenty-first century.

One of the principle catalysts driving e-commerce internationally is the growth in the use of personal computers (PCs), up from 30 million in 1987 to 270 million today. Andy Grove, Intel's former chairman and CEO, estimates that figure will climb to 500 million by 2002. Another powerful force has been the privatization and deregulation of state-owned telecommunications companies and the associated lowering of access costs for users. Similarly the liberalizing and opening of local telephone markets and the explosion of cable and integrated services digital networks (ISDN) telecommunications infrastructure also has reduced costs, expanded capacity, and set the stage for new participants in e-commerce.

Consumers are making increased use of access to services offered by such innovative companies as America Online, IBM, Microsoft, Dell, Cisco Systems, Amazon.com, and countless others. They can go directly to a wide range of suppliers, bypassing traditional retailers and wholesalers. As Internet-connected wireless and non-PC devices proliferate, and as tens of millions of cell phones and portable digital assistants access the Internet, a growing number of new consumers will explore the exploding e-commerce opportunities available.

Through the Internet, even small companies, many of which in the past would have had to limit sales to local markets, can immediately and with relatively little capital investment tap a global market. Using the Internet they instantly have a global reach. By employing this new infrastructure for marketing and leveraging new services and products worldwide, they are in a strong position to challenge more established businesses.

The greatest changes have occurred in business-to-business transactions, the fastest growing form of Internet commerce. Experts forecast this to reach $1.3 trillion by 2003 compared to $40 to $80 billion predicted for business-to-consumer transactions in that year.

E-commerce will have a profound effect not only on the way business is done, but also on national economies. It will greatly intensify competitive pressures in the United States and most other countries. As on-line consumers and businesses shop for and demand competitive products and services around the world, they will force prices down in some sectors, sharply limit increases in others and thereby add to pressures for corporate cost cutting. E-commerce and the Internet are likely to become a powerful force holding down inflation in the United States and other countries as they grow in size and scope. The Internet has also accelerated the transition to competition beyond prices as customers insist on a rich selection of products, rapid service, on-line interaction and increased convenience.[2]

Internet Development

Below we discuss the ongoing development of the Internet. We then set forth the basic elements of the administration's policy initiative. This is followed by a discussion of the implications of the kinds of policies being suggested regarding e-commerce and then by an assessment of the reaction to these policies in other parts of the world. A brief conclusion points to follow-on initiatives that the United States should take to further advance the Internet and e-commerce worldwide.

Growth of Electronic Commerce

The explosive growth of the Internet over the last five years is revolutionizing the way growing numbers of people think about and engage in economic transactions. To highlight the opportunities created by this exploding medium, a consortium of U.S. companies has established the Computer Systems Policy Project. This group produced a White Paper (hereinafter referred to as "CSPP White Paper" with page references included)[3] that offers useful data for understanding the electronic transformation of the world's economies.

Data cited by the CSPP White Paper illustrate the speed and magnitude of the current transformation (CSPP White Paper, p. 1). For example, Labor Department statistics indicate that by the year 2000, 60 percent of American homes will have PCs, creating a broad base for electronic transactions. Moreover, the total number of persons in all nations with access to the World Wide Web is projected to grow tenfold to 550 million within three years. Recent efforts by Brazil, India, China, and other emerging economies to put in place modern telecommunications infrastructure will add tens of millions of people to the Internet and Web in a short period of time.

The CSPP White Paper also suggests that participation in the Internet boom is more than just a marketing opportunity for business; it is necessary to remain competitive (CSPP White Paper, pp. 1–2). It cites surveys that small businesses using the Internet grow at a rate 46 percent higher than small businesses that do not. Data also indicates that companies participating in "collaboration-rich" networks have an average return on investment significantly higher (almost double) than those that have been standing on the sidelines (CSPP White Paper, p.1).

These "competitive strategy" implications are forcing a change in the perspectives of consumers and producers. "Consumers [will be able to] specify preferences, leaving sellers to respond only to particular criteria . . . 24 hours a day, seven days a week" (CSPP White Paper, p. 2). Business will move closer to "just-in-time" models of production. "Global Electronic Commerce [will] foster more robust information exchanges. . . enabling business to more precisely schedule the order and delivery of parts and supplies, reducing on-hand inventory while still meeting customer demands" (CSPP White Paper, p. 3).

Questions

There are, however, numerous questions raised by those who wish to promote this new medium: What type of market access will be available internationally to build the global information infrastructure necessary to achieve the fullest potential for electronic commerce and provide access to it for the widest number of people? Which jurisdictions will claim the right to tax and what will be subject to their taxation? Will taxes in multiple jurisdictions disadvantage growth of the medium? Will taxes or regulations impede opportunities for individuals and business in countries where they are prohibitively high? Will cross-border data and financial transmissions be secure? These and related issues—particularly the

overarching need to boost the level of consumer and business confidence in the security and reliability of Internet transactions—
need to be addressed and the proper scope for government and the
private sector determined.

The Framework

Principles.   The Clinton Administration's E-Commerce Framework initiative is based on five principles. These recognize the
rapid pace of innovation and the reality that government cannot
control technological change. Rather, government's proper role is
said to be assisting individuals to adjust to the opportunities created by a new electronic world.

The first U.S. principle is that "the private sector should lead"
(*Framework*, p. 4). From the U.S. perspective, expanded services
and lower prices that encourage broader participation can only be
achieved through market-driven competition. To that end, industry "self-regulation" is encouraged. Where governmental action is
required, the private sector "should be a formal part of the policy
making process" (*Framework*, p. 4). Reinforcing this point is a report issued by the U.S. Government Working Group on Electronic
Commerce on November 30, 1998. This first annual report on work
done pursuant to the *Framework* (hereafter referred to as FAR)[4]
stressed that "self-regulation in the digital age will require the private sector to engage in much greater collective action to set and
enforce industry guidelines than was characteristic of the Industrial Age" (FAR, p. 8).

Second, the U.S. framework states that "governments should
avoid undue restrictions on electronic commerce" (*Framework*,
p. 4). It points out that unnecessary regulation of the medium will
distort incentives for its rapid development. Indeed, because technology is changing so rapidly, it is not likely that governments
know what the optimal regulatory strategy should be.

Third, the document insists that "where governmental involvement is needed, its aim should be to support and enforce a pre-
dictable, minimalist, consistent and simple legal environment for
commerce" (*Framework*, p. 5). Within the *Framework*, there is a limited
role for policy tools. Such tools would support a decentralized ap-

proach to the development of electronic commerce. Governmental intervention would be used only for a narrow category of supporting functions: maintaining a competitive environment, safeguarding intellectual property, and ensuring effective dispute resolution. These supporting functions represent the institutional foundations necessary for a smoothly functioning market-based system.

Fourth, the initiative calls on "governments [to] recognize the unique qualities of the Internet" (*Framework*, p. 5). As we shall discuss below, Internet-based transactions force a rethinking of political and economic paradigms and prevailing business models. As a result, traditional regulatory approaches need to be updated to effectively meet the challenges posed by the new medium. This requirement ranges across wide areas of business such as cross-border financial services, product liability, and advertising claims. It also raises complicated issues such as how to regulate cross-jurisdictional delivery of legal, healthcare, financial, accounting, and other professional services.

Fifth, the document states that "electronic commerce over the Internet should be facilitated on a global basis" (*Framework*, p. 6). Some markets, such as those involving capital and information, are being linked internationally through the Internet at a rapid pace. Other markets, such as those involving tradable goods, have lagged. Government and the private sector together must take steps to accommodate this fast-moving process of e-commerce or be left behind. Governments that restrict access of their citizens to the Internet reduce vital links to the global commercial and financial system as well as to the information and communication links their companies require to thrive in that system. Moreover, many types of government restrictions probably would be unenforceable anyway and would lead to distortions and evasions.

Policy Issues. Associated with these principles are a variety of issues that the president's *Framework* designates for priority attention. The *Framework* divides these issues into three categories: financial, legal, and market access. Considerable progress has been made on these fronts.

Financial. Financial issues revolve around efforts of governments to tax the Internet or various types of e-commerce. Because special taxes on the medium would distort incentives for its use and development, the United States has insisted that "no new taxes be imposed on Internet commerce" (*Framework*, p. 7).

In particular the *Framework* underscores the U.S. commitment to push in the World Trade Organization (WTO) and other fora for the Internet to be declared a "tariff-free environment" for digital commerce (*Framework*, p. 7). Considerable progress has been made on these fronts.

Customs Duties. In May 1998 a WTO Ministerial Conference in Geneva adopted a declaration committing the organization's 132 member governments to refrain from imposing customs duties on electronic commerce when information and services are delivered digitally. To avoid any confusion it should be noted at this point that the term "e-commerce" embraces two broad categories. Category one is e-commerce such as software and data sold and delivered digitally over the Internet. This is covered by the WTO agreement. Category two is e-commerce that relates to items sold on the Internet but physically delivered, such as books, clothes, computers, or cars, which pose a different set of tariff issues. Thus the WTO moratorium does not exempt from duty a bottle of wine ordered on-line and shipped from France to the United States. Nor does it exempt that bottle from being subject to normal internal taxes in the United States.

Taxes. In the United States, many state and local authorities see taxes on Internet-generated commerce delivered off-line (category two above) as a way to avoid revenue losses as e-shopping displaces store shopping and reduces the sales taxes that are generated thereby. Some also see new lucrative taxing opportunities to boost revenues. Concerned about a rush by many of America's 30,000 tax jurisdictions to tax e-commerce, Congress passed in 1998 the Internet Tax Freedom Act. That act imposed a moratorium on new Internet-related taxes for a three-year period, although states that had previously legislated such taxes had them "grandfathered" so they can continue collecting them during this period. And taxes could be levied if a vendor had a physical presence in the buyer's state. During this time an Advisory Committee on Electronic Commerce created by Congress pursuant to the act will consider and make recommendations to Congress on the subject of appropriate tax treatment of Internet-generated sales.

So far, e-commerce purchases represent only a small fraction, less than 10 percent, of "remote sales," which also includes catalogues, telephone marketing, television, and magazine-generated orders. But as it grows, in the early years of this millennium, the issue of taxation of e-commerce in both the above categories is likely to be a subject of fierce debate. On the one hand, state and local jurisdictions will want to exercise their taxing authorities to avoid threats to their revenue base as store sales are displaced, and on the other, users of the Internet for e-commerce and those jurisdictions who want to promote it will want to minimize taxes. Key issues will revolve around finding ways to avoid an erosion of state and local revenues while also avoiding taxes that impose onerous or discriminatory burdens on e-commerce or that penalize those who conduct transactions over the Internet rather than through traditional channels of commerce. Questions of fairness also will come into play as the "digital divide" separates information "haves" and "have-nots." Higher-income families tend to have computers and on-line connections whereas lower-income families do not. For higher-income families to have a source of tax-free shopping and poorer families not to raises equity issues, unless the latter can be more directly included in the process through increased computer and on-line access.

The U.S. tax debate has international implications because foreign governments might use new, increased, or discriminatory U.S. state taxation of e-commerce as an added argument for their imposing similar taxes. Most foreign governments rely on sales or value-added taxes to a far greater degree for their revenues than does the United States federal government. In this respect they are more like state and local governments, which rely heavily on sales taxes. Roughly 30 percent of Europe's tax revenues come from value-added taxes; government budgets would lose significant sums if a tax-free Internet were to divert sales from stores. Permanent forbearance in collecting taxes on digital e-commerce and on sales of physical goods generated over the Internet is unlikely, as most governments abroad will see this as eroding their tax base.

Questions such as who is to be taxed, what is to be taxed, and where the taxes will be levied will abound. For instance, should a sales tax be applied at the point of sale or at the point of delivery? Should taxation apply only to goods transshipped off-line or to on-line data and services as well? And, if the latter, how would a tax be collected and how would the amount, if any, be determined? An urgent goal should be to reach an international consensus on what kinds of e-commerce should be taxed and on how to tax it in a fair and non-discriminatory way.

Bit Tax.   A particularly troublesome issue was a proposal for a bit tax. As FAR states, "two years ago a number of nations were considering imposing customs duties on digital information sold and distributed via the Internet. The idea of imposing a tax on every bit of information transmitted electronically was gaining momentum" (FAR, p. 7). Support for that idea evaporated after the enormous drawbacks were explained and understood. But the idea has been resurrected in a recent U.N. Development Program Report. Again, it will take a resolute U.S. effort to avoid this going any further.

The U.S. goal internationally is to ensure that no new taxes are imposed that discriminate against Internet commerce; that "existing taxes should be applied in ways that avoid inconsistent national tax jurisdictions and double taxation; and that tax systems treat economically similar transactions equally regardless of whether such transactions occur through electronic means or more conventional channels of commerce" (FAR, p. 13). The U.S. Treasury is leading the work now underway to reach agreement on the principle of tax neutrality between electronic and traditional commerce. This must be a top priority in the next few years: the longer the delay, the greater the risk that discriminatory, administratively burdensome, or inconsistent national tax systems will impede, or Balkanize, the growth of the Internet and e-commerce. Fortunately, the technology and software that facilitate the Internet also can be instrumental in the development of fair and efficient tax collection and of administrative systems that assist taxpayers and tax authorities while avoiding new burdens on e-commerce.

Legal.   While financial issues cluster around taxes, legal issues span a wide variety of topics. The U.S. supports negotiation of a "global uniform commercial code," similar to that which exists among U.S. states; this is needed to facilitate formation and enforcement of international e-commerce contracts (*Framework*, p. 10). In addition, private, voluntary dispute resolution mechanisms are required along with ways to ensure security of contracts and foster digital authentication.

Intellectual property protection requires a legal framework that covers a wide range of issues regarding copyrights, patents, and trademarks. With respect to copyrights, the World Intellectual Property Organization (WIPO) was established to update the Berne Convention. Priorities for international attention will be effective implementation of the 1996 WIPO Copyright Treaty and WIPO Performances and Phonograms Treaty. These treaties are designed to protect intellectual property appearing in digital forms, that is, copyrighted works, musical performances, sound recordings, and computer programs. They also cover movies and other visual material transmitted over the Internet. Such measures are of enormous economic consequence, as worldwide losses from copyright violations approach $20 billion annually and roughly 40 percent of computer software is pirated every year. And governments will need to address equitably the issue of rules regarding the potential liability of network providers in case of piracy.

With respect to patents, the U.S. is seeking agreement with other governments to protect patentable innovations worldwide (FAR, p. 11); stronger enforcement will be needed internationally. An emerging issue requiring international attention is the registration of Internet domain names. The United States aims to "make the governance of the domain name system private and competitive and to create a contractually-based self-regulatory regime that deals with potential conflicts between domain name usage and trademark laws on a global basis" (FAR, p. 12).

The Framework has also identified privacy and security as areas requiring the development of legal protocols. Privacy principles are needed to balance the economic benefits some companies derive from the reuse or sale of information generated by Internet transactions with concerns that such reuse or sale could compromise personal privacy. The U.S. approach builds on the Organization for Economic Cooperation and Development's (OECD) "Guidelines Governing the Protection of Privacy and Transborder Data Flow of Personal Data." It attempts to empower individuals by enabling them to decide whether they want to permit personal data to be disclosed. And it encourages data gatherers to provide information on why the information is being collected and what steps are being taken to ensure privacy. The U.S. goal over the coming months is to "encourage private sector groups to develop and adopt. . . effective codes of conduct, industry developed rules, and technological solutions to protect privacy on the Internet. . . " (FAR, p. 15).

Many leaders of the business community have responded to this challenge. The Online Privacy Alliance, a coalition of nearly ninety companies and associations dedicated to promoting consumer confidence on-line, has played an instrumental role. The earlier mentioned Computer Systems Policy Project (CSPP), as part of a thoughtful report on using new technologies to address public policy challenges posed by the Internet, has put forward creative suggestions for protecting privacy while also protecting the free flow of information. And, a recent Georgetown University study showed that 66 percent of websites and 94 percent of the 100 most popular websites have posted privacy policies to inform users about what information is being collected and how it is being used. As Steve Case, chairman and CEO of America On-line, stated in October 1998, "This new global medium challenges us to create a new model for the industry to govern itself—one that's based on a new partnership among government, industry, and consumers."

With respect to the "security" of e-commerce, the administration's approach recognizes that "strong encryption" (i.e., software that scrambles data so thoroughly that it is virtually impossible to decode without the necessary "key") is essential to build confidence in this medium, but also that it is a "double-edged" sword (*Framework*, p. 20). While the confidentiality of data is enhanced, there can be unintended consequences. Criminals might use strong encryption to deter law-enforcement actions. Terrorists could plot over the Internet without detection by intelligence authorities or police.

The *Framework* identified the goal of working with the OECD to develop international guidelines that address encryption exports. In December 1998, agreement was reached by the United States and 32 other nations to control the export of strong encryption with numerical keys above 64 bytes. Whether limiting sales of encryption technology stronger than 64 bytes will make e-commerce vulnerable to outside taps and thus impair e-commerce is a subject of debate among experts, although most believe that the 64-byte limit is too low and that stronger encryption is needed to protect the security of e-commerce. Until consumers, sellers, and financial institutions have *full confidence* that outsiders cannot tap into their transactions, the potential for e-commerce will not be entirely realized.

Of growing urgency also is the need to protect private and government information, and e-commerce, against cyberattacks. Viruses and other disruptive measures planted by foreign governments, criminals, or terrorists could intercept, cripple, confuse, or disrupt domestic commerce and finance—or government activities and national defense systems. The more economies and societies rely on highly networked, computer-supported communications, the more vulnerable they are to such electronic attacks. Protection against cyberattacks will become a vital issue for U.S. economic and military security in the twenty-first century. It requires high-level attention now and should be a top priority of the G-7 as well as for bilateral talks between the United States and its allies.

Market Access.　Market access issues revolve around provision of services, equipment, and technology. Of the three, provision of services is the most difficult to resolve.

Information infrastructure must be created in a way that encourages its use globally. The Internet can only flourish in a market with low tariffs and taxes on, and high access for, competitive telecom products and services. The administration's *Framework* appropriately stresses that "[g]lobal electronic commerce depends on a modern seamless, global telecommunications network and on the computers and 'information appliances' that connect to it" (*Framework*, p. 22). Trade barriers can restrict the distribution of information technology (IT). National policies often limit foreign or domestic competition in telecommunications services or make them too expensive for customers.

In March 1994, Vice President Gore set forth some basic principles regarding market access at the World Telecommunications Conference in Buenos Aires (*Framework*, p.22). He argued that governmental policies around the world should encourage privatization of telecommunications companies, introduce competition to monopoly phone markets, and create flexible regulatory frameworks with independent regulators. More competition would reduce disincentives for Internet use such as inflated leased line prices to Internet service providers, excessive rates for local phone services, and restrictions on interconnection.

Since 1994, many countries have privatized their national telecommunications companies and attracted foreign partners with world class technology and global linkages. And the United States has used a variety of international fora to translate principles regarding market access into concrete action. The WTO Information Technology Agreement (ITA), which came into force in 1997, and the WTO Basic Telecommunications Agreement, which came into effect in 1998, were important advances. Together these have removed barriers on most types of IT goods and services. Work is now underway to complete an ITA II that would remove tariff and nontariff barriers to trade in remaining technology goods and services. The United States also reached agreement with other members of APEC to develop mutual recognition agreements to eliminate multiple certifications across borders. Similar work is also being done with Latin America. A compelling argument for liberalization is the close correlation between competitive telecom markets and the robustness of a country's Internet environment; for example, Sweden's telecom liberalization has enabled it to become a major European Internet gateway to the United States. For countries to compete in the international race to become hubs for e-commerce traffic, a competitive environment for IT is required.

Standards issues focus on a swirl of considerations: 1) efficiencies brought on by the use of international standards for goods and services; 2) problems created by locking-in obsolescence through inappropriate international or national standards; and 3) difficulties created when standards are used by governments as de facto trade barriers. The United States adheres to the position that "standard setting authorities must be guided by the basic principle that the marketplace, not governments, should set technical standards." Governments, it contends "should refrain from issuing technical standards regulations and instead should rely, to the maximum extent possible, on standards developed by voluntary industry-led consensus-based organizations (at both national and international levels)" (FAR, p. 20).

The EU in its Global Network Ministerial Conference in Bonn in July 1997[5] (hereafter referred to as the Bonn Conference) took a similar view: "standardization is primarily the responsibility of the private sector." It should be "led by the requirements of the market" and "be in line with global standards." But it will be in the U.S. interest to discourage the EU from agreeing internally on standards of its own that could impede access of U.S. companies or systems. That requires, in turn, that the United States reassure the EU that Washington will not set standards aimed at impeding foreign access to the U.S. market. The Transatlantic Business Advisory Committee on Standards represents an ideal forum for a dialogue on this subject.

Content issues present complicated problems as well, involving considerations such as freedom of expression and concerns over censorship. In this case, the administration's position is to call for industry self-regulation and to rely on the availability of "filtering" and "rating" software. Work in the OECD has demonstrated the variety and potential of self-regulatory innovations in this area.

Policy Vision

Importance of Global Development.   The U.S. framework has energized a process that will enable many hundreds of millions of people to harness the power of the emerging global information network—the Internet and the World Wide Web. By pursuing greater openness of economies to flows of information and e-commerce, it will further integrate national markets. And it will lead to the creation of countless new jobs in an explosion of new technologies and the commerce they will facilitate. However, policymakers must also face the fact that many jobs also will be lost as competitive pressures force intense cost-cutting and as sharp alterations in patterns of production, sales, and distribution cause worker displacement, increasing the need for more government supported training and retraining programs. As noted above, the very nature of global production, distribution, sales, advertising, and finance will be permanently and radically changed.

Sharp drops in the cost, speed, and ease of transmitting information and digital services have greatly contributed to the globalization of production, distribution, and finance. In turn, by increasing competitive pressures, the globalization of production, distribution, and finance have added to pressures on business for faster transmission of data and more rapid introduction of new technologies and new business models.

The U.S. framework confirms the enormous economic and social promise of the Internet while recognizing that government's greatest contribution is to let private individuals and businesses lead the way. The era of big government is not only over; in the case of the Internet, it is deemed by the president, quite appropriately, to be downright counterproductive. Government's primary role should be to ensure a framework that promotes competition, protects intellectual property and privacy, prevents fraud, fosters transparency, and facilitates dispute resolution.

But the Internet can only reach its full potential if it can become truly global. The challenge for the United States is to convince other governments of the wisdom of its overall approach and persuade them that their citizens will benefit if they implement policies consistent with it. The time to do that is now—before officials who either do not understand the unique attributes of the Internet or are pressed by revenue, political, cultural, or nationalist considerations impose excessive taxes, regulations, or barriers. Before too long these could become embedded in national laws, budgets, and policies, limiting the Internet and its promise. Avoiding creation of impediments is easier than forcing their removal.

The value of electronic commerce is most readily apparent among the developed countries where information infrastructure and education levels are sufficiently advanced that individuals can readily take advantage of the Internet. Yet, there is a compelling case to be made in the developing world as well. The United States has supported major initiatives to strengthen developing nations' capabilities in this area. In 1998, at the plenary of the ITU in Minneapolis, Vice President Gore urged a government and private sector effort to dramatically increase the number of people in the developing world who participate in the digital economy. In this spirit, George Soros' *Open Society* has created Internet training centers in the New Independent States (NIS), Sun Microsystems has provided support to ninety overseas JAVA training centers, and Cisco has established virtual "network academies" to build competency in network management. In addition, USAID, the Peace Corps, and the U.S. Information Agency (USIA) have embarked on programs to improve the capabilities of citizens of emerging nations to increase their computer and Internet skills and access. Particularly impressive is the U.S. government-led "Leland Initiative" aimed at helping African countries build Internet capacity provided they adjust their policy frameworks to take advantage of the Internet; so far, it has helped establish 40 Internet service providers on that continent. And in June 1994, Vice President Gore announced the United States would provide additional assistance to ten developing countries to expand Internet services.

James Wolfensohn, president of the World Bank, has stressed that both simple technologies, such as radio, and more sophisticated technologies, such as the Internet, must be introduced in developing countries. Without such introduction, an ever-widening gap between the information rich and information poor is likely. Internet availability can create markets anywhere; it can be a conduit for the sale of goods and services from rural areas in developing nations to urban markets in developed countries. As such, the potential use of the Internet will support the global trend toward microentrepreneurship and small business. It also enables large numbers of people in these countries to sell their software capabilities, accounting skills, architectural expertise, and other professional services on a worldwide scale.

If successful, the commerce, information, and entertainment that flow over the Internet, and the international rules needed to protect intellectual property, ensure privacy, and facilitate competition, could form the warp and woof of the fabric that binds societies together in the next century. But this is far from inevitable. First, these societies must see an interest in weaving that fabric.

Values. One of the greatest obstacles to creating an open, global information environment is not so much that governments resist the economic competition that such an environment triggers. It is rather that they are concerned about the social and political implications of free flows of information and ideas across their borders. Deng Xiaopeng described his concerns: "When the door opens, some flies are bound to come in." How the clash of values created by the Internet is resolved will play a major role in determining its long-term economic prospects.

The Internet erodes government control over information. It joins the printing press, radio, television, and the fax in the Pan-

theon of Technologies of Freedom. Of these, it is the least centralized, most international, and least controllable. It promotes freedom from government as the most influential source or arbiter of
information. It also gives citizens access to entertainment or material that governments or other private citizens might find offensive.
Such access raises collateral moral issues, as demonstrated by the
concerns of those in the United States who supported the 1996
Communications Decency Act (signed by the president but struck
down by the Supreme Court) or the similarly motivated 1998 Child
Online Protection Act.

Persuading foreign governments of the virtues of permitting
their citizens to be on-line and connected with millions of people
outside their borders through the Internet and Web cannot be done
only by diplomatic pressure or lofty rhetoric about the virtues of
free markets and electronic commerce. The United States is hampered because its dominant position in software and hardware, its
deregulated telecommunications sector, and its world-class entertainment and content make it suspect in some quarters abroad. But
any suspicions that the United States is only promoting its self-interest can be, and on most occasions have been, dispelled if U.S.
negotiators convince the country in question that U.S. proposals
will produce a win-win outcome from which their citizens benefit
greatly.

To overcome resistance, and shape the new e-commerce environment to achieve maximum openness and minimum regulation and
low barriers, United States government and private sector representatives will need to work with advocates of economic growth
and reform in other countries—businesses, policy visionaries, scientists, entrepreneurs, students and consumer groups as well as
government officials. Businesses in every country need real-time,
on-line information on changes in tastes, cost of materials, consumers' needs, competitors' prices, and financing opportunities
abroad. They will need to be connected to the international information infrastructure to participate in the hundreds of billions of
dollars worth of electronic commerce that will take place early in
this century. The foreign investors that all nations seek to attract
will require connections to global information, the world market
and their headquarters. And consumers need access to the Internet
and Web to receive information on prices, quality, and service to

make sound choices. The strongest argument with governments will be that popular support depends heavily on their ability to create jobs and growth. Restrictions on flows of information and electronic commerce are incompatible with that objective.

Strategy for Global Adoption of the Framework

The United States is actively engaged in an international dialogue to shape the future global environment for electronic commerce with its partners in the WTO, OECD, and three geographic areas: Asia, Latin America, and Europe. With Africa, as noted above, the primary emphasis is on economic and technical assistance.

One key administration goal is to ensure that other nations agree on policies consistent with U.S. objectives. Progress was made at an OECD Ministerial Conference in October 1998. That meeting reinforced an emerging consensus on protection of privacy on the Internet, the need for strong consumer protection, ways to promote and develop the use of authentication devices, and principles for taxation policy for e-commerce. The ministers concluded, inter alia, that "the development of electronic commerce should be led primarily by the private sector in response to market forces and that governments should recognize and reinforce this role." They agreed also that business is leading the way by using "sophisticated tools designed to protect and empower consumers without government over regulation" and "developing transparent procedures for the protection of personal information."[6] Further use of the OECD can promote greater consistency of practice and philosophy.

With respect to Asia, electronic commerce was discussed with APEC leaders in November 1997. While several Asian countries had expressed an interest in learning more about the U.S. approach, a few argued that the United States was pushing its framework too hard without giving them time to study its implications for their respective societies. Issues such as taxation, intellectual property, and regulation of content produced significant division. Modest agreement was reached to continue the discussion and work toward consensus using APEC's e-commerce steering committee.

Such resistance was surprising in that Asian countries have been leaders in investing in information infrastructure. One explanation may be that the "social" dimension of the Internet—greater individual empowerment—has raised fears in Asian countries. In the financial-crisis environment of 1998 little additional progress was made. It will be particularly important to work with China, where the internal Intranet is expanding dramatically. U.S. concerns about intellectual property protection in that country make recent statements by its officials that they are ready to expand cooperation with WIPO and patent offices in other countries particularly noteworthy and follow-up particularly urgent. Agreement and implementation of credible intellectual property rights protection with China could help in other parts of Asia as well.

With respect to Latin America, there have been a variety of efforts to promote the *Framework*. The April 1998 Santiago Summit placed electronic commerce on the hemisphere's economic agenda by setting up a public and private committee to recommend ways to increase and broaden the benefits of e-commerce.[7] Its task was to focus on ways to reduce barriers to electronic commerce as part of the Free Trade Area of the Americas agreement that is targeted for signature by the hemisphere's leaders in 2005. Like Asian countries, the general feeling has been one of interest in the *Framework* but reluctance to proceed expeditiously for fear of not understanding its implications for Latin societies and industries.

As with Asia, the politics of persuading the Latins about the virtues of the *Framework* are entangled with other policy issues. In this hemisphere, strained trade relations, resulting in part from failure of President Clinton to gain fast track authority from Congress, have created an impediment to quick adoption of an electronic commerce framework. Moreover, these broader trade difficulties have made some aspects of the *Framework* a hostage to the competing agendas of trade ministries. Some do not see it as working to their benefit.

The tangle of competing agendas in the hemisphere was seen most clearly in October 1997, when the president traveled to South America. Argentina, with its Communications Ministry taking the lead, appeared ready to sign a joint statement on electronic commerce, adopting the U.S. framework. Days before the president was to arrive, Argentina withdrew its support. Trade and foreign ministries in Argentina and Brazil applied strong pressure on the Argentine Communications Ministry, arguing that more time was needed to study the broader commercial implications of the Clinton Administration's *Framework*. In general, this experience is indicative of the tug of war among trade and telecommunications bureaucracies around the world in defining the domain of electronic commerce.

In contrast to Latin America, the United States has made considerable progress with the EU. On December 5, 1997, the United States and EU capped several months of negotiations with a joint statement on electronic commerce. Most importantly, agreement was reached that global electronic commerce be "essentially market-led and driven by private initiative." An agreed-on workplan identified issues such as copyright and domain names. Also, in setting the boundaries on tariffs, the United States and EU agreed to work toward two key objectives: 1) when goods are ordered electronically and delivered physically, there would be no additional import duties applied in relation to the use of electronic means; and 2) in all other cases relating to electronic commerce, the absence of duties on imports should remain. These elements created momentum toward gaining international support for the U.S. proposal to make digital commerce tariff free at the WTO Ministerial Meeting in May 1998.

In general, the EU and United States see most issues regarding e-commerce in a similar fashion, as their joint statement underscored. The Bonn Conference, for instance, stressed that "regulation should be as light handed and flexible as possible; telecommunication markets should be opened up rapidly to effective competition," and "development of electronic commerce should be market driven" (Bonn Conference Declaration, pp. 1–2). However the EU often feels more comfortable with arrangements that embody a greater degree of bureaucratic intervention than does the United States.

For example, EU regulators believe that Internet service providers should be subject to the same or similar regulatory constraints as telecom service providers. The Internet has flourished largely because it has not been subject to such constraints and to impose them could undermine its vitality. This philosophical/regulatory issue is a major topic in U.S.-EU discussions.

One pending issue between the United States and EU concerns privacy. An EU directive seeks to protect personal information; this includes, inter alia, databases, and networks. Among other things, it prohibits the sharing of data with countries—for example, the United States—that in the EU's eyes do not have "adequate protection of privacy." Each EU member state would be required to establish a "supervisory authority" charged with enforcing the directive. This directive, while not yet implemented against the United States, is indicative of the kinds of international differences that could emerge among Internet regulations.

The United States has a strong interest in working with the EU to reach agreement on e-commerce issues. It is particularly important that this be done before the EU establishes regulations, standards, or practices inconsistent with those of the United States and puts them forward as the basis of a global agreement. Major differences between these two regions could impede the globalization of the Internet and e-commerce. If, on the other hand, as seems more likely, the United States and EU can agree on major issues, they have a good chance of obtaining a broad international consensus in favor of their common position.

Conclusion

We live in the formative period of the Internet and electronic commerce. The Internet-electronic commerce era is only in its infancy. The potential for expansion of the number and range of users, and of the type of business conducted over this new medium, is enormous. The degree to which the full potential of this technology can be realized will depend on how issues such as taxation, market access, regulation, privacy, and security are resolved in the United States and abroad.

The Internet demands new attitudes toward regulation and government policy. As noted earlier, emphasis should be on self-regulation and market-based solutions that engage users, entrepreneurs, and technical experts in an active dialogue and lead to a policy environment that permits them great latitude to advance this new technology and the way businesses and consumers use it. The private sector faces its own challenge—to take advantage of the opportunities presented to it in a way that is economically profitable as well as socially responsible; one key challenge is to produce a high level of public confidence in the protection of privacy and security on the Internet and in e-commerce.

The United States took a significant step forward with the administration's July 1997 *Framework* and the new initiatives of the Working Group on Electronic Commerce in its First Annual Report. But this can be only the beginning. Success will require action across a wide range of fora. The United States will be negotiating on multiple fronts, in multiple organizations, with multiple regions, regarding multiple subjects all at once. Strategic coherence will be essential, along with strong leadership at high levels. The enormous stakes that many individuals, businesses, and groups of citizens have in the success of the Internet, and the need to shape it in its formative years to ensure that it realizes its economic and social potential, make a strong U.S. leadership role a national and international imperative. In light of the breakdown of the trade meetings in Seattle in December 1999, an early test for U.S. leadership will be achieving an extension of the moratorium on tariffs on digital commerce over the Internet.

The future strength of the U.S. economy depends increasingly on its ability to generate new technologies and on access to new and growing foreign markets. Electronic commerce, and the Internet that supports it, are vital to both. Success in using this technology to the fullest will depend not only on getting U.S. policy right at home, including far greater emphasis on education, training, and computer access for lower-income groups so they can participate, but also on convincing citizens and governments of other nations that they can benefit greatly by plugging into the Internet and the commerce it facilitates. Hundreds of billions of dollars of business for small, medium, and large enterprises, millions of jobs, and expanding opportunities for countless consumers in this country and abroad early in the next century will depend directly on how successful the United States will be.

The full integration of the private sector—business groups, entrepreneurs, consumers, and technical experts—in governmental talks designed to promote cooperation on electronic commerce policy is a necessity to ensure that such discussions evolve in a way that encourages continued dynamism in the global expansion of e-commerce. As noted above, for the Free Trade Area of the

Americas initiative, a public and private e-commerce expert committee was set up in July 1998 to make recommendations to trade negotiators. With Europe, the Transatlantic Business Dialogue and Transatlantic Economic Partnership also offer opportunities for public and private cooperation. These efforts and others of a similar nature will be necessary to allow the private sector—the arena in which the greatest use and innovation will occur—to continue to lead.

It is becoming increasingly clear that e-commerce represents a radically new way of conducting business. If its full potential is realized it will be a powerful engine for increasing economic opportunity, growth, and development throughout the world. As in most areas of international economic policy, U.S. leadership will be essential. In shaping the future of international e-commerce and the Internet, the United States will in many ways be shaping the world of the twenty-first century.

Notes

1. *A Framework for Global Electronic Commerce*, The White House, July 1, 1997.

2. For an excellent analysis of how the Internet relates to the U.S. economy as a whole, see "The New Economy Index: Understanding America's Economic Transformation" by Robert D. Atkinson and Randolph H. Court for the Progressive Policy Institute's Technology, Innovation and New Economy Project.

3. *Global Electronic Commerce*, Computer Systems Policy Project, November, 1997.

4. U.S. Government Working Group on Electronic Commerce, First Annual Report, November, 1998.

5. Global Information Networks, Ministerial Conference, Bonn, Germany, July 6–8, 1997.

6. OECD Ottawa Conference on Electronic Commerce, Final News Release, October 13, 1998.

7. *Prosperity and Free Trade at the Santiago Summit*, Press Release, Office of the Press Secretary, The White House, April 19, 1998.

Chapter 15

International Venture Capital

The Role of Start-Up Financing in the United States, Europe, and Asia

Jeffrey D. Nuechterlein

Introduction

The United States solidified its position as the world's most successful entrepreneurial economy during the second half of the twentieth century. U.S. companies have dominated several critical new technologies, including the computer, software, and Internet industries. This article describes and analyzes the role of venture capital as a key source of financing for start-up companies in the United States and compares the success of the U.S. venture capital industry with the venture capital industries in Europe and Asia. In preceding articles, Robert Hormats and David McCurdy have noted the important advisory role that the United States can play in the "networked" economy of the next century. As governments become more aware that venture financing can promote entrepreneurial activity and drive economic growth, they increasingly will look to the United States for guidance in how to support their venture capital sectors.

Venture capitalists provide equity financing to private companies with rapid-growth potential for a variety of purposes, including product development, production, marketing, sales, and expansion. In essence, venture capital is high-risk, high-reward finance designed for young companies that have different asset structures, cash flows, and growth rates than mature companies. Companies backed by venture capital historically have produced a disproportionate share of new jobs, particularly well paid and highly skilled jobs. Moreover, U.S. venture capital-backed companies generate about three times more export sales per dollar of equity than more established companies and are a key source of research and development (R&D) spending and applied technological innovation. Consequently, governments are increasingly aware that venture capital is an important source of economic growth and a means of developing targeted sectors of the economy.

U.S. venture capitalists pioneered and continue to dominate the venture capital business. In 1998, U.S. venture capitalists again raised and had more capital under management than venture capitalists in any other region of the world. While European and Asian venture capitalists have an increasing amount of capital under management, much of this capital is dedicated to buyouts of established companies, as opposed to start-up and expansion financing. In addition, most venture capital investments in Europe and Asia are in safer, more mature, and less dynamic companies than venture-financed firms in the United States. In fact, most European and Asian countries have had relatively little success in early-stage venture capital. The U.S. lead in venture financing for start-up companies partly explains the U.S. dominance in developing many new technologies, including software (nine of the top ten companies are American) and the Internet.

Background

Venture capital is defined herein as early and expansion-stage financing, as opposed to financing for buyouts (the outright purchase of a company, usually with borrowed funds) and workouts (the turnaround of a troubled company). Venture capitalists provide equity financing rather than loans to young companies in exchange for ownership of part of the company. As a result, entrepreneurs avoid interest payments and can more quickly achieve profitability. Entrepreneurs seeking venture financing typically prepare a business plan that provides a description of the product and the market, financial statements and projections, as well as the background of key managers and directors. Venture capitalists assess the quality of the management team and the competitive position and financial prospects of the company. On average, venture capitalists invest in only about 1 percent of the opportunities presented. Once they invest, venture capitalists actively work with the company's management by contributing their business experience and industry knowledge gained from helping other young companies.[1]

During the first few years, before significant revenues are generated, about two-thirds of the average venture capital-backed company's total equity is supplied by venture financing. The average U.S. venture-backed company raises about $16 million of venture capital during its first five years.[2] Start-ups typically use initial financing to develop a prototype and fund marketing and sales. Later financing allows companies to grow more quickly than proceeds from sales alone would allow. At this point, the company could be ready to go public, putting financing in the market's hands and allowing venture capitalists to realize a return on their investment.

In the United States, however, it is as common for a venture capitalist to sell a start-up to another firm as to offer it to the public through an initial public offering. For example, 101 venture-backed firms were sold to other companies in 1996, 152 were sold in 1997, and 190 were sold in 1998. By contrast, 275 venture-backed firms went public in 1996, 136 went public in 1997, and 77 went public in 1998.[3] In Europe, which lacks a liquid, transnational stock market on a par with the U.S. National Association of Securities Dealers Automated Quotation (NASDAQ) market and which has an underdeveloped equity culture, venture-backed companies are more likely to be acquired by another company than sold to the public through an initial public offering. The time from start-up to an initial public offering varies considerably from country to country. In the United States, the average time is about five years, whereas in Japan the average has been about 30 years because of regulations that make if difficult for young companies to list on the Tokyo Stock Exchange.[4]

In addition to the institutional venture capital market analyzed in this article, there are approximately 250,000 so-called "angel" investors (generally wealthy individuals) in the United States who invest about $20 billion in 30,000 companies annually. Angel investors generally operate as individuals, but some angels meet informally in groups to consider investments. The best known group of angel investors is the Band of Angels, comprised of more than 100 Silicon Valley high-tech executives who meet monthly to hear business presentations and make investments. The Band of Angels has invested $45 million in 86 companies over the last four years with a rate of return of 30 percent.[5]

Venture Capital in the United States

U.S. venture capitalists pioneered the venture capital business immediately after World War II, roughly three decades before venture capital grew to a significant size in any other country. Milestones in the development of venture capital in the United States include the formation in 1946 of American Research and Development (ARD)—the first publicly traded company specializing in equity investing in start-up companies—which had some spectacular early successes, particularly on the $70,000 it invested in 1957 for a 77 percent equity stake in the Digital Equipment Corporation that produced a 5,000-fold return over 14 years.[6] The founders of ARD believed that scientists at the Massachusetts Institute of Technology (MIT) and elsewhere who had developed promising new technologies during the war years needed financing and hands-on assistance to successfully commercialize their research.

In 1958, Congress—reacting in part to a 1957 Federal Reserve Bank study that revealed a lack of equity capital for new companies—enacted the Small Business Investment Company (SBIC) Act. SBICs are private corporations licensed by the Small Business Administration (SBA) to provide venture capital to new companies. SBICs can lever their private capital with loans from, or guaranteed by, the SBA; the additional funds made available through SBA guarantees may equal two to three times the invested private capital. By 1963, the 692 SBICs licensed by the SBA managed $464 million of private capital and included 47 publicly owned SBICs that raised $350 million through public offerings. By comparison, ARD raised only $7.4 million in its first 13 years.[7] In the 1960s and 1970s, SBICs accounted for as much as one-third of venture financing, but by 1990 accounted for less than 5 percent of such financing.

After years of mismanagement and abuse, culminating in numerous SBICs going bankrupt between 1986 and 1992, Congress restructured the SBIC program by enacting the Small Business Equity Enhancement Act of 1992 and its 1994 implementing legislation. In addition to correcting a number of structural problems in the program, the 1992 Act enables SBICs to defer paying the accrued costs on their debenture leverage until the SBICs realize sufficient capital gains and income to achieve cumulative profitability. As a result of this legislation, the licensing of new SBICs has increased dramatically. Between 1994 and 1998, 138 new SBICs were licensed with initial private capital of $1.8 billion. Combined with additions to the private capital of existing SBICs, this resulted in a doubling of private capital in the program from $2.3 billion in 1993 to $5.8 billion in 1998. In 1997, SBICs accounted for 45 percent of the total number of venture financings and 20 percent of the total dollar volume of venture financings in the United States. By mid-1998, there were 242 active regular SBICs and 78 Specialized SBICs (which finance businesses owned by socially or economically disadvantaged persons). Of the regular SBICs, 83 are owned by banks, which are limited by banking regulations in their ability to make large equity investments except through an SBIC subsidiary. Bank-owned SBICs represent 63 percent of the private capital in the program and generally do not use SBA-guaranteed leverage. Companies that trace their initial financing to SBICs include America Online, Apple, Federal Express, and Intel.[8]

In addition to the creation of the SBIC program, the late 1950s and the 1960s also saw the establishment of the first venture capital limited partnerships where professional venture capital managers acting as general partners invest funds on behalf of limited partners, which are commonly institutional investors like pension funds. Limited partners are so-called because their liability extends only to the capital they contribute. Limited partnerships typically have a 10-year life, during which the limited partners forgo nearly all control over the management of the partnership. Limited partnerships now manage about 80 percent of all private equity investments.

Technology companies like AT&T, Intel, Lucent, Microsoft, and Xerox also are large providers of venture capital. Intel has one of Silicon Valley's largest venture funds. It has invested $300 million in more than 100 companies and recently raised a $300 million fund. Intel targets start-ups that are developing new applications for faster Intel semiconductors. In addition to its direct investments, Microsoft is investing $5 million to $10 million in several venture capital funds, partly to track new technologies and partly to help potential partners grow. Large technology companies also are an important birthing ground for new companies. For example, Lucent formed a new ventures group in 1997 to nurture an assortment of products that are not focused on Lucent's core telecommunications business. In 1989, Xerox created an in-house venture-financing arm that incubates and capitalizes on Xerox's non-core research and development discoveries.[9]

U.S. venture capital funds grew markedly in the 1980s, in part because of six key legislative acts between 1978 and 1981: the Revenue Act of 1978, which reduced the capital gains tax rate from 49.5 percent to 28 percent; the 1981 Economic Recovery Tax Act, which further reduced the capital gains rate to 20 percent; 1979 and 1980 legislation that allows pension funds to invest in private equity; the 1980 Small Business Investment Incentive Act, which reduced the regulatory burden on venture capitalists; and the 1981 Incentive Stock Option Act, which allows holders of stock options to defer tax liability to the date when the stocks are sold rather than the date when the options are exercised. The U.S. venture capital industry also profited enormously from the boom in personal computers in the 1980s. Between 1980 and 1990, the value of the personal computer industry grew from virtually zero to $100 billion. More than 70 percent of these firms were venture-backed.[10] Cisco, Compaq, Cray, Genentech, Lotus, Microsoft, Netscape, Starbucks, and Sun Microsystems are some of the well-known U.S. companies nurtured by venture capital.

U.S. venture capitalists raise about three times more venture funding each year than those in any other country. In 1997, U.S. venture capitalists raised more than $10 billion (up from $4.4 billion in 1995 and $7.5 billion in 1996), largely from pension funds (55 percent), corporations (13 percent), and endowments and foundations (10 percent) flush with capital from the rapid increase in the S&P 500 over the last few years.[11] U.S. venture capitalists raised an additional $25 billion in 1998 (largely from pension funds—60 percent) and $9.5 billion during the first six months of 1999.[12] Investors have increased their allocations to venture capital in part because of historical figures showing average annual returns of approximately 20 percent for venture capital investments compared to 11 percent for the S&P 500.[13] As a result of 1998's inflow, net capital under management by U.S. venture capital firms increased to about $70 billion, up from $3 billion in 1980. Moreover, the internal rate of return of venture capital investments historically is considerably higher in the United States (approximately 20 percent) than elsewhere in the world (e.g. Britain and France where returns have averaged about 10 percent).[14]

U.S. venture capitalists invested a record $14 billion in nearly 3,000 companies in 1998, compared to $12 billion in 1997, $10 billion in 1996, and $8 billion in 1995. The average size of each financing in 1998 was $5 million. There was more venture capital invested in California ($5.8 billion), Massachusetts ($1.7 billion), and Texas ($800 million) than in all of Europe. Venture capital investments in the United States, unlike in Europe and Asia, are highly concentrated in technology. In 1997, U.S. software companies captured 22 percent of the total invested, networking and communications companies 19 percent, Internet companies 18 percent (up from just 2 percent in 1994), healthcare services 9 percent, biotechnology 8 percent, and medical devices 6 percent. Retailing and consumer products companies combined accounted for only 8.8 percent of the total.[15] U.S. venture capitalists invested an additional $11.4 billion during the first six months of 1999. During the second quarter of 1999 alone, U.S. venture capitalists invested $6.8 billion; 56 percent of that amount went to Internet companies.[16]

The United States has the world's most successful venture capital industry in large part because of a strong entrepreneurial culture that allows managers to take substantial ownership positions in their companies. U.S. managers are much more likely than their European and Asian counterparts to join a rapidly growing start-up that cannot afford to pay large salaries but can attract top talent by offering equity ownership through generous stock option grants.[17] European and Asian managers, on the other hand, generally prefer the security of large corporations and are unlikely to have equity interests in their companies. In fact, many European and Asian countries have severely restricted or prohibited the use of stock options.

The United States also has the most competitive market in the world, which produces excellent managers and gives U.S. companies a significant advantage in increasingly competitive international markets. In addition, the United States, unlike many European and Asian countries, has well-developed and liquid stock markets, which are critical for a vibrant venture capital sector because venture investors and entrepreneurs must have an exit mechanism for realizing capital gains. The U.S. venture capital industry also benefits from ready access to institutional financing, a relatively flexible labor market that allows companies to hire and fire workers more easily than can European and Asian companies, bankruptcy laws that do not prohibit failed entrepreneurs from starting another company, a tax system that generally allows entrepreneurs to retain a higher percentage of profits than their European and Asian counterparts, strong intellectual property rights protection, the world's preeminent business schools,[18] and a merit-oriented business culture that directs capital to good ideas usually without regard to the entrepreneur's pedigree.

U.S. entrepreneurs also have benefited enormously from relatively close links among universities, government laboratories, and private companies. The transfer of research and development and technology innovations from research universities (e.g. Stanford and MIT) and government laboratories (e.g. Oak Ridge in Tennessee)[19] to the private sector has led to clusters of entrepreneurial companies and venture capitalists in areas like Silicon Valley in Northern California, the Route 128 corridor in Boston, the Research Triangle Park in Raleigh-Durham, North Carolina, northern Virginia, and Austin, Texas where much of the development of the semiconductor, software, computer, biotech, and Internet industries has occurred. While there are some examples of universities in other countries transferring technology research to the private sector (e.g. the relationship between Cambridge University and the 1,000 high-technology companies in Silicon Fen in England), there generally is little cooperation between universities and the private sector in Europe and Asia. Unlike U.S. universities, most European and Asian universities do not encourage the commercialization of research, focus more on theory and less on applied innovation, and rarely recruit from the private sector to fill academic positions.

Venture Capital in Europe

Venture capital did not become a significant source of financing in Europe until the 1980s. In the last few years, however, the amount of venture capital under management has grown steadily. By 1997, the approximately 500 European venture capital firms had made cumulative investments of about $30 billion in 20,000 companies.[20] The level of venture capital financing in Europe, however, would need to be three or four times its current level for venture capital as a percentage of the region's GDP to match the equivalent ratio in the United States. Baan, British Biotech, Business Objects, Filofax, Parker Pen, and Zodiac are some of the well-known European companies nurtured by venture capital.

For a number of reasons the greater use of venture capital in Europe over the last few years has not resulted in the same kind of dynamic start-ups that venture capitalists in the United States have helped nurture.

First, much of what is classified as venture capital in Europe (and Asia) is dedicated to buyouts and workouts, as opposed to start-up and expansion financing. More than half of Europe's $11.5 billion in venture financing in 1997 went to management buyouts as opposed to start-up or expansion funding.[21] Less than 10 percent of Europe's venture financing is invested in start-ups, compared to about 37 percent in the United States, in large part because investments in European start-ups have produced low rates of return.[22] In 1997, European venture capitalists invested about $840 million in early stage companies, whereas U.S. venture capitalists invested $2.5 billion in such companies.[23]

Second, venture capitalists in Europe tend to fund safer, more mature, and less dynamic companies than venture capitalists in the United States. In 1995 and 1996, European venture capitalists allocated only about 2 percent of their investments to biotechnology firms and less than 20 percent to various technology sectors, including communications, computer, and electronics firms.[24] In 1996, U.S. venture capitalists invested 12 times more funds in technology companies than their European counterparts.[25] In fact, a larger percentage of venture financing in Europe goes to consumer-related industries than to technology companies. In Europe as a whole, less than 10 percent of venture financing is invested in technology companies. By comparison, in 1997, U.S. venture capitalists invested more than 70 percent of their funds in technology-based companies and only 9 percent in retailing and consumer products companies.

Compared to their U.S. counterparts, most European institutional investors (outside of Britain and the Netherlands) are much more wary of equity investments in start-up firms and prefer the relative safety of fixed income investments. In addition, while the United States has allowed pension funds to invest in private equity since 1979, some European and Asian countries prohibit pension funds from participating in the private equity market. Consequently, pension funds supply more than 50 percent of venture capital raised in the United States compared to 25 percent in Europe (up from 16 percent in 1993) and 5 percent in Japan. Because many European countries allow banks to lend money and make equity investments in the same company, banks are still the leading source (26 percent) of venture capital funding in Europe. The other main sources of venture capital funding in Europe are insurance companies (16.4 percent) and corporations (11.3 percent).[26] In the United States, banks account for a much smaller percentage of venture capital financing because U.S. banking laws (e.g. the Glass-Steagall Act) have imposed more restrictions on banks making equity investments in companies in their loan portfolios. Banks, particularly in Europe, however, are much more likely than venture capitalists to invest in relatively safe investments and normally do not bring the type of expertise needed to nurture young entrepreneurial companies.

Germany

In Germany, the commercial banks, insurance companies, and venture capital firms that invest in start-ups historically have had limited success. The total amount of venture capital that has been invested in Germany is about $4 billion, roughly equivalent to the amount of venture capital invested in the United States in the second quarter of 1998 alone.[27] About $300 million (7 percent) of this total is invested in start-ups and less than 15 percent is invested in high-technology companies (although the amount of venture capital provided to technology start-ups is growing rapidly).[28] German banks provide 58 percent of all venture financing and favor large investments in expansion stage companies.[29] Techno Venture Management, established in 1984 as an offshoot of Siemens, is Germany's oldest venture capital firm, while Deutsche Bank's venture capital arm is Germany's largest provider of venture financing.

The primary problems facing German entrepreneurs have been excessive government regulation, relatively high capital gains taxes, high labor costs, inflexible labor laws (supported by powerful labor unions) that limit the ability to hire and fire employees and a general political concern with protecting workers from layoffs, inadequate exit mechanisms for investors, a lack of management talent to nurture early stage companies, a dearth of employees willing to leave the safety of well paid jobs with large German companies to join a start-up (in part because of the stigma associated with failure in Germany), and an underdeveloped entrepreneurial culture. In part because of these problems, as well as the German preference for bonds over stocks, Germany has less than half the number of quoted companies as Great Britain. Numerous German entrepreneurs have moved their high-tech ventures to the United States to escape Germany's taxation system and to be closer to potential investors and partners.

The German government and business sector have recognized the importance of encouraging entrepreneurial activity and recently have taken steps to bolster support for start-ups. For example, Deutsche Börse, which runs the Frankfurt securities exchanges, established the Neuer Markt in March 1997 to assist young companies in raising capital and to provide venture capitalists with an effective exit route. By August 1999, nearly 150 companies had listed on the exchange.[30] (By comparison, U.S. stock exchanges list approximately 1,500 high-technology companies with a market capitalization twice that of all non-U.S. high-technology companies combined.) Despite the establishment of the Neuer Markt, German venture capitalists still are twice as likely to sell a portfolio company to another company as to offer it to the public through an initial public offering.

In addition, Deutsche Ausgleichsbank, a government-owned bank that is one of the largest start-up financiers in Germany, sponsors the Technology Participation Society that helps finance young technology companies. The German government's BioRegio initiative, begun in 1995, appropriated $90 million to three winning areas (Munich, Rheinland, and Rhein-Neckar-Dreieck) to help develop a more robust biotechnology industry. German banks and investors have agreed to invest an additional $900 million in the initiative over the next five years.[31] On the local level, the Bavarian government has begun funding scientific research to aid the region's growing information technology and biotech sectors.[32] SAP, the German enterprise software maker that is one of the world's largest software companies, is developing a German venture capital arm and recently established four professorships in entrepreneurial studies at German universities. In part because of these developments, Germany's venture capital sector is growing rapidly.

France

France has some of the right elements for a strong venture capital industry, including a strong technology base, an entrepreneurial culture exemplified by a large number of small companies, and a new small company stock market (Le Nouveau Marché).[33] The largest concentration of high-technology companies in France is in Sophia Antipolis, a science park on the Côte d'Azur, which has 1,050 companies with 16,000 employees.[34]

Total venture investments in France, however, are small. In 1996, French venture capitalists invested only about $500 million, less than $200 million of which went to start-ups.[35] In 1997, French venture capitalists invested only about $100 million in start-ups.[36] Banks and corporations provide 34.9 percent and 16.6 percent of venture financing in France, respectively, whereas insurance companies and pension funds provide 3.4 percent and 2.6 percent, respectively.[37]

The primary problems facing the French venture capital industry are relatively poor performance records, the absence of sizable pension funds, the inability of France's financial system to channel significant funds into private equity, relatively high capital gains taxes, a dearth of skilled management teams willing to join start-

ups, and a highly regulated labor market weighed down with social charges.[38] In part because of these problems, nearly 50 French
companies recently have moved or committed to move to Great
Britain, which has a more welcoming business climate.[39]

Great Britain

Great Britain has made the most progress among European countries in stimulating venture capital investments, in part because of
government reforms in the 1980s and 1990s that reduced high tax
rates, promoted more flexible labor markets, and streamlined burdensome regulations that had disproportionately disadvantaged
small companies. In addition, Britain has the most liquid stock
markets in Europe. In 1995, the London Stock Exchange established the Alternative Investment Market in London, which is designed specifically for small growth companies. By 1999, more
than 300 companies had listed on the exchange.[40] Unlike France
and Germany, British pension funds are the dominant source (32.8
percent) of venture financing, whereas insurance companies and
corporations provide 20.6 percent and 16.0 percent, respectively.[41]

In 1996, Britain, with less than half the population, attracted
twice as much venture capital as France and Germany combined;
Britain accounted for 44 percent of total European investment
whereas France and Germany accounted for 12 percent and 10 percent, respectively.[42] In 1997, British venture capital firms invested
about $265 million in 219 early stage companies (whereas U.S. ven-
ture capitalists invested $2.5 billion in more than 700 early stage
companies).[43] British venture capitalists invest about 5 percent of
their funds in start-ups and about 16 percent in technology companies.[44] Although small by U.S. standards, Britain is the second-
largest high-technology venture capital market in the world after
the United States. Britain also has Europe's largest biotechnology
industry, with more than 180 companies, about twice the size of the
biotech sectors in France and Germany.[45] More than any other
country in Europe or Asia, Britain offers an experienced array of
entrepreneurial managers who are available for new start-ups as
their older venture-backed companies mature.[46]

One of the centers of Britain's technology venture boom is Cambridge Science Park ("Silicon Fen") in and around Cambridge,

which is home to about 1,000 high-technology companies that employ 30,000 people and produce more than $3 billion in annual revenues. (By comparison, Silicon Valley's high-tech workforce numbers 480,000 and its exports are 20 times larger than Silicon Fen's.)[47] In 1997, Microsoft established an $80 million research laboratory in Cambridge to take advantage of Cambridge University's strengths in the sciences and its long history of collaborating with industry. Microsoft's links with Cambridge are particularly close—the head of the University's computer laboratory also heads the Microsoft facility. (The Gates Foundation also donated $20 million to the University's computer science department and Microsoft committed $8 million—plus an additional $8 million for possible co-investments—to a Cambridge and London-based venture capital fund managed by Amadeus Capital Partners.)[48] Cambridge University recently established a management school, after years of ambivalence about business as an academic discipline, and has announced that it will establish a school of entrepreneurship modeled on the entrepreneurship program at the Massachusetts Institute of Technology.

A second concentration of venture-backed companies in Britain is in Oxford and the Thames Valley (the M4 corridor), west of London. The Oxford Science Park (established in 1991, 21 years after Cambridge's) and the Oxfordshire region generally are home to 730 high-technology companies that employ about 26,400 people. In addition, eight of the top 10 U.S. information technology companies have their British or European headquarters in the Thames Valley and the other two, Apple and Sun Microsystems, are on the outskirts of the region. Numerous other electronics, telecommunications, and biotechnology companies also are based in the Valley. For many years, a large percentage of Oxford University academics were hostile to the commercialization of research and, like many Cambridge academics, questioned whether business should be part of the academic curriculum. Nevertheless, Oxford established a graduate business school in the 1980s and, after a fierce debate, recently established an undergraduate business school. In addition, Oxford formed Isis Innovation in 1988 to help the university's 2,500 funded researchers and 2,000 doctoral candidates in science and medicine commercialize their research. Since its inception, Isis Innovation has filed 200 patents, completed 50 licensing deals, and attracted venture capital to help establish several biotechnology companies that employ intellectual property developed in the university's laboratories.[49]

European Small-Company Stock Markets

Many European countries have an imbalance between venture capital investments and divestments, indicating that while there is a large supply of venture capital, the exit mechanisms for these investments have been insufficient. Efficient exit mechanisms are critical for a vibrant venture capital sector because venture investors and entrepreneurs must have a mechanism for realizing capital gains. One reason for the imbalance in Europe is that, until 1996, European venture capitalists were hampered by the lack of a liquid, transnational stock market designed for start-up firms on a par with the U.S. NASDAQ market.

Although a number of European countries (Belgium, Britain, Denmark, France, Germany, Ireland, Italy, and the Netherlands) established stock markets in the 1980s and 1990s that are designed to broaden the supply of capital to small companies that do not meet the requirements of the primary markets, these small-company markets have not lived up to expectations for a number of reasons. First, unlike in the United States and Japan, the European small-company markets are under the same management as the primary markets. In general, managers of the European markets are more interested in promoting the primary markets than the secondary markets. Second, European companies generally seek to move their listings to the primary markets as soon as possible (unlike in the United States where many large companies—e.g. Cisco, Dell, Intel, and Microsoft—have retained their listings on NASDAQ). Third, European institutional investors are much less likely to have significant holdings of small-capitalization stocks than U.S. institutional investors, which has depressed the liquidity of the small-company markets. While some European venture-backed companies are listed on NASDAQ, such cross-border offerings represent only a small percentage of European small companies. For all these reasons, a venture-backed company in Europe is much more likely to be acquired by another company than sold to the public through an initial public offering (the preferred exit mechanism in the United States and Japan).

In September 1996, Europe created the European Association of Securities Dealers Automated Quotation (EASDAQ) market, which is intended to make it much easier for European entrepreneurs and venture capitalists to offer start-up companies to the public. EASDAQ, modeled on NASDAQ, seeks to bring together high-growth companies, their investors, and financial intermediaries into one highly liquid, well-regulated, pan-European stock market. Companies listed on EASDAQ have direct access to, and an increased profile with, a wider range of capital sources than can be found in any one national stock market in Europe. Based in Brussels, EASDAQ operates across 14 European countries and is independent of all other European stock markets. EASDAQ is off to a slow start—by August 1999, it had attracted only 49 companies with a combined market capitalization of $21 billion.[50]

EASDAQ's competition in the effort to create a European version of NASDAQ is the EURO.NM market, also created in 1996 to allow cross-border trading by the five small company markets in Amsterdam, Brussels, Frankfurt, Milan, and Paris. The small company markets in Denmark, Italy, Sweden, and Switzerland are scheduled to join the EURO.NM market in 1999. EURO.NM has more than 150 listed companies with a combined market capitalization of more than $30 billion.[51] The companies listed on EASDAQ, however, are generally larger and face tougher listing and disclosure requirements, and the exchange has a fast-track trading link with NASDAQ, all of which appeals to institutional investors. In choosing whether to list on EASDAQ or EURO.NM, nationality continues to plays a role, which illustrates one of the key issues that must be overcome before Europe succeeds in creating a single stock market to complement a single European currency.[52]

Venture Capital in Asia

The amount of venture financing in Asia has grown steadily in the 1980s and 1990s. By late 1997, Asia's 800 venture capital firms (up from 50 in 1989) had $38 billion under management (up from $21 billion in 1991). Asian venture capitalists invested $5.5 billion in

1996; of that total, Japanese venture capitalists invested about $1.4 billion. By comparison, U.S. venture capitalists invested nearly $4 billion in Silicon Valley alone in 1997. Historically, Japan has been the most popular destination for venture capital with about two-thirds of the total. Excluding Japan, Korea (17 percent), Hong Kong (11 percent), and Singapore (8 percent) are the largest recipients of venture financing. Funds are distributed across the spectrum with industrial products (17 percent), consumer-related products (16 percent), and other manufacturing industries (15 percent) attracting the most capital. In 1996, more than 18,000 Asian companies had venture capital backing.[53]

As is the case in Europe, however, much of what is classified as venture capital in Asia is either long-term debt or is dedicated to later-stage financing, as opposed to start-up financing. About 70 percent of Asia's venture capital goes to later-stage financing, while only 21 percent is invested in start-ups.[54] The latter number is misleading, however, because the start-up category in Asia includes new ventures incorporating long-standing state or family-run businesses. By comparison, about 37 percent of all venture financing in the United States is dedicated to actual start-ups. Asian venture capitalists are much more likely to invest in older, more mature companies than U.S. venture capitalists. For example, more than 60 percent of venture investments made by Nippon Investment & Finance Company, an established venture capital company, are made in companies 10 years old or older.[55]

Unlike the United States, three of the largest sources of venture capital in Asia are corporations (41 percent), banks (16 percent), and government agencies (7 percent).[56] Non-Asians are among the largest venture investors in the region—about 25 percent of all venture capital invested in Asia is sourced from outside the region. Excluding Japan (which historically has not readily welcomed foreign venture capital), about 50 percent of Asian venture capital is raised locally, 35 percent is raised outside Asia, and 15 percent is raised in other Asian countries.[57] U.S. venture capitalists, and the pension and other large funds that back them, are among the largest investors backing Asian entrepreneurs. U.S. investors have been attracted to Asia because of the high growth rates across the region in the 1990s and because returns on investment in the U.S. private equity market are coming under pressure as competition for deals among U.S. venture capitalists drives up valuations.

Japan

In Japan, the largest sources of venture capital are corporations (46 percent), banks (30 percent), and insurance companies (10 percent).[58] Japanese venture capital firms allocate a much smaller share of funds to technology companies (35 percent) than do U.S. venture capitalists (70 percent). Japan's largest venture capital firm is the Japan Associated Finance Company (JAFCO), a publicly-traded company founded in 1973 and associated with the Nomura Securities house. JAFCO has made more than 1,800 investments worldwide and its portfolio companies represent about 30 percent of the initial public offerings in Japan. It has offices throughout Japan, as well as in eight other Asian countries, Britain, and the United States. JAFCO America has $265 million under management and has made more than 100 investments, including investments in 30 companies that have gone public.[59]

Most Japanese venture capital firms are subsidiaries of large corporations. For example, in 1996, Toyota Motor Corporation created one of Japan's largest venture capital funds (nearly $400 million) to finance companies inside and outside the Toyota keiretsu. Like most Japanese corporations, Toyota's primary goal for its venture capital unit is not capital gains, but rather the development of new technologies.[60] In 1996, Nippon Telephone and Telegraph, Nippon Life Insurance, Sanyo, and several other large corporations created Nippon Venture Capital Company; to date, it has invested $64 million in 122 companies inside and outside of Japan.[61] Several other Japanese corporations recently established venture capital arms, including Mitsui and Mitsubishi.

Similarly, Japanese companies—seeking high-technology R&D and partners to facilitate their overseas expansion—have invested substantial amounts of venture capital abroad, particularly in the United States and, to a lesser extent, in Europe. This investment includes both direct investment in portfolio companies and indirect investment through U.S. venture capital firms. For most venture capital firms associated with Japanese corporations, exposure to new technologies takes precedence over financial returns.

The Japanese government, like many governments in Asia, continues to work closely with the private sector to formulate business strategy. Japan's reaction to the growth of the Internet is illustrative. Although U.S. government researchers created the Internet in the 1960s to enable scientists around the country to communicate with each other, U.S. entrepreneurs—and the venture capitalists that have rushed to fund them—are responsible for the tremendous growth in Internet services over the last few years. What has most impressed Japan's Ministry of International Trade and Industry (MITI), however, is the U.S. government's initial role in creating the Internet. Consequently, the Japanese government's emphasis has been on funding a government-industry partnership to integrate the operations of Japanese manufacturing facilities worldwide, an initiative that MITI says it eventually will turn over to the private sector.

Although Japan has the largest venture capital market in Asia, a venture capital industry has never developed in Japan on a par with the United States for numerous reasons. First, Japan's Ministry of Finance long has maintained tight regulation of financial markets, which limits the ability of Japanese entrepreneurs to obtain capital, and has prohibited Japanese pension funds from investing in venture capital funds. Second, Japanese banks are reluctant to lend to new businesses, in part because bank lending generally is contingent on ownership of land as collateral and few entrepreneurs can afford Japan's high-priced real estate. Third, Japanese entrepreneurs confront a high tax rate that can take 50 percent of taxable income. Fourth, Japan's culture has hindered the development of an entrepreneurial sector backed by venture capital. It is often said that the nail that sticks out gets hammered down in Japan.

The Japanese emphasis on order, conformity, and seniority contrasts with the U.S. tradition of supporting individualism and limited government power. Japan has spent years nurturing and protecting big manufacturing exporters rather than emulating the entrepreneurial spirit that has driven the high-technology boom in Silicon Valley. Although Japan has had some entrepreneurial heroes—like Soichiro Honda, who created Honda Motor Company, and Akio Morita, who co-founded Sony Corporation—most emerged in the years just after WW II. The current environment is not designed to foster entrepreneurial activity. Because most Japanese favor lifetime employment at major companies like Sony or a major bank and view jobs at start-ups as second rate, it is difficult for entrepreneurs to attract good management. Americans, on the other hand, are generally more willing to accept risk and tolerate career shifts. The result is that the United States, with about twice the population of Japan, produces more than seven times as many new companies each year as Japan.[62]

The Japanese government, however, recently has taken a number of significant steps to increase support for Japanese entrepreneurs. For example, in 1991, Japan established JASDAQ, a stock market designed for start-up firms that is modeled on NASDAQ. In 1995, Japan approved the use of stock options and, in 1997, amended tax laws to make options more attractive to employees at Japanese start-ups. As a result, more than 160 Japanese companies, including Sony, have adopted stock option plans (although most of the plans account for only a small fraction of a worker's earnings).[63] U.S. start-ups, which often have limited cash flow and are forced to pay low salaries to employees, have used stock options for years to attract and retain talented managers, software engineers, and scientists.

In addition, MITI recently created a program that provides grants of up to $500,000 to start-ups and another program that provides loan guarantees.[64] In the last several years, most other Japanese government ministries, as well as local and regional governments, have also adopted programs to encourage Japanese entrepreneurs, including setting up venture-business incubator programs that bring capital, facilities, and entrepreneurs together. The Japanese venture incubators are modeled in part on the 300 venture incubators that U.S. states have established with mixed success. Moreover, MITI recently rescinded the law prohibiting Japanese venture capitalists from serving on and appointing others to the boards of their portfolio companies. MITI and the Finance Ministry also are drafting a limited liability law (similar to that which exists in the United States) that would enable pension funds and other institutional investors to invest in venture capital funds by providing some protection from poor investments.

Recognizing the important role that university research has had in advancing U.S. entrepreneurial activity, the Japanese Ministry of

Education and Science and MITI recently began funding more than 20 so-called venture business laboratories in Japan's largest universities through the Original Industrial Technology R&D Promotion Program, which is designed to promote original research and development that will seed new industries and train new researchers. Significantly, MITI broke with its long-standing practice of unilaterally identifying important new technologies for research and development and now openly solicits proposals for university research projects and encourages researchers to compete for funding.[65]

Despite these efforts by the Japanese government, venture capital activity recently has been declining in Japan. The Japanese recession and the instability of the financial system have led to the failure of numerous venture-backed businesses. Unlike the United States, where venture capitalists increased investments from $8 billion in 1995 to $10 billion in 1996, Japanese venture investments were flat, $1.4 billion in both years.[66]

China

Although Japan accounts for the majority of venture capital activity in Asia, venture investments have been increasing in a number of other Asian nations. For example, a number of Chinese, Asian, and U.S. venture funds have been investing in China over the last several years, primarily in provinces on the coast and near Hong Kong. China has some of the right elements for a strong venture capital industry, including an entrepreneurial culture (exemplified by Chinese living not just in China, but in Taiwan, Indonesia, and numerous other Asian countries),[67] as well as an educational system that directs large numbers of Chinese students to programs in engineering and business at Chinese and U.S. universities.

Nevertheless, venture investors face an array of obstacles in China, in large part because of decades of communist policies that have curtailed entrepreneurial activity. A key difficulty is finding experienced managers to run entrepreneurial companies in a country that only recently began adopting capitalism. In addition, the relationship between venture capitalists and companies is often different in China than in the United States and Europe; Chinese entrepreneurs welcome investment but may chafe at the degree of influence that venture capitalists want over the company's activities. Moreover, China does not have accounting and reporting standards, credit ratings, or a legal system on a par with the United States, and China's two major stock markets in Shanghai and Shenzhen—like most exchanges in Asia—are primitive. Consequently, venture capital returns in China are generally in the single digits.[68]

Taiwan

Elsewhere in Asia, the Taiwanese government established a national laboratory—the Industrial Technology Research Institute (ITRI)—in the mid-1970s in order to focus Taiwan's attention on critical technology markets. It has actively embraced venture capital since 1983, when it formally began encouraging formation of a venture capital industry by easing government restrictions and providing financial backing for venture funds. Taiwan's government has financed and recruited managers for scores of young companies. For example, in 1986, ITRI supplied about 50 percent of the start-up capital, lined up other investors, and recruited Morris Chang, a 25-year veteran of Texas Instruments, to establish the Taiwan Semiconductor Manufacturing Corporation, now one of the world's largest producers of semiconductors. Numerous other Taiwanese citizens, educated in the United States and trained at U.S. companies, have returned home to run Taiwanese technology companies. In addition to the thousands of Taiwanese studying in U.S. universities, Taiwan's universities produce nearly 50,000 new engineers a year, more than a quarter of all graduates.[69]

Although the Taiwanese government provides start-up capital and offers young companies subsidized land-lease rates and generous tax credits, it does not, unlike most of its Asian counterparts, offer much help after companies are up and running. In fact, one key to Taiwan's success is that uncompetitive companies are not shielded from market forces and are allowed to fail. Unlike Japan, declaring bankruptcy in Taiwan does not carry an overwhelming stigma; many failed entrepreneurs immediately start new companies.

In addition to the Taiwanese government's support, major Taiwanese companies have provided venture financing to Taiwanese start-ups for years. Acer, the world's third largest personal computer manufacturer, has announced that it will provide venture financing to create 100 Taiwanese software companies by 2010.[70] An increasing number of Taiwan's approximately 100 venture capital firms are establishing branch offices in Silicon Valley, in part to prospect for cutting-edge technologies that can be commercialized by Taiwanese companies. One of Taiwan's largest venture capital firms is Crimson Asia Capital Holdings, which raised a $400 million fund in 1997. In large part because of the strong entrepreneurial mindset of Taiwan's 22 million people, Taiwan has the highest concentration of small to medium-sized technology companies in Asia, whereas the Japanese and South Korean economies are dominated by large conglomerates. Small to medium-sized enterprises make up 98.5 percent of Taiwan's companies, 75–80 percent of all employment, and 47 percent of the total economy. There is one company for every 18 people in Taiwan, the highest density in the world.[71] Taiwanese workers are much more likely than their Japanese or Korean counterparts to take a low-salaried position with a start-up in exchange for payment in stock (options are still illegal) and the hope of gaining wealth through a successful initial public offering. Since the beginning of 1997, 32 of the 82 companies that have gone public on Taiwan's over-the-counter market have been technology-based.[72]

In addition to the main stock exchange and the over-the-counter market, Taiwan has a gray market comprised of a network of local brokers who are market makers for promising new companies, primarily in the high-technology sector. Although liquidity is generally low, the gray market enables start-ups to more easily raise capital and helps position start-ups for listing on the other two exchanges.

South Korea

Unlike Taiwan, South Korea's government has long maintained high barriers to entry and exit and shielded uncompetitive companies from market forces by offering generous government loans and allowing creative accounting. The lack of exposure to constantly changing markets has plagued the country's chaebol conglomerates. Nevertheless, the South Korea government recognized the role that U.S. venture capital plays in spawning high-technology companies. Consequently, the government set up Korea's first four venture capital firms between 1974 and 1984 in an attempt to help commercialize technologies developed by state-financed research institutes. Although the first venture capital firms met with mixed success, there were 60 independent venture capital firms in South Korea by the early 1990s. Between 1987 and 1997, South Korea venture capitalists invested about $1 billion in 1,891 firms, three-quarters of which were electronics and communications companies. In early 1998, the government announced that it would appropriate $620 million to help finance 2,000 venture-backed firms. In addition, a recently enacted law grants tax concessions to venture investors, lifts the usual ceiling on foreign investment, and, for the first time, allows the country's pension funds to invest in venture capital.

Despite the progress that South Korea has made in fostering a venture capital industry, Korea's high-technology firms have proved much less innovative than Taiwan's, in part because of the oppressive presence of the chaebol, which dominate most sectors of the economy. In addition, although the number of venture capital firms is increasing, their profitability is decreasing, in part because of a lack of managerial experience in running entrepreneurial companies. Moreover, South Korea has yet to develop much of a shareholder culture. On average, South Korea's venture-backed companies take 10 years to list on the Korea Security Dealers Association Automated Quotation (KOSDAQ), the country's small-company equivalent to the U.S. NASDAQ market. (One third of the companies listed on KOSDAQ are venture-backed.) Most companies also seek the added credibility that comes with leaving the KOSDAQ for the larger Korea Stock Exchange. Consequently, KOSDAQ lacks liquidity, which makes it difficult for venture capitalists to sell their stake in portfolio companies that trade on the smaller market.[73]

Government and Venture Capital

Governments are becoming more aware that venture capital investing is critical to the health of their economies and increasingly are looking to the United States for guidance in how to stimulate entrepreneurial activity and promote their venture capital sectors. The United States can play an important advisory role in supporting efforts to increase entrepreneurial activity. Such sharing of "best practices" will help create the "networked" economy of the next century, as David McCurdy noted in an earlier article.

Venture-backed companies historically have produced a disproportionate share of new jobs, particularly well paid and highly skilled jobs, and are a key source of research and development spending. For example, from 1991 through 1995, U.S. venture-backed companies created new jobs at a rate of about 34 percent annually while Fortune 500 companies reduced jobs at a rate of about 4 percent annually. During the same time period, venture-backed companies' revenues increased 38 percent while Fortune 500 companies' revenues increased only 3.5 percent. U.S. venture-backed companies also have increased their annual research and development budgets at about three times the rate of Fortune 500 companies and are an important source of applied technological innovation. In addition, U.S. venture capital-backed companies generate about three times more export sales per dollar of equity than more established corporations.[74] Moreover, venture capitalists have helped create entirely new industries by financing companies like biotechnology pioneer Genentech and overnight shipping provider Federal Express.

Similarly, European venture-backed companies outperform the 500 largest European companies in a number of categories. From 1991 through 1995, venture-backed companies created new jobs at a rate of about 15 percent annually, compared to 2 percent for the top 500 European companies. During the same time period, venture-backed companies' revenues increased 35 percent, while the top 500 companies' revenues increased by only 14 percent. In 1995, research and development expenditures by European venture-backed companies represented 8.6 percent of total sales compared to 1.3 percent for the top European companies.[75] In Britain, the number of people employed in venture-backed companies has increased by 15 percent annually, compared to a national growth rate of less than 1 percent. Companies currently using venture capital employ more than 1 million people in Britain. In addition, venture-backed companies in Britain increased their sales by 34 percent annually, five times faster than FTSE 100 companies.[76] In countries like France, Germany, Italy, and Spain, which have unemployment rates ranging from 11 percent to 16 percent and which need more new companies that can compete globally and contribute to Europe's economic revival, venture financing can play an enormously positive role.

The staggering difference in job growth between the United States and Europe is at least partly due to much higher levels of venture financing in the United States during the last 25 years. Between 1970 and 1995, the European Union, which has one-third more people than the United States, added only 8.5 million jobs or 6 percent of the work force, whereas the United States increased its work force by 46 million or 65 percent.[77] Since 1993, the United States has created more than 13 million new jobs net, whereas the nations of Europe have lost 1 million jobs.[78] The EU's unemployment rate is more than double the U.S. rate. One of the EU's primary problems is that while large companies are cutting jobs, there is relatively little new business formation. Between 1992 and 1996, 3,000 U.S. companies went public raising more than $150 billion, whereas only 150 EU companies went public between 1990 and 1996.[79] The European Commission recognizes the importance of venture capital to Europe's economy and, in May 1998, called for an "action plan" to remove various barriers to venture financing, including a review of national tax systems.

Governments can encourage venture investing by offering legal, fiscal, and financial support that benefits both venture capitalists and entrepreneurs. In fact, government incentives often have been crucial to attracting venture capital to risky, cutting-edge start-ups that may result in job and wealth creation that otherwise would not occur.

For example, although an increasingly large percentage of venture financing comes from tax-exempt investors like pension funds, the capital gains tax rate is an important factor determining the overall level of venture financing. In the United States, for example, venture financing increased significantly after the government lowered the capital gains tax rate from 49 percent to 28 percent in 1978 and to 20 percent in 1981. By comparison, capital gains tax rates in Europe and Asia can reach 60 percent and higher. U.S. tax law also permits owners of closely-held companies to make so-called "sub-S" elections and to issue section 1244 stock, provisions that allow for favorable tax treatment of losses.

The taxation of stock options also has an important effect on entrepreneurs. Start-ups, which cannot afford to pay large salaries, often offer stock options to attract skilled managers. Securities laws governing the issuance of options and fiscal laws governing the level of taxation determine whether managers will be willing to leave the security of larger companies to risk working for a start-up. In the United States, wealth accumulated from stock options is taxed as a capital gain when the stock is sold, whereas in many European countries (including France and Germany) options are taxed as regular income when granted, even though the employee may not be able to cash in the options for several years. To curtail the drain of executive talent to their U.S. rivals, European and Asian companies have begun lobbying their governments to modify tax and securities laws and accounting practices that discourage stock options.[80]

State governments also can use tax incentives to target certain points in the investment cycle (i.e. start-ups) or encourage venture investing by certain types of investors. For example, Louisiana, Missouri, and New York have enacted legislation allowing Certified Capital Companies (CAPCO), which are venture capital funds that invest at least 60 percent of their capital in private, in-state companies. They are funded primarily by insurance companies, which are given tax credits as an incentive to become limited partners. Several other states have CAPCO bills under consideration.[81] Such incentive programs are particularly helpful to entrepreneurs in states (e.g. Missouri) that traditionally have not received large amounts of venture capital. State-funded venture capital efforts have a mixed record. For example, Iowa recently abolished Iowa Seed Capital Corporation, which invested $14 million in 72 companies in an effort to help diversify the state's economy. Poor investments led to large losses that exhausted legislators' support for the program.[82]

Governments also can target certain types of venture financing by offering loan guarantees, project finance, and insurance to investors. For example, the Overseas Private Investment Corporation (OPIC) has offered financial support to U.S. investors who are developing and expanding business operations in certain emerging markets that have the effect of creating U.S. jobs and increasing U.S. exports. This OPIC program is designed, among other things, to support U.S. foreign policy objectives, assist in the economic development of emerging countries, and support the transfer of ownership of businesses from state to private hands. By 1998, 26 U.S.

investment funds had been approved for OPIC loan guarantees for their investment activities in emerging markets ranging from Latin America to Asia to the Newly Independent States. OPIC has committed $2.2 billion in loans, or two-thirds of its $3.26 billion funds program. For example, OPIC currently is providing a guarantee of $100 million to an investment fund managed by Olympus Capital Asia that is investing in Bangladesh, India, Indonesia, Laos, the Philippines, South Korea, Sri Lanka, Thailand, and Vietnam. Under this public-private partnership, OPIC guarantees $100 million of financing that is used to support a $50 million equity fund, providing a total of $150 million available for investment. If the investments fail and OPIC must pay on its guarantee, OPIC could lose up to $100 million.[83]

In some cases, U.S. government agencies directly fund entrepreneurs. For example, the U.S. Department of Agriculture's Alternative Agricultural Research and Commercialization Corporation has provided $33 million in venture capital financing over the last five years to companies to help commercialize bio-based industrial products from agricultural and forestry materials and animal byproducts.[84] Governments also can fund research and development consortiums like the Semiconductor Manufacturing Technology Initiative (SEMATECH), a U.S. government-industry R&D project designed to advance semiconductor equipment manufacturing techniques, and ESPRIT and JESSI, EU efforts to stimulate transnational research and development efforts in information technology. In addition, governments can grant venture capitalists the right to acquire the government's share of an investment at reduced rates if the investment succeeds. If improperly administered, however, public venture financing can have the detrimental effect of displacing or retarding the development of private venture capital and can cause economic distortions by creating unfair competition or by sustaining unprofitable projects.

Governments also can assist entrepreneurs and venture capitalists by establishing adequate institutions, such as strong intellectual property rights protection regimes. For many entrepreneurs, intellectual property rights are their only assets. Consequently, it is essential that patents and copyrights be processed efficiently and that there is adequate enforcement. The United States provides the strongest patent protection in the world and has taken the lead in the World Trade Organization in encouraging other countries to adopt similar protection. In Europe and Asia, however, intellectual property often is not adequately protected. For example, in Europe, there are three patent systems—national, European, and community—that can conflict with each other and with international obligations. Currently no European court has jurisdiction over patents. The European patent system is the most effective system in Europe, but the lengthy patent protection process costs $120,000 compared to $13,000 in the United States.[85] In Japan, patents are narrower in scope than in most other developed economies, which allows competitors more latitude in inventing around existing patents. In China, the enforcement of intellectual property rights is often completely inadequate.

Governments also can support entrepreneurial companies by helping to create efficient exit mechanisms, such as stock markets for young companies, which are critical for a vibrant venture capital sector because they increase liquidity and allow for realization of capital gains. In addition, governments can establish regulatory systems to ensure that new drugs and biotech products are given a timely review.

Bankruptcy laws also have an important effect on entrepreneurs. The U.S. bankruptcy law is designed to give those who suffer bankruptcy an opportunity for a fresh start and quickly channels resources away from companies that are not competitive. In some cases, managing a company that goes bankrupt is viewed as a useful apprenticeship for starting another company.[86] Declaring bankruptcy in many European and Asian countries, on the other hand, carries a stigma that frequently destroys an entrepreneur's future.[87] In addition, some Asian countries either have inadequate bankruptcy laws or no law at all.

Throughout much of Europe and Asia, pension funds are prohibited from investing in venture capital, denying entrepreneurs a significant source of financing. The United States and Britain, on the other hand, allow pension fund portfolio managers to diversify into venture capital. In the United States, "prudent man" guidelines first allowed pension funds to invest in venture capital in 1979. Although only a small percentage of U.S. pension fund assets are invested in venture capital, the amount invested is substantial and has greatly benefited U.S. entrepreneurs.

Although the United States is widely recognized as the world's most entrepreneurial economy, U.S. companies face a number of legal and regulatory impediments. For example, U.S. companies are much more likely to be sued than their European and Asian counterparts, and many small U.S. companies, which lack the resources of larger companies, often settle rather than incur the high and growing costs of litigation. Fear of lawsuits also has affected the freedom of small U.S. companies to hire and fire employees; employment practices liability insurance has become a $100 million a year business.[88] In addition, U.S. companies face increasing health care costs and a wide array of federal, state, and local government regulations, not to mention a convoluted U.S. tax code. Nevertheless, it is virtually impossible to find a U.S. entrepreneur who would rather incorporate abroad.

Conclusion

The United States will continue setting the standard in the venture capital business for many years to come. No other country offers entrepreneurs as welcoming an environment to do business. U.S. start-ups enjoy ready access to institutional financing, the world's most liquid stock markets, a flexible labor market, a large pool of experienced managers trained in the world's preeminent business schools, strong intellectual property rights protection, a favorable capital gains tax, a bankruptcy law that does not permanently stigmatize those who fail, and a regulatory environment that allows managers to take substantial ownership positions in their companies through stock options.

In Europe, Britain will continue to outpace France, Germany, and other Continental economies in entrepreneurial activity. Prime Minister Tony Blair has embraced most of the economic reforms put in place by Margaret Thatcher and John Major in the 1980s and early 1990s that reduced high tax rates, promoted more flexible labor markets, and streamlined government regulations. The Blair government also has supported a number of new initiatives designed to encourage entrepreneurial activity, including a proposal to teach entrepreneurship in schools.[89] In France and Germany, on the other hand, the social democratic governments led by French Prime Minister Lionel Jospin and German Chancellor Gerhard Schröeder have put on hold many of the efforts by their predecessors to reduce high capital gains taxes, reform excessive and rigid regulatory environments, and restructure highly regulated labor markets and welfare systems. In fact, the Jospin government submitted an expansionary budget for 1999 with a heavy emphasis on social spending and has proposed reducing the workweek to 35 hours,[90] and the Schröeder government proposed increasing some taxes on companies and reversing Helmut Kohl's labor market reforms.

In Asia, Taiwan's entrepreneurial culture and vibrant small company sector have helped the island weather the Asian economic storm better than most. One of the keys to Taiwan's success is that, unlike Japan and South Korea, where government ministers identify and fund high-technology initiatives (and shield uncompetitive enterprises), Taiwanese companies have largely made their own way without government interference. Although Japan would benefit from emulating Taiwan's entrepreneurial environment, Prime Minister Keizo Obuchi, like his predecessors, appears to lack the will or ability to reform a regulatory system that puts start-ups at a disadvantage. China's potential is enormous, particularly given the entrepreneurial vigor of the Chinese people, but it will be some time before China's government moves to a market economy and reverses decades of communist policies that have stunted entrepreneurial activity. In sum, European and Asian governments will need to remove myriad regulatory impediments to entrepreneurs in order to foster venture capital activity on a par with the United States.

Notes

1. See B. Zider, "How Venture Capital Works," *Harvard Business Review* (Nov.-Dec. 1998): 131–39.

2. Coopers & Lybrand, "Economic Impact of Venture Capital Study," 1997, p. 1.

3. VentureOne, "1998 Investment Highlights," www.v1.com; National Venture Capital Association, "1997 Annual Report," pp. 54–55.

4. N. Weinberg, "Small Is Ugly: Problems Small Businesses Face in Japan," *Forbes* (Dec. 18, 1995).

5. M. Gannon, "Financing in Purgatory," *Venture Capital Journal* (May 1999), 40–42; C. Darwall and M. Roberts, "The Band of Angels," Harvard Business School, case note (1998); M. Perkins, "Angels on High," *Red*

Herring (supplement) (June 1997); SBA report on the Angel Capital Electronic Network (ACE-Net) (1996), www.sba.gov/advo/acenet.

6. S. Abbott and M. Hay, *Investing for the Future: New Firm Funding in Germany, Japan, the UK and the USA*, Pitman Publishing, 1995, pp. 5–6.

7. G. Fenn, *et. al.*, "The Economics of the Private Equity Market," Board of Governors of the Federal Reserve System, Dec. 1995, p. 8.

8. See SBA, "Small Business Investment Company Program," www. sba.gov/INV.

9. "Intel Wraps Up $300 Million Fund," *Venture Capital Journal* (July 1999): 5; C. Deutsch, "When a Big Company Hatches a Lot of Little Ideas," *New York Times* (Sept. 23, 1998): D4.

10. "Venture Capitalists: A Really Big Adventure," *The Economist* (Jan. 25, 1997): 20.

11. Coopers & Lybrand, "Money Tree Report—1997 Results," p. 1.

12. Joshua Prager, "Venture Capitalists Pour Record Amount into Start-Ups," *Wall Street Journal.* (Aug. 3, 1999): B2; S. Reyes, "Returns Slump, Commitments Soar," *Venture Capital Journal* (July 1999): 44.

13. Venture capital returns over the last several years have been unusually high. For the year ending December 31, 1997, U.S. venture capital funds formed from 1969 to 1997 returned 28.7% to their investors after management fees and carried interest, compared to a 41.7% return in 1996 and 48.5% in 1995. J. Reyes, "Venture Capital Performance Takes a Breather," *Venture Capital Journal*, July 1998, pp. 44–46.

14. European Venture Capital Association, "Europe Private Equity Update," Jan. 1998, www.evca.com; "European Performance Surveyed—A Tentative First Step," *Venture Capital Journal*, Feb. 1997, p. 30.

15. PricewaterhouseCoopers, "Money Tree Report—1998 Results," pp. 1–4; Coopers & Lybrand, "Money Tree Report—1997 Results," pp. 2–3; Price Waterhouse, "National Venture Capital Survey—Full Year 1997," pp. 1–2. Figures detailing the level of venture investing in the U.S., Europe, and Asia include venture investments made from abroad.

16. VentureOne, "Q2 1999 Investment Hightlights," www.v1.com.

17. See generally B. Gross, "The New Math of Ownership," *Harvard Bus. Rev.*, Nov.–Dec. 1998, pp. 68–74.

18. Academic programs in entrepreneurship studies have expanded rapidly in the United States in the last 20 years. In 1980, there were 18 entrepreneurship chairs at U.S. business schools; today, there are more than 200. In 1990, only about two dozen U.S. business schools offered course work in entrepreneurship; today, about 120 business schools offer entrepreneurship studies as a major. E. Bronner, "Students at B-Schools Flock to the E-Courses," *New York Times*, Sept. 23, 1998, p. D6. Despite its suc-

cess at the graduate business school level, the United States lags behind many other developed countries in math and science performance in K–12 education.

19. The Oak Ridge National Laboratories, which enriched uranium for the first nuclear weapons, has helped form Technology 2020, a nonprofit incubator designed to foster high-technology ventures. Similarly, Sandia National Laboratories in Albuquerque has spawned 60 new companies, and Rocky Flats outside Denver has nurtured companies that are working on products as diverse as optical communications and a vaccine to combat AIDS. See C. Wohlwend, "Bomb's Birthplace Gets Down to Business," *New York Times*, Sept. 23, 1998, p. D3.

20. European Venture Capital Association, "White Paper on Priorities for Private Equity," 1998. European venture capitalists make about 12% of their investments outside their national borders. European Venture Capital Association, "1998 Yearbook," pp. 84–85, 89. See also K. Campbell, "Europe Hits Venture Capital Record," *Financial Times*, June 5, 1997, p. 20.

21. European Venture Capital Association, "1998 Yearbook," pp. 87, 105.

22. *Id*. at pp. 57, 105. One study found that European early-stage venture funds raised between 1980 and 1992 produced returns of only 5.7% per annum to the end of 1996. *Id*. at p. 57 (citing the "1997 Investment Benchmarks Report: International Private Equity"). See also "Europe's Great Experiment," *The Economist*, June 13, 1998, p. 67; "Behind America's Small-Business Success Story," *The Economist*, Dec. 13, 1997, p. 51; "Fresh Interest in Technology Funds," *Financial Times*, Oct. 10, 1997.

23. *Id*. at p. 29; Price Waterhouse, "National Venture Capital Survey (1997)," p. 11.

24. K. Campbell, "Europe Hits Venture Capital Record," *Financial Times*, June 5, 1997; "Venture Capitalists: Europe's Tentative Ventures," *The Economist*, Jan. 25, 1997, p. 21.

25. "Fresh Interest in Technology Funds," *Financial Times*, Oct. 10, 1997.

26. European Venture Capital Association, "1998 Yearbook," p. 88. See also S. Abbott and M. Hay, *Investing for the Future: New Firm Funding in Germany, Japan, the UK and the USA*, Pitman Publishing, 1995, p. 18.

27. Steinmetz, "Venture Capitalists Find Opportunities in German Stocks," *Wall Street Journal*, Mar. 20, 1998; K. Campbell, "Europe Hits Venture Capital Record," *Financial Times*, June 5, 1997, p. 20; Pricewaterhouse-Coopers, "Money Tree Survey—Q2 1998," p. 1.

28. Campbell, "Germany Surges Ahead in Venture Capital," *Financial Times*, May 28, 1998, p. 18; W. Kuemmerle, "Survey of Private Equity in Germany," Harvard Business School Working Paper, 1998; Fisher, "German Banking and Finance: Seed Finance Feels the Cold," *Financial Times*, May 29, 1996.

29. Pension funds and insurance companies provide 11.7% and 11.3% of all venture financing, respectively. European Venture Capital Association, "1998 Yearbook," pp. 95, 112.

30. Deutsche Börse, www.neuer-markt.de; "Neuer Markt: Runaway Success Story," *Financial Times*, June 24, 1998, p. IV.

31. "Europe's Great Experiment," *The Economist*, June 13, 1998, p. 67.

32. *Id.* at p. 68.

33. See Le Nouveau Marché, www.nouveau-marche.fr.

34. See B. Groom, "Oxford Closes High-Technology Gap on Cambridge," *Financial Times*, June 30, 1998, p. 10.

35. "France Sees Swing Back to Early-Stage," *Venture Capital Journal*, Sept. 1997, p. 25.

36. European Venture Capital Association, "1998 Yearbook," p. 141; K. Campbell, "Germany Surges Ahead in Venture Capital," *Financial Times*, May 28, 1998.

37. *Id.* at p. 142.

38. Public spending as a proportion of gross domestic product is 54.1% in France compared to an average of 38.3% for the G-7 countries. See R. Graham, "Dose of Realism for France," *Financial Times*, Aug. 17, 1998, p. 11.

39. See W. Hoge, "Ah, Britain! The Light at the End of the Tunnel," *New York Times*, Mar. 9, 1998, p. A4; "Tale of Two Job Markets: Why England Works, France Doesn't," *Wall Street Journal*, Aug. 7, 1997, p. A10.

40. London Stock Exchange, www.londonstockex.co.uk.; British Venture Capital Association, "Report on Investment Activity (1997)," pp. 24–25. In 1997, 217 British companies went public compared to 82 French companies and 35 German companies. European Venture Capital Association, "1998 Yearbook," p. 34. In 1999, the London Stock Exchange launched Techmark, a new market designed specifically for high tech companies.

41. European Venture Capital Association, "1998 Yearbook," p. 207.

42. British Venture Capital Association, "Report on Investment Activity (1997)," p. 26; www.bvca.co.uk.

43. *Id.* at p. 5; Price Waterhouse, National Venture Capital Survey (1997)," p. 11.

44. *Id.* at p. 11; "New Funds Focus on IT Companies," *Financial Times*, Oct. 10, 1997. The largest and most established venture capital company in Britain (and in Europe) is 3i. Created more than 50 years ago by the Bank of England and the major British banks to serve the long-term investment needs of industry, 3i has 28 offices throughout Europe and has invested about $16 billion in more than 13,000 businesses. 3i is listed on the London Stock Exchange and is a FTSE 100 company. See www.3i.com.

45. In terms of total revenue, Europe's biotech sector is about one-seventh the size of the U.S. biotech sector. See "The Cloning of U.S. Success," *Financial Times*, May 15, 1997, p. 15.

46. See Global Entrepreneurship Monitor, "1999 UK Executive Report," (1999): 1–26.

47. B. Groom, "Cambridge Overview," *Financial Times*, July 16, 1998, p. VII. See generally M. Peel, "Cambridge: "Helping to Change the World," *Financial Times*, July 16, 1998, p. IX.

48. See N. Itoi, "Two-Timing," *The Red Herring*, May 1998, p. 28; Y. Ibrahim, "In Old England, A Silicon Fen," *New York Times*, Jan. 4, 1998, sec. 3, p. 1. Gordon Moore, co-founder of Intel, recently committed $12.5 million to Cambridge to establish Europe's most advanced science and technology library. See S. Targett, "Intel Founder Gives $12m to University," *Financial Times*, Oct. 1, 1998, p. 11. The total amount of venture capital under management in Cambridge is about $250 million. B. Groom, "Cambridge to Receive $80m Venture Capital," *Financial Times*, Aug. 29–30, 1998, p. 5.

49. Isis Innovation, www.isis-innovation.com; B. Groom, "Oxford Closes High-Technology Gap on Cambridge," *Financial Times*, June 30, 1998, p. 10.

50. EASDAQ, www.easdaq.be.

51. EURO.NM, www.euro-nm.com.

52. V. Boland, "Gloves Come Off in Battle for Europe's Answer to NASDAQ," *Financial Times*, June 22, 1998, p. 28. See generally A. Swardson, "Discord in Europe's Unity: Plan to Link London, Frankfurt Exchanges Sows Strife," *Washington Post*, Oct. 13, 1998, p. C1. As of August 1999, U.S. equities accounted for 53.5% of the total capitalization of world stock markets, Britain 10.6%, Japan 10.9%, Germany 3.8%, France 3.5%, and the rest of the world 17.7%. Goldman Sachs, "Viewpoint Supplement," *U.S. Research*, Aug. 3, 1999, p. 12.

53. "1996/97: The Year in Review," *Asia Venture Capital Journal*, Dec. 1997, www.asiaventure.com.

54. *Id.*

55. S. Sugawara, "Upstarts and Start-Ups; Japanese Entrepreneurs Gain Attention and Incentives," *Washington Post*, July 28, 1996 p. H1.

56. "1996/97: The Year in Review," *Asia Venture Capital Journal*, Dec. 1997, www.asiaventure.com.

57. *Id.*

58. "JAFCO's Dai Ichi Looks to the Long Term," *Asia Venture Capital Journal*, Dec. 1997, www.asiaventure.com.

59. JAFCO, www.jafco.com.

60. "Toyota Offers to Support Outside Venture Companies," *Asia Pulse*, June 13, 1997.

61. "NVCC: Japan's Rising Venture Capitalist," *Asia Venture Capital Journal*, Nov. 1997, www.asiaventure.com.

62. N. Weinberg, "Small Is Ugly: Problems Small Businesses Face in Japan," *Forbes*, Dec. 18, 1995. A survey conducted by the Organization for Economic Cooperation and Development found that entrepreneurs have a much higher status in the United States and Britain than in Japan, France, or Germany. See "Entrepreneurs to Order," *The Economist*, March 14, 1998, p. 61.

63. "Japan Tries to Encourage Entrepreneurs and VCs," *Venture Capital Journal*, Nov. 1997, p. 38; D. Johnston, "American-Style Pay Moves Abroad: Importance of Stock Options Expands in a Global Economy," *New York Times*, Sept. 3, 1998, p. C1.

64. S. Sugawara, "Upstarts and Start-Ups; Japanese Entrepreneurs Gain Attention and Incentives," *Washington Post*, July 28, 1996, p. H1.

65. D. Normile, "Japan Hopes to Cash in on Industry-University Ties," *Science*, Nov. 29, 1996, pp. 1457–1458.

66. "1996/97: The Year in Review," *Asia Venture Capital Journal*, Dec. 1997; www.asiaventure.com.

67. In 1997, ethnic Chinese accounted for less than 4% of Indonesia's population, but controlled more than two-thirds of its economy. J. Laing, "No Relief," *Barron's*, July 27, 1998, p. 18; "An Army of Ants," *The Economist*, Nov. 7, 1998, p. 9 (Taiwan Survey).

68. D. Lau, "Behind the Great Wall: China Opens its Doors to Domestic and Foreign Venture Capital Funds," *Venture Capital Journal*, (July 1999): 48–50.

69. "Silicon Valley (East)," *The Economist*, Nov. 7, 1998, pp. 14–16 (Taiwan Survey).

70. L. Tyson, "The High Priest of Taiwanese High-Tech," *Financial Times*, May 18, 1998, p. 9.

71. "An Army of Ants," *The Economist*, Nov. 7, 1998, pp. 8–9 (Taiwan Survey). The Hsinchu Science Park near Taipei is the center of the world's third largest high-technology industry, accounting for a third of Taiwan's manufacturing exports and a huge share of the world's computer production. Similarly, Hong Kong, Malaysia, and Singapore are investing billions of dollars to build industrial parks to attract and retain high-tech companies. M. Landler, "Mapping Out Silicon Valley East," *New York Times*, April 5, 1999, C1. See "Silicon Valley (East)," *The Economist*, Nov. 7, 1998, p. 14.

72. See "Made in Taiwan: Entrepreneurs," *USA Today*, June 23, 1998, p. 1B; "The Guide to Venture Capital in Asia," *Asia Venture Capital Journal*, 1998.

73. "South Korean Firms: Wild Careers," *The Economist*, Feb. 14, 1998, p. 67. Although the United States, Europe, and Asia produce the vast majority of technology start-ups, there are several other centers of high-tech innovation. For example, Bangalore, India is home to the Indian Institute of Science and about 250 software and networking companies, including Texas Instruments and Infosys. Israel's venture capitalists have raised about $2.0 billion since 1991 and invested $567 million in 250 companies in 1998. Tel Aviv is home to about 1,000 high-tech firms. Pricewaterhouse-Coopers, "Money Tree Report—1998 Results," pp. 7–8; See generally D. Claymon, "Israel," *Red Herring*, Oct. 1998, pp. 30–34; A. Machlis, "Watershed for Israeli High-Tech Funds," *Financial Times*, Sept. 15, 1998, p. 24; "Venture Capital in India," *The Economist*, Jan. 18, 1997, p. 70.

74. Coopers & Lybrand, "Economic Impact of Venture Capital," 1997, p. 1.

75. Coopers & Lybrand, "The Economic Impact of Venture Capital in Europe," 1998.

76. British Venture Capital Association, "Report on Investment Activity," 1997, p. 3.

77. P. Lynch, "The Upsizing of America," *Wall Street Journal*, Sept. 20, 1996.

78. Goldman, Sachs & Co., "Investment Strategy—1999: Issues and Outlook."

79. P. Lynch, "The Upsizing of America," *Wall Street Journal*, Sept. 20, 1996.

80. D. Johnston, "American-Style Pay Moves Abroad: Importance of Stock Options Expands in a Global Economy," *New York Times*, Sept. 3, 1998, p. C1; Tax legislation can affect venture investments in many other ways. For example, in July 1998, the U.S. Congress passed a bill that will reduce taxes for individuals who invest in small companies through venture capital funds. At issue is the tax treatment of investments in companies with less than $50 million in assets that are sold at a profit, with part or all of the gains reinvested in another small company. Currently, solo private investors can defer capital gains taxes on many such invesments. The tax code, however, has not clearly allowed individuals investing in venture capital funds to enjoy the same tax benefits. Under the new legislation, individuals who invest in venture capital funds will enjoy the same tax treatment. See G. Anders & J. Schlesinger, "IRS Bill Clears Senate, Aids Venture Capitalists," *Wall Street Journal*, July 10, 1998, p. A2.

81. S. Fineberg, "CAPCOs Come of Age," *Venture Capital Journal*, Nov. 1997, pp. 44–46.

82. See generally "California Considers State Venture Fund," *Venture Capital Journal*, July 1998, p. 6.

83. See generally S. Fineberg, "The Battle of OPIC," *Venture Capital Journal*, March 1998, pp. 41–43.

84. AARC Corp., "Source Book," 1998, www.usda.gov/aarc.

85. European Commission, "Background Report—Innovation for Growth and Development in Europe," Apr. 21, 1997.

86. J. Maloney, "Failure May Not Be So Bad After All," *New York Times*, Sept. 23, 1998, p. D12; Despite a booming U.S. economy, personal bankruptcy filings jumped 40% in 1997 over 1996, to 1.4 million. Although only one in five personal bankruptcy filings involve a failed entrepreneur, such cases account for 50% of the total debt written off. "America Goes Bust," *The Economist*, July 4, 1998, p. 78.

87. See S. Sugawara, "Shame of Bankruptcy: Suicide and Hiding Rise in Japan," *International Herald Tribune*, Aug. 21, 1998, p. 13. Bankruptcy laws in Japan and South Korea are much tougher on existing management than the U.S. bankruptcy law. In Japan and Korea, when a company files for bankruptcy, management is dismissed, the court appoints trustee management, and there is no automatic protection from creditors. Consequently, there is little incentive to declare bankruptcy and many crippled companies continue operations. Even when companies do declare bankruptcy, many Asian countries do not have adequate procedures to protect creditors and distribute a bankrupt company's remaining assets. See S. WuDunn, "Bankruptcy the Asian Way," *New York Times*, Sept. 8, 1998, p. C1.

88. On occasion, the U.S. government has acted to curtail abusive litigation that adversely affects entrepreneurial activity. For example, on August 13, 1998, President Clinton signed into law the Biomaterials Access Assurance Act of 1998, which is designed to protect the suppliers of raw materials to medical device companies from frivolous product liability lawsuits. Similarly, the Private Securities Litigation Reform Act of 1995 was designed to curb meritless securities lawsuits that frequently are filed against high-technology companies.

89. See "Britain: Entrepreneurs to Order," *The Economist*, March 14, 1998, p. 61. See generally "Growth Agenda for Small Firms," *Financial Times*, Oct. 29, 1998, p. 11. This is the first time since 1929 that the three largest European states—Britain, France, and Germany—are simultaneously headed by left-of-center governments. Prime Minister Blair, however, stands decidedly to the right of the French prime minister and the German chancellor on economic policy and places more trust in the market.

90. See A. Swardson, "A Job in France? No Sweat: Laws Banning Overwork Trim Executives' Hours," *Washington Post*, Dec. 9, 1998, p. A27.

Chapter 16

Danger.com: National Security in a Wired World

Lawrence Greenberg

The Information Technology Explosion

Over the last twenty years, the development and diffusion of information technology (IT), including computers, telecommunications, and networks, has been explosive and astounding. Twenty years ago the personal computer (PC) barely existed; now PCs are spread generously throughout homes and offices in the developed or semi-developed world and typewriters are hard to find. Once, only elite researchers and defense personnel had access to the Internet; now it is a commodity, available to the millions of people in the United States and around the world who can get their hands on a computer, a modem, and a monthly account with an Internet service provider. Only a handful of countries do not have at least some access to the global network of computer networks, and some of them, such as Burma and North Korea, have chosen to isolate themselves from the flow of threatening ideas that washes across borders from computer screen to computer screen. Today there are probably more than half as many computers on the planet as there are cars, trucks, and buses.

As discussed throughout this volume, but especially by McCurdy, Beese, and Hormats, IT is revolutionizing daily life, particularly in the United States. Computers and networks permit us to control traffic, conduct increasing amounts of electronic commerce, track individuals' purchasing habits, transfer hundreds of billions of dollars between financial institutions daily, monitor corporate inventories, automate factories, design new products, assess water pollution, work collaboratively with distant colleagues, and make friends with distant strangers (many of whom we wouldn't like if we actually met them).

These technologies and the companies that create them have become drivers of the U.S. economy. Computing and telecommunications have grown from 4.9 percent of U.S. Gross Domestic Product (GDP) in 1985 to an estimated 8.2 percent in 1998, and IT's share of total nominal GDP growth is almost 15 percent.[1] IT companies create jobs, and, although such an effect is hard to measure (and is debatable), some observers, including Alan Greenspan, even attribute the remarkable growth of the U.S. economy and productivity in the 1990s to improvements in computing and telecommunications.[2]

The IT sector is one in which U.S. companies can compete, and even crush, their foreign competitors. Major U.S. technology companies routinely derive 40 to 60 percent of their revenues from sales to foreign customers. For example, Intel, which manufactures the chips that are the central processing units (CPU) of most PCs, earned about 55 percent of its $26 billion in revenues from sales outside the Americas in 1998. Microsoft, the software giant, made 58 percent of its $11 billion net revenue from foreign sales in its fiscal 1997. Cisco Systems, the leading networking supplier, made 43.5 percent of its $6.4 billion in sales abroad in 1997. Indeed, some U.S. IT giants face little or no foreign competition. And they are dedicated to preserving their leads over potential market entrants. Perhaps the most extreme examples are Microsoft, which holds more than 90 percent of the market for operating systems in Japan, and Intel, whose global market share for the PC CPU is over 80 percent.

IT has also made tremendous contributions to U.S. national security. Advanced ITs are incorporated into virtually all weapons and command, control, and intelligence (C3I) systems that the U.S. military uses, from the precision guided missiles that made for popular television during the Persian Gulf War, to the sensors that would warn U.S. troops of a bacteriological attack, to the Global Positioning System (GPS), which now can also show civilian drivers where they should have turned off the highway if they hadn't been listening to the radio and talking on their cellular phones. U.S. forces should now know more about their foes, their own forces, and the battlespace than ever before. Moreover, IT, especially through networks, has had a greater effect on U.S. security than just making military systems work better. As networks have spread throughout the United States and the world, they have become critical for the communication, control, and coordination of national militaries and civilian economies. In fact, as McCurdy developed earlier, we are likely to see the paradigm of "networked societies" early in this century.

These contributions to security and the economy have come with often overlooked costs. The very openness that contributes to the ubiquity, utility, and power of networked systems may make those systems vulnerable to intrusions or other attacks that seek to ruin, manipulate, or steal the data that travels through them, or cause damage to other systems that depend on them or that they control. As society increasingly depends on such systems, the potential damages resulting from such intrusions soar. Furthermore, as U.S. industry helps spread IT products and systems globally, foreign actors, including governments, terrorists, or transnational criminal organizations are more likely to gain access to tools that could be used as weapons against U.S. interests.

Dangers in a Wired World

The Rise of Information Warfare. As information systems become significant for military and economic functioning and coordination, they inevitably become the targets and weapons in conflicts. IT is diffusing into virtually all military weapons and C3I systems, as well as the civilian systems that support modern industrial (or post-industrial) economies. The use and targeting of such systems in conflict has been labeled information warfare (IW), which (according to a broad definition put forward by the U.S. Air

Force) may include "any action to deny, exploit, corrupt, or destroy the enemy's information and its functions; protecting ourselves against those actions; and exploiting our own military information functions."[3]

IW includes new techniques, such as computer intrusion and telecommunications spoofing, and old ones, such as ruses, camouflage, and physical attacks on observation posts and lines of communication. Some of the newer forms of information attacks may use electrons and manipulation of data, rather than bullets and explosives, and they may target critical civilian infrastructure systems, such as power, telephone, and transportation systems, as well as purely military targets.

The results of IW attacks on largely civilian systems could range from simple inconvenience, to localized disruption, to apocalyptic, cascading disasters. The prospect of major attacks or combinations of smaller ones has inspired scenarios of massive destruction and disruption, as critical systems malfunction, people panic, and governments are paralyzed, unable to provide emergency services. Scenarios[4] for such attacks sound like (and mostly are, so far) science fiction, but they could include:

- During a time of international tension, a "trap door" hidden in the code controlling switching centers of the Public Switched Network might cause larger portions of it to fail on command, disrupting U.S. communications.
- A mass dialing attack by PCs might overwhelm a local phone system.
- A "logic bomb" or other intrusion into railroad computer systems might cause trains to be misrouted and crash.
- A computer intruder might disrupt the computers that control a portion of the electric power grid, causing cascading blackouts that would degrade emergency services, financial markets, government systems, and even transportation and water delivery.
- Computer intruders might divert funds from bank computers, or corrupt data in bank databases, stealing money or causing disruption or panic, as banks need to shut down to address their problems.
- Computer intruders might steal and disclose confidential personal, medical, or financial information, as a tool of

blackmail, extortion, or to cause widespread social disruption or embarrassment.

- A " worm" could travel from computer to computer across a network, damaging data and disrupting systems.
- Attackers might disrupt a nation's command and control infrastructure, hindering military units' ability to communicate with each other, or with a central command.
- Attackers could manipulate or disrupt stock exchanges, electric power grids, municipal traffic control systems, and air traffic control or navigation systems, with accompanying economic or societal disruption, physical destruction, or loss of life.

The apocalyptic prophets of IW may forget that information attacks do not seem to have occurred on a grand scale outside popular fiction. Still, there are indications that such attacks are possible and potentially crippling. First, there have been small attacks, mostly from hackers, who may be hobbyists, criminals, or both. As early as 1988, when the Internet was tiny and insignificant compared to its status today, Robert Morris, a Cornell University graduate student, created a "worm." It spread over the Internet to thousands of computers, including some military and intelligence systems, paralyzing over 6,000 computers. Eleven years later, in the spring of 1999, the "Melissa" and "Chernobyl" viruses spread explosively through e-mail to hundreds of thousands of computers, disrupting businesses and governments. Losses in China, for example, reportedly totaled more than $120 million. Although banks are reluctant to report or publicize them, attackers have reportedly succeeded in diverting funds electronically: Most notoriously, in 1996, hackers from Russia, in league with gangsters, reportedly invaded Citibank's computers and diverted $10 million to accounts in Europe, the United States, and the Middle East before they were tracked and caught.[5]

The air traffic control system has been similarly vulnerable. In March 1997, a Massachusetts teenager allegedly hacked into an airport computer, perhaps inadvertently shutting down part of the airport. U.S. Department of Defense (DoD) computers and networks have been repeatedly invaded and even taken over through the Internet and the phone network. In February 1998, for example, two California teenagers, guided by an Israeli counterpart called the "Analyzer," allegedly hacked their way into several DoD systems, prompting the Pentagon to warn President Clinton that the United States might be under foreign cyberattack, before the culprits were traced and arrested. Even "cyberterrorism" has reportedly occurred. An offshoot of the Liberation Tigers of Tamil Eelam mounted a "suicide e-mail" attack to overwhelm the computers of Sri Lankan embassies in 1997. More horrifying, according to the Christian Science Monitor, a baby-food manufacturer discovered that a computer intruder had caused its systems to increase one ingredient in a batch of its product to toxic levels.[6]

Second, apparently unintentional accidents have shown what can happen when something goes wrong in complex, interlinked systems. For example, the AT&T long distance network failed for nine hours on Martin Luther King Day in 1990 because of a faulty software update. Many at the time, though, blamed the failure on hackers.[7] Similarly, in August 1996, tree limbs shorted out local powerlines setting off a cascading series of shorts that knocked out power in nine Western states.

That the nightmarish scenarios have not occurred makes it harder for people to believe that they are coming, or even that they are possible. If apocalyptic, destructive attacks are possible and forthcoming, though, it is not hard to grasp the potential damage that they could cause. Airplane crashes, for example, are bloody and terrifying, and the systematic corruption of the international system of financial transfers is horrible to contemplate. At the same time, it may be hard to believe that such attacks are likely; they do not seem to have occurred so far, and it seems logical to assume that the systems whose failures would be most terrible are most likely to be guarded effectively. However, even attacks that would mainly cause disruption and inconvenience, such as communications failures and temporary blackouts (as all blackouts are temporary) have costly consequences, and can be particularly damaging when they occur at the command of a U.S. adversary.

Furthermore, even seemingly noncritical systems, such as logistics or even heating, ventilation, and air conditioning systems can shut down the critical systems that depend on them. Even inconvenience, if inflicted on enough people, could cause social or economic disruption and could certainly be expensive to fix. The U.S. government believed strongly enough in the danger to U.S.

infrastructure systems that it established a President's Commission on Critical Infrastructure Protection (PCCIP) in 1996. The Japanese Ministry of International Trade and Investment established a similar group in 1997. As information systems become increasingly critical everywhere, it seems likely that the United States will choose to wage IW, or suffer information attacks, in future conflicts.

Increasing U.S. Vulnerabilities. The United States' technological advantages may actually endanger the country. Ironically, because the United States military and society are most dependent on information systems, they may be more vulnerable to attack. Attacks against communications, power, transportation, or financial systems could greatly disrupt U.S. society; countries with systems that do not work well enough to be taken for granted might barely notice attacks against them. With the "death of distance,"[8] the sanctuary of the U.S. homeland, formerly protected by oceans, could be endangered, as the very networks that make U.S. systems efficient and effective may open them up to danger. Foreign adversaries and others may also choose to pursue IW against the United States because the Persian Gulf War demonstrated that it was difficult to oppose the United States with traditional, kinetic force. In fact, at least ten countries, including some U.S. foes with comparatively weak conventional forces, such as Iran, Iraq, and Libya are believed to have IW programs.

The increasing interdependence of important infrastructure systems may exacerbate U.S. vulnerability. For example, the air traffic control system, or National Airspace System (NAS), has been relatively secure against attacks, as it is made up of old, specialized subsystems. As the NAS is modernized, though, it will gain a more efficient, open architecture that will depend on more conventional telecommunications and commercial off-the-shelf (COTS) hardware and software. The NAS will thus be cheaper, more efficient, and potentially more vulnerable.[9] Similarly, the electric grid and other energy systems were once mostly vulnerable to physical attacks, such as bombs at generation plants or under transmission pylons. Now, as power companies enter an era of competition, they will control their systems through Supervisory Control and Data Acquisition (SCADA) systems. These systems rely on standard telecommunications or even the Internet, opening themselves up to new vulnerabilities.

The intertwining of civilian and military communications infrastructures may also permit threats to military preparedness and civil life. Because of their reliance on insecure, civilian systems, military systems may be attacked with relative ease; conversely, primarily civilian systems may be attacked as a way to get at the military. For example, about 95 percent of the telecommunications of the DoD travel through the Public Switched Network, and during the Persian Gulf War, commercial communications satellites reportedly carried almost a quarter of the U.S. Central Command's transcontinental telecommunications. U.S. military forces are also particularly dependent on nonmilitary systems for deployment and logistics. As Vice Admiral Arthur Cebrowski stated in 1995, "There is no logical distinction . . . between military or civil systems or technologies. [Therefore] there is also no technical distinctions between exploitation, attack or defense of the information warfare target set."[10]

New Enemies. Just as IT enables new ways of doing business, it may empower new adversaries for the United States. International networks give nations, groups, and even individuals the ability to act over great distances and strike against their enemies from places of sanctuary. If, as appears to be the case, all that is necessary for successful "cyber" attacks is knowledge of the target systems, a readily obtainable amount of computing power, and access to such networks as the Internet or the international telephone grid, then anyone, from a teenage "hacker" in Argentina, to the bin Laden terrorist organization, to the Russian *mafiya,* to Iraq can strike against systems that are continents away. Even individuals with few resources or little expertise may be able to obtain these "weapons"; hardware and software are cheap, and any necessary expertise may also be available for purchase. As Paul A. Strassmann, former director of defense information and principal deputy assistant secretary of defense for C3I, has stated, "Info-assassin paraphernalia is booming, and it's gory stuff you can buy. . . . There is also a wide range of people available for hire to carry things out, many of them ex-intelligence agency people."[11] Indeed, hacker tools, or "warez," are becoming simpler to use and can be found using any web search engine.

The cheapness and availability of information "weapons," combined with the fact that international networks make it possible to attack targets on distant continents, may make information-based attacks particularly attractive to terrorists. This availability could even reduce the need for terrorists or similar actors to seek state support; it should also strengthen the "plausible deniability" of states that support terrorism. The fact that Western societies are so dependent on information systems, along with the fact that those systems may symbolize the triumph of the capitalist West, may contribute to those systems' appeal as terrorist targets. By way of precedent, Western European radical terrorist groups conducted many conventional attacks against computer systems during the 1970s.

Some observers, including McCurdy, have speculated that technology may enable the development of new types of nonstate actors, such as decentralized, horizontally organized "tribes" or "clans" that may use networks to coordinate, or even carry out, attacks.[12] Already, the Zapatista rebels in Chiapas, Mexico are believed to communicate among themselves and with their loose network of supporters through the Internet and faxes. More traditionally, some terrorist and insurgent organizations proselytize through sites on the World Wide Web, increasing their reach well beyond those who once saw their hastily mimeographed and stealthily placed posters.[13]

The Problem of International Networks in a World of Sovereign States

Tracing Attackers

A collision between fundamental principles of physics and those of international law may stymie attempts to cope with international attacks and thus exacerbate the vulnerability of U.S. systems: Electrons may flow freely through networks across international borders, but the authority of national governments' agents does not. Simply, an attack may come from a foreign country or may be routed through computers in several, but law enforcement or national security personnel cannot unilaterally launch pursuit into networks in other countries. Under the principle of sovereignty each government has exclusive authority over events within its borders. Investigators will thus need foreign cooperation (or they will need to operate covertly). Indeed, governments may go so far as to consider foreign investigation of criminal misuse of their systems to be a form of computer crime, or worse.

A 1994 intrusion into the computers at the U.S. Air Force's Rome Laboratory in New York hinted at the problem of the collision between sovereignty and networks. That spring, two hackers, now believed to have been British, weaved their way through phone switches in Colombia and Chile before entering Rome Labs through commercial sites in the United States, then broke into and took control of the operational network at the U.S. Air Force's command and control research facility. Air Force investigators were observing one attacker in the Rome computer when he accessed a system at the [South] Korean Atomic Research Institute, obtained all of its stored data, and deposited that data into the Rome Labs system. The investigators, initially fearing that the system belonged to North Korea, were concerned that the North Korean government would interpret the intrusion and transfer of data to the U.S. system as an invasion, at a time of sensitive negotiations with North Korea over its nuclear weapons program.[14]

The wide availability of the cheap technology necessary for international attacks across computer networks, combined with the anonymity that the technology may provide its users, may complicate investigators' efforts to determine whether responsibility for an attack rests with a foreign government. It would certainly make it difficult to convince other nations or international organizations of that government's role. Indeed, the ability of users (or abusers) of computer networks to hide their identities through such techniques as "spoofing" may make it almost impossible for governments to find them. Actually, given the complexity of many of the interconnected computer systems, investigators may not be able to determine whether a failure is a result of an attack, a software "bug," or just bad luck.

Catching Malefactors.   Even when it can identify its attackers, the victim state may not be able to reach them. The relative novelty of computer networks exacerbates the difficulties arising from the collision between sovereignty and networks. For a country to obtain the apprehension of a criminal in a foreign country and his transportation to the requesting country for trial, an extradition treaty must bind both countries, as there is no underlying right of extradition under international law. Virtually all extradition treaties contain a "double criminality" requirement that mandates that the act that is the basis for the extradition request be an offense under the laws of both the requesting country and the one to which the request is directed. This requirement has been a significant obstacle to U.S. efforts to try those who have intruded into sensitive U.S. data systems, as many nations have not enacted adequate computer crime statutes. For example, when a young Argentine reached into computers containing sensitive information at the Naval Command Control and Ocean Surveillance Center, the Navy Research Laboratory, and Los Alamos National Laboratory, among others, the United States could not obtain his extradition, even though Argentine police cooperated with U.S. authorities, because Argentina's legal system, faced with new technology, had not yet classified such intrusions as criminal.

The potential ability of attackers to conduct devastating attacks from a distant sanctuary may make extradition of their fellows particularly difficult to obtain. Even when they are not complicit in wrongdoing, governments sometimes reject extradition requests out of fear that the alleged criminals' comrades will retaliate against them for their cooperation. In 1977, for example, France released Abu Daoud, the architect of the 1972 Munich Olympic massacre, despite West German and Israeli efforts to obtain his extradition, apparently because France feared retaliation. The threat of such retaliation might appear particularly grave, especially for nations that depend on sophisticated information infrastructures.

Policy Responses.   As U.S. firms drive the continuing diffusion of IT into more and more systems at home and abroad, they may be introducing vulnerabilities into U.S. systems, just as they are providing foreign entities with the resources necessary to take advantage of those vulnerabilities. To paraphrase Lenin, U.S. firms may be selling U.S. adversaries the wires, rather than the ropes, by which the United States will be hanged. An obvious policy solution, then, would be to control the exports of dangerous technologies or, failing that, to ban the sort of attacks that might endanger our critical systems. But obvious solutions can be obviously wrong. Arms control and weapons bans would be pointless and ineffective.

Obvious, Yet Bad, Ideas

Stemming the Tide of IT.   Except when applied to purely military equipment or the highest end products, such as supercomputers, efforts to slow the spread of IT would be hopeless. Keeping technological "weapons" out of the hands of potential U.S. adversaries will be difficult, at best. Because much of the significant technology is embodied in COTS products, or even consumer goods, potential "weapons" may be readily accessible to foreign interests, who certainly will have access to the international telecommunications networks.

U.S. efforts to apply rigorous export controls to everything that might be useful for IW attacks, including the CPU chips, networking hardware, and software would devastate a vital sector of the U.S. economy, be unenforceable, and would promote the development of foreign competitors to U.S. companies. U.S. controls on cryptography, for example, have spurred the development of products in Israel, the NIS, and Western Europe, costing U.S. companies an estimated $37 billion to $96 billion in lost sales over the next five years, according to industry advocates.[15] Additionally, much technical development takes place in U.S. universities, which train thousands of foreign students in advanced fields; many of those students stay in the United States and contribute to the efforts of U.S. companies, but many others return home with their knowledge. Furthermore, modern telecommunications, including the Internet, make it easy for knowledge to disseminate across borders: nobody really knows what flows over the Internet.

The argument against export controls for such products really attacks a straw man. No credible figure is suggesting major controls on exports of such items as PC CPUs. But that makes the point even stronger: Given the limited technology necessary for IW attacks, there is no way to keep that technology out of the hands of U.S. adversaries.

Arms Control?   Some observers have postulated that the United States might pursue some sort of international ban on IW attacks or control of the weapons of IW.[16] Indeed, the Russian Federation has already proposed such controls to the United States and the United Nations. Such an approach might seem particularly appealing if the United States were to determine that its vulnerabilities outweigh its offensive technological advantages.

But the benefits of information arms control in this arena could be illusory. First and most significantly, the weapons of IW are primarily COTS technology, with largely civilian uses. Constraints on the development or sale of such products could impose extraordinary costs on one of the most vital and competitive sectors of the U.S. economy. Second, because of technological diffusion, the small size of much IT, and its primary incorporation into consumer goods, an arms-control regime would seem impossible to enforce. Third, although arms controls and weapons bans have been applied to new technologies before they were widely used or their military ramifications understood, as in the bans on bacteriological or blinding laser weapons, it does seem premature to limit weaponry that promises to bring some measure of nonlethality to conflict, and in which the United States apparently holds a lead. Fourth, in any event, arms controls or weapons bans would not apply to the nonstate actors, such as terrorists or criminal organizations, who would not be parties to the agreements and who may make up the gravest near-term IW threat. Such bans, then, would not eliminate the need for defensive measures, so countries might still need to explore offensive capabilities, if only to test their own defenses through the use of "red teams."

Obvious, Yet Good, Ideas

If systems are vulnerable and defensive and responsive capabilities are limited, then it makes sense for the United States to try to reduce those vulnerabilities and improve those capabilities.

Enhancing Defensive and Responsive Capabilities. In the wake of the PCCIP report, the U.S. government has launched several initiatives to fortify critical infrastructure systems and enhance responsiveness. The National Infrastructure Protection Center (NIPC), based in the FBI, will gather threat and vulnerability information, disseminate warnings of dangers to the public and private sectors, and coordinate the federal government's response to incidents, including investigations of attacks. The Critical Infrastructure Assurance Office (CIAO) was established in May 1998 to coordinate a national infrastructure assurance plan, as well as conduct educational and security awareness programs. Additionally, DoD, the intelligence agencies, and each of the armed services are paying increased attention to offensive and defensive IW.

It is too soon to evaluate the NIPC and CIAO's public efforts,[17] and most of DoD's and the intelligence community's activities are too secret for outsiders to judge, but it seems likely that their defensive and protective measures will not be sufficient. The vast bulk of critical infrastructure systems is not under governmental control; the telephone and electric grids, for example, are almost entirely private, as are the information systems and components that control them. The most important activities of the NIPC and CIAO may thus be their efforts to inform private actors of dangers and promote security consciousness.

International Computer Crime Initiatives.   Even if it cannot protect all systems, the government can improve its ability to punish attackers. The United States needs to address the current conflict between the realities of international networks and the principles of the international state system. To improve detection, pursuit, and prosecution of information attackers and ultimately deter such attacks, especially by terrorists and other criminals, the United States needs to convince other nations to criminalize their activities and cooperate in investigations. The justice ministers of the seven leading industrial nations and Russia agreed to pursue such a course in December 1997, but the global reach of networks demands that such prohibitions be applied as universally as possible.

U.S. development aid, including telecommunications and legal assistance, may provide diplomatic levers to extract concessions and practical methods to improve states' abilities to cooperate in protecting the global networks. Of course, some countries may refuse to participate in a formal or informal regime. They may wish to use such intrusions or other attacks for their own political, economic, or other ends and thus may value maintaining their offensive capacity more than they do the incremental security that their systems would receive, particularly where the systems are poorly developed or relatively unimportant; they may have ideological reasons to resist rules, such as differing conceptions of privacy in electronic systems or data, or distrust of any system that would appear to preserve the advantages of the developed nations; or they may even want to attract hackers as a development strategy.

As the United States pursues harmonization of computer crime laws, it should also explore mechanisms for cooperation in investigations and sharing of information about threats, vulnerabilities, and attacks within the government and with private sector and foreign governmental entities.[18] Critically, though, if the government is to obtain the cooperation of industry while it is sharing information with foreign governments, it will need to ensure that industry's competitive, proprietary information does not fall into the hands of foreign governments that will share those secrets with their own national companies.

Hardening Targets.   If the United States cannot prevent the spread of information "weapons," it can promote the use of technologies that will reduce the damage that they can cause. Strong cryptography, for example, could improve security for virtually all significant infrastructure systems, and industry could provide useful products quickly. Unfortunately, such cryptography has not been widely available, as it has been caught in a stalemate between the U.S. government and industry. The U.S. government has refused to permit general exports of robust encryption unless those products would permit speedy governmental access to decrypted messages for law enforcement or intelligence purposes; many companies resist, out of distrust of the government and the belief that customers will not embrace cryptographic products that may not be as secure as advertised. These rigorous export controls have made it impossible for industry to include advanced cryptography in products that might be exported. The merits of the debate between government and industry are beyond the scope of this chapter (and the U.S. government has softened its position significantly, although the details of U.S. policy are not yet final and may disappoint industry, but the need for some form of robust cryptography is manifest. The relative security of international banking communications, which can use robust cryptography, hints at cryptography's potential value.[19]

Pursuing U.S. Advantages

Rather than trying to clamp down on the fruits of its technological lead, the United States should embrace its advantages:

The U.S. Lead in Information Warfare

Just as U.S. dependence on information systems increases its vulnerability, U.S. experience with those systems gives the United States significant advantages in the offensive and defensive use of those systems. Most observers agree that the United States likely leads the world in developing IW tools and strategy—certainly U.S. defense strategists talk more about IW than do their foreign counterparts, and they seem to have made more progress in converting their discussions to doctrine. Of course, the secrecy shrouding IW efforts makes it difficult to evaluate the relative strength of such programs just as it is hard to compare rival intelligence agencies. Yet, as Emmet Paige, assistant secretary of defense for C3I, stated in 1995, "We have an offensive capability, but we can't discuss it. . . . [However] you'd feel good if you knew about it."[20] It seems likely that in future conflicts U.S. forces will be able to disrupt or corrupt their adversaries' C3I systems (assuming the adversary has such systems), undermining their ability to resist the U.S forces or inflict casualties on them.

Advantages of Information Warfare

Information weapons may have appeal to U.S. decisionmakers that goes beyond the "gee whiz" factor that may inspire imaginations and movies. Infowar may be inexpensive, requiring hardware that, while not always cheap, does not approach the cost of, say, a squadron of jet fighters. IW attacks may be politically inexpensive, too. Such attacks should not require large U.S. deployments abroad, sparing presidents the need to gain domestic approval or foreign consent for deployments. Perhaps most important, information attacks should not endanger the U.S. "cybertroops" who carry them out; U.S. information warriors, who may even telecommute into battle, may be unlikely to return home in body bags. As a side benefit, the nonlethal nature of many of the attacks may increase their palatability both at home and in international forums.

In light of U.S. technological advantages and the attractiveness of some methods of information conflict, the United States should continue to pursue the development of its offensive and defensive capacities. The circumstance under which those capacities ought to be deployed is beyond the scope of this paper.

Selling Others the Wires
by Which They'll Hang

If networking and IT are key to economic development in the twenty-first century, countries will face a stark choice: They may incorporate IT into their critical systems and become as dependent on it as is the United States, and thus as vulnerable; or they may reject the technologies, or embrace them slowly, lagging behind the United States and other technology leaders. The countries that do embrace IT face further perils in that, because much of the technology comes from the United States, the United States may understand it and its vulnerabilities better.

Perhaps the greatest danger to many potential U.S. adversaries is a softer one. IT has improved communication between individuals and groups within and across borders, and it can increase the difficulty that governments face in trying to control the spread of information, including political organization, dissidence, or even blasphemy. Such technologies as radio, television, telephone, and fax made it easier for citizens of the Soviet bloc countries to obtain information about the outside world and coordinate dissident activities, thus contributing, in some way, to the Soviet Union's collapse.[21]

The Internet, which promises to permit virtually unfettered communication between individuals and groups, particularly complicates governments' efforts to control the flow of information. For the United States, which does not really even attempt to regulate the flow of political information and has an open, decentralized society, that difficulty may not pose a problem; China, Iran, Iraq, and the like (and even friendly states such as Saudi Arabia) may find the technology destabilizing, as it weakens governments' ability to control what their people know about themselves, their rulers, and the outside world, and what outsiders know about them, as well as helping opposition groups to coalesce and coordinate activities. Furthermore, to the extent the Internet whets nations' appetites for U.S. popular culture, it may make it harder for nations to cut their links with the United States.

Dancing with the One That Brung You

The spread of technology, largely driven by the private sector, has contributed to U.S. power and prosperity but has exposed the United States to potential dangers. The same market dynamics that created the problem can help address it, as the innovative dynamism that has created so much remarkable technology can be applied to security concerns. Already, companies are using security as a competitive aspect of their products and services. Many companies, of course, are developing cryptographic products, and it seems likely that increasing security awareness, as well as liberalization of U.S. export control policy, will increase the market for such products. Companies are already competing as to the security and reliability of their goods and services. In the wake of stories about the Citibank intrusion, for example, other banks reportedly approached that bank's customers, promising better security.[22] Similarly, Internet access providers advertise their reliability and availability as a way to distinguish themselves from competitors, and Cisco introduced security features into some of its networking products to differentiate them from those of Cisco's larger telecommunications equipment competitors.

Concern about liability for disasters may also drive security measures. The issue of how computer systems will deal with the year 2000 (Y2K) is already focusing the attention of the U.S. legal system on the allocation of responsibility for the effects of system failures. In the security realm, technology providers such as Cisco and NetSolve, Inc. are teaming with CIGNA Property & Casualty to provide integrated security and risk management programs for important information systems. As consciousness of the need for security spreads, demand for products will grow and the market will provide solutions. It would be better for everyone if such security consciousness develops because of education than because of some catastrophic attack.

Conclusion

As it seems futile and self-defeating to attempt to stop either the flow of relatively open networks into U.S. systems or the international flow of IT that might make IW attacks against U.S. targets likely, the United States will need to go with those flows. At the same time, though, the United States will need to harden its systems and drive the development of international legal regimes so that they can cope with technological evolution. When discussing cyberspace it is easy to fall into the habit of calling things "new," "unique," or "revolutionary," (mostly because they often are) and assuming that old rules do not apply. Certainly IT can be "new," "unique," or "revolutionary," but in dealing with the new, unique, and revolutionary security threats that arise in a networked world, it is important to recognize that there is no singular solution to U.S. vulnerabilities. Just as the atom bomb gave the U.S. tremendous power, but then also posed a grave threat, the U.S. will have to adjust to the dangers that its technological talents bring it. In cyberspace, as in the old, physical world, there are no substitutes for vigilance, vigor, and ingenuity.

Notes

1. U.S. Department of Commerce, The Emerging Digital Economy (1998), p. 4.

2. *Id.,* at A1–1.

3. U.S. Department of the Air Force, *Cornerstones of Information Warfare* (1995), p. 2.

4. These scenarios are based upon reported events and ideas suggested in a number of works, including: James Adams, *The Next World War* (New York: Simon & Schuster) 1998, Roger C. Molander, Andrew S. Riddile, and Peter A. Wilson, *Strategic Information Warfare: A New Face of War* (1996), and Tom Clancy, *Debt of Honor* (1994).

5. Adams, pp. 174–175.

6. Tim Regan, "Wars of the future...today," *The Christian Science Monitor* (June 24, 1999): 13.

7. E.g., "Cyber Wars," *The Economist*, (Jan. 13, 1996), at 77; See also Peter G. Neumann, *Computer Related Risks*, 126–128 (1995).

8. "The Death of Distance," *The Economist*, September 30, 1995, p. S5.

9. President's Commission on Critical Infrastructure Protection, Critical Foundations (hereinafter "PCCIP Report") (1997), pp. A17–18.

10. Information Revolution Spawns "Revolution in Security Affairs," *Defense Daily*, June 8, 1995, p. 1.

11. Gary H. Anthes, "Info-Terrorist Threat Growing," *Computerworld*, January 30, 1995, p. 1.

12. E.g., John Arquilla and David Ronfeldt, *The Advent of Netwar* (1996).

13. For example, while its personnel were holding hostages in the residence of the Japanese ambassador to Peru, the Tupac Amaru Revolutionary Movement (MRTA) posted messages to their Website, and in Colombia, the Marxist rebels, right wing paramilitary forces, and national army all maintain Websites.

14. U.S. General Accounting Office, Computer Attacks at Department of Defense Pose Increasing Risks, GAO/AIMD–96–84 (May 1996) 22.

15. Aaron Pressman, U.S. Encryption Export Limits Cost Economy $96 Billion, April 1, 1998, http://www.crypto.com/reuters/show.cgi?article=891552074.

16. See, e.g., John Arquilla, "The Great Cyberwar of 2002," *Wired* (February 1998), pp. 122–127, 160–170. The possible applicability of arms control for information warfare is discussed in David Elliott, Lawrence Greenberg, and Kevin Soo Hoo, "Strategic Information Warfare: A New Arena for Arms Control?" (Stanford Center for International Security and Arms Control, 1997).

17. In the summer of 1999 privacy activists attacked CIAO's first draft national plan, before it was even formally released, as a recipe for increased governmental intrusion into private systems.

18. For a more complete discussion of proposed information sharing mechanisms, see PCCIP Report, pp. 25–47.

19. For a discussion of the U.S. cryptography debate and international cryptography regulation, see Stewart A. Baker and Paul R. Hurst, *The Limits of Trust* (Cambridge, MA: Kluwer Law International, 1998).

20. Neil Munro, "Pentagon Developing Cyberspace Weapons," *Washington Technology* (June 22, 1995).

21. Adams, p. 30.

22. Adams, p. 175.

Part V

Emerging Markets

Unfinished Business and the Future

Chapter 17

Economic Dimensions of Security in Russia

John E. Tedstrom

Introduction

Perhaps nowhere in the world have the economic dimensions of international security become so prominent as in the post-Soviet space commonly referred to as the New Independent States (NIS). This is true in the context of these countries' efforts to build successful states and in the context of U.S. policy toward them. Whether the focus is on internal recovery and stability, regional cooperation, or global integration, economic issues are of central importance. Moreover, even when the United States engages Russia on more traditional security threats such as nonproliferation or arms control, economic levers and logic often emerge as some of our most effective foreign policy tools.

The United States' fundamental, long-term interest in all the transition countries is their development from transition states to modern market democracies that play constructive, collaborative international roles, rather than their decline into rogue or failed states. While none of countries of the region will emerge as peer competitors to the United States in the next generation, it is possible that one or more of the states could stumble on its path toward modernity and target its limited resources on rogue activities. Likewise, a failed transition could result in an unstable state that would become the source of security problems within and beyond its borders. As Europe expands eastward, and our interests in East-Central Europe increase, instability inside neighboring countries take on increased importance.

Additionally, as pointed out elsewhere in this volume, the United States has a strong interest in identifying and fostering new and emerging opportunities for U.S. businesses in markets abroad. Efforts to expand foreign trade and investment, both from and to the U.S., promotes job growth, encourages constructive competition, and diversifies our portfolio of economic partners, minimizing the effect of shocks that may arise from any one country or region of the world. By forging closer economic ties we also promote better international understanding and robust, productive relations with countries abroad. Russia, closed to Western trade and investment for so long, and opposed to Western interests because of ideological competition, thus represents a unique and historic opportunity to expand commerce and promote a more stable and secure international environment.

From the perspective of next generation policy issues, two distinct strategic challenges with respect to Russia stand out, both of which have key economic dimensions. The first priority is Russia's recovery from crisis to stability. Failure to make progress on this cardinal task will impede, if not jeopardize, reform throughout the region, prevent Russia's eventual integration into the global system, and leave important U.S. national security concerns unresolved. As we shall see, Russia's chief obstacle to participating in the global economy are the difficulties it faces in state-building at home.

The second priority is Ukraine's integration into Europe. Although Ukraine faces many serious domestic challenges, with leadership and commitment it could achieve this objective in the next 20 years. Ukraine's principal advantage in this regard is its emerging identity as a European state. Over time this focus will increasingly shape Ukraine's policies and reforms in a European direction. Ukraine is also relatively small—its economy is smaller than Poland's—and is therefore relatively easy to encourage from the outside. Ukraine's success has critical implications for European security and U.S. interests there; a strong, stable Ukraine can help ensure security in Europe, contribute to regional prosperity, and serve as a positive model for other states in the region, including Russia.

Russia: From Crisis to Stability

As important as economics is to Russia's national security and U.S.-Russian relations, much of the discussion in this volume about globalization of capital, new industries, economic cooperation, and vital new markets is only of longer-term relevance to Russia. While U.S. interests are best served by Russia's full integration into the global economy, the next generation of Russian leaders are best advised to grapple first and foremost with the more basic, interrelated questions of national identity and state building. This is not to say that opportunities in the international economic system will not motivate or inform Russian choices. To the contrary, the promises of the global economic system will strongly (and positively) influence and shape the Russian debate. Achieving a broad and sustained social consensus on the fundamental issues of identity and state building—the Russian versions of the issues explored earlier in this volume by McCurdy and Hart—nevertheless needs to be Russia's top priority. Once it begins to consolidate its domestic reforms and build a system of stable social, political, and economic institutions, Russia will be better positioned to address the task of global integration.

A large part of the West's strategy toward Russia since 1992 has been premised on the notion that the collapse of the USSR resolved many of Russia's fundamental state-building and identity questions. Inherent in this was an assumption that there existed a meaningful domestic consensus on the type of state Russia should create for itself, and what role Russia would play internationally. To the contrary, the collapse of the USSR and the emergence of the Russian Federation and 14 other states in its wake only highlighted these questions and brought them to the fore.

As Russia's first post-Soviet decade draws to a close, the only consensus to be found among its citizens is despair about the future and nostalgia for Russia's former position as global superpower counterbalancing the United States. Russian public opinion polls from early 1999 document a strong rejection of markets and reforms, strong pessimism about the foreseeable future, strong disdain for major political figures (especially reformers), and a strong animosity toward the United States, the International Monetary Fund (IMF), and the West generally, which are often blamed for Russia's troubles. All of these sentiments must be reversed for Russia to succeed in the twenty-first century; Russia will not be able to reap the benefits of the global economy if it insists on creating an incompatible economic system and playing a mischievous role in international political and security affairs.

Although the U.S.-Russia agenda is and will be multifaceted, the challenges for U.S. policymakers in the next generation will center on two interrelated issues: First, protecting and strengthening U.S. security, and second, supporting reforms that promote democratic values and economic recovery. Virtually all of the other issues in our bilateral relationship, including Russia's relations with its neighbors, cooperation with the North Atlantic Treaty Organization (NATO), crime and corruption, and Russia's eventual global integration, are derivative of these two strategic problems.

Protecting American Security

Of most immediate relevance to U.S. national security is the bundle of nonproliferation and arms control challenges posed by Russia. These problems are of fundamental importance for the direct threat they represent to U.S. security, but also because their status helps to define the rest of the U.S.-Russian relationship. Unless there is steady progress on these issues, it is difficult to see how the broader bilateral relationship can achieve its full potential. These difficult problems will not be resolved in the near term. To the contrary, they are bound to be prominent parts of the U.S.-Russian relationship for the next generation of policymakers, and some of the most frustrating dimensions of these problems are rooted in economics. As a result, economic policy—in Moscow and Washington—will play a large role in achieving sustainable solutions.

Readers in the West are by now quite familiar with the plight of Russian scientists, engineers, and technicians who used to develop weapons of mass destruction for the Soviet Union. As these programs were scaled back or terminated by the Russian government, thousands of these specialists became under- or unemployed.

These former elites of the Soviet military-industrial complex today face severe economic hardship on a daily basis. Alcoholism and suicide are increasingly commonplace. Less tragic on a human level but more dangerous for international security is the potential temptation for these people to sell their expertise to whomever will pay. Usually, this means rogue states like Iran or Iraq. Similarly, Russians with access to military technologies are sorely tempted to sell to the highest bidder. Often enough, this, too, means selling to states or groups that would threaten our security. This problem will be with us as long as Russia's economy continues to fail, forcing weapons specialists and arms traders to find buyers.

The United States has, for the last several years, attempted to provide alternative economic opportunities to as many of these people as possible, including bringing them to the West and promoting joint ventures that turn their expertise to civilian production. Our success has been uneven, and the cooperation from the Russian government has been sporadic, despite the fact that Russia faces proliferation threats itself. Next generation policymakers will need to build on this early experience and devise new strategies to deal more effectively with the proliferation challenge.

Less well-known are the economics of strategic arms control. The defining arms control agreement for the foreseeable future is START II, which, along with its successor, START III, will determine the pace and direction of nuclear force reductions well into the next century. In January 1996 the U.S. Senate ratified START II, but the Duma has repeatedly delayed a vote. Implementing START II is now expected to run through 2007 at which time further cuts envisioned in START III would begin and take Russia and U.S. nuclear forces to roughly 20 percent of their Cold War peaks.

Economics are key to Russia's nuclear dilemma as well as to the START treaties. First, it was the Soviet Union's economic deterioration since the 1980s—caused in no small part by excessive militarization of its economy—that forced deep cuts in its conventional forces. These cuts shifted Russia's force structure in favor of land-based Inter-Continental Ballistic Missiles (ICBM), the weapons most restricted by START II. Second, Russia's nuclear forces are deteriorating anyway because the military does not have the financial resources to maintain them. As Russian Minister of Defense Sergeev puts it, "To draw up a budget like Mozambique but demand armed forces like the United States is not entirely logical."[1] In fact, with or without START II, most experts agree that financial constraints will eventually force reductions in Russia's strategic nuclear forces to levels below those anticipated in START III.

Third, many Russians object to START II because of the short-term financial costs associated with implementing the treaty. Indeed, it isn't cheap to dismantle an ICBM. But in the longer term these costs will be more than offset by savings associated with lower levels of nuclear weapons. Implementing START II in the context of more radical cuts envisioned by most START III scenarios would without doubt reduce budgetary pressures in the long run and free up resources for investing in more productive endeavors that would improve the quality of life for all Russians. The U.S. has made concessions to the Russians to address their concerns about the short-term costs of implementing START II. One of the agreements reached between Presidents Clinton and Yeltsin in their September 1997 summit was to extend the implementation period of the treaty from 2003 to 2007 to lower the average annual cost of implementation. Of course the total cost to Russia will be higher, but that is seemingly of less concern to Moscow.

Russia's economic restructuring, recovery, and integration into global markets will be important to the ultimate and sustained resolution of problems like these. Integration will help clarify Russia's international interests and agenda in a way that promotes constructive business competition and security collaboration with the West. This will alter Russia's strategic calculations in a way that facilitates nuclear reductions. Economic recovery will allow for more reliable and reasonable defense planning and budgeting, critical for the long-term stability and effectiveness of the Russian Armed Forces. Without Russia's economic recovery it is difficult to see how sustainable progress on these issues will be achieved.

Supporting Domestic Reforms

Of all the states in the region, Russia has suffered the most debilitating economic setback since independence, especially since catching the "Asian flu" of 1998. The ramifications of the economic crisis since August 1998, in particular, have been far-reaching, and it will be difficult to reverse the temporary effects of higher oil prices and a devalued ruble notwithstanding. It is not now clear when Russia's leaders will embark on a decisive program of reform to set the economy on the right track. Until they do, it will be very difficult for the West to engage Russia economically and for Russians to have any real hope for economic recovery.

Three interrelated, deep-rooted dynamics obstruct Russia's transition to a stable, prosperous market democracy in the next few decades. The first is the predominance of personal over national interests. Few people in Russia have enough confidence in the future to invest in it. Instead, they seek short-term gain wherever possible, with little apparent concern for the longer term. Entrepreneurs seek rents instead of sustainable profits. Investment of new capital has stagnated at historically low levels since independence, adding years if not decades to Russia's recovery process. Bureaucrats and politicians at all levels have been reduced to bribery and corruption, discrediting themselves and the state. Ordinary people work multiple jobs just to survive, and then hide their income from the government; Russia's informal economy has grown to something like 50 percent of total Gross Domestic Product (GDP), and many Russians equate reforms with stealing.

A second worrisome dynamic exists in the relationship between center and periphery. Chechnya is a useful, if extreme, example of center-periphery tensions gone very wrong. Chechnya had had a chilling effect on other NIS regions as well as on neighboring countries and has sharply shaken the West's confidence in Russia's government. Tens of thousands ultimately died in the first Chechen conflict alone.

The crisis in Chechnya points to fundamental problems throughout Russia's federal system. Dozens of regions have distanced themselves from Moscow to one degree or another. Many have even signed individual "treaties" with the federal government, spelling out their own political and economic relations. These problems have had a serious and negative effect on economic reform and political development in the NIS and their resolution is important to any hopes of creating a stable state and integrating the NIS into the global system.

There are many facets to Russia's center-periphery disequilibrium, some of which are predominantly economic. First, most people in the NIS have little or no confidence in the ability of the national government to govern effectively, and Moscow has lost its credibility at the regional and local levels. Voters have demanded that their local representatives step in to protect local interests, even if this means adopting policies that run counter to Federation laws. Second, many regions withhold financial payments they owe to Moscow, often because Moscow fails to pay what it owes to regional and local budgets. This, in turn, exacerbates the NIS's fiscal crisis, limiting Moscow's ability to govern and to interact successfully with international organizations such as the IMF and the World Bank. Thus, even seemingly local economic problems eventually influence Russia's international position.

The third dynamic that threatens the transition in Russia is the easy, fluid relationship between actors in business, government, and organized crime. Crime and corruption undermine confidence in the state and ultimately weaken legitimate leaders' ability to govern. Moreover, organized crime in Russia has taken on regional and global proportions. Drug smuggling, money laundering, and arms trafficking by Russian organized crime are growing problems with global effects and have received increased attention at senior government levels in Russia, the United States, and other Western states. The strength and influence of organized crime groups will likely grow as they amass greater wealth, employ new technologies, and expand their networks.

These three dynamics have conspired to create an unstable equilibrium. Russia suffers from wide and growing wealth gaps that are creating a resentful underclass. Center-periphery relationships are tense and unsustainable. Crime and corruption undermine reform and reformers, as well as the legitimacy of the state. An additional problem, just beginning to gain the attention of observers in the West, is Russia's looming health crisis.

The root causes of the healthcare crisis are manifold and range from decades of terrible environmental mismanagement to stress associated with unemployment.[2] Combine these with a broken healthcare delivery system and severe shortages of basic medications and medical equipment, and the Russian health tragedy begins to take shape. Nuclear radiation and chemical contamination associated with civilian and military programs have killed or mutilated entire Russian cities. Simple lead emissions in Russia are about 50 times higher than in the European Union (EU), even though Russia produces a fraction of the EU's GDP. Tuberculosis is on a seemingly uncontrolled rise and has been dubbed an epidemic by Russia's Interior Ministry. Some Western experts predict that between 1.5 million and 2 million Russians will die of tuberculosis in the year 2000. Deaths from AIDS are predicted to skyrocket early in the next century because Russia can't afford to provide the expensive treatments that keep HIV at bay in the West. Syphilis and other sexually transmitted diseases are also at high levels and spreading among Russia's youth who don't have adequate access to condoms or information about safer sex. Only about half of Russia's 16-year-old boys can expect to reach 60, and Russia's population is shrinking year by year. These statistics describe the tip of the iceberg. Russia's health problems could easily emerge as a major international issue in the next decade not only because of the humanitarian challenge they represent inside the region, but because of the threat they pose beyond its borders.

These problems of domestic reform and state building must become the priority for NIS leaders. For its part, the West underestimated the difficulties inherent in changing the mindset of people who had absolutely no understanding of what markets and democracies are or how they work, let alone how to build them or why they should want them. The West also under-appreciated the degree to which political competition would undermine economic reform. Although analysts and government officials all said "Russia's transformation will take a generation or more and will suffer many false starts and missteps," after just six years of post-Soviet reform the West has lost its strategic patience with the area. The IMF, reeling from criticisms that it was perpetuating bad behavior in Russia by ignoring the moral hazard of lending money without assurance of structural reform, by turning a blind eye to the dangers of corruption in the Russian government, and by covering the losses of Western investors who took calculated risks in Russia has distanced itself from Moscow, at least for the time being. IMF lending programs are smaller now and designed only to service Russia's existing IMF debt. Russia, convinced that the West doesn't want it to recover, finds little to lose from trying to revive its traditional competitive role in the world.

Our common goal must be to find a more stable and sustainable course of assistance, one that is informed not just by good economics, but by a better understanding of what makes Russia tick. Russia's problems will persist over the long-term and they will pose important and daunting challenges not only for the next generation of policymakers but for those who will follow.

Ukraine: Returning to Europe

Ukraine's transformation into a successful European market democracy is integral to its security, to the development of Central Europe, and to U.S. interests in the region. If Ukraine gets its transition right, it will emerge as an important contributor to stability, prosperity, and security in this increasingly promising and important region. Importantly, it will also serve as a positive example for Russia. If it fails, Ukraine will become a major consumer of European security and wealth, hindering progress not only in Central Europe but in Eurasia as well.

Although Ukraine and Russia share many common problems, the differences between the two are far more salient to U.S. national security strategy and foreign policy. Most important, Ukraine has officially articulated its intent to return to Europe as a sovereign, independent country. Historically, this implies a fundamental departure from many centuries during which it was dominated by various empires and torn from modern Europe by the Soviet Union. Practically, it means that Ukraine intends to harmonize its legal, political, and economic framework with those of Europe. This strategy will pay enormous dividends in the future, not least of which is greatly enhanced national security.

Ukraine's progress toward this goal since gaining independence in December 1991 has been uneven. Over the course of the last decade, Ukraine has played a constructive role in international security and regional affairs. Domestically, however, Ukraine's economic reforms have been insufficient to generate either growth or the confidence of foreign investors. More than anything, the slow pace of reforms has impeded Ukraine's integration with the European Union and the West more generally.

Among Ukraine's international accomplishments are its implementation of the Trilateral Agreement with the United States and Russia. This agreement led to the transfer of all nuclear weapons from Ukrainian territory. Ukraine also signed the Nuclear Nonproliferation Treaty (NPT). Ukraine has also supported NATO enlargement. These advances in Ukrainian security policy have led to successful collaboration with the United States on specific proliferation problems, the most prominent of which concerned the Busher reactor in Iran.

Ukraine's successful management of relations with key neighbors, most important Russia, Poland, Hungary, and Romania, has advanced regional security and stability. In the early 1990s, Ukraine's relations were strained with a number of its Central European neighbors and with Russia. Ukraine's cooperation and skillful diplomacy transformed thorny problems into promising opportunities for regional cooperation, many of which are already bearing fruit. Many of Ukraine's Central European neighbors have expressed a new interest in its transition efforts and have begun to organize programs of technical assistance and economic cooperation.

Ukraine's intensive cooperation within the Partnership for Peace framework, including participation in peacekeeping activities in Bosnia and later in Kosovo, and signing and developing a "distinctive relationship" with NATO, signals its recognition of the unique role NATO plays in European security. Likewise, by signing a Partnership Cooperation Agreement with the EU (1998), Ukraine signaled its desire to more deeply and systematically pursue its integration with the EU.

Domestically, reforms in Ukraine have come slower than many would have wanted, limiting its ability to generate growth and to integrate economically and politically with Europe. The limiting effect of domestic stagnation is true not only for Ukraine's relations with the EU. Indeed, resource constraints have impeded Ukraine's efforts to reform its military establishment and to cooperate with NATO and other partner countries.

The centrality of economic reforms to Ukraine's international aspirations—including its security agenda—has been a difficult but important lesson for Ukraine to learn. After announcing their strategic objective of full European integration in early 1998, Ukrainian leaders believed that Ukraine's unique geostrategic juxtaposition was enough to qualify it for special consideration by its Western counterparts, especially the EU. This was not to be. Indeed, Ukrainian overtures to Brussels and other European capitals based on this logic were roundly rebuffed. The message Ukrainian diplomats received instead, and have since begun to internalize, is that European integration is not simply or even mostly about foreign policy. Most important in this regard is the "Europeanization" of the state, that is, domestic reforms in the direction of EU norms.

This process of internal transformation will take at least a generation. To be sure, Ukraine's economy suffers many of the same economic problems facing Russian leaders. And like Russia's economy, Ukraine's has contracted every year since independence, inflicting hardship on its people and weakening public support for reforms. Though there is a political consensus that Ukraine must remain free and important impulses that its future lies in Europe, most Ukrainians have little notion of what it means to be part of modern Europe. The short-term task for Ukrainian leaders and their Western partners is to increase public support for reforms by educating Ukraine's citizens on the advantages of European integration and then to accelerate reforms in that direction.

The best way to accomplish this task is to make a strategic adjustment in our policy toward Ukraine. Although we have consistently and correctly supported Ukraine's independence and transformation, the West generally has couched its policies in the wrong context. Instead of thinking about Ukraine in terms of what it was—a Soviet republic—we should think about Ukraine in terms of what it should become—a modern European state. This shift in thinking will inform our policies and programs and encourage the Ukrainians to think more and more in European terms as well. Such a strategic adjustment has other advantages, not least of which is the ability to draw more on the experience and interest of Ukraine's Central European neighbors. There are no good models of transition in the NIS today. And there are no resources in the NIS that can be marshaled to Ukraine's advantage. In Europe, there is an abundance of experience and a considerable resource base, not to mention serious national security interests in Ukraine's success.

Economics and Security
in 2000 and Beyond

The purpose of this essay has been less to chart the recent economic history of Russia and Ukraine than to identify and explore strategically important areas where economics impinge on security, East-West relations, and on the place and role of these countries in the global community. The underlying message is that all states in the NIS have a great deal to do in terms of state building and consolidating public support for reforms. Doing this will improve these states' own national security and make them better international actors.

This rule holds for the countries of the Caspian basin and Central Asia as well as for Russia and Ukraine. Until Azerbaijan, Kazakhstan, Turkmenistan, and other countries consolidate their reforms and become stable, reliable international partners, they will not come close to realizing the economic benefits inherent in their energy resources. Pipelines will not bring peace to the region. Regional cooperation, respect for borders, and democratic institutions will, however, make it possible for foreign investors to engage these countries in mutually beneficial projects.

Russia and Ukraine—and the other states in the region—will present the next generation of U.S. policymakers with a mix of traditional security problems such as proliferation and arms control, and new challenges such as international health crises and European integration. Economic policy is bound to figure prominently in the resolution of each of these issues as well as shape our overall strategic agenda.

Notes

1. Quoted in the *St. Louis Post-Dispatch*, April 22, 1998.

2. See, in particular, the works by Murray Feshbach, including his *Environmental and Health Atlas of Russia* and *Ecological Disaster: Cleaning Up the Hidden Legacy of the Soviet Regime*, Brookings, Washington, DC, 1994.

Chapter 18

Changing China— A Search for Perspective

James E. Bass

During much of the past decade, the American public has been saturated with two images of China: economic miracle and human-rights wasteland. For convenience, the media rarely strays from these two polar axes, and in response, U.S. foreign policymakers and public policy commentators in Washington endlessly debate which focus should be privileged. Recently, one caricature has begun to unravel, as it is no secret that the inflated expectations for profit opportunities in China were naive when conceived. Regarding China's economic development, U.S. perceptions suffer from hot and cold pendulum swings, lacking a middle distance for gauging China's landscape. To lend perspective, it may be helpful to look to the U.S. past. With a deeper comparative perspective, we may be better able to frame a next-generation approach to economic relations with China.

A Sense of History

Whether in the economic or human rights spheres, Americans and their policymakers need a greater sense of history in discussing China's development. Unfortunately, instant gratification through media images jettisons historical context. There are, however, a number of events from the United States' past that should give us pause. I call on two for consideration, stretching to our familiar poles of human rights and economic development.

First, a recent article in the *Far Eastern Economic Review* by John Keenan recalled an incident when thousands of disgruntled citizens marched to the center of their government, camped out and agitated for several months, insisting the government live up to commitments it had made. After gathering in the open flats during April and May, the country's leader ordered the military to put down the demonstrations by any means and to clear the flats. The general followed his leader's orders, using tear gas, tanks, and small arms. Total casualties are not known, but scores of people were estimated killed or wounded. Tiananmen Square? No, the Bonus March. The leader was Herbert Hoover, the general was Douglas MacArthur, the flats were near the Capitol in Washington, and the year was 1932.

The Bonus March erupted because the U.S. government had inequitably delayed bonus payments to World War I veterans. In contrast, the Tiananmen crackdown was fomented by broader social and economic concerns (inflation, corruption, and a yearning for independent student and worker unions) that were not being adequately addressed by the Chinese government. Whereas the Bonus March has slipped from the pages of almost all history textbooks, Tiananmen gave rise to U.S. sanctions against China, provided CNN with spectacular graphic footage, and continues to be the battle cry of various interest groups, both in China and the United States. As Mr. Keenan notes in his article, query whether China has taken more steps to address particular concerns that drove the Tiananmen protests than the city of Los Angeles has taken to address the fracturing fault lines that gave rise to riots in Los Angeles in 1992. And then query whether replayed images of riots in Los Angeles will be backdrops for President Clinton's next visit to Hollywood.

Turning from the human rights axis, tales from the U.S. economic past provide parallels for economic events in China today. The stock exchanges of Shanghai and Shenzhen have provided splendid prime-time footage of "capitalism" in China. The two exchanges were created in the early 1990s to provide an alternative method for Chinese companies to raise capital and (what seems) a proxy for Chinese punters to satisfy their hunger for gaming. Public company listings grew rapidly. Within seven years of establishment, China's two primary stock exchanges had a combined market capitalization greater than 80 percent of the market capitalization of the Stock Exchange of Hong Kong, which has enjoyed an 80-year history.

With traders in prim jackets and a big board flashing stock prices, the floor of the Shanghai Exchange has an aura of New York about it. But when scandals occur, Shanghai (and by implication, China) is portrayed as an unscrupulous market center where illegal activities rule the day. In late 1992, the Chinese government decided to assert more central control over the developing securities market activities in China. However, the initial regulations granting oversight authority to the China Securities Regulatory Commission (CSRC) did not promptly translate into *de facto* authority for the new body.

The CSRC had to contend with belligerent leaders of the stock exchanges of Shanghai and Shenzhen. During the first two years of the CSRC's existence, frequent confrontations arose between the CSRC and the two principal stock exchanges in China, with the stock exchanges often able to thwart CSRC directives. Despite efforts by the central government to staunch manipulative and deceptive trading practices, the stock exchanges had their own bases of power and support (primarily from municipal governments) that frustrated central government efforts. In January 1995, a government treasury futures trading scandal involving Shanghai International Securities erupted, leading to the downfall of the head of the Shanghai Securities Exchange and simultaneous assertion of greater control over the stock exchange by the CSRC. Newspapers around the world prominently reported the trading scandals occurring in China, not minding to point out that the story was a tale being twice told.

Characteristically, several U.S. representatives eventually decided it was time to take action. Congress conducted special hearings in November 1997 to investigate the poor disclosure and deceptive trading practices of Chinese companies that had issued stock in the United States. Congressional aides drafted redundant legislation instructing the United States Securities and Exchange

Commission (SEC) to beware of China stock offerings. Although the legislation, titled the U.S. Markets Securities Act, was not enacted, it illustrates the volatile manner in which the United States is adjusting to China's economic development.

Poor disclosure, corrupt trading practices, and lax accounting standards are not unique to China. And harnessing public support for new government agencies to address such shortcomings in the marketplace is also not a challenge unique to China. China needs aggressive, professionally administered institutions overseeing its financial markets, but such new kids on the block have to find a footing, which is often undermined by other ministries there. Instead of receiving constructive encouragement from the United States, our congressional leaders often launch bullying attacks.

If we take a look back, we remember that one of the great challenges for the Roosevelt Administration during the Depression era was asserting federal government control over activities that, for the prior 150 years, had been the province of private parties or state governments. For Wall Street, the struggle was most poignantly illustrated by resistance of the New York Stock Exchange to 1933 and 1934 legislation shifting oversight and compliance requirements for publicly listed companies from the Exchange to the newly created SEC.

In the case of the SEC, like China's CSRC, effective market oversight did not arise simply by cloaking a new agency with federal legislative authority. The SEC's authority during its early years was *de jure*, not *de facto*. Only when a market scandal brought down Dick Whitney, the chairman of the New York Stock Exchange, did public support for SEC authority arise. Dick Whitney had been the lead spokesman for using a private, nongovernmental approach to oversight of securities market activity and had testified forcefully for such an approach before Congress. When Dick Whitney fell in a well-publicized self-dealing scandal, his credibility, and in turn the credibility of the free market argument against central government oversight, fell, enabling the SEC to assert *de facto* authority.

Perhaps there were few representatives attending the special hearings targeting China in November 1997 who remember Dick Whitney and the early era of the SEC. But they should take note of the historically similar circumstances faced by the SEC and CSRC, and further remember that the powers needed to address disclosure problems and trading practices of foreign entities and persons in the United States have long been held by the SEC. We know, for instance, that nondisclosure of economic and governmental risks in connection with the issuance of foreign bonds to U.S. investors in the 1920s was one of the perceived abuses that led to congressional investigation of securities practices in the early 1930s. Bundling Chinese state-owned enterprises into public offering entities and cloaking them with U.S. GAAP financial statements suffers from, as the Chinese would say, having a chicken talk to a duck. China's economic system does not yet approximate a free-market system, and many experts have doubts that it will any time in the near future. That risk is fully disclosed in the offering prospectuses for Chinese companies. Any sensible U.S. pension-fund manager who decides to purchase the stock of these companies understands that in the case of China, or any developing country still shackled by a policy-driven and quasi-planned economy, there is an element of *caveat emptor*. China's bold willingness to expose its companies to the scrutiny of worldwide investors is a step that few developing countries would have taken so soon after establishing domestic securities markets. China should be encouraged, not ridiculed, by U.S. leaders to continue to improve its market-oriented focus and regulating institutions.

These historical analogies do not excuse violent or ineffectual actions by governments and their leaders. They simply illustrate that all nations and peoples have the capacity to fall short. Better to keep that perspective in mind than replay for prime-time consumption seemingly nefarious deeds—incompletely understood.

Labor and Foreign Investment

Incomplete understanding of the challenges faced by Chinese leaders sometimes works to China's advantage. For instance, the economic-miracle story has been effectively stoked by the warm handshakes of China's leaders. The allure of the Chinese market has tempted foreign tradesmen for centuries. What we have seen in the past 15 years is preprandials. Behind the banquet halls lies a less gracious landscape.

China faces an immense challenge for the foreseeable future: creating employment for its enormous population. When China's leaders puff the great profits to be made in China to an increasingly skeptical international business community, such propaganda should be restated in the context of China's desperate need to keep its laboring masses employed. As frequently noted by China analysts, up to 30 percent of the approximate 110 million laborers working for China's state-owned enterprises (SOE) are redundant. Prime Minister Zhu Rongji has declared that the government will do its fair share in addressing over-employment by laying off 4 million people from government ranks. Add numerical estimates of the roaming labor force from the Chinese countryside (approximately 80 million, which number will increase in the decades to come), and China's most pressing policy concern is clear: find ways to keep the masses *gainfully* employed. The magnitude of this challenge dwarfs any domestic policy concern faced by leaders in the United States.

During the past 18 years of China's open-door policy, the government has launched intermittent worldwide propaganda campaigns aimed at attracting foreign investment. Recent promotion campaigns by China's leaders have unfortunately coincided with the severe currency and economic crises gripping Asia and come on the heels of a number of disturbing years (in terms of profitability) for foreign investors and companies in China. China's leaders realize that CEOs of the world's largest multinational companies have been losing enthusiasm for pursuing business prospects in China. From the perspective of such CEOs, China's long-term potential will always be there but the short-term rewards have not been commensurate with the risks.

Foreign direct investment (FDI), through Sino-foreign joint ventures and so-called "wholly foreign-owned enterprises," has been a cornerstone of China's policy to promote rapid economic development. In recent years, the importance of FDI to urban employment has grown, as 300,000 foreign invested enterprises established since 1980 have provided 17 million new jobs. Such enterprises generate 30 percent of China's exports, thereby enhancing the amount of foreign currency held in China—a key for China's future imports of technology and equipment necessary to sustain high growth and, in turn, employment prospects.

More recently, China's government has discovered the benefits of attracting portfolio equity investment through stock offerings by China-related companies. Chinese enterprises were first startled, then delighted, by the prospect of being able to float 25 percent of the "equity" in their enterprises to foreign investors. The boom of such financing activities on the Shanghai, Shenzhen, Hong Kong, and New York stock exchanges in the past six years has led to a stampede of investment banking enthusiasm for "financing" China's huge commercial and infrastructure needs. It is no secret in China that public equity offerings to foreigners seemed like manna from heaven to Chinese enterprise managers: a huge capital injection for the enterprise for seemingly no cost, and certainly none of the foreign control concerns and labor downsizings that arise from FDI ventures. In 1997, FDI brought $45.3 billion to China and public securities offerings attracted an additional $13 billion.

In the year preceding the currency devaluation crises in Asia, it appeared that China was moving away from FDI as the preferred method of attracting foreign investment. Some Chinese opinion shapers surmised that it is better to have passive minority shareholders far away from the country than to have meddling foreign corporate control of enterprises up and down China's eastern coastline. China began reversing the privileges and benefits bestowed on FDI ventures and tightening guidelines governing the channeling of foreign investment.

With portfolio investment comes, however, "hot" money, the type of money that arrives and departs at the whim of institutional investor sentiment. The recent destruction wrought to the economies of Indonesia, Malaysia, Thailand, and Korea by "hot" foreign money has given policymakers in Beijing considerable pause. Even a 25 percent minority foreign stake in a publicly traded Chinese enterprise can prove troublesome if the minority shareholders quickly abandon their holdings. As the price-earnings ratios for "red chips" and "H" share companies (China's publicly listed enterprises in Hong Kong) fall, so go the prospects of using international institutional investment to underwrite China's next stage of rapid development. In contrast, FDI locks investment in China for the longer term, and as such, its attractiveness to China's policymakers is, once again, on the rise.

As China struggles to define the appropriate role for foreign investment in its economy, foreigners will continue to see touting by China's leadership (and, in the case of stock offerings, Western investment banks) of the great investment opportunities to be found in China. We should, as Western CEOs are now doing, cast a cautious eye on these sales pitches. There are opportunities, but they should be measured in the context of crosscurrent pressures that roam China's economic landscape.

Minding the State

The broad array of foreign business activities permitted in China today arise from China's pressing and capacious desire to acquire foreign technology and to attract huge sums of foreign capital. Such appetite has unfortunately been indiscriminate, leading to excessive imports of production equipment. In recent years, as each province encouraged establishment of a large, new factory to manufacture widgets, China's total production capacity for widgets quickly exceeded domestic and international demand. Now, a rising outcry against "ruinous competition" is heard from industry leaders and government officials, echoing the U.S. struggle with such issue in the latter half of the nineteenth century. For two critical industries—telecommunications and energy—China is steering clear of market competition.

Western companies have struggled in recent years to pry open opportunities for participation in China's telecom sector. Chinese policy prohibits foreign ownership and operation of telecom enterprises, but many companies stood patiently at China's door (or rather inside the banquet halls) waiting for the prohibition to fall. With the establishment of China Unicom in 1994 (the first competitor to China's state-owned telecom monopoly), foreign companies and China Unicom entered into creative investment and participation arrangements aimed at reaping equity-like returns while avoiding equity investment regulatory prohibitions for such telecom enterprises. Chinese officials tolerated such investment models built on legal loopholes for several years but abruptly sought termination of the arrangements in September 1998.

China hesitates to permit foreign companies to tap the enormous potential revenues from its telecom sector. China will continue to

invite foreign companies to establish telecom hardware manufacturing enterprises, which businesses will prosper until production overcapacity drowns the market. In the telecom operation and service sector, however, China will separate sources of capital from sources of technology. By looking to domestic and foreign capital markets for money (albeit minority shareholdings) and to leading technology companies for provision of software and hardware technology, China has—in the minds of some leaders—the best of all possible worlds: foreign minority ownership with world-class foreign technology.

Frustrated foreign telecom companies should learn from China's energy sector, where China has, for 18 years, been luring exploration capital and technology from abroad while barring significant operating and service sector activities by foreign companies. China has hundreds of technical institutes training thousands who will contribute to the country's energy exploration, exploitation, and processing businesses. Before the 1990s, China was confident that it could satisfy its domestic energy needs from domestic exploration and production. In 1984, oil constituted China's largest export commodity, surpassing textiles. As one of its first steps in "opening" to the outside world in 1979, China drafted regulations intended to attract foreign oil companies to explore for oil off China's coast. The largest amount of capital committed to China in the early years of its open-door policy came from foreign oil companies. With the collapse of oil prices in 1985 and the relatively disappointing discoveries offshore, foreign oil companies' initial enthusiasm for China foundered.

As years passed, China opened up more and more sections of the country to foreign-invested energy exploration activities. The conservative doctrines reflected in the initial offshore exploration and production regulations, however, were not amended in regulations governing onshore exploration activities. Geographic largesse did not replace regulatory stinginess. As a result of insufficient exploration and development activities in the late 1980s and early 1990s, China's rapidly expanding economy accelerated past the promise of the country's exploitation potential. In 1993, for the first time in many decades, China became a net importer of oil. By the mid-1990s, policymakers recognized that China would not be able to be energy self-sufficient. The country needed to look abroad.

Signaling a noteworthy shift in energy policy, in 1997 China entered contracts to acquire numerous oil and gas reserves around the world and committed to build an expensive pipeline from Kazakhstan to China's western border. Foreign energy companies have been startled by China's international bids, where the China National Petroleum Company has paid premiums far in excess of competing offers. China is having to overpay for oil resources abroad to protect its poorly performing energy sector at home. China's state petroleum and petrochemical entities employ millions of laborers. The on-shore energy service sector work units are split along geographic lines, protecting such units from the cold, chilly winds of competition. More specifically, if foreign companies were permitted to compete through joint ventures in the energy service sector throughout the country, an enormous number of laborers would lose their jobs. And mass unemployment could lead to social unrest.

As China begins the treacherous task of dismantling and downsizing numerous state-owned enterprises, foreign investment will be essential to create the market engine needed to provide new employment opportunities. However, in critical sectors of China's economy, such as energy and telecommunications, foreign capital (raised through IPOs) will be underwriting overemployment at state monopolies rather than generating new employment at agile competitive ventures.

Caveat Emptor:
Beware or Be Aware?

When President Clinton arrived in China in late June 1998, the media juxtaposed images of the straight-laced greeting ceremony in Tiananmen Square with the terror from 1989. But neither of the images underscored the challenge of securing gainful employment for China's enormous population. Better from the perspective of "truth" to proffer images of thousands of rural laborers camping out in the public squares adjacent to China's urban train stations at Spring Festival each year. That is where the action lies in China for decades to come.

As future U.S. administrations attempt to define U.S. foreign policy "interests" in China's economic growth, the private sector and the investing public in the United States will likely alert such administrations to continuing frustration with arbitrary and shifting policies (accompanied by scant profits) inside China. The administrations should suggest to the American people and enterprises that when it comes to China—*caveat emptor*—not unlike what their ancestors encountered during much of U.S. history. The U.S. government will not be able to change China; rather China will tend to that task.

The open-door policy in China has been remarkable. But an open-door policy does not necessarily mean full disclosure, for the truths about China are not evident when first dining in its banquet halls. U.S. companies and investors have two choices: either have great expectations dampened every five or seven years as Chinese policies change or the business cycle runs its course (or both), or manage such expectations by recognizing that China will change at its own pace. Similarly, U.S. policymakers should explain and debate China issues from a more humble perspective, one that does not lose sight of China's enormous population and its intractable historical ways of dealing with itself and others.

Capital raising in the United States during the nineteenth century relied on foreign investment, primarily from England. Market crashes and bankruptcies (primarily railroad companies) were commonplace. Though foreign investors' memories were sometimes short, such investors understood the risks of the United States' great frontier. The attitude of such investors was not only to "beware" but to "be aware." The investments continued coming, and the United States grew immeasurably. The same will, we hope, be said of China.

Chapter 19

Middle Market
Capitalism in China

Nicholas Rockefeller

Introduction

Success for the United States in the first half of the twenty-first century will be a function of the evolution of the Sino-American relationship. China's trajectory to world power transcends any analogy to the rise of Germany, the Soviet Union, and Japan in the first half of the twentieth century. In some ways, China's geopolitical challenges for the United States may be closer to the sum of these three former challenges. During the past year, the geopolitical stage was roiled by public disclosures that offered evidence that, during the 1990s, China has been solicited for financial donations by agents of the United States political system and has succeeded in obtaining nuclear technology from the United States through intelligence operations. The entrance of these dual villains, spotlighted by the U.S.'s tragic bombing of China's Embassy in Belgrade, provided an unsettling introduction to China's role as the primary United States strategic issue for the next generation.

These dramatic news elements cloud the reality that China's rise has been propelled by a constellation of economic factors: a sustained effort to achieve its goals of higher productivity and living standards; an immense population; and a global movement toward free trade, free capital, and free markets. China has been pushing ahead managing these factors and others while attempting to preserve statism and to gain regional hegemony. Critical for any leverage that the United States might hope to have with China is the "new reality" that China's growing strength has brought it into a uniquely important and possibly economically interdependent relationship with the United States.

China and the United States each contribute greatly to the other's economic security through job creation, technology transfer, expanded markets, and higher investment returns. In 1998, the value of exports and imports of goods and services and the return on United States investment in China, adjusted for the inclusion of Hong Kong, equaled almost 6 percent of United States Gross Domestic Product (GDP), up from less than 1 percent in 1970. At the end of the year, the U.S.-China economic relationship supported an estimated 4 million jobs in the United States and 17 million jobs in China.

Despite its growing importance, United States policymakers have yet to determine how to approach China in anything but cookie-cutter fashion derived from the last generation of policymakers. The focus to date has been on government-to-government relations. Although at some level elite contact is important, it has limited scope in trying to influence China in ways that communicate the American vision of the twenty-first century. The ideals of democratic capitalism such as individual liberty, entrepreneurship, and private property seek recognition and encouragement within the various layers of Chinese society. This essay suggests an alternative to the preservation of the status quo through the current policies' almost single-minded focus on governmental elites. It argues that a missing dimension of cultivating civil society in China could be a catalyst for change.

Background

Since the process of normalization began during the 1970s, American leadership has groped uncertainly to create a foreign policy architecture that includes China as an emerging world power. President Richard Nixon's breakthrough for normalization of the

Sino-U.S. relationship was largely an executive action that, by necessity, preceded general acceptance of Chinese integration into our nation's policymaking institutions and thinking. Successive United States administrations have followed less with the creation of a coherent policy and more with a hodgepodge of activities.

These activities have been driven, on the one hand, by pursuit of domestic constituencies to whom international human rights, unionism, and environmental protection are electoral "hot buttons" and, on the other hand, by commercial considerations of the export, technology, and intellectual property sectors of U.S. industry. Jim Bass noted the tensions between "Moralism" and "Mammon" that have produced a schizophrenic Uncle Sam with whom many, here and abroad, are uncomfortable trusting with the task of introducing a new entrant into the global power structure. Still, the full integration of China into international institutions such as the WTO is one of the great unfinished tasks of the post-Cold War and requires the active participation of the United States.

The schizophrenia is worsened by the U.S. choice of policy levers that it has employed to further its influence over China. These levers may be grouped under the rubrics of military force, trade and investment mechanisms, and access to global institutions. However, these different levers and their subsets share a common attribute in that the use of them by the United States must be "binary." The use of each lever, whether alone or in concert with others, is absolute—the lever must be either in the "on" or the "off" position. For example, the United States must grant or withhold most favored nation (MFN) status and must open or close the guarantee programs of the Overseas Private Investment Corporation (OPIC).

The inefficiency of binaryism when different levers are involved is severe even when the goals of the policy are clearly defined. A situation of "multiple binaryism" is created in institutions where, for example, OPIC investment guarantees are prohibited but loan-guarantee programs of the Export-Import Bank are encouraged. Such inefficiencies and, more importantly, ineffectiveness, are compounded when policy goals are indistinct and contradictory. For this reason, the United States must add "nonbinary" strategies to its policy levers. Nonbinary strategies are those actions having many distinct but easily integrated components that can be set toward a goal. The Marshall Plan and the Peace Corps are examples of nonbinary foreign policy strategies.

Civil Society

The search for nonbinary levers need not take us far from U.S. history and traditions. Indeed, the richest vein of such levers can be found in the U.S. relationships with Great Britain and France during the nineteenth century, a period in which the rise of the United States to globalism actually preserved and strengthened these European nations' global influence. The integrated functioning of British and U.S. banking institutions in the half-century following the American Civil War exemplified those relationships. These types of relationships engendered productive world leadership among once combative rivals; these relationships were marked not only by consistent policies, common objectives, and private institutional pairings but also by common possession of a functioning "civil society."

Civil society is somewhat amorphous in its parameters. To some degree, most nations demonstrate a number of voluntary associations of civil society that promote the objectives of prosperity, domestic tranquillity, and global responsibility. These include institutions that sponsor charitable endeavors, youth organizations, and sports clubs. Francis Fukuyama propounds that the presence and strength of these institutions establish the strength of a nation.[1] The formal apparatus of government is too remote from individuals to do more than contain them. It cannot become a part of their conscience and motivate them from within. However, we need not extrapolate greatly from Fukuyama's thesis to observe the degree to which the success of efforts by the United States with respect to the post–World War II ascendancy to responsible globalism of Japan and Germany was a function of the United States' promotion of independently operating institutions of a civil society within these nations.

A full view of civil society shows a broader spectrum of voluntary associations than are represented by bowling leagues and parent-teacher organizations. Civil society is composed of any number of voluntary associations that are larger than the family and smaller than governmental units. For our purposes, we should focus on those voluntary associations that include private, middle market, and economic enterprises. Such organizations play a leading role in most nations' job creation, technology introduction, social mores maintenance, and information dissemination. Yet, these organizations are uncommon in China, leaving the ends of a civil society to be created by governments, larger economic organizations, and family organizations. Nonetheless, few, if any, United States policy initiatives have targeted the stimulation of middle market enterprise in China.

Comparative Context:
The Americas

We may look to a comparative context to gain some perspective on cultivating civil society in China and its effect on communicating the U.S. vision of the twenty-first century. In April 1998, the leaders of the Western hemisphere gathered in Santiago, Chile for the Second Summit of the Americas. In an effort to get away from a "statist" approach to policy development that had marked failed Latin policies, such as import substitution, there was general agreement among the leaders to focus efforts on civil society and private groups. This effort was the culmination of four years of policy development based on the themes of democracy and free markets emphasized at the First Summit of the Americas in Miami. The Santiago Declaration of Principles put it in straightforward fashion: "The strength and meaning of representative democracy lie in the active participation of individuals at all levels of civic life."

To give content to this philosophical approach, the Santiago Summit set forth a strong work plan that offers us some insight into what may be feasible for China. First, in terms of democracy, the governments of the hemisphere committed to building institutions that developed volunteer groups and civic groups, including "transparent" nonprofit and other civil society organizations. The Organization of American States (OAS) was charged with the task of serving as a forum for the sharing of successful practices. In addition, the Inter-American Development Bank was given the responsibility to develop "financial mechanisms" dedicated to implementing such civil society programs.

On the economic side, the Santiago Summit Action Plan also focused on developing civil society initiatives. First, a civil society committee was established as part of the Free Trade Area of the

Americas negotiations to ensure input in trade negotiations from business, environmental, labor, and consumer groups. Second, as McCurdy conceptualized earlier, the Internet will create unique communities that will be networked. Striking a similar theme, the Santiago Action Plan provided that governments work with the private sector to support electronic commerce and entrepreneurship.

Most importantly, in terms of alleviating poverty, the leaders of the hemisphere agreed to "strengthen the development of [the approximately 50 million] micro, small and medium-size enterprises" in the hemisphere. Such strengthening would be accomplished through proposals for improved access to financial services, technology and training, and simplified property registration and labor and tax regulations. In addition, the hemisphere's leaders would work with regional development agencies to provide approximately $500 million over the next three years to promote training and technical assistance so that such enterprises could be sustained.

These efforts are important for consolidating the gains that the hemisphere has made toward freer markets and smaller governments. They project a U.S. vision of individual liberty and enterprise. As discussed earlier in this volume, the U.S. approach to starting and building small- and medium-sized businesses differs, generally, from that of nations in Europe and Asia. Ours is an approach that stresses individualism, innovation, and risk-taking—values important to shaping the world of the twenty-first century.

United States Policy Tools

For decades, China operated without significant numbers of small- and medium-sized private institutions. Now it has seen an explosion of such institutions in the industrial sphere. In Shanghai, for example, more than an estimated 80 percent of the increase in the city's output of goods and services since 1990 has been the result of small- and medium-sized businesses managed independently of state actors.

This phenomenon is consistent with Daniel Yergin's observation that recent decades have seen a worldwide shift in decisionmaking responsibility within markets from governments and toward private actors, even in traditionally regulated areas such as transportation, telecommunications, and health care.[2] Accordingly, the most appropriate agents to stimulate middle market enterprise in China are not United States government agencies but United States private enterprises themselves, preferably enterprises of the same character as those sought to be encouraged in China. The role of government should be to encourage, support, and reward such activity by U.S. private enterprises.

The U.S. government's tools of choice should resemble those that it used to cause private enterprise to advance domestic social policies. Historically, these tools have included the allocation of government tangible and intangible resources to those enterprises that demonstrate certain target levels for employment, subcontracting, and vending by designated groups within society. By analogy, United States companies seeking government assistance in reaching the China market, whether through approvals for import quotas, credit support, technology licensing, and extraterritorial enforcement of property rights, would be required to present, for their qualification, evidence of their economic relationships with middle-market enterprises in China.

Some of the chief repositories of government assistance programs of this nature are found within the Department of Commerce, the Small Business Administration, and the Export-Import Bank. They include market-access programs and financial-assistance programs ranging from working capital guarantees necessary to manufacture goods for export to support for inclusion of United States companies in major project financing. The programs of OPIC also would fall within this scope if they were made available again to China. Moreover, U.S. policy initiatives are not without guiding influence within institutions such as the World Bank and the Asian Development Bank.

The U.S. business community likely will resist the imposition of yet another selection criteria on the grounds that the criteria places a burden on U.S. industry that is not imposed on other nations' industries. However, this burden is insignificant when included with the other competitive burdens that the U.S. government imposes on U.S. business for policy reasons. These policy reasons include exclusion from certain markets, responsibilities for certain environmental and labor standards, corrupt practice limitations, and lack of government subsidized financing. For each of these reasons, the national benefits achieved are thought to exceed the sum of the costs incurred by individual enterprises.

The business community also may point out that China's middle market organizations may be neither the most efficient purchasers and suppliers of goods nor the most efficient operators of industrial organizations. Even if a statistical basis for such a conclusion exists, the argument is outweighed by the longer-term contributions made by middle-market enterprises to their societies. These contributions are recognized and fostered by governmental policies from Japan to the European Union. To be sure, the approaches in these regions are different from that of the United States and rely less on cultivating civil society and entrepreneurship. Furthermore, we see little compelling evidence that China's domestic policies will contradict a strong role for middle-market enterprises.

Finally, the business community may be expected to focus on the anticipated administrative difficulties in defining standards and in measuring results. However, the United States' success in analogous domestic programs provides some guidelines. Initially, definitions should be simple and compliance should be measured by a company's inputs into the middle market system in China. For example, useful criteria would include a company's identifiable volume of business with middle-market suppliers and purchasers, its inclusion of middle-market companies in joint ventures, and the number of licenses entered into with middle-market licensees.

Conclusion

Gary Hart, earlier in this volume, invoked "civic virtue and citizen participation" as the basis for a new ideology for the next generation of policymakers in the United States. Such elements will perhaps enable Americans to think about policy development in ways that will meet twenty-first century challenges brought on by technologies and tribalism. Some of that same civil society spirit could be helpful in our approach to China.

U.S. policymakers must recognize several points. First, China is poised to rise to a position of global prominence in this century. Second, the United States does not have, and is unlikely to establish, a coherent policy toward China because of the irreconcilable differences between the interests of various United States domestic constituencies. This shortcoming is compounded by the failure of the United States to generate and implement nonbinary policy levers. Third, the model for United States policy toward China should draw more heavily from its historical successes with countries rising to global prominence than from its historical failures. A common element of these historical successes has been the presence of functioning civil societies in nations that rise to responsible globalism. Therefore, China would benefit from a civil society of voluntary associations similar to that in other globally responsible nations. The United States should promote civil society within China by focusing its allocation of government benefits to U.S. business entities willing to contribute to the growth of middle market civil institutions within China.

The costs and risks of a policy initiative to promote civil society in China are small. The benefits are great and historically well founded. The United States should act to add this initiative to its China policy.

Notes

1. Francis Fukuyama, *Trust: The Social Virtues and the Creation of Prosperity*, (1995).

2. Daniel Yergin and Joseph Stanislaw, *The Commanding Heights: The Battle between Government and the Market Place That Is Remaking the Modern World* (1998).

Chapter 20

Mainstreaming the Americas

Eric Farnsworth

Introduction

The definition of U.S. national security has been broadened considerably by foreign policy elites and non-elites alike as we cross the threshold of a new century. To be sure, the world will always remain a dangerous place in traditional terms, as the on-again, off-again crises in the Balkans, the ongoing tension between China and Taiwan, the two Koreas, and India and Pakistan so clearly show. These types of threats must continue to be addressed on a priority basis. Even so, new threats are emerging as old ones fade away.

The next generation security agenda is filled with "kitchen-table" issues that deeply affect the people of the United States, as this volume has discussed. Jobs and personal financial security depend on international trade, integrated financial markets, and stable, open-market economies. National energy security depends on an uninterrupted supply of oil from friendly, stable sources. Personal physical security depends on halting nuclear proliferation, stanching the flow of illegal narcotics to our shores, breaking up cross-border criminal gangs and mafias, and protecting against the threat of terrorism. Illegal immigration tests our abilities to secure our own borders, a basic principle of nationhood. Significant global climate change and environmental degradation would cause havoc with our physical well-being and economic base. At the supposed end of history, these have become the new strategic issues for the new century. Our ability to address them will depend—as during two World Wars and the Cold War—on our success in developing true partnerships with like-minded peoples and nations across the globe.

Within this paradigm, the Western Hemisphere, a traditional stepchild in the worldview of the U.S. foreign policy establishment, has become more important than ever to the strategic interests of the United States. Gone are the days when a secretary of state could joke that South America, for example, holds little more significance than being a dagger pointed at the heart of Antarctica. Policymakers must recognize that Canada, Latin America, and the Caribbean are a key to the long-term security and well-being of the United States, and see the region as vital to U.S. national interests. With proper attention and sustained engagement, we have the opportunity to establish a true community of nations in the Americas, building on a foundation of cooperation that has already been laid. Policymakers should seize it before it passes and work to remake the Western Hemisphere into a bulwark of peace and prosperity supporting U.S. economic strategy and national security well into the global twenty-first century.

Elbows Together; Hearts Apart?

On its face, the case is compelling. By the end of 1998 we sent some 40 percent of our exports to the Americas including Canada, while 35 percent of our imports came from there. The region is more important to us tradewise than Japan and Germany combined, and, by the year 2010, it will be more important than Japan and the entire European Union combined. Canada is our top trade partner worldwide, with almost $1 billion in crossborder trade every day. Mexico is our second largest market, $5 billion larger than Japan ($71 billion vs. $66 billion in 1997). Already we do almost $1 billion in crossborder trade with Mexico every two days. Astoundingly, in 1997 we sold more to potential free trade partner Chile ($4.4 billion), with a population of 14 million, than to India ($3.6 billion), with a population of one billion; nearly twice as much to the six Spanish-speaking Central American nations as to the 15 former Soviet Republics including Russia ($9 billion vs. $5.2 billion, respectively); and over $3 billion more to Brazil than China, the favorite "big emerging market" of many U.S. elites.

In the new global economy, where economic security has become a vital aspect of overall national security, and where fully one-third of economic growth has come from international trade, the Americas have become a cornerstone for our economic well being. Even so, the potential for further upside in the equation is substantial. With half of Latin America's population under 21 years old, according to the Inter-American Development Bank, with an affinity for U.S. culture and the goods and services it produces, Latin America promises to be an engine of U.S. export growth—a critical economic security consideration.

Yet, it's not just trade and commercial relations that suggest that the Americas are increasingly important to our success in the global environment. Unlike a few short years ago (generally prior to the 1994 entry into force of the North American Free Trade Agreement [NAFTA]), nations in the region are, for the most part, beginning to share the values we promote and to see their interests aligned with our own. They are also more politically mature, and these new realities together have formed the basis of a new partnership.

For example, at U.S. urging, democratic Argentina and Brazil—historical rivals whose former military governments put them on the road to confrontation—voluntarily gave up their nuclear weapons programs in the early 1990s. Both nations are now cooperating in the peaceful application of atomic energy, as well as undertaking joint conventional military confidence-building measures. They independently condemned Indian and Pakistani nuclear tests in 1998, as did others in Latin America, and are actively supporting the efforts of the international community to establish a workable non-proliferation regime. That directly supports U.S. national security interests, and it is a remarkable turnaround from the days when Argentina and Brazil joined together as leaders in the non-aligned movement specifically to frustrate U.S. initiatives.

Peacekeeping missions around the globe have also been meaningfully supported by hemispheric governments—something difficult to envision in the past under traditional Latin ideals of nationalism and sovereignty. From Bosnia and Iraq, to Angola and Mozambique, and closer to home in Haiti, Guatemala, and the border between Peru and Ecuador, governments in the hemisphere have contributed troops on the ground, equipment, logistical support, and appropriate leadership. Such support leverages and expands engagement by the United States. It allows the United States to marshal its resources while providing the political imprimatur of the international community for actions that might be undertaken alone by the United States, but only at significant political cost.

Argentina, for example, has been among the most responsive nations in the world to requests for support from the international community. At the end of 1998, Argentina had 664 troops committed to UN peacekeeping operations, the same number as France and more than any other NATO ally of the United States (more, indeed, than the United States' 583). Uruguay (62), Chile (38), and Brazil (19) were also active, the latter particularly in Lusophone Africa. Working together, traditional rivals Argentina, Brazil, and Chile joined with the United States to bring peace to the long-disputed border between Peru and Ecuador, one of the most successful peacekeeping operations anywhere, ever. Canada, of course (297 troops committed to UN peacekeeping), remains a reliable ally in multiple fora besides the UN.

In terms of energy, a critical national and economic security issue in the modern age, three of our top four petroleum suppliers come from the hemisphere. Venezuela is number one; Canada and Mexico follow Saudi Arabia. During periods of crisis or instability elsewhere, such as the two oil embargoes in the 1970s, the United States has been able to count on its hemispheric neighbors to offer steady and stable supplies. Venezuela actually increased its production to help the United States during those difficult times. Bold efforts by the Venezuelan government to re-open Venezuela's energy sector to foreign investment beginning with the mid-1990s *apertura* have been mutually rewarding. Simply put, low energy costs have contributed to low inflation and fueled the uninterrupted economic expansion that the United States continues to enjoy.

Less traditional aspects of foreign policy, such as the effort to reduce greenhouse gasses and to protect the environment, have also benefited from cooperation in the hemisphere. Previously, in the absence of promises of massive resource transfers, Latin and Caribbean nations would have lined up to see who could denounce U.S. efforts on global warming the loudest. But at the global environmental conference in Kyoto, Japan in late 1997, Latin American nations participated in a consensus position on this divisive issue, after Argentina brokered agreement among competing interests. The follow-on conference in Buenos Aires in November 1998 actually opened with an Argentine proposal for developing countries to adopt self-imposed restraints, a constructive alternative to the usual stale North/South debate.

Likewise, Costa Rica is remaking itself into an international model for sustainable development, encouraging the notion that economic progress and environmental protection can be mutually supportive. In 1994, at the Miami Summit of the Americas, Central America as a sub-region signed the CONCAUSA agreement with the United States to protect environmental areas and provide much needed U.S. support for Central America's innovative but under-resourced Alliance for Sustainable Development. South American countries such as Bolivia, Brazil, and Peru are also getting into the act, looking at new ways to protect their respective environments through land set-asides and robust national park systems. In Brazil's case, this includes a new, 2.35 million hectare Amazon forest reserve which, when aggregated with two existing parks, creates a total reserve larger than Switzerland.

From trade and investment to nuclear non-proliferation and global peacekeeping, energy security, and the environment, North America, Latin America, and the Caribbean have reached the point where we now share broadly similar values and see our interests aligned.

In a true geo-strategic sense, if Samuel Huntington is correct in arguing that the global system will increasingly be defined by social and cultural cleavages, it is in our national interest to find ways to solidify our relationships with these like-minded peoples and nations.

Consequently, we should not squander the opportunity that now exists to mold Western Hemisphere nations into a true community of the Americas, to address the economic and national security challenges that will increasingly affect our national well-being in the twenty-first century.

The Changing Face of the Americas

Only a few short years ago, discussion of partnership or even co-operation in the Americas would have been unthinkable. Old stereotypes defined the region, including crony capitalism and cor-ruption, economic contraction (–0.4 percent real per capita growth between 1980 and 1990), and crushing debt burdens and debt re-payment moratoria that began with Mexico's debt rescheduling in 1982. Every Latin American nation except Chile and Colombia de-faulted on its debt or was forced to reschedule to forestall default. Inflation was out-of-control (five percent daily in Brazil, almost 5000 percent annually in Argentina). The pattern of income in-equality was unsustainable and arguably unjust (in the mid-1980s in Brazil, the wealthiest 10 percent of the population held a 67 per-cent share of household income, according to the World Bank, al-most 10 times that of its poorest 40 percent). Stagnant, closed economies throughout the region were built on the quirky ideas of *dependencia* theorists that decreed import substitution, restricted foreign investment, and state ownership of key economic sectors.

Politically, military dictators of both the left and the right tram-pled human rights in virtually every country in Latin America and in many Caribbean states, employing grisly methods to silence in-surgents and agitators leading to the disappearance of thousands. Untold others (estimates vary) lost their lives in guerrilla conflicts in El Salvador, Guatemala, Nicaragua, Colombia, and Peru, which were fueled by billions of dollars in secret and overt military and economic assistance from the Soviet Union and Cuba. Courts up-held no law but that which could be bought or intimidated. The non-official press was muzzled.

Correspondingly, a deep, unifying mistrust of the United States ran throughout the region. It was based on an almost allergic fear of U.S. hegemonic ambitions and perceived meddling on issues from human rights to drug trafficking to civil wars; a fear of the ef-fects of U.S. culture and influence; and in some cases, more than a touch of envy given the economic and military disparities that di-vided our nations. Contemporary U.S. military interventions in Grenada (1983) and Panama (1989) and, to a lesser extent Haiti (1994) reinforced these perceptions. Countries and their leaders de-fined themselves by their anti-*yanqui* attitudes, paralyzing hemispheric relations and the institutions of the Inter-American system such as the Organization of American States. Such institutions were designed to bring the hemisphere closer together, not wedge it further apart. Consequently, until the early 1990s observers could characterize our hemisphere as dysfunctional, a model to be avoided, not copied, and a virtual monument to the failed utopian ideals of pan-Americanists such as Bolivar and Jefferson.

The region, however, is shedding this difficult past. Political scientists, economists, sociologists, and others will debate the reasons for change, but the facts are immutable.

Most importantly, peace has come at last. In December 1996, Guatemala's peace accords ended 36 years of continuous conflict in Central America, a somber yet ardently hopeful occasion I shall never forget. Colombia is now the only country with a national guerrilla insurgency. Border disputes throughout Latin America have largely been resolved; Peru and Ecuador, which fought a brief but bloody border war in 1995, signed a comprehensive peace agreement in November 1998 midwifed by the hemispheric community. El Salvador and Honduras, belligerents in the so-called "soccer war" of 1969, used a decision by the International Court of Justice handed down in 1992 as the basis for resolution of their border differences. Even the Falklands/Malvinas dispute that led to war in 1982 between Argentina and Great Britain is being discussed after a breakthrough visit by President Carlos Menem to London in early 1999. As noted above, the threat of nuclear proliferation, a significant destabilizer, has dramatically diminished.

Now, every nation but Cuba is democratic. Direct elections of national and sub-national leaders like Mexico City's opposition Mayor Cuauhtemoc Cardenas are increasingly common; Mexico's longtime ruling party, the PRI, lost control of the lower house of Congress for the first time in 1997 and held a presidential primary for the first time in November 1999 to prepare for elections in 2000. In 1998, Fernando Henrique Cardoso was handily re-elected in Brazil, Venezuelan Hugo Chavez won a clean election despite the united opposition of Venezuela's established political parties, and Costa Rica enjoyed yet another seamless presidential transition between competing political parties. In 1999 Argentina, Chile, Guatemala, and Uruguay all held scheduled elections. The list could go on. In addition, vital institutions of democracy such as fair and independent judiciaries and a free, unfettered press are being built from the ground up as in Bolivia. Human rights and the rule of law are increasingly monitored and respected in each country.

Economically, inflation across the region now averages around 30 percent, one-tenth what it once was. In Argentina and Panama, it has dipped below one percent per year. In Brazil, it has been below five percent annually. As a result of an aggressive program of privatization, particularly in the telecommunications, energy, and transportation sectors, among others, direct foreign investment to Latin America reached a record $50 billion in 1997. Brazil, Mexico, and Argentina, respectively, headed the list. Before the Asian financial flu spread to Latin America, international credit ratings had inched up. Tough financial decisions made by a new cadre of educated, world-class leaders such as Brazil's Cardoso, Argentina's Menem, Mexico's Zedillo, and Chile's Frei, among others, supported strong economic growth through mid-1998, when Russia defaulted on its international obligations and the Asian crisis began to take its toll. (For example, economic model Chile, which began far-reaching economic reforms earlier than most, grew at an average of 7 percent annually for 15 years.)

Significant economic challenges remain, of course. Cardoso's retreat from his inflation-beating *real* plan bears particularly close watch, as does Chavez' implementation of an uncertain political and economic program and the Colombian guerrilla conflict which has intensified, throwing its economy into deep recession. Nonetheless, the region taken as a whole is better prepared than ever before to participate and succeed in the new global economy, and to meet its obligations economically and politically in the worldwide community of responsible nations. Simply put, the face of the Americas has changed.

The Need for Sustained Engagement

To be sure, intractable problems exist. Reforms, while impressive, are not irreversible. Optimism must be tempered with reality. As a result of the Asian crisis, many observers project stagnant or even negative 1999 growth for the region. The debt to GDP burden remains far too high. Up to 40 percent of the people still live in poverty, even with the broad-based economic growth that has occurred over the past several years. The income gap remains the world's largest, and the gap between the Latin American and Caribbean region and North America guarantees continued immigration flows—legal or illegal—well into the future. The threat of narcotics is a constant debilitating presence that corrupts governments, engenders violence, and attacks the social fabric of hemispheric communities. Focused investment in infrastructure is desperately needed just to sustain growth in the short term.

In the cases of Central America in the aftermath of Hurricane Mitch, which literally redrew the topographical map of Honduras and Nicaragua, and in the cases of the Dominican Republic and Haiti in the wake of Hurricane Georges, all in 1998, massive investment is needed just to return the affected countries to a minimum acceptable level of basic economic activity. (When fully funded and implemented, the Clinton Administration's comprehensive hurricane relief program will have totaled over $1.2 billion, just to lay the groundwork for future sustainable growth.) Institutional concerns such as long-term judicial reform, financial sector and banking restructuring, and the reduction of common crime and corruption must also be addressed on a priority basis.

Nonetheless, despite such hardships, the people of the Americas have shown remarkable determination in making the social sacrifices needed to shift over the last decade from state-led to open market economies, from one-party rule to vibrant competitive elections. Based on these new realities, President Clinton committed the United States to a mature partnership with the region at the 1994 Summit of the Americas in Miami, an unprecedented gathering of the hemisphere's 34 democratically-elected leaders. In addition, the president traveled to the region *six times* between May 1997 and March 1999, and, as a show of tangible ongoing support, he made the determination to appoint his first chief of staff, Thomas (Mack) McLarty, as his personal envoy to the hemisphere.

During the president's travels he made a point of supporting democracy, democratic institutions, and economic reform and integration. For example, in Mexico City in May 1997, the president met with key leaders of the PAN and PRD opposition, in addition to the government, just prior to the elections that broke the PRI legislative monopoly. He did the same with government and opposition leaders in Buenos Aires in October 1997 and in Brasilia, where he met with a broad spectrum of leaders of the Brazilian legislature. In Valparaiso in April 1998, the president made the sensitive but sensible decision to address the full Chilean legislature—minus General Pinochet and his boycotting political allies—in addition to meeting with government officials in Santiago. The president's trips to the region also included Summits in Costa Rica and Barbados (May 1997), a bilateral visit to Venezuela (October 1997), the Asia-Pacific Economic Cooperation Summit in Vancouver (November 1997), a second visit to Mexico (February 1999), and travel to hurricane-ravaged Central America (March 1999). This intensive travel schedule complemented numerous meetings with hemispheric leaders in Washington, New York, Miami, and even Atlanta during the 1996 Summer Olympic Games, as well as Cabinet-level meetings too numerous to count.

Despite the failure to gain fast track trade authority from Congress, the president has publicly committed his administration to further enhancing hemispheric economic integration through the Free Trade Area of the Americas (FTAA). It must also be underscored that Presidents Bush and Clinton showed extraordinary national security vision and political courage in negotiating and pushing through, respectively, NAFTA. As Fishlow and DeSouza noted in an earlier essay, NAFTA is an important building block for global trade leadership. Continued U.S. support for hemispheric trade and investment expansion is a critical factor reinforcing the sacrifice that hemispheric economic restructuring has entailed. Sustainability requires constant nurturing, and the champions of politically difficult reforms must be rewarded if reform is to continue. That is why it is so important that this administration and the next finish the bipartisan process of hemispheric trade integration begun by Presidents Bush and Clinton. Hopes are high, expectations have been raised. Unless they are met—unless democracy delivers—the political and economic gains of the recent past may be lost. That would be a significant setback to the national security interests of the United States.

Historical Antecedents

Traditionally, opinion leaders, policymakers, and the press in the United States have tended to focus primarily on the negative aspects of the hemisphere—to the extent they focus on Canada, Latin America, and the Caribbean at all—and as a result they have simply missed the change in the underlying character of the hemisphere. This misperception stems in part from the way our histories have intertwined. The Monroe Doctrine, declared on December 2, 1823, suggested the United States would reject European colonization of the Americas, defend the independent nations in the region from European domination, and refuse to recognize transfers of hemispheric territory from one European nation to another. The *quid pro quo* would be U.S. neutrality in Europe's political affairs. Later, in 1904, Teddy Roosevelt expanded the scope of the Monroe Doctrine with the Roosevelt Corollary, justifying U.S. intervention in Latin America and the Caribbean on the basis of Europe's avowed tendency to intervene in other governments' internal affairs. Later U.S. policymakers targeted Soviet and Cuban adventurism rather than the traditional European powers, but the effect was the same: to reserve for the United States a free hand in the hemisphere. Indeed, a free hand was used with some frequency throughout the twentieth century in Chile, the Dominican Republic, Grenada, Guatemala, Haiti, Mexico, Nicaragua, Panama and elsewhere. The attempted Bay of Pigs invasion of Cuba also fit within this framework.

Whether the Monroe Doctrine and later the Roosevelt Corollary achieved their desired effect is debatable. Nevertheless, the important point is that they provided the outward, somewhat paternalistic manifestation of U.S. policymakers' conceptualizations of the hemisphere and its place in the world. Consequently, they provided the context for U.S. relations with Latin America and the Caribbean. Along with the practical realities established by the Spanish-American War in 1898, they defined U.S. policy toward the region as one of protection from external threat, coupled with a propensity to intervene, not partnership, for more than 150 years.

Only twice in this century did the United States seriously attempt to put relations on a more even, sustainable footing: during the period of the Good Neighbor Policy enunciated by Franklin Roosevelt, and during John Kennedy's Alliance for Progress. Both programs failed in the end, in large part because they raised expectations in the region to a level that ultimately could not be met when the United States became distracted by events elsewhere.

They also failed because U.S. decision-makers did not view the Latin American and Caribbean region as strategically important in and of itself. To be sure, the promise of trade expansion made during the Miami Summit, which has languished absent fast track, has had somewhat similar deflating effects.

Of course, it is also true that the rest of the hemisphere was simply not ready for closer partnership with the United States and that additional U.S. overtures for improved relations were frequently rebuffed. We did not share common values such as the importance of democratic governance and respect for human rights. We did not see our interests in parallel; rather than working together toward a common goal such as market-based prosperity, the region believed its interests would be best served by developing infant industries at home, keeping U.S. investment out, and keeping relations cold. Such thinking ensured that a true partnership was difficult, if not impossible.

That is why the Miami Summit in December 1994 and the follow-on Santiago Summit in April 1998 were such watershed events in hemispheric affairs. In Miami, the democratically elected leaders gathered together for the first time to launch a comprehensive program of shared commitments. The process launched by the Miami Summit would not have been possible absent a "first generation" of reforms that established democracy and open markets as the basic framework for hemispheric affairs.

In Santiago, leaders committed their respective governments to the implementation of a so-called "second generation" of reforms: judicial reforms to stem corruption; emphasis on primary and secondary education and distance learning through information technology to build twenty-first century skill-sets; and commitments to strengthen democracy and make it more relevant to the daily lives of citizens in the Americas. Leaders also met a key Miami commitment by launching actual negotiations to establish a hemispheric free trade area by the year 2005.

The course established in Miami and continued in Santiago has led to other successes. For example, as a direct result of the Summit process and the leadership of Venezuela's President Rafael Caldera, the hemisphere passed the world's first comprehensive anti-corruption convention in 1995, anticipating even that of the Organization of Economic Cooperation and Development (OECD).

Similarly, in 1997 the hemisphere passed a groundbreaking convention to stop the illegal trade in guns, and countries are now working together on implementation. Hemispheric nations have also adopted a region-wide anti-drugs strategy and a coordinated action plan to combat money laundering.

Supporting Summit commitments, the Inter-American Development Bank (IDB) has loaned some $1.4 billion for private infrastructure development since 1995, mobilizing investment in that sector for a total of $4 billion. It has also committed close to $1 billion in the promotion of microenterprises and small businesses throughout the hemisphere. The IDB, the World Bank, and the U.S. Agency for International Development have pledged billions of dollars in new resources for education and other Summit priorities.

After years of disappointment and conflict, two hemispheric Summits and extensive presidential travel have confirmed the basis of a vibrant American partnership to address new opportunities and threats. The next Summit has already been scheduled for Canada in 2001. Our success in promoting U.S. national security and economic interests is now inextricably linked to the health of a hemispheric community of open market democracies. Simply put, achieving our goals in the global environment of the twenty-first century depends more than ever before on our willingness to engage fully with our hemispheric partners.

Toward the Future

Several recommendations for U.S. policymakers flow from this framework. First, the United States must be resolute in standing with democrats against those who would return to the authoritarianism of the past. Specifically, we must continue to uphold democratic governance and open markets by word and deed as the ideal for the hemisphere. Those nations, such as Cuba, which reject the basic tenets of the Americas we are collectively attempting to create, must continue to be excluded by the United States and its hemispheric partners from the community of hemispheric nations.

As the OAS Washington Protocol makes clear, we must also be prepared as a hemisphere to take action against those who attempt to overthrow their nations' democratically-elected leaders by extra-constitutional means, as in Guatemala in 1993.

Where guerrillas and narco-traffickers threaten democracy, as in Colombia, it is imperative we engage more aggressively with the international community and responsible government elements such as the Colombian national police to bring peace and shore up the democratically-elected government. Over 80 percent of the co-caine on the streets of the United States comes from or through Colombia. Collapse of democracy there would do significant harm to long-term U.S. interests. Where democracy is threatened by eco-nomic stagnation or financial collapse, such as that engendered by the Asian crisis, we have no sound alternative but to be prepared to lead multilateral efforts to stave off contagion and support eco-nomic growth, as the U.S. government did in October 1998, and early 1995 in Brazil and Mexico respectively. Where democracy re-mains in its infancy, as in Paraguay and Haiti, the United States should continue to join with the international community to sup-port such countries financially and rhetorically.

Finally, U.S. policy must be sensitive to the unique challenges of democracy in the Caribbean Basin, from increasingly aggressive narcotics trafficking and the corruption that follows, to waves of immigrants, to the vexing issue of bananas and economic diver-sification, to open questions such as the integration of micro-economies into the global economy.

One of the strongest tangible signals of our support for democ-racy would be a renewed push to open trade and investment in the Americas as a whole. Open markets support open governance. They provide the resources necessary for democratic governments to meet the expectations of their citizens, while helping establish a middle class with political interests apart from traditional oli-garchic elites. It is a mistake to view the FTAA merely as a jobs pro-gram for the United States, although increasing trade will indeed increase national economic well being. Rather, progress toward an FTAA will also support hemispheric reformers in their efforts to open their societies to the emerging global economy, while strengthening democratic institutions. Trade agreements also help stabilize economies and political relationships while holding off the worst of a potential financial collapse. Tellingly, after its 1982 fi-nancial crisis, Mexico—without NAFTA—took seven *years* to re-turn to conventional international financing methods. Following the peso crisis in 1995, Mexico—with NAFTA—took seven *months*.

That is why fast track negotiating authority for the president is so important. As noted above, it is a potent signal of collective resolve. When used, it will support robust, open-market democracies, including the United States. Without it, we cannot conclude an FTAA on U.S. terms; with it, we can lead and shape a final agreement to open markets for U.S. exporters while supporting democracy in the hemisphere. Fast track should therefore be granted as soon as possible, despite acknowledged political difficulties, and its first use in the hemisphere should be to consummate a free trade agreement with Chile, as promised by the three NAFTA leaders during the Miami Summit. To address the unique challenges of the Caribbean Basin, efforts should be finalized to provide the region reciprocal benefits broadly similar to NAFTA. This would counteract the unintended trade and investment diversion from the Caribbean Basin to Mexico as a result of NAFTA's success, and would also be an appropriate stepping-stone for the hemispheric FTAA. Additionally, early extension of the Andean Trade Preferences is critical to assist Andean nations fight the illegal narcotics trade and provide opportunities for alternative development.

Second, because traditional rivalries in the hemisphere still exist—for example, regarding regional permanent representation on the UN Security Council—it would be counterproductive to single out a particular country or grouping in the hemisphere for strategic partnership. Clearly, some of the countries in Latin America are more important to the United States geostrategically than others. Brazil, for example, produces half of Latin America's economic output. The financial crisis of 1998 and early 1999 points to Brazil's importance as an indicator of confidence in emerging markets. We should pay more attention to Brazil than we do. But such heightened attention risks alienating several of our closest allies in South America, for example Argentina and Chile—Brazil's traditional rivals. A hemispheric condominium with Brazil would be unworkable. Benefits would be uncertain, the costs would be substantial.

The same is true of regional groupings such as MERCOSUR, the Common Market of the South, which includes Argentina, Brazil, Paraguay, and Uruguay, and, as associate members, Chile and Bolivia. Sub-regional groupings, currently in vogue, must be dealt with on their own merits. Nonetheless, they do not necessarily have U.S. interests as the basis for cooperation (NAFTA is an obvious exception). As a result, our focus in the hemisphere must be clear: partnership with the Americas as a whole, based on the FTAA as the driving force for building a strong community of open-market democracies.

The U.S. relationship with Mexico, including NAFTA, is perhaps the one exception that calls for special nurturing. Relations with Mexico impact U.S. citizens more than any other in the hemisphere, including Canada. We must find a way to put our relations on an even keel for the long run. Our bilateral relationship is a reality, given our 1,800-mile border, legally crossed over 250 million times every year. Some 800,000 good paying U.S. jobs depend on exports to Mexico. On the negative side, Mexico is geographically caught between Andean narcotics suppliers and North American consumers, and immigration issues are a perennial concern. Additionally, general perceptions of the hemisphere held by many U.S. policymakers and citizens are colored by their perceptions of Mexico, due in part to the increasing number of Mexican citizens in the United States. In fact, Los Angeles boasts the second largest population of Mexican descent after Mexico City itself. It is thus important that the U.S. government continue to be fully engaged with Mexico's leadership, and working with the U.S. Congress, a critical player, pursue an agenda vis-à-vis Mexico to make overall hemispheric engagement politically sustainable. In this way, the drumbeat of negative news on illegal immigration, narcotics, and the environment might be managed in a more productive way.

The implications for successful management of the U.S.-Mexico relationship are profound. Arguably, U.S. inability to move forward on additional trade legislation such as fast track stems from public (mis)perceptions regarding NAFTA. It is the prism through which the U.S. public has now come to view trade. In some ways, NAFTA has become the "El Niño" of economic integration, the target for opponents of an increasingly global economy. Conventional wisdom considers NAFTA to have been a failure, promoting a hollowed-out U.S. economy, hundreds of thousands of lost jobs, a deteriorating environment, and an irreparable diminution of U.S. sovereignty. Of course, the reality is more nuanced, and the congressionally-mandated three-year review of NAFTA by the Clinton Administration found in 1997 that, on balance, NAFTA has been a net positive for each party: the United States, Canada, and Mexico. Trade and investment among all three partners is higher now than ever before. Some jobs have been lost but more have been gained, and the foreign policy benefits of a closer linkage with a more stable Mexico have frequently been overlooked in the heated exchanges surrounding the issue. With U.S. unemployment at its lowest level in 30 years, it is difficult to make a compelling argument that NAFTA has hollowed out the U.S. economy. Still, perception often becomes reality in politics, and the failure of both presidential campaigns in 1996 to defend NAFTA against the increasingly pointed attacks of the left and the right abandoned the public square to the opponents of trade. We must not repeat that mistake in the next presidential campaign.

Rather, the time is ripe for a new American foreign policy doctrine, stressing democratic partnership with the responsible nations of the hemisphere through a policy of sustained political and economic engagement.

The way to approach the new century in the Americas will be similar to the course we pursued for much of the twentieth century—cooperation and coordination with like-minded nations to address the opportunities and threats that collectively concern us. Bold pursuit of our national interests will continue to require partnership with those who most closely share our values. In the end, therefore, our ability to achieve our economic, political, and, importantly, security aspirations in the modern world will depend in part on our ability to build a true community of the Americas, based on mutual trust and mutual respect.

If we are to encourage economic growth and improve the livelihood of our citizens, for example, we must find a way to encourage mutual trade and investment with the region of the world that already takes almost half of our exports, and provides the energy resources we need to keep our economy growing. If we are to address fully the threat of illegal narcotics, we must find a new, cooperative way to work with drug producer nations in the Andes, and transit nations between South America and the United States. If we want to address the issue of illegal immigration, we must find a new way to work more effectively with Mexico and the nations of the Caribbean Basin. If we want to prevent global warming, we must find a way to work cooperatively together with Brazil and other Amazonian nations. If we want to contain military threats posed by outlaw regimes such as Iraq or lessen human misery and suffering from the Balkans to Rwanda, we need to work together underneath the umbrella afforded by the international community with nations committed to peacekeeping, an area in which Latin nations have excelled. And if we want to prevent the re-opening of a nuclear arms race, we must work together to contain nuclear proliferation with nations such as Argentina and Brazil, which have led the way.

If U.S. foreign policy is truly to serve the *people* of the United States, we must engage on a sustained basis with our neighbors in the Americas, *mainstreaming* the region in U.S. foreign policy efforts and in calculations of U.S. strategic interests. Perhaps for the first time in history, not only is the region ready for a deeper partnership with us, but also for U.S. strategic reasons, the time is right to pursue a deeper partnership with the region. Opportunities and threats have changed, and we must be prepared to join together with like-minded states—wherever they are—to meet them as effectively as possible. To paraphrase Lord Palmerston, our interests should determine our allies. In short, the success or failure of the United States in building a true community of the Americas will directly affect the shape of the world, and our position in it, for many years to come. It should be a priority for the next—and current—generations of foreign and economic policy leaders in the United States.

Chapter 21

Conclusion

Patrick J. DeSouza and *Laura Hills*

Continuity and Change
In U.S. Foreign Policy

In the essays and discussions that contributed to this volume, one question kept cropping up: Were the economic, political, and technological changes that we were discussing really new, catapulting us into unfamiliar territory? Or, were such changes simply old wine in new bottles? Put differently, in terms that Dave McCurdy and Gary Hart have outlined, do we need to make a break with the past to address effectively the "new realities" brought on by technology and globalization?

Part of the answer depends on what level of generality one is considering. First, at the level of the individual, in thinking about human nature, the fundamentals regarding the need for power and control over one's environment remain, as always, a "basic instinct." However, there is a unique aspect in that, as never before, new technologies will empower individuals to carry out their desires for good or evil.

For example, within the next decade, significant numbers of individuals will be able to choose their own "virtual" communities untethered to territory. In some regards, such choices will be to the good of society. Empowerment through new technologies will make one proud to be part of the twenty-first century. As illustrated during President Clinton's trip to the Mangueira school in

Rio de Janiero in October 1997, children there could discuss issues or fads through the Internet with their counterparts in Virginia. And what was remarkable about this event was that the Mangueira school was located in an extremely poor section of the city. With the help of corporate sponsors and some new technology, poor children could visualize a different world. To that extent, the Microsoft commercial "Where would you like to go today" strikes a responsive chord. It dramatizes that every citizen will have enormous possibilities available in the twenty-first century.

At the same time, the fragmentation of community through Internet technologies could also create the possibilities for evil to spread as never before. Child pornography, the spread of terrorism through the dissemination of knowledge regarding nuclear or biological weapons, and the cultivation of intolerant "communities" that give form to racial or ethnic hatreds may now incubate outside of the reach of societal institutions.

As one moves to higher levels of political aggregation, the "new realities" will not affect some "traditional" modes of behavior. At the governmental level, there will be no escaping the machinery of the state. Globalization, though, will produce new winners and losers, thus increasing the stakes of political mobilization. As always, foreign economic policy will be determined to some extent by traditional political in-fighting in attempts to capture access points of governments. Interest groups from the technology sector, financial sector, and smokestack sector have already begun to align themselves based on new labels of "integrationists" and "economic nationalists."

Yet, here as well, the "new realities" are changing the forms of public discourse. Governments will be responsible for a more difficult balancing act that is qualitatively different from prior times. Information technologies now make citizens aware in real time about political, economic, and military events creating different pressures on leaders to explain complex issues in a relatively short time. And such awareness has ramifications for political control that will have serious consequences in the twenty-first century. For example, the U.S.–China trade pact signed on November 15, 1999, allows American firms to invest in Chinese Internet firms and to own up to 50 percent in Chinese telecommunications firms. While such concessions were inevitable to bring China into the global economy, they will allow information and purchasing decisions to evade the purview of central authorities and create interesting possibilities for the growth of democracy. More broadly, unfiltered information is distributed across the globe in seconds spinning reality in ways that change the dimensions of policy and conflict.

In addition, the nature of governmental institutions will change in the twenty-first century. It is likely that technology will force governments to be more responsive to the people. Already the Gore Commission on Reinventing Government has tried to think through ways that technology can make bureaucracies more responsive. Various academics have gone further and tried to rethink the nature of democracy itself. For example, information technology may make it possible in the near term to have direct democracy in which individuals may express their preferences on discrete issues.

How widespread the effect of "new realities" will be on the nature of governmental institutions will to some extent depend on the political character of technological advance. As we have discussed, the regulatory frameworks that are being put in place around the world are influencing the current evolution of electronic commerce. For example, in the United States the development of the Internet is primarily private-sector driven; in the European Union it is led to a greater extent by governmental bureaucracies. As a result, one hypothesis is that U.S. political institutions will come under comparatively greater pressures to be responsive to the "new realities" than will the Europeans. Whether such greater pressures will yield institutional efficiencies will be an empirical question for the next generation.

Finally, at the highest level of political aggregation—the international system—it will be interesting to see if the "new realities" of the twenty-first century produce significant changes in the structure of the international system. The twentieth century ended with only one country—the United States—capable of being a hegemon and enforcing a multilateral political order. Yet, we are likely to be facing choice points in the near term regarding alternative futures in which the international system may take on a different character.

On one hand, the fundamentals of international relations may still reflect the change in the balance of power. With the seeming rise of China, we may be faced, as Rockefeller points out, with a return to the same political dynamics with which we began the last century: a challenger to the international order with a set of grievances—in this case regarding Taiwan and regional influence—that causes other nations to form coalitions out of fear. In fact, this dynamic of the balance of power and the reactions of states driven by changes in power is as old as Thucydides' explanation for the causes of the Peleponnesian War.

On the other hand, as described most profoundly by McCurdy, the emergence of a "networked" world may change the requirements for security adding centrifugal forces as power becomes more decentralized. It is possible that such forces will produce a degree of political fluidity that the modern world has never experienced. With such diffusion of authority and loyalties, a greater degree of chaos is possible.

The Road Ahead

For the seventy-fifth anniversary of *Foreign Affairs*, James Hoge and Fareed Zakaria put together a collection of influential essays that had appeared in the magazine over the course of the twentieth century. The volume, titled *The American Encounter*, was intended by the editors as an intellectual history of the "American century."

Hoge and Zakaria point out that

> [t]he current scene bears marked similarities to the opening years of *Foreign Affairs*. Once again we are in a post-war era in which relief at the end of a protracted struggle and the immediate absence of security threats has bred public complacency. The public's disinterest is mirrored in the behavior of politicians and government officials, who make little effort to persuade the American people of the importance of foreign policy and the need to handle early on the conditions that breed threats.[1]

Today, as McCurdy points out, American leaders in Congress are proud of the fact that they have never traveled outside of the country. Many do not even have passports. Hoge and Zakaria argue against such complacency. They point out that globalization may well turn out to represent the most powerful force we face today. In this light, they argue that no stable world order can exist without U.S. active participation. Moreover, "for America to play its natural role in the world, the American public must be led, and by the president."[2]

We could not agree more with their analysis. As we have discussed in this volume, it is important for the United States at the beginning of this new century to focus more directly on the problems of interdependence. New realities brought on by information technology, advances in communications, and integrated markets must be addressed and their implications discussed with the American people through presidential leadership. As McCurdy emphasizes, U.S. leadership in the world will require the president to exercise his most important weapon in this new age—moral persuasion. This task may prove increasingly difficult as working men and women seek assurances that democracy will deliver security in a volatile and sometimes brutal global economy.

In closing, we underscore two points that were highlighted by stewards of American foreign policy that have gone before us. Each point is elaborated in the *The American Encounter*.

First, Secretary of State Elihu Root in 1922, in the lead essay in the first issue of *Foreign Affairs*, pointed out that foreign affairs in a world of democracies was the people's business requiring an effort in public education.[3] We hope that the issues discussed herein advance public knowledge and debate of new issues facing us in the next generation.

Second, captain of industry Walter Wriston wrote presciently in 1988 about issues discussed in this volume:

> When major tides of change wash over the world, power structures almost inevitably reject the notion that the world really is changing, and they cling to their old beliefs . . . in the last years of the century, however, the velocity of change in the world has become so great that there are literally no precedents to guide us. The information revolution is changing our global economy, transforming national political and business institutions, and altering national foreign policy objectives and methods of achieving them. . . . The mismatch between the fruits of new technology and the operation of the political process, whether in government, business or the family, has often produced unrest, changing value systems, and sometimes, indeed, revolution.[4]

With respect to our beginning efforts to think about and discuss the intersection of economic strategy and national security issues facing the next generation, enough said.

Notes

1. James F. Hoge, Jr. and Fareed Zakaria, *The American Encounter*, 1997 at p. 8.
2. *Ibid.*
3. *Ibid.* at 13.
4. *Ibid.* at 503, 505.

About the Authors

Thomas F. (Mack) McLarty III is Vice Chairman of Kissinger McLarty Associates. He was President Clinton's first Chief of Staff, Counselor to the President, and Special Envoy for the Americas with over five years of service in the Cabinet and on the National Economic Council. Mr. McLarty helped enact the historic 1993 deficit reduction package, NAFTA, and the Family and Medical Leave Act. He helped organize the Miami and Santiago Summits of the Americas, and the 1996 Summer Olympic Games. Earlier, Mr. McLarty was chairman and CEO of Arkla, Inc, a Fortune 500 natural gas company, and president of the McLarty Companies, a diversified transportation group. He was a member of the St. Louis Federal Reserve Board and the Arkansas State Legislature. Mr. McLarty graduated *summa cum laude* from the University of Arkansas.

Patrick J. DeSouza is a banker with Violy, Byorum & Partners LLC, an investment bank focused on Latin America. During 1997–1998, he served in the White House as Director for Inter-American Affairs on President Clinton's National Security Council. Prior to his work in the Clinton Administration, Dr. DeSouza practiced corporate law focusing on cross-border mergers and acquisitions and venture capital. He clerked for the Hon. Thomas Gibbs Gee, U.S. Court of Appeals for the Fifth Circuit. Dr. DeSouza received his B.A. from Columbia, an M.A. in International Relations from Yale Graduate School, a J.D. from the Yale Law School, and his Ph.D. from Stanford. In addition, Dr. DeSouza has been a term member, International Affairs Fellow, and the inaugural Next Generation Fellow at the Council on Foreign Relations.

Dave McCurdy is the President of the Electronics Industries Alliance (EIA), a leading voice of the $500 billion electronics industry. Prior to joining EIA, he was the Chairman of the McCurdy Group, a business consulting and investment firm (1995–1998). Mr. McCurdy served for fourteen years (1981–1995) in the U.S. House of Representatives from the fourth district of Oklahoma. During his time in Congress, he attained numerous leadership positions, including chairmanship of the House Intelligence Committee, subcommittees of both the Armed Services Committee and Science and Space Committee. He was also the national chairman of the Democratic Leadership council. He is a member of the Council on Foreign Relations.

Gary Hart is presently Counsel to Coudert Brothers, an international law firm. He was recently appointed to co-chair the U.S. National Security Commission for the Twenty-First Century by Secretary of Defense William S. Cohen.

Gary Hart represented the state of Colorado in the United States Senate from 1975 to 1987. In 1984 he was a candidate for the Democratic Party's nomination for President. During his 12 years in the Senate, he served on the Armed Services Committee, where he specialized in nuclear arms and naval issues, and he was an original founder of the military reform caucus. He also served on the Senate Environment Committee, Budget Committee, and Intelligence Oversight Committee.

Senator Hart is the author of ten books. Among them are *The Double Man* (1984), co-authored with former senator and current Secretary of Defense, William Cohen, and his latest book, *The Minuteman*, published by The Free Press in early 1998. He was a founding member of the Board of Directors of the U.S.-Russia Investment Fund; a member of the Defense Policy Board; and a member of the Board of Directors of Eagle Wireless International. He is a member of the Council on Foreign Relations. Senator Hart is a graduate of the Yale Law School, the Yale Divinity School, and Southern Nazarene University.

Antony Blinken is Special Assistant to the President and Senior Director for European Affairs at the White House on the National Security Council staff. Prior to this position, he served as President Clinton's chief speechwriter on foreign policy. A graduate of Harvard College and Columbia Law School, Mr. Blinken has practiced law in New York and Paris and has written widely on foreign policy. The views expressed in his contribution are his own and do not necessarily reflect those of the Clinton Administration.

Albert Fishlow is Senior Economist at Violy, Byorum & Partners LLC and professor at the Yale School of Management. He was formerly the Paul A. Volcker Senior Fellow of International Economics, Council on Foreign Relations. Until 1994 he was professor of economics at the University of California at Berkeley and has served as chairman of its Economics Department. He has been Berkeley's first dean of International and Area Studies and professor of economics and director of the Center for International and Area Studies at Yale University. During the Ford Administration, he served as Deputy Assistant Secretary of State for Inter-American Affairs and has been a member of many public task forces related to Latin American affairs. He is on the board of the Social Science Research Council, and serves as chair of its executive committee. He received his doctorate in economics from Harvard University.

Brian VanDeMark teaches history at the United States Naval Academy, Annapolis, and serves as Freeman Professor of American History at the Hopkins-Nanjing Center in China during 1999–2000. A Ph.D. graduate of the University of California, Los Angeles, his publications include *In Retrospect: The Tragedy and Lessons of Vietnam*; *Counsel to the President: A Memoir*; and *Into the Quagmire: Lyndon Johnson and the Escalation of the Vietnam War*. He is currently at work on a new book, *Pandora's Keepers: The Atomic Scientists and Their Creation*. Dr. VanDeMark has been a member of the Council on Foreign Relations.

Deroy Murdock is an MSNBC columnist. He also regularly contributes his op-ed feature, "This Opinion Just In. . . ." to, among other publications, the *Washington Times, Philadelphia Inquirer, Orange County Register*, and *Dallas Morning News*. He has appeared on ABC's "Nightline," the "NBC Nightly News," CNN, Fox News Channel, C-Span, and "Politically Incorrect." Among other publications, Mr. Murdock was a contributor to *Black and Right: The Bold New Voice of Black Conservatives in America* (Praeger). He served as an intern on the U.S. Senate Judiciary Committee under Senator Orin Hatch (R-Utah) between 1982 and 1985 and was a member of the National Advisory Board on International Educational Programs from 1987–1989. Mr. Murdock is a Senior Fellow with the Atlas Economic Research Foundation and a Media Fellow with the Hoover Institution at Stanford University. Mr. Murdock received an AB in Government from Georgetown University and an MBA in Marketing and International Business from New York University. He is a member of the Council on Foreign Relations.

M. Diana Helweg is an International Affairs Fellow, a Hitachi International Affairs Fellow and the 1999 Franklin International Affairs Fellow at the Council on Foreign Relations in New York City, where she is working on international economic policy issues. She served as the Executive Assistant to the Deputy Advisor to the President for National Security Affairs at the National Security Council from 1997 to 1998, and as the Special Assistant to the Under Secretary for Economic, Business, and Agricultural Affairs at the State Department from 1996 to 1997. She has also lived and worked in Japan, both as a lawyer and as a research fellow. She is a graduate of Yale College and Boston University School of Law.

Jeffrey R. Shafer is a Managing Director of Solomon Smith Barney and Vice-Chairman of Solomon Smith Barney International. Dr. Shafer served as Assistant Secretary of the U.S. Treasury for International Affairs from 1993 to 1995 and as Under Secretary from 1995 to 1997. From 1984 until 1993, Dr. Shafer was in the economics department of the Organization for Economic Cooperation and Development (OECD). Prior to the OECD, he served with the Federal Reserve Bank of New York, the Federal Reserve Board, and the Council of Economic Advisors. Dr. Shafer received a B.A. in Economics from Princeton University and M.Phil. and Ph.D. degrees in Economics from Yale University. He is a member of the Council on Foreign Relations.

J. Carter Beese Jr. is President of Riggs Capital Partners, a $100 million venture capital fund. He is also the vice-chairman of Riggs & Co. Both groups are part of Riggs National Corporation of Washington, D.C. Prior to joining Riggs, Mr. Beese was vice-chairman of the Global Banking Group at Bankers Trust and chairman of Alex, Brown International. In 1992, he was nominated by President Bush and confirmed by the U.S. Senate as the 71st Commissioner of the U.S. Securities and Exchange Commission (SEC). While at the SEC, Mr. Beese was particularly active in the areas of cross-boarder capital flows, the derivatives market, and corporate governance.

Julie T. Katzman is head of Merchant Banking and a partner at Violy, Byorum & Partners LLC, an investment bank focused on Latin America. Previously Ms. Katzman was a Managing Director at Lehman Brothers where she participated in numerous leveraged buyouts and principal investments. With a prior background in the Middle East and Africa, Ms. Katzman has successfully conceived of and executed numerous cross-border merger and acquisition transactions and equity investments in Latin America over the past four years. Ms. Katzman is a member of the Board of Visitors of Georgetown University's School of Foreign Service as well as the boards of other philanthropic endeavors. She graduated *summa cum laude* from the School of Foreign Service at Georgetown University and With Honors from Northwestern University's Kellogg School of Management.

Eugene A. Sekulow was President of NYNEX International Company from 1986 to 1991, and Executive Vice-President International, NYNEX Corporation from December 1991 to December 1993. He then founded his own telecommunications consultancy. Dr. Sekulow received his M.A. and Ph.D. from The Johns Hopkins University. He was a member of the State Department Task Force on Telecommunications in Europe and is currently an adjunct professor at the Columbia University Graduate School of Business. Dr. Sekulow is a member of the Council on Foreign Relations.

Robert D. Hormats is Vice-Chairman of Goldman Sachs (International) and managing director of Goldman, Sachs & Co. He served as Senior Staff Member for International Economic Affairs on the National Security Council from 1970 to 1977 and as Senior Economic Advisor to Dr. Henry Kissinger, General Brent Scowcroft, and Dr. Zbigniew Brzezinski. He also served as Senior Deputy Assistant Secretary for Economic and Business Affairs at the Department of State from 1977 to 1979, Ambassador and Deputy U.S. Trade Representative from 1979 to 1981, and Assistant Secretary of State for Economic and Business Affairs from 1981 to 1982. He was a recipient of the French Legion of Honor in 1982 and the Arthur Fleming Award in 1974.

Mr. Hormats is a board member of the Council on Foreign Relations, Engelhard Hanovia, Inc., and Human Genome Sciences, Inc. He is also a member of the Board of Visitors of the Fletcher School of Law and Diplomacy. Mr. Hormats is a member of the advisory boards of *Foreign Policy* and *International Economics* magazines. He was appointed by President Clinton in 1993 to the board of the U.S.-Russia Investment Fund. Mr. Hormats' publications include: *American Albatross: The Foreign Debt Dilemma* and *Reforming the International Monetary System*.

Jeffrey D. Nuechterlein is Managing Director at National Gypsum Company, where he manages public and private equity investments. He is an active investor in early stage Internet companies. Dr. Nuechterlein received his M.A. and D. of Phil. from Oxford University and his B.A. and J.D. from the University of Virginia. Before joining National Gypsum, Dr. Nuechterlein was outside legal counsel to several U.S. semiconductor companies, counsel to the U.S. Senate's Technology & Law Subcommittee, and senior counsel to the U.S. Trade Representative. He lectures frequently at Oxford and at U.S. business schools on venture capital investing. Dr. Nuechterlein is a member of the Council on Foreign Relations. His e-mail address is: jdneuchterlein@nationalgypsum.com.

Lawrence T. Greenberg is General Counsel of The Motley Fool, Inc., a leading multimedia provider of personal finance information, education, and entertainment. He has practiced securities and intellectual property law at Wilson, Sonsini, Goodrich, and Rosati and was affiliated with the Stanford Center for International Security and Arms Control, where he helped found the Project on Information Technology and International Security. He clerked for the Hon. Jerry E. Smith, U.S. Court of Appeals for the Fifth Circuit, and has served as an attorney at the National Security Agency and as a Graduate Fellow analyst for counterterrorism at the Central Intelligence Agency. He is a graduate of Harvard College and Stanford Law School and received an M.A. in political science from Stanford University. He is the author (with Seymour Goodman and Kevin Soo Hoo) of *Information Warfare and International Law* (Institute for National Strategic Studies, 1998).

John E. Tedstrom is Director for Russian, Ukrainian, and Eurasian Affairs for President Clinton at the National Security Council. His chief responsibilities include economic, trade, and assistance policies for the

New Independent States as well as overall policy for Ukraine and Belarus. From 1992 until March 1999, he was an international economist at RAND where he was research leader for Russian, Ukrainian, and Eurasian Affairs. His publications include *Socialism, Perestroika, and the Dilemmas of Soviet Economic Reform* published by Westview Press in 1990. He earned a Ph.D. in Economics and Russian Area Studies from the University of Birmingham, England. Dr. Tedstrom has been a term member of the Council on Foreign Relations. The views expressed in his contribution are his own and do not necessarily reflect those of the Clinton Administration.

James E. Bass is an Executive Director of FB Gemini Limited, an Asian investment bank with headquarters in Hong Kong. He was previously the Managing Partner of the Hong Kong office of Gibson, Dunn & Crutcher LLP. Mr. Bass has been a term member and an International Affairs Fellow of the Council on Foreign Relations. He clerked for the Hon. Thomas Gibbs Gee, U.S. Court of Appeals for the Fifth Circuit. Mr. Bass received a B.A., *magna cum laude*, from Yale University and a J.D. from Stanford Law School.

Nicholas Rockefeller is Of Counsel to the law firm of Troop Steuber Pasich Reddick & Tobey, LLP, where his practice emphasizes financial transactions. He is also Managing Director of Rockvest Development Company, an investment group with multinational interests in banking and venture capital. He serves on the boards of a number of companies, universities, and foundations and is active in the affairs of Yale University. He is a graduate of the Yale Law School. Mr. Rockefeller is a member of the Council of Foreign Relations.

Eric Farnsworth is an international strategic consultant with Manatt, Phelps & Phillips, LLP in Washington D.C. focusing on Latin America and Asia and an adjunct fellow with the Americas Program of the Center for Strategic and International Studies. Prior to joining Manatt, Mr. Farnsworth was policy director to Thomas (Mack) McLarty, Counselor to the President and Special Envoy for the Americas, at the White House. Mr. Farnsworth has served at the U.S. department of state where he received the Superior Honor Award three times for his efforts to help shape U.S. policy toward Latin America and the Caribbean, and at the Office of the U.S. Trade Representative where he was a member of the NAFTA negotiation team. He holds an M.A. in Public Affairs from Princeton and a B.A. with honors from Ball State University.

Laura Hills is Assistant General Counsel in Overseas Private Investment Corporation's ("OPIC") Office of Legal Affairs. Before joining OPIC in 1992, Ms. Hills was an associate at the law firm Patton, Boggs & Blow. In 1987, she graduated from Stanford Law School with a joint J.D./M.A.

degree in Latin American Studies. At Stanford Law School, Ms. Hills was the Editor-in-Chief of the *Stanford Journal of International Law*. Ms. Hills received her B.A. in Political Science and Spanish from Stanford University in 1983. She is a member of the District of Columbia Bar, the Federal Bar Association (co-chair, International Finance and Banking Committee, 1997–98), and the Washington Foreign Law Society (President, 1995–96). Ms. Hills has been a term member of the Council on Foreign Relations.

Index

Abortion, 169
Abu Daoud, 309
Abyssinia, 148(n4)
Acer, 282–283
Accountability. *See* Generational accountability
Accounting standards, 197, 198, 199–200, 282, 338
Advisory Committee on Electronic Commerce, 244
Advisory Council on Social Security, 181
Africa, 133, 177, 253, 255, 360
   populations over 60, 179
Agency on Global Aging, 187
"Age of Social Transformation, The" (Drucker), 48
Age of Transition, 69, 70, 72
Aging populations, 173, 174, 176, 178–181, 187. *See also* Seniors
Agreement on Basic Telecommunications Services, 28, 228
Agriculture, 106, 111, 114
Agriculture Department, 123
   Alternative Agricultural Research and Commercialization Corporation, 288
AID. *See* United States, Agency for International Development
AIDS, 329
Air Force Rome Laboratory, 308
Airline passengers, 80
Air traffic control, 303, 305
Albright, Madeleine K., 145, 151(n34)
Alex Brown, 193
Alliance for Progress, 367
Alliance for Sustainable Development, 361
Alternative Investment Market (London), 273
Amadeus Capital Partners, 274
American Encounter, The (Hoge and Zakaria), 378, 379
American Research and Development (ARD), 264
American Stock Exchange, 191
Andean Pact countries, 103
APEC. *See* Asia-Pacific Economic Cooperation Forum
Apple (corporation), 265, 274
Arab League, 140
ARD. *See* American Research and Development

Argentina, 103, 104, 119, 185, 194, 210–211, 211–212, 213–214, 256–257, 309, 359, 360, 362, 363, 364, 371, 374
Arms control, 85, 310–311, 324, 325
Army After Next wargames, 55
ASEAN. *See* Association of Southeast Asian Nations
Asia, 6, 7, 95, 100, 133, 137, 171, 174, 177, 229, 255–256, 262, 267–268, 286, 291
   Asian crisis, 2, 22, 97, 162, 166, 195, 197, 203, 229, 326, 340, 364, 365, 370. *See also* Crises
   bankruptcy in, 289
   East Asia, 26, 92
   venture capital in, 276–284
Asian Development Bank, 353
Asia-Pacific Economic Cooperation Forum (APEC), 28, 29, 104, 105, 158, 250, 255
   Working Group on Telecommunications, 229
Asia-Pacific Economic Cooperation summit (1997), 366
Association of Southeast Asian Nations (ASEAN), 104
Australia, 133, 167, 222, 225, 238
Automobiles, 97, 98, 102
Autonomy, 52, 61, 62
Azerbaijan, 333

Balance of payments, 158, 184
Balance of power, 377, 378
Bananas, 8, 104, 125–126, 370
Band of Angels, 264
Bangladesh, 288
BankAmerica, 194
Bankers Trust, 193
Bank for International Settlements (BIS), 167, 210
Bankruptcies, 268, 282, 289, 290, 297(n87), 345
Banks, 13, 143, 158, 167, 190, 193, 194, 206, 265, 270, 271, 272, 277, 279, 294(n44), 302, 303, 313, 316
Barbados, 366
Barber, Benjamin, 50
Baxter, Frank, 192
Belgium, 275
BellSouth, 227
Bergsten, Fred, 10–11

389